GREAT
CAT TALES

GREAT
CAT TALES

To Anna
Happy birthday

Knowing how much you
love Lola.
I thought this would be
a great coffee table
book to dip in and
out of
Love
Lenora
xx.

CHANCELLOR PRESS

First published in Great Britain in 1992 by
Chancellor Press an imprint of
Reed International Books Limited
Michelin House
81 Fulham Road
London SW3 6RB

ISBN 1 85152 112 7

Printed in Great Britain by The Bath Press

CONTENTS

Contents

Contents

Acknowledgements

The publishers wish to thank the following for permission to reprint previously published material. Every effort has been made to locate all persons having any rights in the stories appearing in this book. Any omissions will be corrected in future reprints upon written notification to the publishers.

The Trustees of the Wodehouse Estate, A.P. Watt Ltd. and Barrie & Jenkins, Ltd. for 'The Story of Webster', from *Mulliner Nights* by P.G. Wodehouse. Copyright © 1933 by Barrie & Jenkins Ltd.

Martin Secker and Warburg, Ltd. and Farrar, Strauss and Giroux, Inc. for 'Three Cats', from *Creatures Great And Small* by Colette. Copyright © 1951 by Martin Secker and Warburg Ltd.

Douglas Sealy for 'How the First Cat Was Created', from *Legends Of Saints And Sinners* by Douglas Hyde, first published in 1915. Copyright © by Douglas Sealy.

Curtis, Brown, Ltd. for 'The Fat Cat', by Quentin Patrick, from *This Week Magazine* Copyright © 1944 by Quentin Patrick.

The estate of the late Marguerite Steen and Michael Joseph Ltd. for chapter two of *Little White King* by Marguerite Steen. Copyright © 1956 by Michael Joseph Ltd.

William Heinemann Ltd. and Warner Books, Inc. for 'Ming's Biggest Prey', from *The Animal Lover's Book Of Beastly Murder* by Patricia Highsmith. Copyright © 1975 by Patricia Highsmith.

Souvenir Press Ltd. and Crown Publishers, Inc. for permission to reprint 'Speech' from *The Silent Miaow* by Paul Gallico and Suzanne Scatz. Copyright © 1964 by Paul Gallico.

Anon

I WISH she wouldn't ask me if
I love the kitten more than her.
Of course I love her –
          But I love the kitten too,
And it has fur . . .

Slippers. The White House Cat

Jacob A. Riis

Doubtless there never was, and never will be, another cat that has had respectful homage paid it by representatives of so many great and little powers of the world. But such was the experience of 'Slippers' in the year of grace 1906. Slippers was the name of the White House cat. Gray in colour, and having six toes, it was this unusual foot-furnishing that earned him his name. Perhaps because of a surplusage of dogs in this generation; perhaps because of an inbred Americanism that makes him assert his independence as a democratic cat, even in the White House under a Republican administration, and long to perch upon the back fence with others of his kind; perhaps just because he was a cat – Slippers had a habit of absenting himself from his post for days and weeks at a time. But, however long he stayed away, he never failed to turn up just before a big diplomatic dinner. How he knew, I cannot tell. No one can. But that he did know is certain. Anyone who kept a steady eye on the White House did not need to be told by the newspapers when a State dinner was impending. When he saw Slippers sunning himself on the front steps, that was enough. The cards were out.

Thus came about the historic occasion I hinted at. The dinner was over, and the President, with the wife of a distinguished Ambassador on his arm, led the procession from the state dining-room along the wide corridor to the East room at the other end of the building: Ambassadors and the plenipotentiaries and ministers following, according to their rank in the official world, all chattering happily with their ladies, seeing no cloud on the diplomatic horizon; when all of a sudden the glittering procession came to a halt. There, on the rug, in the exact middle of the corridor, lay Slippers, stretched out at full length and blinking lazily at the fine show which no doubt he thought got up especially to do him honour. The President saw him in time to avoid treading on him and stopped. His first impulse was to pick Slippers up, but a little shiver of his lady and a half suppressed exclamation, as he bent over the cat, warned him that she did not like cats, or was afraid, and for a moment he was perplexed. Slippers, perceiving the attention bestowed on him, rolled luxuriously on the rug, purring his delight. No thought of moving out of the path was in his mind. There was but one thing to do, and the man who found the way to make peace between Russia and Japan did it quickly. With an amused bow, as if in apology to the Ambassadress, he escorted her round Slippers, and kept on his way toward the East Room. Whereupon the representatives of Great Britain, and of France, of Germany, and Italy, of all the Empires and of the little kingdoms, followed suit, paying their respects to Slippers quite as effectually as if the warships of their nations had thundered out a salute at an expenditure of powder that would have kept a poor man comfortable for a year, and certainly have scared even a White House cat almost to death. But the honours the fates had in store for Slippers on that memorable night were not yet exhausted. There was a peril lurking in his sudden elevation of which, basking there in the electric light, he little dreamed, but which the President had made out at once. As soon as he had reached the East Room, he excused himself, went back to Slippers, and carried him to Mrs Roosevelt, that she might pet and admire him. So he was safe from the vengeance of any White House servant. For Slippers had acquired official status, so to speak, and not only in the house, but in the family.

There used to be a story of the President's father, who was a man of rare strength and lovableness of character, telling how one day, going to a meeting of the Chamber of Commerce, he found a little kitten some thoughtless boys had worried, and carefully wrapping it in his handkerchief, put it in his pocket and carried it in with him to the meeting and back to his home, where it was safe.

The Story of Webster

P. G. Wodehouse

'Cats are not dogs!'

There is only one place where you can hear good things like that thrown off quite casually in the general run of conversation, and that is the bar-parlour of the Anglers' Rest. It was there, as we sat grouped about the fire, that a thoughtful Pint of Bitter had made the statement just recorded.

Although the talk up to this point had been dealing with Einstein's Theory of Relativity, we readily adjusted our minds to cope with the new topic. Regular attendance at the nightly sessions over which Mr Mulliner presides with such unfailing dignity and geniality tends to produce mental nimbleness. In our little circle I have known an argument on the Final Destination of the Soul to change inside forty seconds into one concerning the best method of preserving the juiciness of bacon fat.

'Cats,' proceeded the Pint of Bitter, 'are selfish. A man waits on a cat hand and foot for weeks, humouring its lightest whim, and then it goes and leaves him flat because it has found a place down the road where the fish is more frequent.'

'What I've got against cats,' said a Lemon Sour, speaking feelingly, as one brooding on a private grievance, 'is their unreliability. They lack candour and are not square shooters. You get your cat and you call him Thomas or George, as the case may be. So far, so good. Then one morning you wake up and find six kittens in the hat-box and you have to reopen the whole matter, approaching it from an entirely different angle.'

'If you want to know what's the trouble with cats,' said a red-faced man with glassy eyes, who had been rapping on the table for his fourth whisky, 'they've got no tact. That's what's the trouble with them. I remember a friend of mine had a cat. Made quite a pet of that cat, he did. And what occurred? What was the outcome? One night he came home rather late and was feeling for the keyhole with his corkscrew; and, believe me or not, his cat selected that precise moment to jump on the back of his neck out of a tree. No tact.'

Mr Mulliner shook his head.

'I grant you all this,' he said, 'but still, in my opinion, you have not got quite to the root of the matter. The real objection to the great majority of cats is their insufferable air of superiority. Cats, as a class, have never completely got over the snootiness caused by the fact that in Ancient Egypt they were worshipped as gods. This makes them too prone to set themselves up as critics and censors of the frail and erring human beings whose lot they share. They stare rebukingly. They view with concern. And on a sensitive man this often has the worst effects, inducing an inferiority complex of the gravest kind. It is odd that the conversation should have taken this turn,' said Mr Mulliner, sipping his hot Scotch and lemon, 'for I was thinking only this afternoon of the rather strange case of my cousin Edward's son, Lancelot.'

'I knew a cat – ' began a Small Bass.

My cousin Edward's son, Lancelot (said Mr Mulliner) was, at the time of which I speak, a comely youth of some twenty-five summers. Orphaned at an early age, he had been brought up in the home of his Uncle Theodore, the saintly Dean of Bolsover; and it was a great shock to that good man when Lancelot, on attaining his majority, wrote from London to inform him that he had taken a studio in Bott Street, Chelsea, and proposed to remain in the metropolis and become an artist.

The Dean's opinion of artists was low. As a prominent member of the Bolsover Watch Committee, it had recently been his distasteful duty to be present at a private showing of the super-super-film, *Palettes of Passion*; and he replied to his nephew's communication with a vibrant letter in which he emphasized the grievous pain it gave him to think that one of his flesh and blood should deliberately be embarking on a career which must inevitably lead sooner or later to the painting of Russian princesses lying on divans in the semi-nude with their arms round tame jaguars. He urged Lancelot to return and become a curate while there was yet time.

But Lancelot was firm. He deplored the rift between himself and a relative whom he had always respected; but he was dashed if he meant to go back to an environment where his individuality had been stifled and his soul confined in chains. And for four years there was silence between uncle and nephew.

During these years Lancelot had made progress in his chosen profession. At the time at which this story opens, his prospects seemed bright. He was painting the portrait of Brenda, only daughter of Mr and Mrs B. B. Carberry-Pirbright, of 11, Maxton Square, South Kensington, which meant thirty pounds in his sock on delivery. He had learned to cook eggs and bacon. He had practically mastered the ukulele. And, in addition, he was engaged to be married to a fearless young *vers libre* poetess of the name of Gladys Bingley, better known as The Sweet Singer of Garbidge Mews, Fulham – a charming girl who looked like a pen-wiper.

It seemed to Lancelot that life was very full and beautiful. He lived joyously in the present, giving no thought to the past.

But how true it is that the past is inextricably mixed up with the present and that we can never tell when it may not spring some delayed bomb beneath our feet. One afternoon, as he sat making a few small alterations in the portrait of Brenda Carberry-Pirbright, his fiancée entered.

He had been expecting her to call, for today she was going off for a three weeks' holiday to the South of France, and she had promised to look in on her way to the station. He laid down his brush and gazed at her with a yearning affection, thinking for the thousandth time how he worshipped every spot of ink on her nose. Standing there in the doorway with her bobbed hair sticking out in every direction like a golliwog's she made a picture that seemed to speak to his very depths.

'Hullo, Reptile!' he said lovingly.

'What ho, Worm!' said Gladys, maidenly devotion shining through the monocle which she wore in her left eye. 'I can stay just half an hour.'

'Oh, well, half an hour soon passes,' said Lancelot. 'What's that you've got there?'

'A letter, ass. What did you think it was?'

'Where did you get it?'

'I found the postman outside.'

Lancelot took the envelope from her and examined it.

'Gosh!' he said.

'What's the matter?'

'It's from my Uncle Theodore.'

'I didn't know you had an Uncle Theodore.'

'Of course I have. I've had him for years.'

'What's he writing to you about?'

'If you'll kindly keep quiet for two seconds, if you know how,' said Lancelot, 'I'll tell you.'

And in a clear voice which, like that of all the Mulliners, however distant from the main branch, was beautifully modulated, he read as follows:

'The Deanery,

'Bolsover,

'Wilts.'

'MY DEAR LANCELOT,

'As you have, no doubt, already learned from your *Church Times*, I have been offered and have accepted the vacant Bishopric of Bongo-Bongo in West Africa. I sail immediately to take up my new duties, which I trust will be blessed.

'In these circumstances, it becomes necessary for me to find a good home for my cat Webster. It is, alas, out of the question that he should accompany me, as the rigours of the climate and the lack of essential comforts might well sap a constitution which has never been robust.

'I am dispatching him, therefore, to your address, my dear boy, in a straw-lined hamper, in the full confidence that you will prove a kindly and conscientious host.

'With cordial good wishes,

'Your affectionate uncle,

'THEODORE BONGO-BONGO.'

For some moments after he had finished reading this communication, a thoughtful silence prevailed in the studio. Finally Gladys spoke.

'Of all the nerve!' she said. 'I wouldn't do it.'

'Why not?'

'What do you want with a cat?'

Lancelot reflected.

'It is true,' he said, 'that, given a free hand, I would prefer not to have my studio turned into a cattery or cat-bin. But consider the special circumstances. Relations between Uncle Theodore and self have for the last few years been a bit strained. In fact, you might say we had definitely parted brass-rags. It looks to me as if he were coming round. I should describe this letter as more or less what you might call an olive-branch. If I lush this cat up satisfactorily, shall I not be in a position later on to make a swift touch?'

'He is rich, this bean?' said Gladys, interested.

'Extremely.'

'Then,' said Gladys, 'consider my objections withdrawn. A good stout cheque from a grateful cat-fancier would undoubtedly come in very handy. We might be able to get married this year.'

'Exactly,' said Lancelot. 'A pretty loathsome prospect, of course, but still, as we've arranged to do it, the sooner we get it over, the better, what?'

'Absolutely.'

'Then that's settled. I accept custody of cat.'

'It's the only thing to do,' said Gladys. 'Meanwhile, can you lend me a comb? Have you such a thing in your bedroom?'

'What do you want with a comb?'

'I got some soup in my hair at lunch. I won't be a minute.'

She hurried out, and Lancelot, taking up the letter again, found that he had omitted to read a continuation of it on the back page.

It was to the following effect:

'P.S. In establishing Webster in your home, I am actuated by another motive than the simple desire to see to it that my faithful friend and companion is adequately provided for.

'From both a moral and an educative stand-point, I am convinced that Webster's society will prove of inestimable value to you. His advent, indeed, I venture to hope, will be a turning-point in your life. Thrown, as you must be, incessantly among loose and immoral Bohemians, you will find in this cat an example of upright conduct which cannot but act as an antidote to the poison cup of temptation which is, no doubt, hourly pressed to your lips.

'P.P.S. Cream only at midday, and fish not more than three times a week.'

He was reading these words for the second time, when the front door-bell rang and he found a man on the steps with a hamper. A discreet mew from within revealed its contents, and Lancelot, carrying it into the studio, cut the strings.

'Hi!' he bellowed, going to the door.

'What's up?' shrieked his betrothed from above.

'The cat's come.'

'All right. I'll be down in a jiffy.'

Lancelot returned to the studio.

'What ho, Webster!' he said cheerily. 'How's the boy?'

The cat did not reply. It was sitting with bent head, performing that wash and brush up which a journey by rail renders so necessary.

In order to facilitate these toilet operations, it had raised its left leg and was holding it rigidly in the air. And there flashed into Lancelot's mind an old superstition handed on to him, for what it was worth, by one of the nurses of his infancy. If, this woman had said, you creep up to a cat when its leg is in the air and give it a pull, then you make a wish and your wish comes true in thirty days.

It was a pretty fancy, and it seemed to Lancelot that the theory might as well be put to the test. He advanced warily, therefore, and was in the act of extending his fingers for the pull, when Webster, lowering the leg, turned and raised his eyes.

He looked at Lancelot. And suddenly with sickening force, there came to Lancelot the realization of the unpardonable liberty he had been about to take.

Until this moment, though the postscript to his uncle's letter should have warned him, Lancelot Mulliner had had no suspicion of what manner of cat this was that he had taken into his home. Now, for the first time, he saw him steadily and saw him whole.

Webster was very large and very black and very composed. He conveyed the impression of being a cat of deep reserves. Descendant of a long line of ecclesiastical ancestors who had conducted their decorous courtships beneath the shadow of cathedrals and on the back walls of bishops' palaces, he had that exquisite poise which one sees in high dignitaries of the church. His eyes were clear and steady, and seemed to pierce to the very roots of the young man's soul, filling him with a sense of guilt.

Once, long ago, in his hot childhood, Lancelot, spending his summer holidays at the deanery, had been so far carried away by ginger-beer and original sin as to plug a senior canon in the leg with his air-gun – only to discover, on turning, that a visiting archdeacon had been a spectator of the entire incident from his immediate rear. As he had felt then, when meeting the arch-deacon's eye, so did he feel now as Webster's gaze played silently upon him.

Webster, it is true, had not actually raised his eyebrows. But this, Lancelot felt, was simply because he hadn't any.

He backed, blushing.

'Sorry!' he muttered.

There was a pause. Webster continued his steady scrutiny. Lancelot edged towards the door.

'Er – excuse me – just a moment . . . ' he mumbled. And, sidling from the room, he ran distractedly upstairs.

'I say,' said Lancelot.

'Now what?' asked Gladys.

'Have you finished with the mirror?'

'Why?'

'Well, I – er – I thought,' said Lancelot, 'that I might as well have a shave.'

The girl looked at him, astonished.

'Shave? Why, you shaved only the day before yesterday.'

'I know. But, all the same . . . I mean to say, it seems only re-spectful. That cat, I mean.'

'What about him?'

'Well, he seems to expect it, somehow. Nothing actually said, don't you know, but you could tell by his manner. I thought a quick shave and perhaps change into my blue serge suit – '

'He's probably thirsty. Why don't you give him some milk?'

'Could one, do you think?' said Lancelot doubtfully. 'I mean, I hardly seem to know him well enough.' He paused. 'I say, old girl,' he went on, with a touch of hesitation.

'Hullo?'

'I know you won't mind my mentioning it, but you've got a few spots of ink on your nose.'

'Of course I have. I always have spots of ink on my nose.'

'Well . . . you don't think . . . a quick scrub with a bit of pumice-stone . . . I mean to say, you know how important first impressions are. . . . '

The girl stared.

'Lancelot Mulliner,' she said, 'if you think I'm going to skin my nose to the bone just to please a mangy cat – '

'Sh!' cried Lancelot, in agony.

'Here, let me go down and look at him,' said Gladys petulantly.

As they re-entered the studio, Webster was gazing with an air of quiet distaste at an illustration from *La Vie Parisienne* which adorned one of the walls. Lancelot tore it down hastily.

Gladys looked at Webster in an unfriendly way.

'So that's the blighter!'

'Sh!'

'If you want to know what I think,' said Gladys, 'that cat's been living too high. Doing himself a dashed sight too well. You'd better cut his rations down a bit.'

In substance, her criticism was not unjustified. Certainly, there was about Webster more than a suspicion of *embonpoint*. He had that air of portly well-being which we associate with those who dwell in cathedral closes. But Lancelot winced uncomfortably. He had so hoped that Gladys would make a good impression, and here she was, starting right off by saying the tactless thing.

He longed to explain to Webster that it was only her way; that in the Bohemian circles of which she was such an ornament genial chaff of a personal order was accepted and, indeed, relished. But it was too late. The mischief had been done. Webster turned in a pointed manner and withdrew silently behind the chesterfield.

Gladys, all unconscious, was making preparations for departure.

'Well, bung-oh,' she said lightly. 'See you in three weeks. I suppose you and that cat'll both be out on the tiles the moment my back's turned.'

'Please! Please!' moaned Lancelot. 'Please!'

He had caught sight of the tip of a black tail protruding from behind the chesterfield. It was twitching slightly, and Lancelot could read it like a book. With a sickening sense of dismay, he knew that Webster had formed a snap judgment of his fiancée and condemned her as frivolous and unworthy.

It was some ten days later that Bernard Worple, the neo-Vorticist sculptor, lunching at the Puce Ptarmigan, ran into Rodney Scollop, the powerful young surrealist. And after talking for a while of their art –

'What's all this I hear about Lancelot Mulliner?' asked Worple. 'There's a wild story going about that he was seen shaved in the middle of the week. Nothing in it, I suppose?'

Scollop looked grave. He had been on the point of mentioning Lancelot himself, for he loved the lad and was deeply exercised about him.

'It is perfectly true,' he said.

'It sounds incredible.'

Scollop leaned forward. His fine face was troubled.

'Shall I tell you something, Worple?'

'What?'

'I know for an absolute fact,' said Scollop, 'that Lancelot Mulliner now shaves every morning.'

Worple pushed aside the spaghetti which he was wreathing about him and through the gap stared at his companion.

'Every morning?'

'Every single morning. I looked in on him myself the other day, and there he was, neatly dressed in blue serge and shaved to the core. And, what is more, I got the distinct impression that he had used talcum powder afterwards.'

'You don't mean that!'

'I do. And shall I tell you something else? There was a book lying open on the table. He tried to hide it, but he wasn't quick enough. It was one of those etiquette books!'

'An etiquette book!'

'*Polite Behaviour*, by Constance, Lady Bodbank.'

Worple unwound a stray tendril of spaghetti from about his left ear. He was deeply agitated. Like Scollop, he loved Lancelot.

'He'll be dressing for dinner next!' he exclaimed.

'I have every reason to believe,' said Scollop gravely, 'that he does dress for dinner. At any rate, a man closely resembling him was seen furtively buying three stiff collars and a black tie at Hope

Brothers in the King's Road last Tuesday.'

Worple pushed his chair back, and rose. His manner was determined.

'Scollop,' he said, 'we are friends of Mulliner's, you and I. It is evident from what you tell me that subversive influences are at work and that never has he needed our friendship more. Shall we not go round and see him immediately?'

'It was what I was about to suggest myself,' said Rodney Scollop.

Twenty minutes later they were in Lancelot's studio, and with a significant glance Scollop drew his companion's notice to their host's appearance. Lancelot Mulliner was neatly, even foppishly, dressed in blue serge with creases down the trouser-legs, and his chin, Worple saw with a pang, gleamed smoothly in the afternoon light.

At the sight of his friends' cigars, Lancelot exhibited unmistakable concern.

'You don't mind throwing those away, I'm sure,' he said pleadingly.

Rodney Scollop drew himself up a little haughtily.

'And since when,' he asked, 'have the best fourpenny cigars in Chelsea not been good enough for you?'

Lancelot hastened to soothe him.

'It isn't me,' he exclaimed. 'It's Webster. My cat. I happen to know he objects to tobacco smoke. I had to give up my pipe in deference to his views.'

Bernard Worple snorted.

'Are you trying to tell us,' he sneered, 'that Lancelot Mulliner allows himself to be dictated to by a blasted cat?'

'Hush!' cried Lancelot, trembling. 'If you knew how he disapproves of strong language!'

'Where is this cat?' asked Rodney Scollop. 'Is that the animal?' he said, pointing out of the window to where, in the yard, a tough-looking Tom with tattered ears stood mewing in a hardboiled way out of the corner of its mouth.

'Good heavens, no!' said Lancelot. 'That is an alley cat which comes round here from time to time to lunch at the dustbin. Webster is quite different. Webster has a natural dignity and repose of manner. Webster is a cat who prides himself on always being well turned out and whose high principles and lofty ideals shine from his eyes like beacon-fires. . . . ' And then suddenly, with an abrupt change of manner, Lancelot broke down and in a low voice added: 'Curse him! Curse him! Curse him! Curse him!'

Worple looked at Scollop. Scollop looked at Worple.

'Come, old man,' said Scollop, laying a gentle hand on Lancelot's bowed shoulder. 'We are your friends. Confide in us.'

'Tell us all,' said Worple. 'What's the matter?'

Lancelot uttered a bitter, mirthless laugh.

'You want to know what's the matter? Listen, then. I'm cat-pecked!'

'Cat-pecked?'

'You've heard of men being hen-pecked, haven't you?' said Lancelot with a touch of irritation. 'Well, I'm cat-pecked.'

And in broken accents he told his story. He sketched the history of his association with Webster from the letter's first entry into the studio. Confident now that the animal was not within earshot, he unbosomed himself without reserve.

'It's something in the beast's eye,' he said in a shaking voice. 'Something hypnotic. He casts a spell upon me. He gazes at me and disapproves. Little by little, bit by bit, I am degenerating under his influence from a wholesome, self-respecting artist into . . . well, I don't know what you would call it. Suffice it to say that I have given up smoking, that I have ceased to wear carpet slippers and go about without a collar, that I never dream of sitting down to my frugal evening meal without dressing, and' – he choked – 'I have sold my ukulele.'

'Not that!' said Worple, paling.

'Yes,' said Lancelot. 'I felt he considered it frivolous.'

There was a long silence.

'Mulliner,' said Scollop, 'this is more serious than I had supposed. We must brood upon your case.'

'It may be possible,' said Worple, 'to find a way out.'

Lancelot shook his head hopelessly.

'There is no way out. I have explored every avenue. The only thing that could possibly free me from this intolerable bondage would be if once – just once – I could catch that cat unbending. If once – merely once – it would lapse in my presence from its austere dignity for but a single instant, I feel that the spell would be broken. But what hope is there of that?' cried Lancelot passionately. 'You were pointing just now to that alley cat in the yard. There stands one who has strained every nerve and spared no effort to break down Webster's inhuman self-control. I have heard that animal say things to him which you would think no cat with red blood in its veins would suffer for an instant. And Webster merely looks at him like a Suffragan Bishop eyeing an erring choirboy and turns his head and falls into a refreshing sleep.'

He broke off with a dry sob. Worple, always an optimist, attempted in his kindly way to minimize the tragedy.

'Ah, well,' he said. 'It's bad, of course, but still, I suppose there is no actual harm in shaving and dressing for dinner and so on. Many great artists . . . Whistler, for example - '

'Wait!' cried Lancelot. 'You have not heard the worst.'

He rose feverishly, and, going to the easel, disclosed the portrait of Brenda Carberry-Pirbright.

'Take a look at that,' he said, 'and tell me what you think of her.'

His two friends surveyed the face before them in silence. Miss Carberry-Pirbright was a young woman of prim and glacial aspect. One sought in vain for her reasons for wanting to have her portrait painted. It would be a most unpleasant thing to have about any house.

Scollop broke the silence.

'Friend of yours?'

'I can't stand the sight of her,' said Lancelot vehemently.

'Then,' said Scollop, 'I may speak frankly. I think she's a pill.'

'A blister,' said Worple.

'A boil and a disease,' said Scollop, summing up.

Lancelot laughed hackingly.

'You have described her to a nicety. She stands for everything most alien to my artist soul. She gives me a pain in the neck. I'm going to marry her.'

'What!' cried Scollop.

'But you're going to marry Gladys Bingley,' said Worple.

'Webster thinks not,' said Lancelot bitterly. 'At their first meeting he weighed Gladys in the balance and found her wanting. And the moment he saw Brenda Carberry-Pirbright he stuck his tail up at right angles, uttered a cordial gargle, and rubbed his head against her leg. Then, turning, he looked at me. I could read that glance. I knew what was in his mind. From that moment he has been doing everything in his power to arrange the match.'

'But, Mulliner,' said Worple, always eager to point out the bright side, 'why should this girl want to marry a wretched, scrubby, hard-up footler like you? Have courage, Mulliner, It is simply a question of time before you repel and sicken her.'

Lancelot shook his head.

'No,' he said. 'You speak like a true friend, Worple, but you do not understand. Old Ma Carberry-Pirbright, this exhibit's mother, who chaperons her at the sittings, discovered at an early date my relationship to my Uncle Theodore, who, as you know, has got it in gobs. She knows well enough that some day I shall be a rich man. She used to know my Uncle Theodore when he was Vicar of St Botolph's in Knightsbridge, and from the very first she assumed towards me the repellent chumminess of an old family friend. She was always trying to lure me to her At Homes, her Sunday luncheons, her little dinners. Once she actually suggested that I should escort her and her beastly daughter to the Royal Academy.'

He laughed bitterly. The mordant witticisms of Lancelot Mulliner at the expense of the Royal Academy were quote from Tite Street in the south to Holland Park in the north and eastward as far as Bloomsbury.

'To all these overtures,' resumed Lancelot, 'I remained firmly unresponsive. My attitude was from the start one of frigid aloofness. I did not actually say in so many words that I would rather be dead in a ditch than at one of her At Homes, but my manner indicated it. And I was just beginning to think I had choked her off when in crashed Webster and upset everything. Do you know how many times I have been to that infernal house in the last week? Five. Webster seemed to wish it. I tell you, I am a lost man.'

He buried his face in his hands. Scollop touched Worple on the arm, and together the two men stole silently out.

'Bad!' said Worple.

'Very bad,' said Scollop.

'It seems incredible.'

'Oh, no. Cases of this kind are, alas, by no means uncommon

among those who, like Mulliner, possess to a marked degree the highly-strung, ultra-sensitive artistic temperament. A friend of mine, a rhythmical interior decorator, once rashly consented to put his aunt's parrot up at his studio while she was away visiting friends in the north of England. She was a woman of strong evangelical views, which the bird had imbibed from her. It had a way of putting its head on one side, making a noise like someone drawing a cork from a bottle, and asking my friend if he was saved. To cut a long story short, I happened to call on him a month later and he had installed a harmonium in his studio and was singing hymns , ancient and modern, in a rich tenor, while the parrot, standing on one leg on its perch, took the bass. A very sad affair. We were all much upset about it.'

Worple shuddered.

'You appal me, Scollop! Is there nothing we can do?'

Rodney Scollop considered for a moment.

'We might wire Gladys Bingley to come home at once. She might possibly reason with the unhappy man. A woman's gentle influence . . . Yes, we could do that. Look in at the post office on your way home and send Gladys a telegram. I'll owe you for my half of it.'

In the studio they had left, Lancelot Mulliner was staring dumbly at a black shape which had just entered the room. He had the appearance of a man with his back to the wall.

'No!' he was crying. 'No! I'm dashed if I do!'

Webster continued to look at him.

'Why should I?' demanded Lancelot weakly.

Webster's gaze did not flicker.

'Oh, all right,' said Lancelot suddenly.

He passed from the room with leaden feet, and proceeding upstairs, changed into morning clothes and a top hat. Then, with a gardenia in his buttonhole, he made his way to 11, Maxton Square, where Mrs Carberry-Pirbright was giving one of her intimate little teas ('just a few friends') to meet Clara Throckmorton Stooge, authoress of *A Strong Man's Kiss*.

Gladys Bingley was lunching at her hotel in Antibes when Worple's telegram arrived. It occasioned her the gravest concern.

Exactly what it was all about, she was unable to gather, for emotion had made Bernard Worple rather incoherent. There were moments, reading it, when she fancied that Lancelot had met with a serious accident; others when the solution seemed to be that he had sprained his brain to such an extent that rival lunatic asylums were competing eagerly for his custom; others, again, when Worple appeared to be suggesting that he had gone into partnership with his cat to start a harem. But one fact emerged clearly. Her loved one was in serious trouble of some kind, and his best friends were agreed that only her immediate return could save him.

Gladys did not hesitate. Within half an hour of the receipt of the telegram she had packed her trunk, removed a piece of asparagus from her right eyebrow, and was negotiating for accommodation on the first train going north.

Arriving in London, her first impulse was to go straight to Lancelot. But a natural feminine curiosity urged her, before doing so, to call upon Bernard Worple and have light thrown on some of the more abstruse passages in the telegram.

Worple, in his capacity of author, may have tended towards obscurity, but, when confining himself to the spoken word, he told a plain story well and clearly. Five minutes of his society enabled Gladys to obtain a firm grasp on the salient facts, and there appeared on her face that grim, tight-lipped expression which is seen only on the faces of fiancées who have come back from a short holiday to discover that their dear one has been straying in their absence from the straight and narrow path.

'Brenda Carberry-Pirbright, eh?' said Gladys, with ominous calm. 'I'll give him Brenda Carberry-Pirbright! My gosh, if one can't go off to Antibes for the merest breather without having one's betrothed getting it up his nose and starting to act like a Mormon Elder, it begins to look a pretty tough world for a girl.'

Kind-hearted Bernard Worple did his best.

'I blame the cat,' he said. 'Lancelot, to my mind, is more sinned against than sinning. I consider him to be acting under undue influence or duress.'

'How like a man!' said Gladys. 'Shoving it all off on to an innocent cat!'

'Lancelot says it has a sort of something in its eye.'

'Well, when I meet Lancelot,' said Gladys, 'he'll find that I have a sort of something in my eye.'

She went out, breathing flame quietly through her nostrils. Worple, saddened, heaved a sigh and resumed his neo-Vorticist sculping.

It was some five minutes later that Gladys, passing through Maxton Square on her way to Bott Street, stopped suddenly in her tracks. The sight she had seen was enough to make any fiancée do so.

Along the pavement leading to Number Eleven two figures were advancing. Or three, if you counted a morose-looking dog of a semi-Dachshund nature which preceded them, attached to a leash. One of the figures was that of Lancelot Mulliner, natty in grey herring-bone tweed and a new Homburg hat. It was he who held the leash. The other Gladys recognized from the portrait which she had seen on Lancelot's easel as that modern Du Barry, that notorious wrecker of homes and breaker-up of love-nests, Brenda Carberry-Pirbright.

The next moment they had mounted the steps of Number Eleven, and had gone in to tea, possibly with a little music.

It was perhaps an hour and half later that Lancelot, having wrenched himself with difficulty from the lair of the Philistines, sped homeward in a swift taxi. As always after an extended *tête-à-tête* with Miss Carberry-Pirbright, he felt dazed and bewildered, as if he had been swimming in a sea of glue and had swallowed a good deal of it. All he could think of clearly was that he wanted a drink and that the materials for that drink were in the cupboard behind the chesterfield in his studio.

He paid the cab and charged in with his tongue rattling dryly against his front teeth. And there before him was Gladys Bingley, whom he had supposed far, far away.

'You!' exclaimed Lancelot.

'Yes, me!' said Gladys.

Her long vigil had not helped to restore the girl's equinimity. Since arriving at the studio she had had leisure to tap her foot three thousand, one hundred and forty-two times on the carpet, and the number of bitter smiles which had flitted across her face was nine hundred and eleven. She was about ready for the battle of the century.

She rose and faced him, all the woman in her flashing from her eyes.

'Well, you Casanova!' she said.

'You who?' said Lancelot.

'Don't say "Yoo-hoo!" to me!' cried Gladys. 'Keep that for your Brenda Carberry-Pirbrights. Yes, I know all about it, Lancelot Don Juan Henry the Eighth Mulliner! I saw you with her just now. I hear that you and she are inseparable. Bernard Worple says you said you were going to marry her.'

'You mustn't believe everything a neo-Vorticist sculptor tells you,' quavered Lancelot.

'I'll bet you're going back to dinner there tonight,' said Gladys.

She had spoken at a venture, basing the charge purely on a possessive cock of the head which she had noticed in Brenda Carberry-Pirbright at their recent encounter. There, she had said to herself at the time, had gone a girl who was about to invite – or had just invited – Lancelot Mulliner to dine quietly and take her to the pictures afterwards. But the shot went home. Lancelot hung his head.

'There was some talk of it,' he admitted.

'Ah!' exclaimed Gladys.

Lancelot's eyes were haggard.

'I don't want to go,' he pleaded. 'Honestly I don't. But Webster insists.'

'Webster!'

'Yes, Webster. If I attempt to evade the appointment, he will sit in front of me and look at me.'

'Tchah!'

'Well, he will. Ask him for yourself.'

Gladys tapped her foot six times in rapid succession on the carpet, bringing the total to three thousand, one hundred and forty-eight. Her manner had changed and was now dangerously calm.

'Lancelot Mulliner,' she said, 'you have your choice. Me, on the one hand, Brenda Carberry-Pirbright on the other. I offer you a home where you will be able to smoke in bed, spill the ashes on the floor, wear pyjamas and carpet-slippers all day and shave only on Sunday mornings. From her, what have you to hope? A house in South Kensington – possibly the Brompton Road – probably with her mother living with you. A life that will be one long round of stiff collars and tight shoes, of morning-coats and top hats. '

Lancelot quivered, but she went on remorselessly.

'You will be at home on alternative Thursdays, and will be expected to hand the cucumber sandwiches. Every day you will air the dog, till you become a confirmed dog-airer. You will dine out in Bayswater and go for the summer to Bournemouth or Dinard. Choose well, Lancelot Mulliner! I will leave you to think it over. But one last word. If by seven-thirty on the dot you have not presented yourself at 6A, Garbidge Mews ready to take me out to dinner at the Ham and Beef, I shall know what to think and shall act accordingly.'

And brushing the cigarette ashes from her chin, the girl strode haughtily from the room.

'Gladys!' cried Lancelot.

But she had gone.

For some minutes Lancelot Mulliner remained where he was, stunned. Then, insistently, there came to him the recollection that he had not had that drink. He rushed to the cupboard and produced the bottle. He uncorked it, and was pouring out a lavish stream, when a movement on the floor below him attracted his attention.

Webster was standing there, looking up at him. And in his eyes was that familiar expresson of quiet rebuke.

'Scarcely what I have been accustomed to at the Deanery,' he seemed to be saying.

Lancelot stood paralysed. The feeling of being bound hand and foot, of being caught in a snare from which there was no escape, had become more poignanat than ever. The bottle fell from his nerveless fingers and rolled across the floor, spilling its contents in an amber river, but he was too heavy in spirit to notice it. With a gesture such as Job might have made on discovering a new boil, he crossed to the window and stood looking moodily out.

Then, turning with a sigh, he looked at Webster again – and, looking, stood spellbound.

The spectacle which he beheld was of a kind to stun a stronger man than Lancelot Mulliner. At first, he shrank from believing his eyes. Then, slowly, came the realisation that what he saw was no mere figment of a disordered imagination. This unbelievable thing was actually happening.

Webster sat crouched upon the floor beside the widening pool of whisky. But it was not horror and disgust that had caused him to crouch. He was crouched because, crouching, he could get nearer to the stuff and obtain crisper action. His tongue was moving in and out like a piston.

And then abruptly, for one fleeting instant, he stopped lapping and glanced up at Lancelot, and across his face there flitted a quick smile – so genial, so intimate, so full of jovial camaraderie, that the young man found himself automatically smiling back, and not only smiling but winking. And in answer to that wink Webster winked, too – a wholehearted, roguish wink that said as plainly as if he had spoken the words:

'How long has this been going on?'

Then with a slight hiccough he turned back to the task of getting his quick before it soaked into the floor.

Into the murky soul of Lancelot Mulliner there poured a sudden flood of sunshine. It was as if a great burden had been lifted from his shoulders. The intolerable obsession of the last two weeks had ceased to oppress him, and he felt a free man. At the eleventh hour the reprieve had come. Webster, that seeming pillar of austere virtue, was one of the boys, after all. Never again would Lancelot quail beneath his eye. He had the goods on him.

Webster, like the stag at eve, had now drunk his fill. He had left the pool of alcohol and was walking round in slow, meditative circles. From time to time he mewed tentatively, as if he were trying to say 'British Constitution.' His failure to articulate the syllables appeared to tickle him, for at the end of each attempt he would utter a slow, amused chuckle. It was at about this moment that he suddenly broke into a rhythmic dance, not unlike the old Saraband.

It was an interesting spectacle, and at any other time Lancelot would have watched it raptly. But now he was busy at his desk, writing a brief note to Mrs Carberry-Pirbright, the burden of which was that if she thought he was coming within a mile of her foul house that night or any other night she had vastly underrated the dodging powers of Lancelot Mulliner.

And what of Webster? The Demon Rum now had him in an

iron grip. A lifetime of abstinence had rendered him a ready victim to the fatal fluid. He had now reached the stage when geniality gives way to belligerence. The rather foolish smile had gone from his face, and in its stead there lowered a fighting frown. For a few moments he stood on his hind legs, looking about him for a suitable adversary: then, losing all vestiges of self-control, he ran five times round the room at a high rate of speed and, falling foul of a small footstool, attacked it with the utmost ferocity, sparing neither tooth nor claw.

But Lancelot did not see him. Lancelot was not there. Lancelot was out in Bott Street, hailing a cab.

'6A, Garbidge Mews, Fulham,' said Lancelot to the driver.

Puss in Boots

Charles Perrault

A miller, dying, divided all his property among his three children. This was a very simple matter, as he had nothing to leave but his mill, his Ass, and his Cat; so he made no will, and called in no lawyer, who would probably have taken a large slice out of these poor possessions. The eldest son took the mill, the second the Ass, while the third was obliged to content himself with the Cat, at which he grumbled very much. 'My brothers,' said he, 'by putting their property together, may gain an honest livelihood; but there is nothing left for me, except to die of hunger – unless, indeed, I were to kill my Cat and eat him, and make a coat out of his skin, which would be very scanty clothing.'

The Cat, who heard the young man talking to himself, sat up on his four paws, and looking at him with a grave and wise air, said, 'Master, I think you had better not kill me; I shall be much more useful to you alive.'

'How so?' asked his master.

'You have but to give me a sack, and a pair of boots such as gentlemen wear when they go shooting, and you will find you are not so ill off as you suppose.'

Now, though the young miller did not much depend upon the Cat's words, still he thought it rather surprising that a Cat should speak at all. And he had before now seen him show so much adroitness and cleverness in catching Rats and Mice that it seemed advisable to trust him a little further; especially as, poor young fellow! he had nobody else to trust.

When the Cat got his boots, he drew them on with a grand air; and slinging his sack over his shoulder, and drawing the cords of it around his neck, he marched bravely to a Rabbit warren hard by, with which he was well acquainted. Then, putting some bran and lettuces into his bag, and stretching himself out beside it as if he were dead, he waited till some fine fat young Rabbit, ignorant of the wickedness and deceit of the world should peer into the sack to eat the food that was inside.

This happened very shortly, for there are plenty of foolish young Rabbits in every warren; and when one of them, who really was a splendid fat fellow, put his head inside, Master Puss drew the cords immediately, and took him and killed him without mercy.

Then, very proud of his prey, he marched directly up to the palace, and begged to speak with the king. He was desired to ascend to the apartment of his majesty, where, making a low bow, he said, –

'Sire, here is a magnificent Rabbit, killed in the warren which belongs to my lord the Marquis of Carabas, which he has desired me to offer humbly to your majesty.'

'Tell your master,' replied the king politely, 'that I accept his present, and am very much obliged to him.'

Another time, Puss went and hid himself and his sack in a wheat field, and there caught two splendid fat Partridges in the same manner as he had done the Rabbit. When he presented them to the king, with a smilar message as before, his majesty was so pleased that he ordered the Cat to be taken down into the kitchen and given something to eat and drink; where, while enjoying himself, the faithful animal talked in the most cunning way of the large preserves and abundant game which belonged to 'my lord the Marquis of Carabas.'

One day, hearing that the king was intending to take a drive along the riverside with his daughter, the most beautiful princess in the world, Puss said to his master, 'Sir, if you will only follow my advice, your fortune is made.'

'Be it so,' said the miller's son, who was growing very disconsolate, and cared little what he did, 'say your say, Cat.'

'It is but little,' replied Puss, looking wise, as Cats can. 'You have only to go and bathe in the river, at a place which I shall show you, and leave the rest to me. Only remember that you are no longer yourself, but my lord the Marquis of Carabas.'

'Just so,' said the miller's son, 'it's all the same to me'; but he did as the Cat told him.

While he was bathing, the king and all the court passed by, and were startled to hear loud cries of 'Help! help! my lord the Marquis of Carabas is drowning.' The king put his head out of the carriage, and saw nobody but the Cat, who had, at different times, brought him so many presents of game; however, he ordered his guards to fly quickly to the succour of 'my lord the Marquis of Carabas.' While they were pulling the unfortunate marquis out of the water, the Cat came up, bowing to the side of the king's carriage, and told a long and pitiful story about some thieves, who, while his master was bathing, had come and carried away all his clothes, so that it would be impossible for him to appear before his majesty and the illustrious princess.

'Oh, we will soon remedy that,' answered the king kindly; and immediately ordered one of the first officers of the household to ride back to the palace with all speed, and bring the most elegant supply of clothes for the young gentleman, who kept in the background until they arrived. Then, being handsome and well-made, his new clothes became him so well that he looked as if he had been a marquis all his days, and advanced with an air of respectful ease to offer his thanks to his majesty.

The king received him courteously, and the princess admired him very much. Indeed, so charming did he appear to her that she hinted to her father to invite him into the carriage with them, which, you may be sure, the young man did not refuse. The Cat, delighted at the success of his scheme, went away as fast as he could, and ran so swiftly that he kept a long way ahead of the royal carriage.

He went on and on till he came to some peasants who were mowing in the meadow. 'Good people,' said he in a very firm voice, 'the king is coming past here shortly; anad if you do not say that the field you are mowing belongs to my lord the Marquis of Carabas, you shall all be chopped as small as mincemeat.'

So when the king drove by, and asked whose meadow it was where there was such a splendid crop of hay, the mowers all answered, trembling, that it belonged to my lord the Marquis of Carabas.

'You have very fine land, Marquis,' said his majesty to the

miller's son; who bowed, and answered 'that it was not a bad meadow, take it altogether.'

Then the Cat came to a wheatfield, where the reapers were reaping with all their might. He bounced in upon them: 'The king is coming past today, and if you do not tell him that this wheat belongs to my lord the Marquis of Carabas, I will have you every one chopped as small as mincemeat.' The reapers, very much alarmed, did as they were bid, and the king congratulated the Marquis upon possessing such beautiful fields, laden with such an abundant harvest.

They drove on, the Cat always running before and saying the same thing to everybody he met – that they were to declare the whole country belonged to his master; so that even the king was astonished at the vast estate of 'my lord the Marquis of Carabas.'

But now the Cat arrived at a great castle where dwelt an Ogre, to whom belonged all the land through which the royal equipage had been driving. He was a cruel tyrant, and his tenants and servants were terribly afraid of him; which accounted for their being so ready to say whatever they were told to say by the Cat, who had taken pains to inform himself of all about the Ogre.

So, putting on the boldest face he could assume, Puss marched up to the castle with his boots on, and asked to see the owner of it, saying that he was on his travels, but did not wish to pass so near the castle of such a noble gentleman without paying his respects to him. When the Ogre heard this message, he went to the door, received the Cat as civilly as an Ogre can, and begged him to walk in and repose himself.

'Thank you, sir,' said the Cat; 'but first I hope you will satisfy a traveller's curiosity. I have heard in far countries of your many remarkable qualities, and especially how you have the power of changing yourself into any sort of beast you choose – a Lion, for instance, or an Elephant.'

He did so, and the Cat was so frightened that he sprang up to the roof of the castle and hid himself in the gutter – a proceeding rather inconvenient on account of his boots, which were not exactly fitted to walk with upon tiles. At length, perceiving that the Ogre had resumed his original form, he came down again stealthily, and confessed that he had been very much frightened.

'But, sir,' said he, 'it may be easy enough for such a big gentleman as you to change yourself into a large animal. I do not suppose you can become a small one – a Rat or a Mouse, for instance. I have heard that you can; still, for my part, I consider it quite impossible.'

'Impossible?' cried the other indignantly. 'You shall see!' and immediately the Cat saw the Ogre no longer, but a little Mouse running along on the floor.

This was exactly what he wanted; and he did the very best a Cat could do, and the most natural under the circumstances – he sprang upon the Mouse, and gobbled it up in a trice. So there was an end of the Ogre.

By this time, the king had arrived opposite the castle, and was seized with a strong desire to enter it. The Cat, hearing the noise of the carriage wheels, ran forward in a great hurry and standing at the gate, said in a loud voice, 'Welcome, sire, to the castle of my lord the Marquis of Carabas.'

'What!' cried his majesty, very much surprised, 'does the castle also belong to you? Truly, Marquis, you have kept your secret well up to the last minute. I have never seen anything finer than this courtyard and these battlements. Indeed, I have nothing like them in the whole of my dominions.'

The Marquis, without speaking, offered his hand to the princess to assist her to descend, and standing aside that the king might enter first – for he had already acquired all the manners of a court – followed his majesty to the great hall, where a magnificent collation was laid out, and where without more delay, they all sat down to feast.

Before the banquet was over, the king, charmed with the good qualities of the Marquis of Carabas – and likewise with his wine, of which he had drunk six or seven cups – said, bowing across the table at which the princess and the miller's son were talking very confidentially together, 'It rests with you, Marquis, whether you will not become my son-in-law.'

'I shall be only too happy,' said the complaisant Marquis, and the princess's cast-down eyes declared the same.

So they were married the very next day, and took possession of the Ogre's castle, and everything that had belonged to him.

As for the Cat, he became at once a grand personage and had never more any need to run after Mice, except for his own diversion.

Jephson's Cat Stories

Jerome K. Jerome

'Cats,' remarked Jephson to me, one afternoon, as we sat in the punt discussing the plot of our novel, 'cats are animals for whom I entertain a very great respect. Cats and Nonconformists seem to me the only things in this world possessed of a practicable working conscience. Watch a cat doing something mean and wrong – if ever one gives you the chance; notice how anxious she is that nobody should see her doing it; and how prompt, if detected, to pretend that she was not doing it – that she was not even thinking of doing it – that, as a matter of fact, she was just about to do something else, quite different. You might almost think they had a soul.

'Only this morning I was watching that tortoiseshell of yours on the houseboat. She was creeping along the roof, behind the flower-boxes, stalking a young thrush that had perched upon a coil of rope. Murder gleamed from her eye, assassination lurked in every twitching muscle of her body. As she crouched to spring, Fate, for once favouring the weak, directed her attention to myself, and she became, for the first time, aware of my presence. It acted upon her as a heavenly vision upon a Biblical criminal. In an instant she was a changed being. The wicked beast, going about seeking whom it might devour, had vanished. In its place sat a long-tailed, furry angel, gazing up into the sky with an expression that was one-third innocence and two-thirds admiration of the beauties of nature. What was she doing there, did I want to know? Why, could I not see, playing with a bit of earth. Surely I was not so evil-minded as to imagine she wanted to kill that dear little bird – God bless it.

'Then note an old Tom, slinking home in the early morning, after a night spent on a roof of bad repute. Can you picture to yourself a living creature less eager to attract attention? "Dear me," you can all but hear it saying to itself, "I'd no idea it was so late; how time does go when one is enjoying oneself. I do hope I shan't meet any one I know – very awkward, it's being so light."

'In the distance it sees a policeman, and stops suddenly within the shelter of a shadow. "Now what's he doing there," it says, "and close to our door too? I can't go in while he's hanging about. He's sure to see and recognise me; and he's just the sort of man to talk to the servants."

'It hides itself behind a post and waits, peeping cautiously round the corner from time to time. The policeman, however, seems to have taken up his residence at that particular spot, and the cat becomes worried and excited.

'"What's the matter with the fool?" it mutters indignantly; "is he dead? Why don't he move on, he's always telling other people to. Stupid ass."

'Just then a far-off cry of "milk" is heard, and the cat starts up in an agony of alarm. "Great Scott, hark at that! Why, everybody will be down before I get in. Well, I can't help it. I must chance it."

'He glances round at himself, and hesitates. "I wouldn't mind if I didn't look so dirty and untidy," he muses; "people are so prone to think evil in this world."

'"Ah, well," he adds, giving himself a shake, "there's nothing else for it, I must put my trust in Providence, it's pulled me through before: here goes."

'He assumes an aspect of chastened sorrow, and trots along with a demure and saddened step. It is evident he wishes to convey the idea that he has been out all night on work connected with the Vigilance Association, and is now returning home sick at heart because of the sights that he has seen.

'He squirms in, unnoticed, through a window, and has just time to give himself a hurried lick down before he hears the cook's step on the stairs. When she enters the kitchen he is curled up on the hearth-rug, fast asleep. The opening of the shutters awakes him. He rises and comes forward, yawning and stretching himself.

'"Dear me, is it morning, then?" he says drowsily. "Heigh-ho! I've had such a lovely sleep, cook; and such a beautiful dream about poor mother."

'Cats! do you call them? Why, they are Christians in everything except the number of legs.'

'They certainly are,' I responded, 'wonderfully cunning little animals, and it is not by their moral and religious instincts alone that they are so closely linked to man; the marvellous ability they display in taking care of 'number one' is worthy of the human race itself. Some friends of mine had a cat, a big black Tom: they have got half of him still. They had reared him from a kitten, and, in their homely, undemonstrative way, they liked him. There was nothing, however, approaching passion on either side.

'One day a Chinchilla came to live in the neighbourhood, under the charge of an elderly spinster, and the two cats met at a garden wall party.

'"What sort of diggings have you got?" asked the Chinchilla.

'"Oh, pretty fair."

'"Nice people?"

'"Yes, nice enough – as people go."

'"Pretty willing? Look after you well, and all that sort of thing?"

'"Yes – oh yes. I've no fault to find with them."

'"What's the victuals like?"

'"Oh, the usual thing, you know, bones and scraps, and a bit of dog-biscuit now and then for a change."

'"Bones and dog-biscuits! Do you mean to say you eat bones?"

'"Yes, when I can get 'em. Why, what's wrong about them?"

'"Shade of Egyptian Isis, bones and dog-biscuits! Don't you ever get any spring chickens, or a sardine, or a lamb cutlet?"

'"Chickens! Sardines! What are you talking about? What are sardines?"

'"What are sardines! Oh, my dear child (the Chinchilla was a lady cat, and always called gentlemen friends a little older than herself 'dear child'), these people of yours are treating you just shamefully. Come, sit down and tell me all about it. What do they give you to sleep on?"

'"The floor."

'"I thought so; and skim milk and water to drink, I suppose?"

'"It *is* a bit thin."

'"I can quite imagine it. You must leave these people, my dear, at once."

'"But where am I to go to?"

'"Anywhere."

'"But who'll take me in?"

'"Anybody, if you go the right way to work. How many times do you think I've changed my people? Seven! – and bettered myself on each occasion. Why, do you know where I was born? In a pig-sty. There were three of us, mother and I and my little brother. Mother would leave us every evening, returning generally just as it was getting light. One morning she did not come back. We waited and waited, but the day passed on and she did not return, and we grew hungrier and hungrier, and at last we lay down, side by side, and cried ourselves to sleep.

'"In the evening, peeping through a hole in the door, we saw her coming across the field. She was crawling very slowly, with her body close down against the ground. We called to her, and she answered with a low 'crroo'; but she did not hasten her pace.

'"She crept in and rolled over on her side, and we ran to her, for we were almost starving. We lay long upon her breasts, and she licked us over and over.

'"I dropped asleep upon her, and in the night I awoke, feeling cold. I crept closer to her, but that only made me colder still, and she was wet and clammy with a dark moisture that was oozing from her side. I did not know what it was at that time, but I have learnt since.

'"That was when I could hardly have been four weeks old, and from that day to this I've looked after myself: you've got to do that in this world, my dear. For a while, I and my brother lived on in that sty and kept ourselves. It was a grim struggle at first, two babies fighting for life; but we pulled through. At the end of about three months, wandering farther from home than usual, I came upon a cottage, standing in the fields. It looked warm and cosy through the open door, and I went in: I have always been blessed with plenty of nerve. Some children were playing round the fire, and they welcomed me and made much of me. It was a new sensation to me, and I stayed there. I thought the place a palace at the time.

'"I might have gone on thinking so if it had not been that, passing through the village one day, I happened to catch sight of a room behind a shop. There was a carpet on the floor, and a rug before the fire. I had never known till then that there were such luxuries in the world. I determined to make that shop my home, and I did so."

'"How did you manage it?" asked the black cat, who was growing interested.

'"By the simple process of walking in and sitting down. My dear child, cheek's the 'Open sesame' to every door. The cat that works hard dies of starvation, the cat that has brains is kicked downstairs for a fool, and the cat that has virtue is drowned for a scamp; but the cat that has cheek sleeps on a velvet cushion and dines on cream and horseflesh. I marched straight in and rubbed myself against the old man's legs. He and his wife were quite taken with what they called my 'trustfulness,' and adopted me with enthusiasm. Strolling about the fields of an evening I often used to hear the children of the cottage calling my name. It was weeks before they gave up seeking for me. One of them, the youngest, would sob herself to sleep of a night, thinking that I was dead: they were affectionate children.

'"I boarded with my shopkeeping friends for nearly a year, and from them I went to some new people who had lately come to the neighbourhood, and who possessed a really excellent cook. I think I could have been very satisfied with these people, but, unfortunately, they came down in the world, and had to give up the big house and the cook, and take a cottage, and I did not care to go back to that sort of life.

'"Accordingly I looked about for a fresh opening. There was a curious old fellow who lived not far off. People said he was rich, but nobody liked him. He was shaped differently from other men. I turned the matter over in my mind for a day or two, and then determined to give him a trial. Being a lonely sort of man, he might make a fuss over me, and if not I could go.

'"My surmise proved correct. I have never been more petted than I was by 'Toady,' as the village boys had dubbed him. My present guardian is foolish enough over me, goodness knows, but she has other ties, while 'Toady' had nothing else to love, not even himself. He could hardly believe his eyes at first when I jumped up on his knees and rubbed myself against his ugly face. 'Why, Kitty,' he said, 'do you know you're the first living thing that has ever come to me of its own accord.' There were tears in his funny little red eyes as he said that.

'"I remained two years with 'Toady,' and was very happy indeed. Then he fell ill, and strange people came to the house, and I was neglected. 'Toady' liked me to come up and lie upon the bed, where he could stroke me with his long, thin hand, and at first I used to do this. But a sick man is not the best of company, as you can imagine, and the atmosphere of a sick room not too healthy, so, all things considered, I felt it was time for me to make a fresh move.

'"I had some difficulty in getting away. 'Toady' was always asking for me, and they tried to keep me with him: he seemed to lie easier when I was there. I succeeded at length, however, and, once outside the door, I put sufficient distance between myself and the house to ensure my not being captured, for I knew 'Toady' so long as he lived would never cease hoping to get me back.

'"Where to go, I did not know. Two or three homes were offered me, but none of them quite suited me. At one place, where I put up for a day, just to see how I liked it, there was a dog; and at another, which would otherwise have done admirably, they kept a baby. Whatever you do, never stop at a house where they keep a baby. If a child pulls your tail or ties a paper bag round your head, you can give it one for itself and nobody blames you. 'Well, serve you right,' they say to the yelling brat, 'you shouldn't tease the poor thing.' But if you resent a baby's holding you by the throat and trying to gouge out your eye with a wooden ladle, you are called a spiteful beast, and 'shoo'd' all round the garden. If people keep babies, they don't keep me; that's my rule.

'"After sampling some three or four families, I finally fixed upon a banker. Offers more advantageous from a worldly point of view were open to me. I could have gone to a public-house, where the victuals were simply unlimited, and where the back door was left open all night. But about the banker's (he was also a churchwarden, and his wife never smiled at anything less than a joke by the bishop) there was an atmosphere of solid respectability that I felt would be comforting to my nature. My dear child, you will come across cynics who will sneer at respectability: don't you listen to them. Respectability is its own reward – and a very real and practical reward. It may not bring you dainty dishes and soft beds, but it brings you something better and more lasting. It brings you the consciousness that you are living the right life, that you are doing the right thing, that, so far as earthly ingenuity can fix it, you are going to the right place, and that other folks ain't. Don't you ever let any one set you against respectability. It's the most satisfying thing I know of in this world – and about the cheapest.

'"I was nearly three years with this family, and was sorry when I had to go. I should never have left it I could have helped it, but one day something happened at the bank which necessitated the banker's taking a sudden journey to Spain, and, after that, the house became a somewhat unpleasant place to live in. Noisy, disagreeable people were continually knocking at the door and making rows in the passage; and at night folks threw bricks at the windows.

'"I was in a delicate state of health at the time, and my nerves could not stand it. I said goodbye to the town, and making my way back into the country, put up with a county family.

'"They were great swells, but I should have preferred them had they been more homely. I am of an affectionate disposition, and I like every one about me to love me. They were good enough to me in their distant way, but they did not take much notice of me, and I soon got tired of lavishing attentions on people that neither valued nor responded to them.

'"From these people I went to a retired potato merchant. It was a social descent, but a rise so far as comfort and appreciation were concerned. They appeared to be an exceedingly nice family, and to be extremely fond of me. I say they 'appeared' to be these things, because the sequel proved that they were neither. Six months after I had come to them they went away and left me. They never asked me to accompany them. They made no arrangements for me to stay behind. They evidently did not care what became of me. Such egotistical indifference to the claims of friendship I had never before met with. It shook my faith – never too robust – in human nature. I determined that, in future, no one should have the opportunity of disappointing my trust in them. I selected my present mistress on the recommendation of a gentleman friend of mine who had formerly lived with her. He said she was an excellent caterer. The only reason he had left her was that she expected him to be in at ten each night, and that hour didn't fit in with his other arrangements. It made no difference to me – as a matter of fact, I do not care for these midnight *réunions* that are so popular amongst us. There are always too many cats for one properly to enjoy oneself, and sooner or later a rowdy element is sure to creep in. I offered myself to her, and she accepted me gratefully. But I have never liked her, and never shall. She is a silly old woman, and bores me. She is, however, devoted to me, and, unless something extra attractive turns up, I shall stick to her.

'"That, my dear, is the story of my life, so far as it has gone. I tell it you to show you how easy it is to be 'taken in.' Fix on your house, and mew piteously at the back door. When it is opened run in and rub yourself against the first leg you come across. Rub hard, and look up confidingly. Nothing gets round human beings, I have noticed, quicker than confidence. They don't get much of it, and it pleases them. Always be confiding. At the same time be prepared for emergencies. If you are still doubtful as to your reception, try and get yourself slightly wet. Why people should prefer a wet cat to a dry one I have never been able to understand; but that a wet cat is practically sure of being taken in and gushed over, while a dry cat is liable to have the garden hose turned upon it, is an undoubted fact. Also, if you can possibly manage it, and it is offered you, eat a bit of dry bread. The Human Race is always stirred to its deepest depths by the sight of a cat eating a bit of dry bread."

'My friend's black Tom profited by the Chinchilla's wisdom. A catless couple has lately come to live next door. He determined to adopt them on trial. Accordingly, on the first rainy day, he went out soon after lunch and sat for four hours in an open field. In the evening, soaked to the skin, and feeling pretty hungry, he went mewing to their door. One of the maids opened it, he rushed under her skirts and rubbed himself against her legs. She screamed, and down came the master and the mistress to know what was the matter.

'"It's a stray cat, mum," said the girl.

'"Turn it out," said the master.

'"Oh no, don't," said the mistress.

'"Perhaps it's hungry," said the cook.

'"Try it with a bit of dry bread," sneered the master, who wrote for the newspapers, and thought he knew everything.

'A stale crust was proferred. The cat ate it greedily, and afterwards rubbed imself gratefully against the man's light trousers.

'This made the man ashamed of himself, likewise of his trousers. 'Oh, well, let it stop if it wants to,' he said.

'So the cat was made comfortable, and stayed on.

'Meanwhile, its own family were seeking for it high and low. They had not cared over much for it while they had had it; now it was gone, they were inconsolable. In the light of its absence, it appeared to them the one thing that had made the place home. The shadows of suspicion gathered round the case. The cat's disappearance, at first regarded as a mystery, began to assume the shape of a crime. The wife openly accused the husband of never having liked the animal, and more than hinted that he and the gardener between them could give a tolerably truthful account of its last moments; an insinuation that the husband repudiated with a warmth that only added credence to the original surmise.

'The bull-terrier was had up and searchingly examined. Fortunately for him, he had not had a single fight for two whole days. Had any recent traces of blood been detected upon him, it would have gone hard with him.

'The person who suffered most, however, was the youngest boy. Three weeks before, he had dressed the cat in doll's clothes and taken it round the garden in the perambulator. He himself had forgotten the incident, but Justice, though tardy, was on his track. The misdeed was suddenly remembered at the very moment when unavailing regret for the loss of the favourite was at its deepest, so that to box his ears and send him, then and there, straight off to bed was felt to be a positive relief.

'At the end of a fortnight, the cat, finding he had not, after all, bettered himself, came back. The family were so surprised that at first they could not be sure whether he was flesh and blood, or a spirit come to comfort them. After watching him eat half a pound of raw steak, they decided he was material, and caught him up and hugged him to their bosoms. For a week they over-fed him and made much of him. Then, the excitement cooling, he found himself dropping back into his old position, and didn't like it, and went next door again.

'The next door people had also missed him, and they likewise greeted his return with extravagant ebullitions of joy. This gave the cat an idea. He saw that his game was to play the two families off one against the other; which he did. He spent an alternate fortnight with each, and lived like a fighting cock. His return was always greeted with enthusiasm, and every means were adopted to induce him to stay. His little whims were carefully studied, his favourite dishes kept in constant readiness.

'The destination of his goings leaked out at length, and then the two families quarrelled about him over the fence. My friend accused the newspaper man of having lured him away. The newspaper man retorted that the poor creature had come to his door wet and starving, and added that he would be ashamed to keep an animal merely to ill-treat it. They have a quarrel about him twice a week on the average. It will probably come to blows one of these days.'

Jephson appeared much surprised by this story. He remained thoughtful and silent. I asked him if he would like to hear any more, and as he offered no active opposition I went on. (Maybe he was asleep; that idea did not occur to me at the time.)

I told him of my grandmother's cat, who, after living a blameless life for upwards of eleven years, and bringing up a family of something like sixty-six, not counting those that died in infancy and the water-butt, took to drink in her old age, and was run over while in a state of intoxication (oh, the justice of it!) by a brewer's dray. I have read in temperance tracts that no dumb animal will touch a drop of alcoholic liquor. My advice is, if you wish to keep them respectable, don't give them a chance to get at it. I knew a pony – But never mind him; we are talking about my grandmother's cat.

A leaky beer-tap was the cause of her downfall. A saucer used to be placed underneath it to catch the drippings. One day the cat, coming in thirsty, and finding nothing else to drink, lapped up a little, liked it, and lapped a little more, went away for half an hour, and came back and finished the saucerful. Then sat down beside it, and waited for it to fill again.

From that day till the hour she died, I don't believe that cat was ever once quite sober. Her days she passed in a drunken stupor before the kitchen fire. Her nights she spent in the beer cellar.

My grandmother, shocked and grieved beyond expression, gave up her barrel and adopted bottles. The cat, thus condemned to enforced abstinence, meandered about the house for a day and a half in a disconsolate, quarrelsome mood. Then she disappeared, returning at eleven o'clock as tight as a drum.

Where she went, and how she managed to procure the drink, we never discovered; but the same programme was repeated every day. Some time during the morning she would contrive to elude our vigilance and escape; and late every evening she would come reeling home across the fields in a condition that I will not sully my pen by attempting to describe.

It was on Saturday night that she met the sad end to which I have before alluded. She must have been very drunk, for the man told us that, in consequence of the darkness, and the fact that his horses were tired, he was proceeding at little more than a snail's pace.

I think my grandmother was rather relieved than otherwise. She had been very fond of the cat at one time, but its recent conduct had alienated her affection. We children buried it in the garden under the mulberry tree, but the old lady insisted that there should be no tombstone, not even a mound raised. So it lies there, unhonoured, in a drunkard's grave.

I also told him of another cat our family had once possessed. She was the most motherly thing I have ever known. She was never happy without a family. Indeed, I cannot remember her when she hadn't a family in one stage or another. She was not very particular what sort of a family it was. If she could not have kittens, then she would content herself with puppies or rats. Anything that she could wash and feed seemed to satisfy her. I believe she would have brought up chickens if we had entrusted them to her.

All her brains must have run to motherliness, for she hadn't much sense. She could never tell the difference between her own children and other people's. She thought everything young was a kitten. We once mixed up a spaniel puppy that had lost its own mother among her progeny. I shall never forget her astonishment when it first barked. She boxed both its ears, and then sat looking down at it with an expression of indignant sorrow that was really touching.

'You're going to be a credit to your mother,' she seemed to be saying; 'you're a nice comfort to any one's old age, you are, making a row like that. And look at your ears flopping all over your face. I don't know where you pick up such ways.'

He was a good little dog. He did try to mew, and he did try to wash his face with his paw, and to keep his tail still, but his success was not commensurate with his will. I do not know which was the sadder to reflect upon, his efforts to become a creditable kitten, or his foster-mother's despair of ever making him one.

Later on we gave her a baby squirrel to rear. She was nursing a family of her own at the time, but she adopted him with enthusiasm, under the impression that he was another kitten, though she could not quite make out how she had come to overlook him. He soon became her prime favourite. She liked his colour, and took a mother's pride in his tail. What troubled her was that it would cock up over his head. She would hold it down with one paw, and lick it by the half-hour together, trying to make it set properly. But the moment she let it go up it would cock again. I have heard her cry with vexation because of this.

One day a neighbouring cat came to see her, and the squirrel was clearly the subject of their talk.

'It's a good colour,' said the friend, looking critically at the supposed kitten, who was sitting up on his haunches combing his whiskers, and saying the only truthfully pleasant thing about him that she could think of.

'He's a lovely colour,' exclaimed our cat proudly.

'I don't like his legs much,' remarked the friend.

'No,' responded his mother thoughtfully, 'you're right there. His legs are his weak point. I can't say I think much of his legs myself.'

'Maybe they'll fill out later on,' suggested the friend, kindly.

'Oh, I hope so,' replied the mother, regaining her momentarily dashed cheerfulness. 'Oh yes, they'll come all right in time. And then look at his tail. Now, honestly, did you ever see a kitten with a finer tail?'

'Yes, it's a good tail,' assented the other; 'but why do you do it up over his head?'

'I don't,' answered our cat. 'It goes that way. I can't make it out. I suppose it will come straight as he gets older.'

'It will be awkward if it don't,' said the friend.

'Oh, but I'm sure it will,' replied our cat. 'I must lick it more. It's a tail that wants a good deal of licking, you can see that.'

And for hours that afternoon, after the other cat had gone, she sat trimming it; and, at the end, when she lifted her paw off it, and it flew back again like a steel spring over the squirrel's head, she sat and gazed at it with feelings that only those among my readers who have been mothers themselves will be able to comprehend.

'What have I done,' she seemed to say – 'what have I done that this trouble should come upon me?'

Jephson roused himself on my completion of this anecdote and sat up.

'You and your friends appear to have been the possessors of some very remarkable cats,' he observed.

'Yes,' I answered, 'our family has been singularly fortunate in its cats.'

'Singularly so,' agreed Jephson; 'I have never met but one man from whom I have heard more wonderful cat talk than, at one time or another, I have from you.'

'Oh,' I said, not, perhaps without a touch of jealousy in my voice, 'and who was he?'

'He was a seafaring man,' replied Jephson. 'I met him on a Hampstead tram, and we discussed the subject of animal sagacity.

'"Yes, sir," he said, "monkeys is cute. I've come across monkeys as could give points to one or two lubbers I've sailed under; and elephants is pretty spry, if you can believe all that's told of 'em. I've heard some tall tales about elephants. And, of course, dogs has their heads screwed on all right: I don't say as they ain't. But what I do say is: that for straightfor'ard, level-headed reasoning, give me cats. You see, sir, a dog, he thinks a powerful deal of a man – never was such a cute thing as a man, in a dog's opinion; and he takes good care that everybody knows it. Naturally enough, we says a dog is the most intellectual animal there is.

Now a cat, she's got her own opinion about human beings. She don't say much, but you can tell enough to make you anxious not to hear the whole of it. The consequence is, we says a cat's got no intelligence. That's where we let our prejudice steer our judgment wrong. In a matter of plain common sense, there ain't a cat living as couldn't take the lee side of a dog and fly round him. Now, have you ever noticed a dog at the end of a chain, trying to kill a cat as is sitting washing her face three-quarters of an inch out of his reach? Of course you have. Well, who's got the sense out of those two? The cat knows that it ain't in the nature of steel chains to stretch. The dog, who ought, you'd think, to know a durned sight more about 'em than she does, is sure they will if you only bark loud enough.

'"Then again, have you ever been made mad by cats screeching in the night, and jumped out of bed and opened the window and yelled at them? Did they ever budge an inch for that, though you shrieked loud enough to skeer the dead, and waved your arms about like a man in a play? Not they. They've turned and looked at you, that's all. 'Yell away, old man,' they've said, 'we like to hear you: the more the merrier.' Then what have you done? Why, you've snatched up a hair-brush, or a boot, or a candlestick, and made as if you'd throw it at them. They've seen your attitude, they've seen the thing in your hand, but they ain't moved a point. They knew as you weren't going to chuck valuable property out of the window with the chance of getting it lost or spoiled. They've got sense themselves, and they give you credit for having some. If you don't believe that's the reason, you try showing them a lump of coal, or half a brick, next time – something as they know you *will* throw. Before you're ready to heave it, there won't be a cat within aim.

'"Then as to judgment and knowledge of the world, why dogs are babies to 'em. Have you ever tried telling a yarn before a cat, sir?"

'I replied that cats had often been present during anecdotal re-citals of mine, but that, hitherto, I had paid no particular attention to their demeanour.

'"Ah, well, you take an opportunity of doing so one day, sir," answered the old fellow; "it's worth the experiment. If you're tell-ing a story before a cat, and she don't get uneasy during any part of the narrative, you can reckon you've got hold of a thing as it will be safe for you to tell to the Lord Chief Justice of England.

'"I've got a messmate," he continued; "William Cooley is his name. We call him Truthful Billy. He's as good a seaman as ever trod quarter-deck; but when he gets spinning yarns he ain't the sort of man as I could advise you to rely upon. Well, Billy, he's got a dog, and I've seen him sit and tell yarns before that dog that would make a cat squirm out of its skin, and that dog's taken 'em in and believed 'em. One night, up at his old woman's, Bill told us a yarn by the side of which salt junk two voyages old would pass for spring chicken. I watched the dog to see how he would take it. He listened to it from beginning to end with cocked ears, and never so much as blinked. Every now and then he would look round with an expression of astonishment or delight that seemed to say: 'Wonderful, isn't it!' 'Dear me, just think of it!' 'Did you ever!' 'Well, if that don't beat everything!' He was a chuckle-headed dog; you could have told him anything.

'"It irritated me that Bill should have such an animal about him to encourage him, and when he had finished I said to him, 'I wish you'd tell that yarn round at my quarters one evening.'

'"Why?" said Bill.

'"Oh, it's just a fancy of mine,' I says. I didn't tell him I was wanting my old cat to hear it.

'"Oh, all right," says Bill, "you remind me." He loved yarning, Billy did.

'"Next night but one he slings himself up in my cabin, and I does so. Nothing loth, off he starts. There was about half-a-dozen of us stretched round, and the cat was sitting before the fire fussing itself up. Before Bill had got fairly under weigh, she stops washing and looks up at me, puzzled like, as much as to say, 'What have we got here, a missionary?' I signalled to her to keep quiet, and Bill went on with his yarn. When he got to the part about the sharks, she turned deliberately round and looked at him. I tell you there was an expression of disgust on that cat's face as might have made a travelling Cheap Jack felt ashamed of himself. It was that human, I give you my word, sir, I forgot for the moment as the poor animal couldn't speak. I could see the words that were on its lips: 'Why don't you tell us you swallowed the anchor?' and I sat on tenter-hooks, fearing each instant that she would say them aloud. It was a relief to me when she turned her back on Bill.

'"For a few minutes she sat very still, and seemed to be wrestling with herself like. I never saw a cat more set on controlling its feelings, or that seemed to suffer more in silence. It made my heart ache to watch it.

'"At last Bill came to the point where he and the captain between 'em hold the shark's mouth open while the cabin-boy dives in head foremost, and fetches up, undigested, the gold watch and chain as the bo'sun was a-wearing when he fell overboard; and at that the old cat giv'd a screech, and rolled over on her side with her legs in the air.

'"I thought at first the poor thing was dead, but she rallied after a bit, and it seemed as though she had braced herself up to hear the thing out.

'"But a little further on, Bill got too much for her again, and this time she owned herself beat. She rose up and looked round at us: 'You'll excuse me, gentlemen,' she said – leastways that is what she said if looks go for anything – 'maybe you're used to this sort of rubbish, and it don't get on your nerves. With me it's different. I guess I've heard as much of this fool's talk as my constitution will stand, and if it's all the same to you I'll get outside before I'm sick.'

'"With that she walked up to the door, and I opened it for her, and she went out.

'"You can't fool a cat with talk same as you can a dog."'

The Silent Miaow

Paul Gallico

I cannot begin to tell you how effective the Silent Miaow can be for breaking down resistance, always provided you don't overdo it but save it for the right moment.

The technique for this is ridiculously simple. You look up at the subject, open your mouth as you would for a fully articulated miaow, such as you emit if, say, you wish to leave the room and want the door opened, or are hungry or irritated by something, except in this case you permit no sound to issue.

The effect is simply staggering. The man or the woman appears to be shaken to the core, and will give you practically anything, which is why I say you must not use it often, for one of the human traits, in fact reduced to a proverb, is that 'Familiarity breeds contempt.' Whereas in our world, as you know, the proverb reads, 'Familiarity breeds contentment.'

Even I, who have made a lifelong study of the human species, am not able to tell you exactly why the Silent Miaow has this devastating effect, or even the exact emotion it inspires in people. The nearest I can come to it is that it creates a picture of helplessness that the God syndrome is unable to resist. We are already fortunate that certain notes of our spoken language, the miaow, resemble the cries of their own infants, the sound with which their young communicate their need for food, warmth, attention, or whatever it is they may be lacking. People have become conditioned to immediate response to this baby-wauling and thus, by association, a similar desire to do something about it can be evoked by the properly placed and pitiful miaow.

People, it seems, communicate principally vocally, and their clacking and chattering goes on interminably from morn till night and, believe it or not, some of them even continue to talk in their sleep.

Thus they will always think of the sounds we make in terms of theirs, and think of our language as being like theirs which, of course, could not possibly be wider of the mark.

To return, then, to the Silent Miaow. It appears to sum up for them such a burden of unhappiness and need that we are not able even to give voice to it. It is an un-cry of despair and longing that pierces more swiftly and directly to the human heart than the most self-pitying miaow of which we are capable and, I suspect, corresponds in the human mind to their own facial expressions of love, despair, anguish or entreaty, with which they are in the habit of supplementing their speech.

Speaking for myself, I usually confine the use of the Silent Miaow to begging at the dinner table, as indicated in my writing upon that subject, but it can also be used to good effect at other times when you want something you feel they are not inclined to give you.

I have referred in the above section to the pitiful miaow as among the most effective sounds you can produce to get some action out of your people, and to this must be added the sound that all of you will know how to produce, which has a most remarkable softening-up effect; it is that little lilt of ours, a chirrup, which goes, 'Prrrr-maow,' with a rising inflection upon the last syllable. This sound of ours has no specific use vis-à-vis people; except that for some reason or other it just seems to make them feel fine, and puts them into a good humor. We use it naturally from time to time as a kind of a greeting, or when we are in a particularly benign mood, and also when we happen to be carrying kittens, and I simply call it to your attention as yet another item in the armory for keeping our people in a state of subjugation and prepared to wait on us.

Fortunately for us, they are not all unintelligent, in a way, and you will find that it will not take you long to teach them various sounds you make, that is to say certain kinds of miaow, and what you mean by them. As you know, we, of course, have entirely different methods of communicating with one another in our world, but people are mostly dependent upon what they can hear, and hence this is what you use.

For instance, if you will go over and sit by the door and do a kind of short, scratchy miaow and perhaps even touch the door with your paw until they let you out, you will find that after a time your people are able to make the connection between that kind of a miaow and the fact that you want the door opened for you. You can do the same for food, or wanting your toys, or 'Get-off-my-chair,' until you have taught them quite a useful little vocabulary of eight or ten sounds, certainly all you need for *your* purposes, for you obviously won't wish to become any further involved in talk with them. For, and this is only an anthropological sideline upon the species, you will notice after you have lived with them for a long time that it is their constant talk and chatter that seems to land them in most of the trouble into which they get themselves. Remember, it does not matter which sounds or miaows you use for this reason, so long as each time you use the *same* one for each purpose. You can invent your own language here, and it is rather a good idea to do so, instead of copying that of some other cat, for here again you convey the desired illusion of exclusiveness, a secret means of communication between your people and yourself that cannot be understood by anyone else and will enable them to boast, 'When our cat wants to go out she goes like this: "——." I never heard any other cat do that.'

The Cameronian Cat

There was a Cameronian cat
   Was hunting for a prey,
And in the house she catched a mouse
   Upon the Sabbath-day.

The Whig, being offended
   At such an act profane,
Laid by his book, the cat he took,
   And bound her in a chain.

'Thou damned, thou curséd creature!
   This deed so dark with thee!
Think'st thou to bring to hell below
   My holy wife and me?

'Assure thyself that for the deed
   Thou blood for blood shall pay,
For killing of the Lord's own mouse
   Upon the Sabbath-day.'

The Presbyter laid by the book,
   And earnestly he prayed,
That the great sin the cat had done
   Might not on him be laid.

And straight to execution
    Poor pussy she was drawn,
And high hanged up upon a tree –
    The Preacher sang a psalm.

And when the work was ended,
    They thought the cat was dead;
She gave a paw, and then a mew,
    And stretchéd out her head.

'Thy name', said he, 'shall certainly
    A beacon still remain,
A terror unto evil ones,
    For evermore. Amen.'

ANON

The Attic

Algernon Blackwood

The forest-girdled village upon the Jura slopes slept soundly, although it was not yet many minutes after ten o'clock. The clang of the *couvre-feu* had indeed just ceased, its notes swept far into the woods by a wind that shook the mountains. This wind now rushed down the deserted street. It howled about the old rambling building called La Citadelle, whose roof towered gaunt and humped above the smaller houses – Château left unfinished long ago by Lord Wemyss, the exiled Jacobite. The families who occupied the various apartments listened to the storm and felt the building tremble. 'It's the mountain wind. It will bring the snow,' the mother said, without looking up from her knitting. 'And how sad it sounds.'

But it was not the wind that brought sadness as we sat round the open fire of peat. It was the wind of memories. The lamplight slanted along the narrow room towards the table where breakfast things lay ready for the morning. The double windows were fastened. At the far end stood a door ajar, and on the other side of it the two elder children lay asleep in the big bed. But beside the window was a smaller unused bed, that had been empty now a year. And tonight was the anniversary. . . .

And so the wind brought sadness and long thoughts. The little chap that used to lie there was already twelve months gone, far, far beyond the Hole where the Winds came from, as he called it; yet it seemed only yesterday that I went to tell him a tuck-up story, to stroke Riquette, the old motherly cat that cuddled against his back and laid a paw beside his pillow like a human being, and to hear his funny little earnest whisper say, 'Oncle, tu sais, j'ai prié pour Petavel.' For La Citadelle had its unhappy ghost – of Petavel, the usurer, who had hanged himself in the attic a century gone by, and was known to walk its dreary corridors in search of peace – and this wise Irish mother, calming the boys' fears with wisdom, had told him, 'If you pray for Petavel, you'll save his soul and make him happy, and he'll only love you.' And, thereafter, this little imaginative boy had done so every night. With a passionate seriousness he did it. He had wonderful, delicate ways like that. In all our hearts he made his fairy nests of wonder. In my own, I know, he lay closer than any joy imaginable, with his big blue eyes, his queer soft questionings, and his splendid child's unselfishness – a sun-kissed flower of innocence that, had he lived, might have sweetened half a world.

'Let's put more peat on,' the mother said, as a handful of rain like stones came flinging against the windows; 'that must be hail.' And she went on tiptoe to the inner room. 'They're sleeping like two puddings,' she whispered, coming presently back. But it struck me she had taken longer than to notice merely that; and her face wore an odd expression that made me uncomfortable. I thought she was somehow just about to laugh or cry. By the table a second she hesitated. I caught the flash of indecision as it passed. 'Pan,' she said suddenly – it was a nickname, stolen from my tuck-up stories, *he* had given me – 'I wonder how Riquette got in.' She looked hard at me. 'It wasn't you, was it?' For we never let her come at night since he had gone. It was too poignant. The beastie always went cuddling and nestling into that empty bed. But this time it was not my doing, and I offered plausible explanations. 'But – she's on the bed. Pan, *would* you be so kind – ' She left the sentence unfinished, but I easily undestood, for a lump had somehow risen in my own throat too, and I remembered now that she had come out from the inner room so quickly – with a kind of hurried rush almost. I put 'mère Riquette' out into the corridor. A lamp stood on the chair outside the door of another occupant further down, and I urged her gently towards it. She turned and looked at me – straight up into my face; but, instead of going down as I suggested, she went slowly in the opposite direction. She stepped softly towards a door in the wall that led up broken stairs into the attics. There she sat down and waited. And so I left her, and came back hastily to the peat fire and companionship. The wind rushed in behind me and slammed the door.

And we talked then somewhat busily of cheerful things; of the children's future, the excellence of the cheap Swiss schools, of Christmas presents, ski-ing, snow, tobogganing. I led the talk away from mournfulness; and when these subjects were exhausted I told stories of my own adventures in distant parts of the world. But 'mother' listened the whole time – not to me. Her thoughts were all elsewhere. And her air of intently, secretly listening, bordered, I felt, upon the uncanny. For she often stopped her knitting and sat with her eyes fixed upon the air before her; she stared blankly at the wall, her head slightly on one side, her figure tense, attention strained – elsewhere. Or, when my talk positively demanded it, her nod was oddly mechanical and her eyes looked through and past me. The wind continued very loud and roaring; but the fire glowed, the room was warm and cosy. Yet she shivered, and when I drew attention to it, her reply, 'I do feel cold, but I didn't know I shivered,' was given as though she spoke across the air to some one else. But what impressed me even more uncomfortably were her repeated questions about Riquette. When a pause in my tales permitted, she would look up with 'I wonder where Riquette went?' or, thinking of the inclement night, 'I hope mère Riquette's not out of doors. Perhaps Madame Favre has taken her in?' I offered to go and see. Indeed I was already half-way across the room when there came the heavy bang at the door that rooted me to the ground where I stood. It was not wind. It was something alive that made it rattle. There was a second blow. A thud on the corridor boards followed, and then a high, odd voice that at first was as human as the cry of a child.

It is undeniable that we both started, and for myself I can answer truthfully that a chill ran down my spine; but what frightened me more than the sudden noise and the eerie cry was the way 'mother' supplied the immediate explanation. For behind the words 'It's only Riquette; she sometimes springs at the door like that; perhaps we'd better let her in,' was a certain touch of uncanny quiet that made me feel she had known the cat would come, and knew also *why* she came. One cannot explain such impressions further. They leave their vital touch, then go their way.

Into the little room, however, in that moment there came between us this uncomfortable sense that the night held other purposes than our own – and that my companion was aware of them. There was something going on far, far removed from the routine of life as we were accustomed to it. Moreoever, our usual routine was the eddy, while this was the main stream. It felt big, I mean.

And so it was that the entrance of the familiar, friendly creature brought this thing both itself and 'mother' *knew*, but whereof I as yet was ignorant. I held the door wide. The draught rushed through behind her, and sent a shower of sparks about the fireplace. The lamp flickered and gave a little gulp. And Riquette marched slowly past, with all the impressive dignity of her kind, towards the other door that stood ajar. Turning the corner like a shadow, she disappeared into the room where the two children slept. We heard the soft thud with which she leaped upon the bed. Then, in a lull of the wind, she came back again and sat on the oilcloth, staring into 'mother's' face. She mewed and put a paw out, drawing the black dress softly with half-opened claws. And it was all so horribly suggestive and pathetic, it revived such poignant memories, that I got up impulsively – I think I had actually said the words, 'We'd better put her out, mother, after all' – when my companion rose to her feet and forestalled me. She said another thing instead. It took my breath away to hear it. 'She wants us to go with her. Pan, will you come too?' The surprise on my face must have asked the question, for I do not remember saying anything. 'To the attic,' she said quietly.

She stood there by the table, a tall, grave figure dressed in black, and her face above the lamp-shade caught the full glare of light. Its expression positively stiffened me. She seemed so secure in her singular purpose. And her familiar appearance had so oddly given place to something wholly strange to me. She looked like another person – almost with the unwelcome transformation of the sleep-walker about her. Cold came over me as I watched her, for I remembered suddenly her Irish second-sight, her story years ago of meeting a figure on the attic stairs, the figure of Petavel. And the idea of this motherly, sedate, and wholesome woman, absorbed day and night in prosaic domestic duties, and yet 'seeing' things, touched the incongruous almost to the point of alarm. It was so distressingly convincing.

Yet she knew quite well that I would come. Indeed, following the excited animal, she was already by the door, and a moment later, still without answering or protesting, I was with them in the draughty corridor. There was something inevitable in her manner that made it impossible to refuse. She took the lamp from its nail on the wall, and following our four-footed guide, who ran with obvious pleasure just in front, she opened the door into the court-yard. The wind nearly put the lamp out, but a minute later we were safe inside the passage that led up flights of creaky wooden stairs towards the world of tenantless attics overhead.

And I shall never forget the way the excited Riquette first stood up and put her paws upon the various doors, trotted ahead, turned back to watch us coming, and then finally sat down and waited on the threshold of the empty, raftered space that occupied the entire length of the building underneath the roof. For her manner was more that of an intelligent dog than of a cat, and sometimes more like that of a human mind than either.

We had come up without a single word. The howling of the wind as we rose higher was like the roar of artillery. There were many broken stairs, and the narrow way was full of twists and turnings. It was a dreadful journey. I felt eyes watching us from all the yawning spaces of the darkness, and the noise of the storm smothered footsteps everywhere. Troops of shadows kept us company. But it was on the threshold of this big, chief attic, when 'mother' stopped abruptly to put down the lamp, that real fear took hold of me. For Riquette marched steadily forward into the middle of the dusty flooring, picking her way among the fallen tiles and mortar, as though she went towards – some one. She purred loudly and uttered little cries of excited pleasure. Her tail went up into the air, and she lowered her head with the unmis-takable intention of being stroked. Her lips opened and shut. Her green eyes smiled. She *was* being stroked.

It was an unforgettable performance. I would rather have wit-nessed an execution or a murder than watch that mysterious crea-ture twist and turn about in the way she did. Her magnified shadow as large as a pony on the floor and rafters. I wanted to hide the whole thing by extinguishing the lamp. For, even before the mysterious action began, I experienced the sudden rush of conviction that others besides ourselves were in this attic – and

standing very close to us indeed. And, although there was ice in
my blood, there was also a strange swelling of the heart that only
love and tenderness could bring.

But, whatever it was, my human companion, still silent, knew
and understood. She *saw*. And her soft whisper that ran with the
wind among the rafters, 'Il a prié pour Petavel et le bon Dieu l'a
entendu,' did not amaze me one quarter as much as the expression I then caught upon her radiant face. Tears ran down the
cheeks, but they were tears of happiness. Her whole figure
seemed lit up. She opened her arms – picture of great Mother-
hood, proud, blessed, and tender beyond words. I thought she
was going to fall, for she took quick steps forward; but when I
moved to catch her, she drew me aside instead with a sudden
gesture that brought fear back in the place of wonder.

'Let them pass,' she whispered grandly. 'Pan, don't you see. . .
. He's leading him into peace and safety . . . by the hand!'
And her joy seemed to kill the shadows and fill the entire attic
with white light. Then, almost simultaneously with her words,
she swayed. I was in time to catch her, but as I did so, across the
very spot where we had just been standing – two figures, I swear,
went past us like a flood of light.

There was a moment next of such confusion that I did not see
what happened to Riquette, for the sight of my companion kneel-
ing on the dusty boards and praying with a curious sort of passionate happiness, while tears pressed between her covering
fingers – the strange wonder of this made me utterly oblivious to
minor details. . . .

We were sitting round the peat fire again, and 'mother' was
saying to me in the gentlest, tenderest whisper I ever heard from
human lips – 'Pan, I think perhaps that's why God took him. . . .'

And when a little later we went in to make Riquette cosy in the
empty bed, ever since kept sacred to her use, the mournfulness
had lifted; and in the place of resignation was proud peace and
joy that knew no longer sad or selfish questionings.

A Parable for Philanthropists

Anon

Christopher and I were motoring through the Adirondacks; and, on the morning in question, were traversing an unusually long stretch of unbroken wilderness. For ten or fifteen miles we had passed not a cottage, not a camp, not even a trail. Nothing but forest on both sides of the road – wild, tangled forest, beautiful, fragrant, and infinitely lonely. Its silence had fallen upon us. We felt as if we had escaped forever from the troubled haunts of men, and could never again be confronted with human problems. We drove slowly, with only a half apprehensive eye on the gray sky, which threatened rain.

I was just thinking that it was strange we saw so little evidence of the wild animal life with which the woods must abound, when suddenly, like an answer to my mental challenge, there came a little stir in the bushes ahead of us. A tiny, discreet stir. No suggestion of a bear or a deer. Perhaps a hedgehog, however. As we passed, I looked closely and, to my astonishment, saw, not a hedgehog, not even a rabbit or squirrel, but – of all things, in that uninhabited wilderness – a shrinking, small gray kitten. I could hardly have been more surprised by the appearance of a woodchuck on Fifth Avenue.

Christopher saw it as soon as I did, and he slid into neutral and stopped the car. An indignant and disdainful look crept about his mouth. I knew what he was thinking. We live in a summer-resorted valley ourselves, – and we have had incredulously disgusted experience with people who abandon pet cats when they close their cottages. But not out in the wilderness like this, at the mercy of all kinds of dangers, and so little and helpless, its mother's milk scarcely dry on its mouth. I was so angry that I could not speak, as I got out of the car and went back along the road.

'I don't know what in the world we'll do with it,' said Christopher.

The point was well taken. We were planning to spend the night in a hotel. Neither of us hesitated, however. Our duty seemed clear.

'I suppose we can leave it at some camp or farmhouse,' I suggested.

'And pay them for taking care of it!' Christopher added, ironically.

The kitten remained just where we had discovered it until we were near enough to look it in the eye. It had evidently been a pet. Its fur was sleek and its face wore the open, candid expression peculiar to well-bred cats. It seemed glad to see us. Steadfastly it returned our gaze, and its pink mouth opened in a plaintive meow.

'Kitty!' I murmured. I'm fond of cats, and this one quite went to my heart. 'Pick her up for me, Christopher. I'll hold her while you drive.'

So Christopher went to pick her up, and for the next hour and a half he continued to repeat the motion.

Who could have believed it would be so hard to make connections with a pet kitten? She was not afraid of us. On the contrary, the minute we let her alone, she came stealing back to the side of the road where she could see us and call to us. But she simply could not make up her mind to let us rescue her.

First Christopher tried, with a confident method which left him staring rather foolishly at his unexpectedly empty hand. Then I tried.

'That's not the way. Evidently, she's been out here long enough to get frightened. Poor little thing! We must coax her into confidence.'

So Christopher sat down on a rock and lighted a cigarette while, slowly, slowly, discoursing, 'Poor kitty! nice kitty!' in my most mellifluous accents, I crossed the road and approached the spot where the kitten crouched. It took me at least ten minutes, and, in the end, she slipped from beneath my very fingers. My discomfiture was worse than Christopher's, for the retreating ball of fur turned and spat at me.

'Hard luck!' said Christopher, sympathetically, if also a little critically, 'when you so nearly had her. I'll try again next; but we'd better sit still for a while till she gets over her scare.'

As we sat waiting, it became evident that it really was going to rain. In fact, already a fine mist was in the air.

'Those bushes will soon be nice and wet,' remarked Christopher.

'Well,' I replied, much subdued, 'she's near the edge now. Go and get her, and get it over with.'

Three minutes later, after a slow approach followed by a plunge on Christopher's part, the kitten was in the heart of the forest.

'Oh, I say!' cried Christopher. 'This is hopeless. We might stay here all day and all night and all another day. Don't you think we'd better conclude that we've done our best? After all, there are plenty of mice and grass-hoppers in the woods.'

I recognized this as sound, sensible masculine advice, and I longed to accept it. The prospect of spending indefinite hours dodging about tangled bushes in the rain was not exhilarating. Moreover, the next inn was leagues ahead, and we were hungry. But the sentiment of my sex was too much for me.

'I'm afraid I could never look Shem in the face again,' I murmured.

Shem is our yellow cat at home.

Christopher was admirable. He always is, but on this occasion he outdid himself. He said nothing further, but took off his hat and coat, turned up his trousers, and went to work. For nearly an hour he pursued that kitten, trying every method he could think of or I could suggest. He stalked and coaxed, he waited and plunged, he withdrew, he circumvented and headed off. The rain fell steadily, and the bushes more than fulfilled their promise of wetness. I was very unhappy. After all, I care more about Christopher than about kittens. But something of the kitten's perversity had infected me. As she could not bring herself to be caught, so I could not bring myself to abandon her.

'Well,' said Christopher finally (he spoke carefully; for the last half hour when he had said anything at all, he had said it carefully), 'I'm going to make one more effort, and then – '

It was a thorough effort. He made a wide détour about the kitten's position, entering a part of the forest which he had not penetrated before, and was about to close in on the maddening outcast, when, to my perplexity, he suddenly desisted from the whole undertaking and returned to the road, shaking the rain from his hair and turning down his trousers with as dark an air of disgust as I have ever seen. I wanted to ask, 'What in the world is the matter?' but I thought I'd better not.

He told me, however, presently. The situation was one which just had to be shared. 'There's a trail over there,' he said concisely, 'leading to an occupied camp. We've spent the morning trying to kidnap that kitten.'

Perhaps there is nothing more to be said. Certainly Christopher and I said nothing for many miles. I was too humbly chastened, and he was too – well, let us call it considerate. But we did some thinking; and, after a most opportunely good dinner at an unexpected wayside inn, I was relieved to hear Christopher begin to meditate aloud.

'It wasn't crying at all,' he reflected. 'It was just saying, as its mother had taught it, "Welcome to our mountain home." How embarrassed it must have been!'

'And frightened,' I added. 'No wonder I thought it looked scared. Several times we nearly had it.'

'Well,' Christopher concluded, with a grave glance at me, 'philanthropy's a ticklish business.'

The White Cat

C. H. Ross

There once was a King, the legend says, who was growing old, and it was told to him that his three sons wished to govern the kingdom. The old King, who did not wish to give up his power just yet, thought the best way to prevent his sons from taking his throne was to send them out to seek for adventures; so he called them all around him, and said: –

'My sons, go away and travel for a year; and he of you who brings me the most beautiful little dog, shall have the kingdom, and be King after me.'

Then the three Princes started on the journey; but it is of the youngest of the three that I have now to tell. He travelled for many days, and at last found himself, one evening, at the door of a splendid castle, but not a man or woman was to be seen. A number of hands, with no bodies to them, appeared: two hands took off the Prince's cloak, two others seated him in a chair, another pair brought a brush to brush his hair, and several pairs waited on him at supper. Then some more hands came and put him to bed in a fine chamber, where he slept all night, but still no one appeared. The next morning, the hands brought him into a splendid hall, where there sat on a throne a large White Cat, who made him sit beside her, and expressed herself glad to see him. Next day, the Prince and the White Cat went out hunting together: the Cat was mounted on a fine spirited monkey, and seemed very fond of the Prince, who, on his part, was delighted with her wit and cleverness.

Instead of dogs, Cats hunted for them. These creatures ran with great agility after rats, and mice, and birds, catching and killing a great number of them; and sometimes the White Cat's monkey would climb a tree, with the White Cat on his back, after a bird, a mouse, or a squirrel. This pleasant life went on for a long time: every day the White Cat became more fond of the Prince, while, on his part, the Prince could not help loving the poor Cat, who was so kind and attentive to him. At last, the time drew near when the Prince was to return home, and he had not thought of looking for a little dog; but the Cat gave him a casket, and told him to open this before the King, and all would be well; so the Prince journeyed home, taking with him an ugly mongrel cur. When the brothers saw this, they laughed secretly to each other, and thought themselves quite secure, so far as their younger brother was concerned. They had, with infinite pains, procured each of them a very rare and beautiful little dog, and each thought himself quite sure to get the prize. When the day came on which the dogs were to be shown, each of the two elder Princes produced a beautiful little dog, on a silk velvet cushion: no one could judge which was the prettier. The youngest now opened his casket, and found a walnut: he cracked this walnut, and out of the walnut sprang a little tiny dog, of exquisite beauty. Still the old King would not give up his kingdom. He told the young Princes they must bring him home a piece of cambric so fine that it could be threaded through the eye of a needle; and so they went away in search of such a piece of cambric. Again the youngest Prince passed a year with the White Cat, and again the Cat gave him a walnut when the time came for him to return home. The three Princes were summoned before their father, who produced a needle. The first and second Princes brought a piece of cambric which would almost, but not quite, go through the needle's eye. The youngest Prince broke open his walnut-shell: he found inside it a small nut-shell, and then a cherry-stone, and then a grain of wheat, and then a grain of millet, and in this grain of millet a piece of cambric four hundred yards long, which passed easily through the eye of the needle. But the old King said: –

'He who brings the most beautiful lady shall have the kingdom.'

The Prince went back to the White Cat, and told her what his father had said. She replied –

'Cut off my head and my tail.'

At last he consented: instantly the Cat was transformed into a beautiful Princess; for she had been condemned by a wicked fairy to appear as a Cat, till a young Prince should cut off her head and tail. The Prince and Princess went to the old King's court, and she was far more beautiful than the ladies brought by the other two Princes. But she did not want the kingdom, for she had four of her own already. One of these she gave to each of the elder brothers of the young Prince, and over the other two she ruled with her husband, for the young Prince married her, and they lived happily together all their lives.

Tobermory

Saki

It was a chill, rain-washed afternoon of a late August day, that indefinite season when partridges are still in security or cold storage, and there is nothing to hunt – unless one is bounded on the north by the Bristol Channel, in which case one may lawfully gallop after fat red stags. Lady Blemley's house-party was not bounded on the north by the Bristol Channel, hence there was a full gathering of her guests round the tea-table on this particular afternoon. And, in spite of the blankness of the season and the triteness of the occasion, there was no trace in the company of that fatigued restlessness which means a dread of the pianola and a subdued hankering for auction bridge. The undisguised open-mouthed attention of the entire party was fixed on the homely negative personality of Mr Cornelius Appin. Of all her guests, he was the one who had come to Lady Blemley with the vaguest reputation. Some one had said he was 'clever,' and he had got his invitation in the moderate expectation, on the part his hostess, that some portion at least of his cleverness would be contributed to the general entertainment. Until tea-time that day she had been unable to discover in what direction, if any, his cleverness lay. He was neither a wit nor a croquet champion, a hypnotic force nor a begetter of amateur theatricals. Neither did his exterior suggest the sort of man in whom women are willing to pardon a generous measure of mental deficiency. He had subsided into mere Mr Appin, and the Cornelius seemed a piece of transparent baptismal bluff. And now he was claiming to have launched on the world a discovery beside which the invention of gunpowder, of the printing-press, and of steam locomotion were inconsiderable trifles. Science had made bewildering strides in many directions during recent decades, but this thing seemed to belong to the domain of miracle rather than to scientific achievement.

'And do you really ask us to believe,' Sir Wilfrid was saying, 'that you have discovered a means for instructing animals in the art of human speech, and that dear old Tobermory has proved your first successful pupil?'

'It is a problem at which I have worked for the last seventeen years,' said Mr Appin, 'but only during the last eight or nine months have I been rewarded with glimmerings of success. Of course I have experimented with thousands of animals, but latterly only with cats, those wonderful creatures which have assimilated themselves so marvellously with our civilization while retaining all their highly developed feral instincts. Here and there among cats one comes across an outstanding superior intellect, just as one does among the ruck of human beings, and when I made the acquaintance of Tobermory a week ago I saw at once that I was in contact with a 'Beyond-cat' of extraordinary intelligence. I had gone far along the road to success in recent experiments; with Tobermory, as you call him, I have reached the goal.'

Mr Appin concluded his remarkable statement in a voice which he strove to divest of a triumphant inflection. No one said 'Rats,' though Clovis's lips moved in a monosyllabic contortion, which probably invoked those rodents of disbelief.

'And do you mean to say,' asked Miss Resker, after a slight pause, 'that you have taught Tobermory to say and understand easy sentences of one syllable?'

'My dear Miss Resker,' said the wonder-worker patiently, 'one teaches little children and savages and backward adults in that piecemeal fashion; when one has once solved the problem of making a beginning with an animal of highly developed intelligence one has no need for those halting methods. Tobermory can speak our language with perfect correctness.'

This time Clovis very distinctly said 'Beyond-rats!' Sir Wilfrid was more polite, but equally sceptical.

'Hadn't we better have the cat in and judge for ourselves?' suggested Lady Blemley.

Sir Wilfrid went in search of the animal, and the company

settled themselves down to the languid expectation of witnessing some more or less adroit drawing-room ventriloquism.

In a minute Sir Wilfrid was back in the room, his face white beneath its tan and his eyes dilated with excitement.

'By Gad, it's true!'

His agitation was unmistakably genuine, and his hearers started forward in a thrill of awakened interest.

Collapsing into an armchair he continued breathlessly: 'I found him dozing in the smoking-room, and called out to him to come for his tea. He blinked at me in his usual way, and I said, "Come on, Toby; don't keep us waiting"; and, by Gad! he drawled out in a most horribly natural voice that he'd come when he dashed well pleased! I nearly jumped out of my skin!'

Appin had preached to absolutely incredulous hearers; Sir Wilfrid's statement carried instant conviction. A Babel-like chorus of startled exclamation arose, amid which the scientist sat mutely enjoying the first-fruit of his stupendous discovery.

In the midst of the clamour Tobermory entered the room and made his way with velvet tread and studied unconcern across to the group seated round the tea-table.

A sudden hush of awkwardness and constraint fell on the company. Somehow there seemed an element of embarrassment in addressing on equal terms a domestic cat of acknowledged mental ability.

'Will you have some milk, Tobermory?' asked Lady Blemley in a rather strained voice.

'I don't mind if I do,' was the response, couched in a tone of even indifference. A shiver of suppressed excitement went through the listeners, and Lady Blemley might be excused for pouring out the saucerful of milk rather unsteadily.

'I'm afraid I've spilt a good deal of it,' she said apologetically.

'After all, it's not my Axminster,' was Tobermory's rejoinder.

Another silence fell on the group, and then Miss Resker, in her best district-visitor manner, asked if the human language had been difficult to learn. Tobermory looked squarely at her for a moment and then fixed his gaze serenely on the middle distance. It was obvious that boring questions lay outside his scheme of life.

'What do you think of human intelligence?' asked Mavis

Pellington lamely.

'Of whose intelligence in particular?' asked Tobermory coldly.

'Oh, well, mine for instance,' said Mavis, with a feeble laugh.

'You put me in an embarrassing position,' said Tobermory, whose tone and attitude certainly did not suggest a shred of embarrassment. 'When your inclusion in this house-party was suggested Sir Wilfrid protested that you were the most brainless woman of his acquaintance, and that there was a wide distinction between hospitality and the care of the feeble-minded. Lady Blemley replied that your lack of brain-power was the precise quality which had earned you your invitation, as you were the only person she could think of who might be idiotic enough to buy their old car. You know, the one they call 'The Envy of Sisyphus,' because it goes quite nicely up-hill if you push it.'

Lady Blemley's protestations would have had greater effect if she had not casually suggested to Mavis only that morning that the car in question would be just the thing for her down at her Devonshire home.

Major Barfield plunged in heavily to effect a diversion.

'How about your carryings-on with the tortoise-shell puss up at the stables, eh?'

The moment he had said it everyone realized the blunder.

'One does not usually discuss these matters in public,' said Tobermory frigidly. 'From a slight observation of your ways since you've been in this house I should imagine you'd find it inconvenient if I were to shift the conversation on to your own little affairs.'

The panic which ensued was not confined to the Major.

'Would you like to go and see if cook has got your dinner ready?' suggested Lady Blemley hurriedly, affecting to ignore the fact that it wanted at least two hours to Tobermory's dinner-time.

'Thanks,' said Tobermory, 'not quite so soon after my tea. I don't want to die of indigestion.'

'Cats have nine lives, you know,' said Sir Wilfrid heartily.

'Possibly,' answered Tobermory; 'but only one liver.'

'Adelaide!' said Mrs Cornett, 'do you mean to encourage that cat to go out and gossip about us in the servants' hall?'

The panic had indeed become general. A narrow ornamental balustrade ran in front of most of the bedroom windows at the

Towers, and it was recalled with dismay that this had formed a favourite promenade for Tobermory at all hours, whence he could watch the pigeons – and heaven knew what else besides. If he intended to become reminiscent in his present outspoken strain, the effect would be something more than disconcerting. Mrs Cornett, who spent much time at her toilet table, and whose complexion was reputed to be of a nomadic though punctual disposition, looked as ill at ease as the Major. Miss Scrawen, who wrote fiercely sensuous poetry and led a blameless life, merely displayed irritation; if you are methodical and virtuous in private you don't necessarily want every one to know it. Bertie van Tahn, who was so depraved at seventeen that he had long ago given up trying to be any worse, turned a dull shade of gardenia white, but he did not commit the error of dashing out of the room like Odo Finsberry, a young gentleman who was understood to be reading for the Church and who was possibly disturbed at the thought of scandals he might hear concerning other people. Clovis had the presence of mind to maintain a composed exterior; privately he was calculating how long it would take to procure a box of fancy mice through the agency of the *Exchange and Mart* as a species of hush-money.

Even in a delicate situation like the present, Agnes Resker could not endure to remain too long in the background.

'Why did I ever come down here?' she asked dramatically.

Tobermory immediately accepted the opening.

'Judging by what you said to Mrs Cornett on the croquet-lawn yesterday, you were out for food. You described the Blemleys as the dullest people to stay with that you knew, but said they were clever enough to employ a first-rate cook; otherwise they'd find it difficult to get any one to come down a second time.'

'There's not a word of truth in it! I appeal to Mrs Cornett - ' exclaimed the discomfited Agnes.

'Mrs Cornett repeated your remark afterwards to Bertie van Tahn,' continued Tobermory, 'and said, "That woman is a regular Hunger Marcher; she'd go anywhere for four square meals a day," and Bertie van Tahn said – '

At this point the chronicle mercifully ceased. Tobermory had caught a glimpse of the big yellow Tom from the Rectory working his way through the shrubbery towards the stable wing. In a flash he had vanished through the open French window.

With the disappearance of his too brilliant pupil Cornelius Appin found himself beset by a hurricane of bitter upbraiding, anxious inquiry, and frightened entreaty. The responsibility for the situation lay with him, and he must prevent matters from becoming worse. Could Tobermory impart his dangerous gift to other cats? was the first question he had to answer. It was possible, he replied, that he might have initiated his intimate friend the stable puss into his new accomplishment, but it was unlikely that his teaching could have taken a wider range as yet.

'Then,' said Mrs Cornett, 'Tobermory may be a valuable cat and a great pet; but I'm sure you'll agree, Adelaide, that both he and the stable cat must be done away with without delay.'

'You don't suppose I've enjoyed the last quarter of an hour, do you?' said Lady Blemley bitterly. 'My husband and I are very fond of Tobermory – at least, we were before this horrible accomplishment was infused into him; but now, of course, the only thing is to have him destroyed as soon as possible.'

'We can put some strychnine in the scraps he always gets at dinner-time,' said Sir Wilfrid, 'and I will go and drown the stable cat myself. The coachman will be very sore at losing his pet, but I'll say a very catching form of mange has broken out in both cats and we're afraid of it spreading to the kennels.'

'But my great discovery!' expostulated Mr Appin; 'after all my years of research and experiment – '

'You can go and experiment on the short-horns at the farm, who are under proper control,' said Mrs Cornett, 'or the elephants at the Zoological Gardens. They're said to be highly intelligent, and they have this recommendation, that they don't come creeping about our bedrooms and under chairs, and so forth.'

An archangel ecstatically proclaiming the Millennium, and then finding that it clashed unpardonably with Henley and would have to be indefinitely postponed, could hardly have felt more crestfallen than Cornelius Appin at the reception of his wonderful achievement. Public opinion, however, was against him – in fact, had the general voice been consulted on the subject it is probable that a strong minority vote would have been in favour of including him in the strychnine diet.

Defective train arrangements and a nervous desire to see matters brought to a finish prevented an immediate dispersal of the party, but diner that evening was not a social success. Sir Wilfrid had had rather a trying time with the stable cat and subsequently with the coachman. Agnes Resker ostentatiously limited her repast to a morsel of dry toast, which she bit as though it were a personal enemy; while Mavis Pellington maintained a vindictive silence throughout the meal. Lady Blemley kept up a flow of what she hoped was conversation, but her attention was fixed on the doorway. A plateful of carefully dosed fish scraps was in readiness on the sideboard, but sweets and savoury and dessert went their way, and no Tobermory appeared either in the dining-room or kitchen.

The sepulchral dinner was cheerful compared with the subsequent vigil in the smoking-room. Eating and drinking had at least supplied a distraction and cloak to the prevailing embarrassment. Bridge was out of the question in the general tension of nerves and tempers, and after Odo Finsberry had given a lugubrious rendering of 'Mèlisande in the Wood' to a frigid audience, music was tacitly avoided. At eleven the servants went to bed, announcing that the small window in the pantry had been left open as usual for Tobermory's private use. The guests read steadily through the current batch of magazines, and fell back gradually on the 'Badminton Library' and bound volumes of *Punch*. Lady Blemley made periodic visits to the pantry, returning each time with an expression of listless depression which forestalled questioning.

At two o'clock Clovis broke the dominating silence.

'He won't turn up tonight. He's probably in the local newspaper office at the present moment, dictating the first instalment of his reminiscences. Lady What's-her-name's book won't be in it. It will be the event of the day.'

Having made this contribution to the general cheerfulness, Clovis went to bed. At long intervals the various members of the house-party followed his example.

The servants taking round the early tea made a uniform announcement in reply to a uniform question. Tobermory had not returned.

Breakfast was, if anything, a more unpleasant function than

dinner had been, but before its conclusion the situation was relieved. Tobermory's corpse was brought in from the shrubbery, where a gardener had just discovered it. From the bites on his throat and the yellow fur which coated his claws it was evident that he had fallen in unequal combat with the big Tom from the Rectory.

By midday most of the guests had quitted the Towers, and after lunch Lady Blemley had sufficiently recovered her spirits to write an extremely nasty letter to the Rectory about the loss of her valuable pet.

Tobermory had been Appin's one successful pupil, and he was destined to have no successor. A few weeks later an elephant in the Dresden Zoological Garden, which had shown no previous signs of irritability, broke loose and killed an Englishman who had apparently been teasing it. The victim's name was variously reported in the papers as Oppin and Eppelin, but his front name was faithfully rendered Cornelius.

'If he was trying German irregular verbs on the poor beast,' said Clovis, 'he deserved all he got.'

Dick Whittington's Cat

. . . But as he went along
  In a fair summer's morne
London bells sweetly rung,
  'Whittington, back return!'

Evermore a sounding so
  'Turn againe Whittington:
For thou in time shall grow
  Lord Mayor of London.'
Whereupon back againe
  Whittington came with speed,
Aprentise to remaine
  As the Lord had decreed.

'Still blessed be the bells'
  (This was his daily song),
'They my good fortune tells
  Most sweetly have they rung.
If God so favour me
  I will not proove unkind;
London my love shall see,
  And my great bounties find.'

But for this happy chance
  Whittington had a cat
Which he a venture sent
  And got his wealth by that

Far from Foreign Land
  Where Rats and Mice abound
They bought him for his cat
  Many a fair thousand pound.

When as they home were come
  With their ships laden so
Whittington's wealth began
  By this cat and thus to grow;
Scullion's life he forsook
  To be a merchant good. . . .

1641 BALLAD

The Cat of the Cherokees

Herbert Ravenel Sass

When Fergus Gilyan came up through the virgin wilderness to the rolling country within sight of the Blue Mountains, he did not place his cabin on any of the wooded knolls that he might have chosen. Instead he made a small clearing in a dense canebreak bordering a creek and built his little log house there in the heart of the canes.

Some say he did this for safety's sake. the Muskogees were making war talks at the time and a house on a height would have been a temptation to roving bands raiding the Overhills as the mountain Cherokees called their high domain of purple peaks and ranges. But there was another reason.

Gilyan was a born hunter, and the canebrake extending for miles along the stream, was alive with game. Around his cabin on every side the smooth straight stems towered thirty feet or more, an evergreen jungle wailing in his tiny clearing, a jungle so dense that he could penetrate it only by following the winding rails made by the buffalo and the deer. These trails were his highways to the outside world. From his cabin door to the creek he cut a straight, wide path through the canes. There was scarcely an hour from dawn to dusk when, sitting in his doorway, he could not see some wild animal moving up or down the creek bed across that path.

One May afternoon, when he was sitting there smoking, he saw a sight more strange. He saw a small Indian boy, a slim, naked youngster of perhaps ten years, back slowly down the creek bed and, still walking backward, turn into the path. Gilyan's right hand reached swiftly for the loaded rifle leaning against the wall just inside the door. In the half light under the over-arching canes there was something deeply uncanny about that backward-walking Indian, but in a moment Gilyan had the answer to the riddle.

A long, gaunt, yellow-brown beast followed the boy; a big she puma or panther, wild-eyed with hunger. At a glance Gilyan knew all he needed to know. The puma's lower jaw had been broken. Some strange mischance – probably a blow from a wild horse's hoof – had shattered it and twisted it awry, so that it hung useless and crooked. The beast had starved for days, perhaps for weeks, and now famine had maddened her.

Yet her madness had not wholly conquered her fear of man. Grimly she dogged the boy's footsteps, but because he kept his face turned to her, she had not yet leaped upon him. Plainly, however, she had now nerved herself for the onset. Gilyan knew that in another instant she would hurl herself upon her victim.

Gilyan did not rise from his stool. He flung the long, heavy rifle to his shoulder, glanced for a fraction of a second along its steady barrel. The bullet passed not six inches from the young Indian and struck the puma between the eyes.

Gilyan was on his feet before she had struck the ground. At top speed he raced down the path past the Indian boy and the dead puma to the point where the path met the creek. There he halted and gazed eagerly up and down the sandy bed of the stream, hedged in by the tall, dense canes.

He saw nothing, but he knew that his eyes had not tricked him. He knew that at the moment when he pulled the trigger he had glimpsed along his rifle barrel another face besides the one at which he aimed – a wide, flat, tawny face, in the midst of which gleamed a round white spot like a gigantic eye. For an instant this face had glared at him from the end of the path close beside the creek. Then, at the crack of the rifle, the face had vanished.

Gilyan was a clean man in those days. The raw, poisonous tafia rum of the traders had not blurred his eye or his brain. The face that he had seen was no phantom, yet he had never seen such a face before. He searched the sands of the creek margin and found certain tracks there in addition to the tracks of the she puma which he had killed. He studied them carefully; then, sure of his woodcraft, announced his conclusion in a gutteral whisper, talking to himself, as was his habit.

'Aye,' he muttered, 'a big he-cub, bigger than the old she and not yet full grown; a big he-cub with a white spot on his forehead. Some day I'll stretch his hide.'

Then he turned and walked back along the path toward the slender copper-coloured lad awaiting him beside the she puma's body.

This was the beginning of two things. It was the beginning of Fergus Gilyan's knowledge of Koe Ishto (as he was afterward known), the puma of Unaka Kanoos, that great rock mountain sometimes called by the Cherokees Sanigilagi; and it was the beginning of a long friendship, if such it could be termed, between Gilyan, the first white man to settle on Gilyan's Creek at the foot of the Blue Mountains, and Corane the Raven, a war captain of the mountain Cherokees.

The Indian boy whose life Gilyan saved was Corane's son. Corane the Raven was no friend of the whites, for long ago, at a time when trouble threatened, they had captured him by trickery and had held him as a hostage until the war drums no longer throbbed in the Overhills. But if the Raven never forgot that injury, neither could he forget what Gilyan had done. Thenceforward he was the white hunter's pledged brother.

There was one other who did not forget. The big he-cub, whose face Gilyan had glimpsed along his rifle barrel that May afternoon in the canebrake, learned that afternoon a lesson which struck deep. Crouching behind the creek bank where the path came down to the stream, he saw his mother meet her end. He saw, too, in that same moment, a man leap from the doorway of the cabin in the clearing – a tall, round-shouldered man, clad in buckskin and wearing a coonskin cap. In an instant the cub was gone, a lithe, yellow-brown shape, speeding in long bounds up the creek bed, hidden from the man's view by the canes.

Thus at the very outset of his independent career – for until then he had hunted with his mother and accepted her guidance – Koe Ishto, the puma of Unaka Kanoos, had his first lesson on the deadly power of the tall, buckskin-clad woodsman with whom, through no desire of his own, he was to wage a long war of craft and cunning. The experience amazed and terrified him. The young puma ran half a mile, a great distance for one if his short-winded race, before he halted, and even then his halt was only temporary. Travelling all the rest of the day and most of the night, he pushed steadily northward through the vast, park-like, virgin forest until, almost suddenly, the rolling hills became mountains. The high humped bulk of the Unaka Kanoos stood well behind the first ridges of the mountain bulwark. Not until he was back on the peak where he had been born – the peak which had been his home until, in an evil moment, his mother had led him down into the foothills – would the big cub feel that he was safe.

Even into that lofty fastness fate followed him swiftly. Within a month after his return to Unaker he heard for the second time the crack of a rifle. He fled from it, yet it seemed to pursue him, for two hours later he heard it again. An hour before sunset he ventured down to the lower slopes in search of game. He was stalking a young buck grazing apart from its fellows in a grassy flat when a crashing roar deafened his ears and a fierce burning pain stabbed his right hind leg.

The wound was a slight one. It healed in less than a week. But the terror of the moment was stamped indelibly upon his consciousness; and even in his panic he recognized the man who had wounded him – a tall, round-shouldered, buckskin-clad man in a coonskin cap, the man who had leaped from the door of the cabin in the canebrake.

Corane the Raven told Gilyan how among certain clans or tribes of the Cherokees the puma was held sacred, and that this puma of Unaka Kanoos had become to the warriors of the Raven's clan more sacred than any other of his race. Klandaghi was the Cherokee name for the puma kind, an honourable name, worthy of the big lion-like cats of the forest who were the greatest of all the wild hunters. But to the puma of Unaka Kanoos an even loftier title had been given – Koe Ishto, the Cat of God.

There were several reasons, Corane explained, for the bestowal of this honour. Not only did Koe Ishto make his home on one of the mountains which the Cherokees held in special reverence – that huge, humped, granite peak which was the throne and couch of the Red Spirit whose weapon was the lightning and whose voice was the thunder. he was too, in his own might and bulk, such a puma as no living hunter of the Overhills had ever seen before.

And this was not all. There was yet another thing which set him apart. he bore upon his flat forehead just above the eyes a round white spot as big as a wild turkey's egg. Against the dark background of his upper face this white spot stood out so vividly that it was visible a long bowshot away. Not even the oldest hunter of the Cherokee had seen or heard of another puma bearing a mark like this upon its face.

To all this, as Corane the Raven told it, Gilyan listened gravely. Yet there was mockery in his heart and deceit upon his lips. The very things that made Koe Ishto sacred to the Cherokee hunters rendered Gilyan all the more desirous of securing the puma's pelt.

Season after season Gilyan searched in vain. At last, although he did not abandon his efforts altogether, he forced himself to admit that only by enlisting Raven's aid could he succeed. This, difficult though it seemed, might not be impossible, for the Raven was bound by the tenets of his tribe to do the will of the man to whom he owed a great debt, the man whom he had made his pledged brother.

Gilyan, confident that his opportunity would come, did not force the issue. Craftily, he bided his time.

Sir Alexander Twining, Special Commissioner of His Majesty King George II to the powerful Cherokee Nation, whose domain was the Blue Mountains, found much to interest him in Charles Town when he landed there from the high-pooped ship which had brought him from London. Yet to Sir Alexander, a sportsman before he had become a diplomat, Charles Town was only a gateway to the mysterious, alluring wilderness which lay beyond.

The preparations for his journey to the Overhills were quickly made. In early spring his caravan set out – himself and his periwigged secretary; four lean, lynx-eyed hunters selected by the governor of Carolina and headed by Fergus Gilyan of Gilyan's Creek, somewhat the worse for rum, now that he was nearing fifty, but still one of the best woodsmen in the province; a half-dozen pack-horse men and Negro grooms; Conerton, the ex-trader, to act as interpreter; and five tall Cherokee warriors sent down by Moytoy of Tellequo, greatest of the chiefs, to make sure that no war party of the Choctaw or the Muskogee lurked beside the trail. Corane the Raven, one of the Moytoy's war captains, commanded the Indian escort.

Of him the king's commissioner saw but little as the cavalcade rode league after league along the narrow trail winding through the endless primeval forest. The Raven, as always distrustful of the Charles Town English, held himself aloof. As a rule, he rode with two of his braves well in advance of the column, and from the first Sir Alexander's keen eyes marked the careless grace of his horsemanship, the feline litheness and strength of his tall, powerful form.

Twining, for all his airs and frills, a good judge of men, sought closer acquaintance with this war captain of Moytoy, the great chief, whom he was presently to meet in conference, but found the task discouraging. The Raven, always respectful, wrapped himself in frigid dignity which effectually rebuffed the commissioner's advances and soon strained his good humour to the breaking point. At last, flushed with anger, Sir Alexander reined in his horse.

'Faith, Gilyan' he exclaimed as the main body of the caravan came up, 'the man's a lump! There's no sense or courtesy in him. You say he understands our English speech, but, if so, he has forgotten how to wag his tongue. I give no thanks to the Cherokee king for sending so unmannerly a minion to escort me to his kingdom!'
Fergus Gilyan, who had watched the play with grim amusement, smiled.

'Corane the Raven is no friend to the English, Sir Alexander', he said slowly. 'He is longer-headed than most of his breed and he knows what the coming of the white man means to his people. He does not favour this treaty which you will offer the Cherokee chiefs. If he could have his way, there would be war, not peace.'

Twining ripped out an oath.

'I guessed as much', he said. 'We had best watch him, then, lest he lead us into some ambush. D'ye think Moytoy plans treachery?'

Gilyan shook his head.

'No fear', he replied. 'Gifts and flattery from Charles Town have blinded Moytoy's eyes. He has been won by your plan to make him emperor of all the Cherokee tribes. Corane will obey Moytoy's commands.'

Sir Alexander pursed his lips and muttered in his curled and scented brown beard, yet quickly forgot his fears. Soon sights and sounds of the springtime wilderness drove weightier matters from his mind. To his English eyes this trail through the teeming virgin forest was an avenue of innumerable wonders; and always, as he rode, he carried in his right hand the long rifle which he had procured in Charles Town and with which, thanks to Gilyan's teaching, he was already fairly proficient.

Again and again he tried his marksmanship. Now his target was a platoon of tall grey canes standing like soldiers on parade in a flower-sprinkled savanna beside the trail. Now he brought down, amid the plaudits of his comrades, a great wild turkey cock which Gilyan had pointed out to him as it perched in fancied security on a high limb of a giant pine. A half-dozen times he wasted powder and shot on flocks of green and yellow parakeets which at frequent intervals flew screeching overhead; and once he rode a quarter of a mile along a sun-dappled forest vista toward a herd of twenty whitetails resting under the trees and starting a small black wolf from its bed in a bunch of boom grass, killed it with a lucky shot as it dashed toward the cover of a wild rose thicket.

'What say you now, Gilyan?' he cried in high elation as he galloped back to his companions. 'What say you now to my skill? Am I good enough yet, d' ye think, to hunt your great tawny cat of the sacred mountain – that Koe Ishto of the white-spotted face whose hide you have promised me when we reach the Overhills?'

It was the time of the midday halt for rest and food. Most of the party had dismounted and were standing around the fire, where the turkey cock which Sir Alexander had killed was roasting, together with several haunches of venison brought in by Gilyan's hunters.

Corane the Raven still sat his wiry Chickasaw pony a little apart from the others, but he was near enough to hear Sir Alexander's words.

For a fraction of a second his brows contracted; and Gilyan, watching the Indian keenly, saw that fleeting shadow of a frown. The white hunter laughed carelessly as he answered Sir Alexander's question.

'Koe Ishto is wise', he said, 'as wise as he is strong – the greatest and wisest of his kind. I have promised you that we shall hunt him when we camp under the Blue Mountains because you wish a panther skin for your lady. But as for promising you his hide, there is only one man here present who could make you that promise.'

King George's commissioner had dismounted while Gilyan was speaking. He turned slowly toward the hunter, his silver snuff-box delicately balanced in his left hand.

'And that man?' he asked eagerly.

Gilyan nodded toward the tall Indian sitting erect and impassive on his claybank pony.

'Corane's town lies in the valley of Sequilla, in the shadow of Koe Ishto's mountain. Corane knows Koe Ishto's ways and can lead us to his lair. Corane the Raven must hunt with us or we shall fail.'

For a moment Twining hesitated. Then, swallowing his pride, he turned with an engaging smile to Moytoy's war captain.

'What say you, my brother?' he asked suavely. 'Wilt lead us to the den of the great cat of the mountain – this Koe Ishto of the spotted face, concerning whom Gilyan has told me many tales?'

For a long half minute Corane the Raven, gazing straight ahead of him, his clear-cut countenance as stern as that of a bronze image, remained silent. Twining's brows drew together in a frown' the blood mounted to his pale handsome face. At last the Indian turned his head slowly and looked at Gilyan – a look which seemed at once to convey a challenge and ask a question.

The white hunter nodded; then, frowning slightly, lowered his eyes. The Raven, addressing himself to Twining, spoke gravely in his own tongue.

'Corane will lead you to Koe Ishto's cave', he said.

While Conerton, the interpreter, was whispering to Sir Alexander the meaning of the words, the Indian wheeled his horse and rode slowly forward along the trail.

A Cherokee woman, pounding corn beside the shallow rock-strewn river which flowed through the Raven's village in the vale of Sequilla, glanced up at the huge, humped mountain towering above the Indian town.

'See', she said to the little naked girl squatting beside her, 'the Thunder God sleeps. He has drawn his robe over him so that the noonday sun will not shine on his face.'

A fleecy cloud hid the upper half of Unaka Kanoos. Only the heavily wooded lower slopes of the mountain were visible, their deep lustrous green appearing almost black in contrast with the brilliant whiteness of the cloud curtain veiling the rocky crest. Three miles to the eastward, on a ridge across the valley, Corane the Raven noted with troubled eyes the blanket of dense vapour hiding the summit and half the bulk of Unaka. To him also this meant that the Spirit was at home on his chosen mountain and was taking his ease there, having first thrown a coverlet of cloud over his couch so that he might not be seen by mortal eyes.

Yet the Raven spoke no word, did not slacken his pace. Fergus Gilyan, spare, wiry, endowed with sinews of steel, strode briskly close behind the tall Indian. But King George's commissioner puffing and blowing as the slope grew steeper, prayed silently for a halt, yet was too plucky to confess his plight.

It was already mid-afternoon. Sir Alexander's caravan had encamped in the foothills the evening before. After a long ride over the first rampart of the Blue Ridge, with but one halt by the high falls of the Whitewater, the Raven and his two companions had left their Chickasaw ponies at the foot of Unaka Kanoos and had at once begun the ascent.

Gilyan noted with silent approval the Raven's plans for the hunt. He knew that, unlike most pumas, Koe Ishto helped his mate kill meat for her little ones and kept watch over the cave which was their home. Evidently the Raven would waste no time seeking his quarry along the runways of the deer or in the bushy meadows where the whitetails grazed. Instead he would go straight to the cave where the puma had his lair, the cave for which Gilyan had so often searched in vain. The white hunter smiled with satisfaction, and his lean brown fingers tightened their grip on the butt of the long rifle crocked across his shoulder.

None of the three, not even Corane the Raven, knew that as they skirted a laurel thicket fringing a precipitous brook, pale yellow eyes, surmounted by a round white spot as bit as a wild turkey's egg, had gazed upon them coldly from the thicket's recesses. None of them knew that when they had passed on up the slope, a long sinuous tawny shape emerged from the laurels and followed in their footsteps, gliding as silently as a ghost amid the massive grey trunks of the burly oaks and the towering tulip trees.

The fear in those pale eyes was stronger than the anger which was in them also. Koe Ishto had learned long since that the Raven was not his foe. But now the Raven was not alone. With him marched two white hunters; and in one of these two Koe Ishto recognized at once his most implacable enemy, the tall round-shouldered, buckskin-clad white man who had wounded him long ago and who camped from time to time on the lower slopes of Unaka Kanoos and ranged widely over the rocky heights as well as the timbered valleys. The big puma feared the tall woodsman in the buckskin shirt and coonskin cap wherever he found him; but when Gilyan ranged high on Unaka or followed some trail which would take him to the mountain's summit, the fear in Koe Ishto's heart became an agony of terror.

This terror clutched him now. Never before had the thing which he dreaded most seemed so imminent. Early that spring torrential rains had drenched Unaka Kanoos. Through some obscure cranny streams of water had found their way into the high cave which Koe Ishto and his mate had used for years. Hating moisture, like all the cat tribe, the two old pumas had removed their cubs to another cave, drier but in other respects much less secure, a cave situated some distance further down the mountain.

The move had scarcely been made when disaster befell, a mischance so strange as to be almost incredible. Salali the Squirrel, the chief conjuror of the Raven's town, had climbed to the top of Unaka Kanoos to gather certain roots and herbs which grew above the clouds. At the edge of the huge precipice near the mountain's summit the conjuror stood in rapture, shaking like a man with a fever, chanting the praises of the Thunder God. Then, when the frenzy had passed, an idle impulse moved him to pick up a heavy rounded stone, as big as a man's head, and hurl it into the abyss.

The stone fell into the treetops far below and bounded on and on down the steep slope. No trunk of oak or poplar arrested its progress. Instead it crashed like a cannon ball into the ribs of Koe Ishto's mate, lying asleep in a shady spot near the cave where soft, fernlike mosses covered the ground. Ten minutes later the life passed out of her, and Koe Ishto, returning to the cave toward evening, found her lying bloody and stiff upon the moss.

The cubs no longer needed their mother's milk. They were old enough now to subsist entirely upon meat, and Koe Ishto easily supplied their wants. He had been hunting deer for them in the deep woods of the lower slopes when he chanced upon the Raven and his companions making their way along the trail leading to the summit, a trail which passed within a hundred yards of the cub's new home. At one he had forgotten the deer and had shadowed the hunters as they pushed upward through the forest.

Sir Alexander Twining was a proud man and sound of wind and limb. But he had never before climbed mountains, and at last his extremity got the better of his pride. He whispered to Gilyan that he could go no further, and when Gilyan had informed the Raven of the fact, the tall Indian stood for a moment in thought. Koe Ishto's lair, he told the white hunter presently, still lay far ahead and above, near the summit of Unaka; but there was a spot near at hand where they might rest and spend the night in comfort, then push on toward their goal before dawn.

King George's commissioner, flat on his back in the shade, gave a great sigh of relief when this news was imparted to him. He was too weary to move, and his heart was pounding like a hammer. They would remain where they were, he proposed, until the sun sank lower, then seek their sleeping place. The view from the spot where he lay entranced him; and the crimson and gold of a mountain sunset, painting the billowy clouds and bathing all the wooded peaks and valleys in magic light, held him there until dusk had fallen. Hence it was black night when the Raven, turning aside from the trail, led the way through the deep woods around a shoulder of the mountain to the place where they would find shelter.

A narrow ledge traversed the face of a great rock mass at the head of a small ravine. Presently the ledge widened, forming a broad, level shelf; and behind this shelf, a long horizontal cleft, ten feet high at the entrance, struck deep into the rock. Kindling a fire, they roasted two ruffed grouse which the Raven had brought down with light can arrows on the way up the mountain. Then the King's commissioner lay down on a bed of odorous spruce boughs.

Already the night chill had descended. Sir Alexander placed his couch well within the cave, where he would escape the dew. Gilyan chose to sleep in the open on the broad shelf directly in front of the cave's entrance, where the branches of a great chestnut oak, springing from the base of the rock, spread themselves ten feet above him like a canopy. Long before the fire flickered out, these two were sleeping soundly.

Corane the Raven, stretched at full length on the bare rock five yards to Gilyan's left, knew that for him there would be no sleep that night. For an hour or more he lay motionless, his eyes closed; but all that while his brain was in turmoil – a turmoil of anger, none the less deep because it was sternly repressed – and sorrow and foreboding.

He was grateful for the respite which Sir Alexander's fatigue had brought. But for Twining's temporary collapse, they would have reached that afternoon the high cave which had been Koe Ishto's den for years. He had planned to station Twining and Gilyan in an ambush near the path which the parent pumas used in passing to and from the den; and probably before nightfall a rifle would have cracked and Koe Ishto's life would have ended. But the respite, after all, meant little. It merely postponed the sacrilege for which the Red Spirit of Unaka Kanoos would assuredly seek vengeance.

What would that vengeance be? What punishment would be visited upon him because through his connivance the Cat of God had been killed? The Raven did not know. But he was very sure that punishment would come, that it was inescapable. He had no choice, it seemed, save to do what he was doing, for such was the law of the gods – that inviolable law, which commanded loyalty to a pledged brother. But his heart blazed with hatred of the man who, taking advantage of that law, had forced this course upon him. And presently, like a spectre dreadful yet somehow welcome, a grim question pushed its way to the threshold of his brain.

Was there a way out, after all, a way which the gods might approve or at least excuse? It was true that, on that May afternoon long ago in the canebrake in the foothills, he had given to Gilyan the pledge of lifelong brotherhood. It was true that his debt to the man who had saved his son's life was a debt so deep that it could never be forgotten. But it was true also that Gilyan had proved himself an enemy to the people of the Overhills, the people of Corane's race.

The white traders, coming up from Charles Town, brought rum to the Blue Mountains, that strong, maddening drink known as tafia, which already had all but ruined the tribes of the lower country. From his cabin in the foothills Gilyan had introduced rum to the Cherokees. For a keg of tafia many deerskins might be had. Stealing away the red hunter's brains with his liquor, Gilyan year after year had robbed them of their pelts. Nor was this the worst. In his long pursuit of Koe Ishto, the puma of Unaka Kanoos, whom the Shamans and the conjurors had declared sacred, Gilyan had flouted the Cherokee's beliefs and insulted their gods; and now, to curry favour with this powerful white chief who had come from beyond the Great Water, he was making the Raven himself a traitor to his own faith and exposing him to the Red God's wrath.

Suddenly there leaped full-formed into the Raven's brain a new thought. What if the vengeance which would surely come were visited not upon him alone but upon all his people? What if the Red Spirit who dwelt upon Unaka Kanoos should punish Corane's nation for Corane's crime?

Into the Raven's heart swept such fear as he had never known before; such fear as a man must feel who opens his eyes suddenly to find himself standing on the brink of a bottomless pit into which he had been about to plunge unawares. And after the fear followed horror of the thing that must now be done; and after the horror came something that was like a terrible, fierce joy.

He had loved Gilyan. Many times in years gone by they had roamed the woods together. But those years had passed, and long ago his love for Gilyan had died. Since then there was a heavy score to settle; and now the time for settling it had come. It was Gilyan's life or Koe Ishto's. The Raven could not, by simply withdrawing from the hunt, undo what he had done. Gilyan now knew too definitely the general location of Koe Ishto's lair. He could find it without further aid, and that he would find it sooner or later was certain. The Raven knew that there was only one way in which he could atone, only one way in which he could save his people from the calamity which he all but brought upon them. And, with that long score to settle, he was glad that there was only one way.

For many minutes he did not move. He lay on his back, his eyes open now, listening to Gilyan's slow, heavy breathing, planning carefully the thing that he was about to do. At last his had groped along the rocky surface to his left and closed upon the long knife which he had placed within easy reach beside his bow and his spear.

There would be no outcry. The King's commissioner would awake at dawn to find a dead man lying at the entrance of his cave; and by that time the Raven would be far on his way toward the unknown wilderness beyond the headwater of Ocono Lufta, where no white man had ever trod.

Still lying on his back, he turned his head very slowly to the right.

For some moments he was not sure of what he saw. The fire had died away to nothing. Overhead a few stars glittered. A half-moon shone feebly through a thin veil of cloud. In the faint light even the Indian warrior's trained vision failed to discern the out-line of the puma's form. Yet something about the shape of the stout chestnut oak limb slanting above the wide ledge in front of the cave fixed his attention. Instinctively he studied it; and all at once he knew that Koe Ishto crouched on the limb ten feet above the spot where Gilyan lay.

Amazement held him motionless, but even in his amazement he understood. Instantly he realized that only one thing could have brought Koe Ishto to that place, that only one thing could have nerved him to mount the chestnut oak at the base of the cliff and take his stand on the limb above the ledge where the hunter was sleeping. Koe Ishto had changed his lair. He had abandoned the high cave near Unaka's summit and had brought his cubs to this other cave which he had never utilized before. The Raven knew that somewhere in the black recesses of that deep slit in the rock the cubs were hiding.

In an instant his plan was formed. It came to him suddenly, complete and perfect, as though some voice had whispered it in his ear. His right hand laid down the knife, groped cautiously for a moment, closed upon the slim, straight shaft of his spear. Very slowly, so slowly that the movement was almost imperceptible, he turned over and began to crawl inch by inch across the ledge toward the cave's entrance.

Always as he crawled he watched the vague bulk of Koe Ishto on the great oak limb almost directly over Gilyan's head. He saw the long body of the puma tremble and stiffen, and immediately he halted and for perhaps five minutes remained motionless. Even more slowly he crept forward again, until he vanished in the obscurity of the cave.

For some minutes there was no sound except the slow breathing of the two sleeping men. Then a shrill, piercing scream split the silence; the scream of a puma cub in fear or pain, a puma cub which had felt the prick of the Raven's spear.

At once Gilyan – a light sleeper, like all wilderness hunters - awoke and sat bolt upright. And at once a long dark shape, dim, shadowy, incredibly huge, launched itself from the oak limb above and fell full upon him, smashing him down upon the rock.

He uttered no sound. His neck was broken; probably his skull was crushed. Koe Ishto, growling savagely, crouched upon the body, his long tail twitching to and fro, his eyes shining like huge emeralds lit with yellow fire. Sir Alexander Twining, awakened by harsh shuddering growls which seemed to shake the air within the cave, raised himself on his elbow. He saw those eyes and the vague bulk behind them, and gave himself up for lost.

Suddenly, from the blackness of the cave, Corane the Raven strode forward, his spear levelled. For an interminable minute puma and Indian faced each other; and, as the slow seconds passed, the Raven knew that behind the emerald eyes, burning like live coals in the darkness, fury and fear were struggling for the mastery.

He could almost read in the changing glare of those eyes the progress of the struggle; and from the beginning he had little doubt as to the outcome. For one reckless moment, as the scream of his cub rang in his ears, Koe Ishto's fury had triumphed. In the madness of that moment he had hurled himself upon his nearest enemy. So much the Raven had foreseen and expected confidently; but knowing the puma kind, he believed that this would be the end.

For as much as a minute he waited motionless, his right hand gripping the levelled spear, ready for what might happen. Then slowly he raised his left hand above his head in the stately gesture of peace and farewell. Next moment the burning eyes vanished and the ledge was empty except for the dead man lying twisted and limp.

It was the Indian who broke the silence. Standing at the cliff's edge, his tall, sinewy form superbly erect, his face lifted to the faint stars, he intoned in the Cherokee tongue a chant of praise to the Spirit of Unaka Kanoos, the Red God of the Thunders, Koe Ishto's master and lord, who had given the great cat courage to serve the Raven's need. Then he turned to King George's commissioner.

'Corane the Raven has fulfilled his promise', he said in English. 'He has led the white chief to Koe Ishto, the Cat of God. Tomorrow he will lead the white chief back to the camp of his people below the Overhills.'

The Cat

My children, you should imitate
  The harmless, necessary cat,
Who eats whatever's on his plate,
  And doesn't ever leave the fat;
Who never stays in bed too late,
  Or does immoral things like that;
Instead of saying, 'Shan't!' or 'Bosh!'
He'll sit and wash, and wash, and wash!

When shadows fall and lights grow dim,
  He sits beneath the kitchen stair;
Regardless as to life and limb,
  A shady lair he chooses there;
And if you tumble over him,
  He simply loves to hear you swear,
And while bad language *you* prefer
He'll sit and purr, and purr, and purr!

HARRY GRAHAM

In Ancient Egypt, Greece and Rome

Dorothy Margaret Stewart

It was from Libya that she made her way into the land of Egypt and into the homes and the temples of the Ancient Egyptians. Aloof, graceful, of unfailing dignity, with mysterious expanding and contracting eyes to which the darkness was not dark, she would have been an obvious candidate for deification even among a people less apt to integrate their animals with their gods. Beauty was not demanded of these sacred beasts. Nobody could have called Ta-urt, the hippopotamus-headed wife of Set, even moderately good-looking. And the dog's head of Anubis was a hideous, grinning head. But the two goddesses, Ubastet (otherwise Bastet, ultimately Bast) and Sekmet, who wore feline masks wore them with a difference. Whether it be in the likeness of a lioness or of a cat the mask could never be described as ugly, for all the bristling whiskers and the slightly sinister slant of the eye.

More ancient than either was yet another cat-goddess Mafdet, who appears as early as the First Dynasty in the act of protecting Pharaoh's house from snakes. In a Twelfth Dynasty tomb at Abydos, Flinders Petrie found seventeen skeletons of cats; in the recess intended for offerings stood a row of the roughest little votive pots, presumably meant to contain milk.

As the long sequence of centuries dawned and darkened over the Nile Valley the cult of the cat-goddess established itself ever more firmly there. It would last well into the Roman period.

Bast typified the kindly, fructifying powers of the sun: she was the Lady of Life, the Soul of Osiris, the Eye of Ra. Her 'opposite number', Sekmet, symbolized his destructive power and wore the features of a lioness. Yet it must be confessed that these two divine ladies sometimes tended to melt into each other after the disconcerting fashion of heathen gods. Each could, if she chose, poise the sun's disc or the sacred uraeus upon her shallow brows; but it is curious that the amiable Bast should have cared to assume the face of the unamiable Sekmet, as she seems occasionally to have done.

Whether she was represented as having a human body with a cat's head or as being incarnate in the complete body of a cat depended upon time, place and religious fashion. The Greeks, the Hellenized Egyptians and the Romans identified her with Artemis or Diana. 'When the gods', wrote Ovid, 'fled into Egypt and hid themselves there under borrowed forms, the sister of Apollo wore the similitude of a cat.' He does not say that she wore the *head* of a cat.

In her heyday Bast was the honoured patroness of the eastern half of the Delta. The centre of her cult was at Per-Ubastet, the 'Bubastis' of Herodotus, in the district now known as Beni-Hassan. Modern archaeologists exploring the site discovered that the mound into which they delved was called Tell-Basta. Centuries of Islamic domination had not robbed the cat-goddess of her ninth life.

To the Jewish prophets all this bowing down to graven images was most repugnant; and the ineradicable tendency of their people to 'go-a-whoring after strange gods' must have lent a sharper edge to their fury. Bubastis under the name of 'Pi-Beseth', is mentioned in one of the most minatory passages in the Book of the Prophet Ezekiel, where he foretells with a certain grim glee of the downfall and desolation of the idolatrous land of Egypt.

Bast received especial honours from the Libyan Pharaohs of the Twenty-Second Dynasty, who were in a sense her compatriots. To this period belongs the delightful bronze figurine in the British Museum where she is shown with large, pricked up ears and wears upon her human body a long, close-fitting garment embroidered with a reticular design and scored with perpendicular stripes. One hand holds the sistrum, the sacred rattle so much used in religious rites, and the other a sort of *pochette* known as her *aegis*. Both objects are ornamented with cat-masks. In the Hermetic Books anciently ascribed to Hermes Trismegistus, otherwise the god Thoth, it is stated that this mask symbolizes the moon, 'on account of the cat's variable nature, nocturnal habits and fecundity': and it seems strange that the Egyptians should have elected to associate Bast with the sun to the exclusion of the moon, who also has what may justly be described as nocturnal habits and a variable nature.

At the feet of the figurine described above sit four charming kittens. These little creatures often appear, with or without their divine mother, in the art of Ancient Egypt. They played a part analogous to that of the *amorini* in Baroque sculpture; they introduce a note almost of gaiety. One finds them on sistra, on sceptre-heads, in amulets of carved crystal, in vivid blue or green faience, even as beads in royal necklaces.

Votive images of cats are usually naturalistic: sometimes a relaxed pose is copied straight from nature: sometimes the animal sits erect, as she so often does in real life, front paws close together, tail primly curved round them. Eyes are inlaid with obsidian, rock-crystal, lapis-lazuli, even with gold. The ears, or even the nose, may be pierced for rings. In some instances these adornments still exist. Collars and necklaces encircled furry necks; these may have been personal trinkets, not any part of a cult offering.

The yearly festival of the cat-headed sun-goddess was held in the spring, when tokens of her unchanging beneficence were everywhere visible. It was, as the late Dr James Baikie gravely observed, 'something in the nature of a beanfeast'. The rowdy element, seldom absent on such occasions, was much in evidence at Bubastis. According to Herodotus more grape-wine was then drunk than in the whole of the years besides.

When seven thousand pilgrims assembled, playing flutes, singing sometimes indecorous songs, eating and drinking, dancing, indulging in boisterous jests and even more boisterous horseplay, the result must have been anything rather than edifying. Some of the visitors would take boats and, paddling as near as possible to the reedy margin of the water, would bandy quips with the crowds on the shore. In this light-hearted exchange women seem to have borne a leading part, as befitted the votaresses of a female divinity.

It seems paradoxical that all this uncouth, noisy fun should have been linked with the image of a cat, an animal who, however playful she may on occasion condescend to be, never stoops to the awkward gambols in which a dog will quite unselfconsciously indulge.

By some persuasion of their own the Egyptians overcame the cat's inherited repugnance towards water, her proverbial reluctance to wet her delicate paws. When some great one, a scribe of Pharaoh's household or a captain of his chariots, went fowling with a throw-stick he often used a trained cat to retrieve the birds as, dazed or dying, they fluttered down among the blue-blossomed papyrus reeds.

Such a scene is shown on several surviving tomb-paintings. There is a well-known example in the British Museum. The hunter, wigged, necklaced, girt with a loin-cloth of fine linen, stands erect in the act of aiming his snake-shaped stick. His womenkind are with him – the Ancient Egyptian equivalent of 'going out with the guns'. His wife, upright in the stern, poises on her head, above the wig, one of those cones of nard which by slowly dissolving were supposed to give comfort in hot weather: his small daughter, with shaven skull and exiguous costume, grasps him firmly by the leg. A single glance at the highly competent retrieving cat is enough to prove that she approached her duties without any reluctance. She has succeeded in seizing three birds at once, one with her hindpaws, one with her forepaws, one in her mouth. Her coat is of a tawny brown handsomely striped with tabby markings. In the water beneath the canoe fish teem: in the sky above butterflies flutter. Such would be the scenes and the delights which the stick-throwing gentleman confidently expected to find in the world to come, where his faithful cat would bear him company.

In another wall-painting, hardly less charming, one of the ladies tethers the canoe by clutching a handful of reeds while the cat, beautifully striped and very life-like, rears up in an attitude of supplication, as if saying, 'Oh pray, can I not get on with my job?'

Her voice, as conveyed by her Egyptian name, must have been very similar to the voice of the cats of today. Her name was *Mau*. When out hunting she would perforce doff her immemorial dignity, but she might not have been pleased if she had known that a tomb-painter had caught her in either a pouncing or an imploring pose. Still less would she have liked to see herself in a 'comic-strip' papyrus, walking along on her hindlegs, a stick grasped in one paw, and driving before her a gaggle of anxious-looking geese.

The *Mau* was a domestic pet as well as a goddess and a huntress and in that character also she is always what Miss Austen would have called 'quite the lady'. Usually she arranges both paws and tail as if in obedience to some feline code of deportment; at other times she hastily devours a fish or a duck beneath the dinner-table, yet never with any real loss of dignity. In the Cairo Museum, there is a carved chair-back which shows Queen Tiy, wife of Ameophis III, taking her pleasure on the water in a narrow skiff, with two fan-waving damsels (one of them a princess) at prow and stern. Under the Queen's chair, cosy and condescending, sits her pet cat.

This queen, Tiy, was the mother of Akhenaton, the Heretic Pharaoh, whose efforts to introduce a monotheistic religion into the most madly polytheistic country in the antique world brought him to destruction. She was not Egyptian-born and it may have been that the Great Heresy was derived indirectly from her lack of enthusiasm for the teeming gods which bedevilled her adopted country.

Tiy had a brother, Onen by name, the walls of whose tomb at Thebes bear the likeness of a cat conjecturally identified with his royal sister's favourite. Of course the lively animal devouring a goose beneath his chair may have been one of his own: but at a later date, when the reaction against Akhenaton was in full swing, the head of this cat was deliberately erased. The close connection between the cat, who could claim kinship with the Aton, the sun-symbol of the One God, may have accounted for the erasure, even if she were not recognizably Queen Tiy's particular pet; but it is remarkable that the goose, sacred to Amon-Ra, should have been left untouched. The monotheistic Aton-sun was taboo, while the Amon-Ra sun blazed in triumph over a vast and varied pantheon; nor is there any indication that Bast fell under suspicion because of her solar affiliations.

Cats must have been permitted – even encouraged – to live, mate and breed in the temple courts of Bubastis; and according to the prophet Baruch they also invaded the sacred places of

Babylon. With vehemence he sets forth the folly of those who put their trust in impotent idols incapable of protecting themselves from moth and rust, 'though they be covered with purple raiment', and whose faces have to be wiped clean from the dust of the temple 'when there is much upon them'. These carven faces, blurred by dust, blackened by smoke, were further befouled by bats, swallows and various birds perching on their bodies and heads, 'and the cats also'. Alice's drowsy question, 'Do cats eat bats?' might well have found its answer in the temples of Babylon.

When we make the obvious transition from Ancient Egypt of Ancient Greece we find a curious dearth of cats. It has been suggested that one of their Greek names, *ailouros*, may have been derived from two words, *ailos*, swift, changing, and *oura*, a tail, 'as expressive of the wavy motion of the tail peculiar to the cat-kind'. The other name was *galen*, but unfortunately this is shared between the cat and the weasel, and some ambiguity follows. Both beasts are sworn foes to mice, and were employed as mice-exterminators in Greek households, but one might have expected the logical Attic mind to draw a clear terminological line between them. A myth of rather late emergence relates how Galinthias, one of the daughters of Proteus, legendary King of Egypt, was changed into a *galen*. Hecate had compassion upon her and made her a priestess. The twofold link with witchcraft and with Egypt suggests that in this instance the word indicated a cat and not a weasel.

The Greeks were not cat-conscious. Their only famous poet to allude to 'the cat-kind' was Theocritus, and he was a Syracusan not a Greek by birth. Also the allusion occurs once only. It is in his fifth Idyll, recording the lively colloquy between Gorgo and Praxinoë, two ladies of Syracuse. Praxinoë, impatient at the awkward fumbling of her slave-girl, flings at her what seems to be a proverbial saying: 'Cats like to sleep soft.' *Galen* must in this context mean a cat and not a weasel. During the time that the poet spent at the court of Ptolemy Philadelphus at Alexandria he would have seen many a cherished royal *Mau* 'sleeping soft' on a bed of blue and purple linen.

Though the days of Egypt's glory had departed when Herodotus sojourned there in the fifth century B.C., the cult of the cat still flourished as it had continued to do while

Macedonian, Greek and Persian conquerors filled the throne of the vanished Pharaohs, and would continue to do after the land became a Roman province.

By the time that the Father of History visited Bubastis the integration of Bast with Artemis was so complete that he could write of the great festivals held there in honour of the Moon-Goddess of the Greeks without even mentioning the feline sun-goddess of the Egyptians. Faithful to his rule of eschewing controversial subjects connected with religion, he does not attempt to explain the Egyptian cult of the cat; but he tells us some curious things. For example: if a house is on fire a 'supernatural impulse' inspires the family pets to leap into the flames. The people, standing at a distance, neglect to put out the fire in their anxiety to deter the cats from committing *felo de se:* but these escape by jumping over their heads in order to accomplish their purpose. When all is over there are great lamentations and the bereaved household shaves off its eyebrows in token of mourning. Dead cats are 'taken to certain sacred houses where being first embalmed they are buried in the city of Bubastis'.

Superintendents, both men and women, were appointed to feed every kind of sacred animal, the office being hereditary. When the father of a family had made a vow to some particular beast he proceeded to shave his children's heads, the whole head, or half, or two-thirds. The clippings were then weighed on scales against silver, and whatever the weight might be the silver was handed to the superintendent, who in return 'cut up some fish' and fed it to the object of the vow. This last clause surely applies to the sacred cats only? The sacred crocodile and the sacred ibis would presumably have 'found themselves' in fish.

Some four centuries later Diodorus Siculus was not less impressed by the cult, and he gives us some endearing little glimpses of it in operation. With an amused eye he watched the Egyptians crumbling bread into milk or cutting up fish for the cats, whom they would summon to the banquet 'with a clucking sound'. He notes that anyone who killed an ibis or a cat might by lynched by the populace, with the result that if an Egyptian should catch sight of either animal lying dead he would at one 'withdraw to a great distance and shout with lamentations and protestations' that it was already dead when he found it. Can it have been from Diodorus that Cicero learned that 'no one had ever heard of an Egyptian laying profane hands on a crocodile, an ibis, or a cat?'

This far-travelled historian describes an incident which he himself witnessed when he sojourned in Egypt at the time when Ptolemy Auletes (Ptolemy the Flute-Player) was seeking recognition from the Roman Senate. This Ptolemy was the last of the Hellenistic Kings: with his daughter, Cleopatra, the line of the Ptolemies was extinguished.

At his accession in 80 B.C. he at once began to angle for the goodwill of Rome. Enormous sums of money changed hands before this grace was won, and protracted negotiations were carried on by Roman envoys whom both the King and the whole of his subjects were extremely anxious to please. By sheer mischance a member of one of these missions happened to kill a cat:

> the multitude rushed to his house, and neither the officials sent by the King to beg the man off nor the fear of Rome (which all the people felt) availed to save him.

Learned gentlemen, both Egyptologists and Zoologists recognize two types of cat among the surviving cat-mummies: a largish animal perhaps only half-tame and resembling a lynx, living among human habitations but feeding itself; and a smaller form, loosely classed as *felis libyca bubastis,** which became completely domesticated without losing its sacred character.

During the benighted period when human mummy-powder was a popular ingredient in the pharmacopoeia of the West we do not hear of the mummified bodies of cats being used in the same way; but thousands of these were decapitated by Arab husbandmen and then spread upon the fields to act as manure. One-hundred-and-ninety of these lopped-off heads were found at Gizeh and scientifically examined by Mr T.C.S. Morrison-Scott.

On the evidence of the tomb-paintings he attributes to this type of cat long ears (sometimes barred with dark stripes), a ginger-coloured coat, and a long tail with dark rings. MM. Lortet and

---

* Because it corresponds to the true Libyan cat and is of the kind found in the great cat-cemetery at Bubastis.

Gaillard call the colour *gris cendré jauneâtre, mêlés de fauve et de noir*, the tails *annelés de jaune et de noir:* the whiskers, if these survive, are a yellowish white.

The family cat and the temple cat were both punctiliously mummified, but not by so lengthy a process or with such a variety of rare spices as were needed to preserve the mortal remains of their human friends. For kittens, steeping in nitron and banding with linen was often considered adequate, with the result that when such mummies are unwrapped there is to be found only a meagre deposit of dust and few slender fragments of bone.

More time, money and skill were accorded to fully-grown cats: their wrappings were of two colours, sometimes wound in intricate patterns as if to indicate the characteristic tabby markings. The face is covered by a sort of linen mask with little sprouts representing the ears and eyes, nostrils and whiskers are carefully indicated.

The outer case containing the mummy was fairly substantial and elaborate. A kitten (or even a cat's foetus) might have a little coffin of bronze with the figure of a cat perched on the lid. An adult cat would probably be enclosed in a bronze or wooden receptacle, painted or else sheathed in painted linen, in the shape of a seated *Mau*. One example in the British Museum has a white body surmounted incongruously by a green head. Another has eyes formed of discs of crystal laid upon a gilded surface: the contracted pupils are of black obsidian, the eyelids of bronze. Another, made entirely of bronze, wears an engraved scarab hanging from its collar and an effort has been made to suggest the markings of its fur.

The actual body was as a rule arranged in a sitting posture, the hindquarters flexed, the forepaws lying flat against the flanks, the tail brought up neatly against the belly: but at least one specimen has survived in which the post is natural and life-like, the cat squatting on its haunches, head up, one paw advanced.

Cat-mummification was practised well into the Roman period.

Aga

Lord Zouche

I went to the house of the aga to seek for a habitation, but the aga was asleep; and who was there so bold as to wake a sleeping aga? Luckily he awoke of his own accord: and he was soon informed by my interpreter that an illustrious personage awaited his leisure. He did not care for a monk, and not much for an agoumenos; but he felt small in the presence of a mighty Turkish aga. Nevertheless, he ventured a few hints as usual about the kings and queens who were my first cousins, but in a much more subdued tone than usual; and I was received with that courteous civility and good breeding which is so frequently met with among Turks of every degree. The aga apologised for having no room to offer me; but he sent out his men to look for a lodging; and in the meantime we went to a kiosk, that is, a place like a birdcage, with enough roof to make a shade, and no walls to impede the free passage of the air. It was built of wood, upon a scaffold eight or ten feet from the ground, in the corner of a garden, and commanded a fine view of the sea. In one corner of this cage I sat all day long, for there was nowhere else to go to; and the aga sat opposite to me in another corner, smoking his pipe, in which solacing occupation to his great surprise I did not partake. We had cups of coffee and sherbet every now and then, and about every half-hour the aga uttered a few words of compliment or welcome, informing me occasionally that there were many dervishes in the place, 'very many dervishes,' for so he denominated the monks. Dinner came towards evening. There was meat, dolmas, demir tatlessi, olives, salad, roast meat, and pilau, that filled up some time; and shortly afterwards I retired to the house of the monastery of Russico, a little distance from my kiosk; and there I slept on a carpet on the boards; and at sunrise was ready to continue my journey, as were also the mules. The aga gave me some breakfast, at which repast a cat made its appearance, with whom the day before I had made acquaintance; but now it came, not alone, but accompanied by two kittens. 'Ah!' said I to the aga, 'how is this? Why, as I live, this is a *she*-cat! a cat feminine! What business has it on Mount Athos? and with kittens too! a wicked cat!'

'Hush!' said the aga with a solemn grin, 'do not say anything about it. Yes, it must be a she-cat: I allow, certainly, that it must be a she-cat. I brought it with me from Stamboul. But do not speak of it, or they will take it away; and it reminds me of my home, where my wife and children are living far away from me.'

I promised to make no scandal about the cat, and took my leave; and as I rode off I saw him looking at me out of his cage with the cat sitting by his side. I was sorry I could not take aga and cat and all with me to Stamboul, the poor gentleman looked so solitary and melancholy.

The White and Black Dynasties

Théophile Gautier

A cat brought from Havana by Mademoiselle Aîta de la Penuela, a young Spanish artist whose studies of white angoras may still be seen gracing the printsellers' windows, produced the daintiest little kitten imaginable. It was just like a swan's-down powder-puff, and on account of its immaculate whiteness it received the name of Pierrot. When it grew big this lengthened to Don Pierrot de Navarre as being more grandiose and majestic.

Don Pierrot, like all animals which are spoilt and made much of, developed a charming amiability of character. He shared the life of the household with all the pleasure which cats find in the intimacy of the domestic hearth. Seated in his usual place near the fire, he really appeared to understand what was being said, and to take an interest in it.

His eyes followed the speakers, and from time to time he would utter little sounds, as though he too wanted to make remarks and give his opinion on literature, which was our usual topic of conversation. He was very fond of books, and when he found one open on a table he would lie on it, look at the page attentively, and turn over the leaves with his paw; then he would end by going to sleep, for all the world as if he were reading a fashionable novel.

Directly I took up a pen he would jump on my writing-desk and with deep attention watch the steel nib tracing black spider-legs on the expanse of white paper, and his head would turn each time I began a new line. Sometimes he tried to take part in the work, and would attempt to pull the pen out of my hand, no doubt in order to write himself, for he was an aesthetic cat, like

Hoffman's Murr, and I strongly suspect him of having scribbled his memoirs at night on some house-top by the light of his phosphorescent eyes. Unfortunately these lucubrations have been lost.

Don Pierrot never went to bed until I came in. He waited for me inside the door, and as I entered the hall he would rub himself against my legs and arch his back, purring joyfully all the time. Then he proceeded to walk in front of me like a page, and if I had asked him, he would certainly have carried the candle for me. In this fashion he escorted me to my room and waited while I undressed; then he would jump on the bed, put his paws round my neck, rub noses with me, and lick me with his rasping little pink tongue, while giving vent to soft inarticulate cries, which clearly expressed how pleased he was to see me again. Then when his transports of affection had subsided, and the hour for repose had come, he would balance himself on the rail of the bedstead and sleep there like a bird perched on a bough. When I woke in the morning he would come and lie near me until it was time to get up. Twelve o'clock was the hour at which I was supposed to come in. On this subject Pierrot had all the notions of a concierge.

At that time we had instituted little evening gatherings among a few friends, and had formed a small society, which we called the Four Candles Club, the room in which we met being, as it happened, lit by four candles in silver candlesticks, which were placed at the corners of the table.

Sometimes the conversation became so lively that I forgot the time, at the risk of finding, like Cinderella, my carriage turned into a pumpkin and my coachman into a rat.

Pierrot waited for me several times until two o'clock in the morning, but in the end my conduct displeased him, and he went to bed without me. This mute protest against my innocent dissipation touched me so much that ever after I came home regularly at midnight. But it was a long time before Pierrot forgave me. He wanted to be sure that it was not a sham repentance; but when he was convinced of the sincerity of my conversion, he deigned to take me into favour again, and he resumed his nightly post in the entrance-hall.

To gain the friendship of a cat is not any easy thing. It is a philosophic, well-regulated, tranquil animal, a creature of habit and a lover of order and cleanliness. It does not give its affections indiscriminately. It will consent to be your friend if you are worthy of the honour, but it will not be your slave. With all its affection, it preserves its freedom of judgement, and it will not do anything for you which it considers unreasonable; but once it has given its love, what absolute confidence, what fidelity of affection! It will make itself the companion of your hours of work, of loneliness, or of sadness. It will lie the whole evening on your knee, purring and happy in your society, and leaving the company of creatures of its own kind to be with you. In vain the sound of caterwauling reverberates from the house-tops, inviting it to one of those cats' evening parties where essence of red-herring takes the place of tea. It will not be tempted, but continues to keep its vigil with you. If you put it down it climbs up again quickly, with a sort of crooning noise, which is like a gentle reproach. Sometimes, when seated in front of you, it gazes at you with such soft, melting eyes, such a human and caressing look, that you are almost awed, for it seems impossible that reason can be absent from it.

Don Pierrot had a companion of the same race as himself, and no less white. All the imaginable snowy comparisons it were possible to pile up would not suffice to give an idea of that immaculate fur, which would have made ermine look yellow.

I called her Seraphita in memory of Balzac's Swedenborgian romance. The heroine of that wonderful story, when she climbed the snow peaks of the Falberg with Minna, never shone with a more pure white radiance. Seraphita had a dreamy and pensive character. She would lie motionless on a cushion for hours, not asleep, but with eyes fixed in rapt attention on scenes invisible to ordinary mortals.

Caresses were agreeable to her, but she responded to them with great reserve, and only to those of people whom she favoured with her esteem, which it was not easy to gain. She liked luxury, and it was always in the newest armchair or on the piece of furniture best calculated to show off her swan-like beauty, that she was to be found. Her toilette took an immense time. She would carefully smooth her entire coat every morning, and wash her face with her paw and every hair on her body shone like new silver when brushed by her pink tongue. If anyone touched her she would immediately efface all traces of the contact, for she could not endure being ruffled. Her elegance and distinction gave one an idea of aristocratic birth, and among her own kind she must have been at least a duchess. She had a passion for scents. She would plunge her nose into bouquets, and nibble a perfumed handkerchief with little paroxysms of delight. She would walk about on the dressing-table sniffling the stoppers of the scent-bottles, and she would have loved to use the violet powder if she had been allowed.

Such was Seraphita, and never was a cat more worthy of a poetic name.

Don Pierrot de Navarre, being a native of Havana, needed a hot-house temperature. This he found indoors, but the house was surrounded by large gardens, divided up by palings through which a cat could easily slip, and planted with big trees in which hosts of birds twittered and sang; and sometimes Pierrot taking advantage of an open door, would go out hunting of an evening and run over the dewy grass and flowers. He would then have to wait till morning to be let in again, for although he might be mewing under the windows, his appeal did not always wake the sleepers inside.

He had a delicate chest, and one colder night than usual he took a chill which soon developed into consumption. Poor Pierrot, after a year of coughing, became wasted and thing, and his coat, which formerly boasted such a snowy gloss, now put one in mind of the lustreless white of a shroud. His great limpid eyes looked enormous in his attenuated face. His pink nose had grown pale, and he would walk sadly along the sunny wall with slow steps, and watch the yellow autumn leaves whirling up in spirals. He looked as though he were reciting Millevoye's elegy.

There is nothing more touching than a sick animal; it submits to suffering with such gentle, pathetic resignation.

Everything possible was done to try and save Pierrot. He had a very clever doctor who sounded him and felt his pulse. He ordered him asses' milk, which the poor creature drank willingly enough out of his little china saucer. He lay for hours on my knee like the ghost of a sphinx, and I could feel the bones of his spine like the beads of a rosary under my fingers. He tried to respond to my caresses with a feeble purr which was like a death rattle.

When he was dying he lay panting on his side, but with a

supreme effort he raised himself and came to me with dilated eyes in which there was a look of intense supplication. This look seemed to say: 'Cannot you save me, you who are a man?' Then he staggered a short way with eyes already glazing, and fell down with such a lamentable cry, so full of despair and anguish, that I was pierced with silent horror.

He was buried at the bottom of the garden under a white rose-bush which still marks his grave.

Seraphita died two or three years later of diphtheria, against which no science could prevail.

She rests not far from Pierrot. With her the white dynasty became extinct, but not the family. To this snow-white pair were born three kittens as black as ink.

Let him explain this mystery who can.

Just at that time Victor Hugo's *Misérables* was in great vogue, and the names of the characters in the novel were on everyone's lips. I called the two male kittens Enjolras and Gavroche, while the little female received the name of Eponine.

They were perfectly charming in their youth. I trained them like dogs to fetch and carry a bit of paper crumpled into a ball, which I threw for them. In time they learnt to fetch it from the tops of cupboards, from behind chests or from the bottom of tall vases, out of which they would pull it very cleverly with their paws. When they grew up they disdained such frivolous games, and acquired that calm philosophic temperament which is the true nature of cats.

To people landing in America in a slave colony all negroes are negroes, and indistinguishable from one another. In the same way, to careless eyes, three black cats are three black cats; but attentive observers make no such mistake. Animal physiognomy varies as much as that of men, and I could distinguish perfectly between those faces, all three as black as Harlequin's mask, and illuminated by emerald disks shot with gold.

Enjolras was by far the handsomest of the three. He was remarkable for his great leonine head and big ruff, his powerful shoulders, long back and splendid feathery tail. There was something theatrical about him, and he seemed to be always posing like a popular actor who knows he is being admired. His movements were slow, undulating and majestic. He put each foot down with as much circumspection as if he were walking on a table covered with Chinese bric-à-brac or Venetian glass. As to his character, he was by no means a stoic, and he showed a love of eating which that virtuous and sober young man, his namesake, would certainly have disapproved. Enjolras would undoubtedly have said to him, like the angel to Swedenborg: 'You eat too much.'

I humoured this gluttony, which was as amusing as a gastronomic monkey's, and Enjolras attained a size and weight seldom reached by the domestic cat. It occurred to me to have him shaved poodle-fashion, so as to give the finishing touch to his resemblance to a lion.

We left him his mane and a big tuft at the end of his tail, and I would not swear that we did not give him mutton-chop whiskers on his haunches like those Munito wore. Thus tricked out, it must be confessed he was much more like a Japanese monster than an African lion. Never was a more fantastic whim carved out of a living animal. His shaven skin took odd blue tints, which contrasted strangely with his black mane.

Gavroche, as though desirous of calling to mind his namesake in the novel, was a cat with an arch and crafty expression of countenance. He was smaller than Enjolras, and his movements were comically quick and brusque. In him absurd capers and ludicrous postures took the place of the banter and slang of the Parisian gamin. It must be confessed that Gavroche had vulgar tastes. He seized every possible occasion to leave the drawing-room in order to go and make up parties in the backyard, or even in the street, with stray cats,

'De naissance quelconque et de sang peu prouvé,'
in which doubtful company he completely forgot his dignity as cat of Havana, son of Don Pierrot de Navarre, grandee of Spain of the first order, and of the aristocratic and haughty Doña Seraphita.

Sometimes in his truant wanderings he picked up emaciated comrades, lean with hunger, and brought them to his plate of food to given them a treat in his good-natured, lordly way. The poor creatures, with ears laid back and watchful side-glances, in fear of being interrupted in their free meal by the broom of the housemaid, swallowed double, triple, and quadruple mouthfuls, and, like the famous dog Siete-Aguas (seven waters) of Spanish *posadas* (inns), they licked the plate as clean as if it had been washed and polished by one of Gerard Dow's or Mieris's Dutch housewives.

Seeing Gavroche's friends reminded me of a phrase which illustrates one of Gavarni's drawings. 'Ils sont jolis les amis dont vous êtes susceptible d'aller avec!' ('Pretty kind of friends you like to associate with!')

But that only proved what a good heart Gavroche had, for he could easily have eaten all the food himself.

The cat named after the interesting Eponine was more delicate and slender than her brothers. Her nose was rather long, and her eyes slightly oblique, and green as those of Pallas Athene, to whom Homer always applied the epithet of γλανκωπκ. Her nose was of velvety black, with the grain of a fine Périgord truffle; her whiskers were in a perpetual state of agitation, all of which gave her a peculiarly expressive countenance. Her superb black coat was always in motion, and was watered and shot with shadowy markings. Never was there a more sensitive, nervous, electric animal. If one stroked her two or three times in the dark, blue sparks would fly crackling out of her fur.

Eponine attached herself particularly to me, like the Eponine of the novel to Marius, but I, being less taken up with Cosette than that handsome young man, could accept the affection of this gentle and devoted cat, who still shares the pleasures of my suburban retreat and is the inseparable companion of my hours of work.

She comes running up when she hears the front-door bell, receives the visitors, conducts them to the drawing-room, talks to them – yes, talks to them – with little chirruping sounds, that do not in the least resemble the language cats use in talking to their own kind, but which simulate the articulate speech of man. What does she say? She says in the clearest way, 'Will you be good enough to wait till monsieur comes down? Please look at the pictures, or chat with me in the meantime, if that will amuse you.' Then when I come in she discreetly retires to an armchair or a corner of the piano, like a well-bred animal who knows what is correct in good society. Pretty little Eponine gave so many proofs of intelligence, good disposition and sociability, that by common consent she was raised to the dignity of a *person*, for it was quite evident that she was possessed of higher reasoning power than mere instinct. This dignity conferred on her the privilege of eating at table like a person instead of out of a saucer in a corner of the room like an animal.

So Eponine had a chair next to me at breakfast and dinner, but on account of her small size she was allowed to rest her two front paws on the edge of the table. Her place was laid, without spoon or fork, but she had her glass. She went right through dinner dish by dish, from soup to dessert, waiting for her turn to be helped, and behaving with such propriety and nice manners as one would like to see in many children. She made her appearance at the first sound of the bell, and on going into the dining-room one found her already in her place, sitting up in her chair with her paws resting on the edge of the tablecloth, and seeming to offer you her little face to kiss, like a well-brought-up little girl who is affectionately polite towards her parents and elders.

As one finds flaws in diamonds, spots on the sun, and shadows on perfection itself, so Eponine, it must be confessed, had a passion for fish. She shared this in common with all other cats. Contrary to the Latin proverb,

'Catus amat pisces, sed non vult tingere plantas,'
she would willingly have dipped her paw into the water if by so doing she could have pulled out a trout or a young carp. She became nearly frantic over fish, and, like a child who is filled with the expectation of dessert, she sometimes rebelled at her soup when she knew (from previous investigations in the kitchen) that fish was coming. When this happened she was not helped, and I would say to her coldly: 'Mademoiselle, a person who is not hungry for soup cannot be hungry for fish,' and the dish would be pitilessly carried away from under her nose. Convinced that matters were serious, greedy Eponine would swallow her soup in all haste, down to the last drop, polishing off the last crumb of bread or bit of macaroni, and would then turn round to look at me with pride, like someone who has conscientiously done his duty. She was then given her portion, which she consumed with great satisfaction, and after tasting of every dish in turn, she would finish up by drinking a third of a glass of water.

When I am expecting friends for dinner Eponine knows there is going to be a party before she sees the guests. She looks at her place, and if she sees a knife and fork by her plate she decamps at once and seats herself on a music-stool, which is her refuge on these occasions.

Let those who deny reasoning powers to animals explain if they can this little fact, apparently so simple, but which contains a whole series of inductions. From the presence near her plate of those implements which man alone can use, this observant and reflective cat concludes that she will have to give up her place for that day to a guest, and promptly proceeds to do so. She never makes a mistake; but when she knows the visitor well she climbs on his knee and tries to coax a tit-bit out of him by her pretty caressing ways.

The Cat and the Rat

Four creatures, wont to prowl, –
　　Sly Grab-and-Snatch, the cat,
Grave Evil-bode, the owl,
　　Thief Nibble-stitch, the rat,
And Madam Weasel, prim and fine, –
Inhabited a rotten pine.
A man their home discover'd there,
And set, one night, a cunning snare.
　　The cat, a noted early-riser,
　　　　Went forth, at break of day,
　　　　To hunt her usual prey.
　　　　　Not much the wiser
　　　　For morning's feeble ray,
　　The noose did suddenly surprise her.
　　　　Waked by her strangling cry,
　　　　Grey Nibble-stitch drew nigh:
　　　　As full of joy was he
　　　　As of despair was she,
　　　　His foe of mortal paw.
'Dear friend,' said Mrs Grab-and-Snatch,
'Do, pray, this cursed cord detach.
　　I've always known your skill,
　　And often your good-will;
Now help me from this worst of snares,
In which I fell at unawares.
　　'Tis by a sacred right,
　　　　You, sole of all your race,

By special love and grace,
Have been my favourite –
  The darling of my eyes.
'Twas order'd by celestial cares,
No doubt: I thank the blessed skies,
  That, going out to say my prayers,
As cats devout each morning do,
This net has made me pray to you.
  Come, fall to work upon the cord.'
  Replied the rat, 'And what reward
    Shall pay me, if I dare?'
    'Why,' said the cat, 'I swear
    To be your firm ally:
    Henceforth, eternally,
    These powerful claws are yours,
    Which safe your life insures.
I'll guard from quadruped and fowl;
I'll eat the weasel and the owl.'
    'Ah,' cried the rat, 'you fool!
I'm quite too wise to be your tool.'
He said, and sought his snug retreat,
Close at the rotten pine-tree's feet.
Where plump he did the weasel meet;
Whom shunning by a happy dodge,
He climb'd the hollow trunk to lodge;
And there the savage owl he saw.
Necessity became his law,
And down he went, the rope to gnaw.
Strand after strand in two he bit,
And freed, at last, the hypocrite.
That moment came the man in sight;
The new allies took hasty flight.

    A good while after that,
    Our liberated cat
    Espied her favourite rat,
  Quite out of reach, and on his guard.
'My friend,' said she, 'I take your shyness hard;
  Your caution wrongs my gratitude;

Approach, and greet your staunch ally.
Do you suppose, dear rat, that I
Forget the solemn oath I mew'd?'
'Do I forget,' the rat replied,
'To what your nature is allied?
To thankfulness, or even pity,
Can cats be ever bound by treaty?'

Alliance from necessity
Is safe just while it has to be.

LA FONTAINE

Tom Connor's Cat

Samuel Lover

There was a man in these parts, sir, you must know, called Tom Connor, and he had a cat that was equal to any dozen of rat traps, and he was proud of the baste, and with rayson; for she was worth her weight in goold to him in saving his sacks of meal from the thievery of the rats and mice; for Tom was an extensive dealer in corn, and influenced the rise and fall of that article in the market, to the extent of a full dozen of sacks at a time which he either kept or sold, as the spirit of free trade or monopoly came over him. Indeed, at one time, Tom had serious thoughts of applying to the government for a military force to protect his granary when there was a threatened famine in the country.'

'Pooh, pooh, sir!' said the matter-of-fact little man. 'As if a dozen sacks could be of the smallest consequence in a whole country – pooh pooh!'

'Well sir,' said Murtough, 'I can't help you if you don't believe; but it's truth what I'm telling you, and pray don't interrupt me, though you may not believe; by the time the story's done you'll have heard more wonderful things than *that* – and besides, remember you're a stranger in these parts, and have no notion of the extraordinary things, physical, metaphysical, and magical, which constitute the idiosyncrasy of rural destiny.'

The little man did not know the meaning of Murtough's last sentence – nor Murtough either; but, having stopped the little man's throat with big words, he proceeded:

'This cat, sir, you must know, was a great pet, and was so up to everything, that Tom swore she was a'most like a Christian, only she couldn't speak, and has so sensible a look in her eyes, that he was sartin sure the cat knew every word that was said to her. Well, she used to set by him at breakfast every morning, and the eloquent cock of her tail, as she used to rub against his leg, said: "Give me some milk, Tom Connor," as plain as print, and the plentitude of her purr afterward spoke a gratitude beyond language. Well, one morning, Tom was going to the neighboring town to market, and he had promised the wife to bring home shoes to the childre' out o' the price of the corn; and sure enough before he sat down to breakfast there was Tom taking the measure of the children's feet, by cutting notches on a bit of stick; and the wife gave him so many cautions about getting a "nate fit" for "Billy's purty feet," that Tom, in his anxiety to nick the closest possible measure, cut off the child's toe. This disturbed the harmony of the party, and Tom was obliged to breakfast alone, while the mother was endeavouring to cure Billy; in short, trying to make a *heal* of his *toe*. Well, sir, all the time Tom was taking measure for the shoes, the cat was observing him with that luminous peculiarity of eye for which her tribe is remarkable; and when Tom sat down for breakfast the cat rubbed up against him more vigorously than usual; but Tom being bewildered, between his expected gain in corn and the positive loss of his child's toe, kept never minding her, until the cat, with a sort of caterwauling growl, gave Tom a dab of her claws, that wen clean through his leathers, and a little further. 'Wow!' says Tom, with a jump, clapping his hand on the part, and rubbing it. 'By this and that, you drew the blood out o' me,' says Tom. 'You wicked divil-tish! – go along!' says he, making a kick at her. With that the cat gave a reproachful look at him, and her eyes glared just like a pair of mail-coach lamps in a fog. With that, sir, the cat, with a mysterious 'meow,' fixed a most penetrating glance on Tom, and distinctly uttered his name.

'Tom felt every hair on his head as stiff as a pump handle; and scarcely crediting his ears, he returned a searching look at the cat, who very quietly proceeded in a sort of nasal twang:

'"Tom Connor," says she.

'"The Lord be good to me!" says Tom. "If it isn't spaking' she is!"

'"Tom Connor," says she again.

'"Yes, ma'am," says Tom.

'"Come here," says she. "Whisper – I want to talk to you, Tom," says she, "the laste taste in private," says she – rising on her hams and beckoning him with her paw out o' the door, with a wink and a toss o' the head aiqual to a milliner.

'Well, as you may suppose, Tom didn't know whether he was on his head or his heels, but he followed the cat, and off she went and squatted herself under the hedge of a little paddock at the back of Tom's house; and as he came round the corner, she held up her paw again, and laid it on her mouth, as much as to say "Be cautious, Tom." Well, divil a word Tom could say at all, with the fright, so up he goes to the cat, and says she:

'"Tom," says she, "I have a great respect for you, and there's something I must tell you, because you're losing character with your neighbors," says she, "by your goin's on," says she, "and it's out o' the respect that I have for you, that I must tell you," says she.

'"Thank you, ma'am," says Tom.

'"You're going off to the town," says she, "to buy shoes for the childre'," says she, "and never thought o' getting me a pair."

'"You!" says Tom.

'"Yis, me, Tom Connor," says she, "and the neighbors wondhers that a respectable man like you allows your cat to go about the counthry barefutted," says she.

'"Is it a cat to ware shoes?" says Tom.

'"Why not?" says she. "Doesn't horses ware shoes? And I have a prettier foot than a horse, I hope," says she with a toss of her head.

'"Faix, she spakes like a woman; so proud of her feet," says Tom to himself, astonished, as you may suppose, but pretending never to think it remarkable all the time; and so he went on discoursin'; and says he: "It's thrue for you, ma'am," says he, "that horses ware shoes – but that stands to rayson, ma'am, you see – seeing the hardship their feet has to go through on the hard roads."

'"And how do you know what hardship my feet has to go through?" says the cat, mighty sharp.

'"But, ma'am," says Tom, "I don't well see how you could fasten a shoe on you," says he.

'"Lave that to me," says the cat.

'"Did anyone every stick walnut shells on you, pussy?" says Tom, with a grin.

'"Don't be disrespectful, Tom Connor," says the cat, with a frown.

'"I ax your pard'n, ma'am," said he, "but as for the horses you wor spakin' about warin' shoes, you know their shoes is fastened on with nails, and how would your shoes be fastened on?"

'"Ah, you stupid thief!" says she, "haven't I illigant nails o' my own?" and with that she gave him a dab of her claw, that made him roar.

'"Ow! murdher!" says he.

'"Now no more of your palaver, Misther Connor," says the cat. "Just be off and get me the shoes."

'"Tare and ouns!" says Tom. "What'll become o' me if I'm to get shoes for my cats?" says he. "For you increase your family four times a year, and you have six or seven every time," says he; "and then you must all have two pair apiece – wirra! wirra! – I'll be ruined in shoeleather," says Tom.

'"No more o' your stuff," says the cat; "don't be standin' here undher the hedge talkin' or we'll lose our characters – for I've re-marked your wife is jealous, Tom."

'"Pon my sowl, that's thrue," says Tom, with a smirk.

'"More fool she," says the cat, "for 'pon my conscience, Tom, you're as ugly as if you wor bespoke."

'Off ran the cat with these words, leaving Tom in amazement. He said nothing to the family, for fear of fright'ning them, and off he went to the town, as he pretended – for he saw the cat watching him through a hole in the hedge; but when he came to a turn at the end of the road, the dickings a mind he minded the market, good or bad, but went off to Squire Botherum's, the magisthrit, to swear examinations agen the cat.'

'Pooh pooh – nonsense!' broke in the little man, who had listened thus far to Murtough with an expression of mingled won-der and contempt, while the rest of the party willingly gave up the reins to nonsense, and enjoyed Murtough's legend and their companion's more absurd common sense.

'Don't interrupt him, Coggins,' said Mr. Wiggins.

'How can you listen to such nonsense!' returned Coggins, 'Swear examinations against a cat, indeed! Pooh pooh!'

'My dear sir,' said Murtough, 'remember this is a fairy story, and that the country all round here is full of enchantment. As I was telling you, Tom went off to swear examinations.'

'Ay, ay!' shouted all but Coggins. 'Go on with the story.'

'And when Tom was asked to relate the events of the morning, which brought him before Squire Botherum, his brain was so bewildered between his corn, and his cat, and his child's toe, that he made a very confused account of it.'

'"Begin your story from the beginning,"' said the magistrate to Tom.

'"Well, your honor," says Tom, "I was goin' to market this mornin', to sell the child's corn – I beg your pard'n – my own toes, I mane, sir."

'"Sell your toes!"' said the Square.

"No sir, takin' the cat to market, I mane – "

'"Take a cat to market!"' said the Squire. '"You're drunk, man."'

"No, your honor, only confused a little; for when the toes began to spake to me – the cat, I mane – I was bothered clane -"

'"The cat speak to you!"' said the Squire. '"Phew! Worse than before. You're drunk, Tom."'

"No, your honor; it's on the strength of the cat I come to spake to you – "

'"I think it's on the strength of a pint of whiskey, Tom."'

"By the vartue o' my oath, your honor, it's nothin' but the cat." And so Tom then told him all about the affair, and the Squire was regularly astonished. Just then the bishop of the diocese and the priest of the parish happened to call in, and heard the story; and the bishop and the priest had a tough argument for two hours on the subject; the former swearing she must be a witch; but the priest denying *that*, and maintaining she was *only* enchanted, and that part of the argument was afterward referred to the primate, and subsequently to the conclave at Rome; but the Pope declined interfering about cats, saying he had quite enough to do minding his own bulls.

'"In the meantime, what are we to do with the cat?"' says Botherum.

'"Burn her,"' says the bishop. '"She's a witch."'

'"*Only* enchanted,"' says the priest, '"and the ecclesiastical court maintains that – '''

'''Bother the ecclesiastical court!''' said the magistrate; '''I can only proceed on the statutes'';' and with that he pulled down all the lawbooks in his library, and hunted the laws from Queen Elizabeth down, and he found that they made laws against everything in Ireland, *except a cat*. The divil a thing escaped them but a cat, which did *not* come within the meaning of any Act of Parliament – *the cats only had escaped.*

'''There's the alien act, to be sure,''' said the magistrate, '''and perhaps she's a French spy in disguise.'''

"She spakes like a French spy, sure enough," says Tom, "and she was missin', I remember, all last Spy Wednesday."

'''That's suspicious,''' says the Squire, '''but conviction might be difficult; and I have a fresh idea,''' says Botherum.

"Faith, it won't keep fresh long, this hot weather," says Tom, "so your honor had better make use of it as wanst."

'''Right,''' says Botherum. '''We'll make her a subject to the game laws; we'll hunt her,''' says he.

"Ow! Elegant!" says Tom; "we'll have a brave run out of her."

'''Meet me at the crossroads,''' says the Squire, '''in the morning, and I'll have the hounds ready.'''

'Well, off Tom went home; and he was racking his brain what excuse he could make to the cat for not bringing the shoes; and at last he hit one off, just as he saw her cantering up to him, half a mile before he got home.

'''Where's the shoes, Tom?''' says she.

"I have not got them today, ma'am," says he.

'''Is that the way you keep your promise, Tom?''' says she. "'I'll tell you what it is, Tom – I'll tare the eyes out o' the childre' if you don't get me those shoes.'''

"Whist, whist!" says Tom, frightened out of his life for his children's eyes. "Don't be in a passion, pussy. The shoemaker said he had not a shoe in his shop, nor a last that would make one to fit you; and he says I must bring you into the town for him to take your measure."

'''And when am I to go?''' says the cat, looking savage.

"Tomorrow," says Tom.

'''It's well you said that, Tom,''' said the cat, or the devil an eye I'd leave in your family this night,''' and off she hopped.

"Tom thrimbled at the wicked look she gave.

'"Remember!"' says she, over the hedge, with a bitter cater-waul.

"Never fear," says Tom.

"Well, sure enough, the next mornin' there was the cat at cock-crow, licking herself as nate as a new pin, to go into the town, and out came Tom with a bag undher his arm and the cat after him.

"Now git into this, and I'll carry into the town," says Tom, opening the bag.

'"Sure, I can walk with you,"' says the cat.

"Oh, that wouldn't do," says Tom. "The people in the town is curious and slandherous people, and sure it would rise ugly remarks if I was seen with a cat after me – a dog is a man's companion by nature, but cats does not stand to rayson."

'Well, the cat, seeing there was no use in argument, got into the bag, and off Tom set to the crossroads with the bag over his shoulder, and he came up, quite innocent-like, to the corner, where the Squire, and his huntsman, and the hounds, and a pack of people were waitin'. Out came the Squire on a sudden, just as if it was all by accident.'

'"God save you, Tom,"' says he.

"God save you kindly, sir," says Tom.

'"What's that bag you have at your back?"' says the Squire.

"Oh nothin' at all, sir," says Tom, makin' a face all the time, as much as to say, I have her safe.

'"Oh, there's something in that bag, I think,"' says the Squire. '"You must let me see it."'

"If you bethray me, Tom Connor"' says the cat, in a low voice, '"by this and that I'll never spake to you again!"'

"Pon my honor, sir" says Tom, with a wink and a twitch of his thumb toward the bag, "I haven't anything in it."

'"I have been missing my praties of late,"' says the Squire, '"and I'd just like to examine that bag,"' says he.

"Is it doubting my character you'd be, sir?" says Tom, pretending to be in a passion.

'"Tom, your sowl!"' says the voice in the sack. '"If you let the cat out of the bag. I'll murther you."'

'"An honest man would make no objection to be sarched,"' said the Squire, '"and I insist on it,"' says he, laying hold o' the bag, and Tom pretending to fight all the time; but, my jewel! before two minutes, they shook the cat out o' the bag, sure enough and off she went, with her tail as big as a sweeping brush, and the Squire, with a thundering view halloo after her, clapped the dogs at her heels, and away they went for the bare life. Never was there seen such running as that day – the cat made for a shaking bog, the loneliest place in the whole country, and there the riders were all thrown out, barrin' the huntsman, who had a web-footed horse on purpose for soft places, and the priest, whose horse could go anywhere by reason of the priest's blessing; and sure enough, the huntsman and his riverence stuck to the hunt like wax; and just as the cat got on the border of the bog, they saw her give a twist as the foremost dog closed with her, for he gave her a nip in the flank. Still she went on, however, and headed them well, toward an old mud cabin in the middle of the bog, and there they saw her jump in at the window, and up came the dogs the next minit, and gathered round the house, with the most horrid howling ever was heard. The huntsman alighted, and went into the house to turn the cat out again, when what should he see but an old hag lying in bed in the corner!

'"Did you see a cat come in here?"' says he.

'"Oh, no-o-o-o!"' squealed the old hag in a trembling voice. '"There's no cat here,"' says she.

'"Yelp, yelp, yelp!"' went the dogs outside.

'"Oh, keep the dogs out of this,"' says the old hag – '"oh-o-o-o!"' and the huntsman saw her eyes glare under the blanket, just like a cat's.

'"Hillo!"' says the huntsman, pulling down the blanket – and what should he see but the old hag's flank all in a gore of blood.

'"Ow, ow! you old divil – is it you? You old cat!"' says he, opening the door.

'In rushed the dogs. Up jumped the old hag and, changing into a cat before their eyes, out she darted through the window again, and made another run for it; but she couldn't escape, and the dogs gobbled her while you could say "Jack Robinson." But the most remarkable part of this extraordinary story, gentlemen, is that the pack was ruined from that day out; for after having eaten the enchanted cat, *the devil a thing they would ever hunt afterward but mice.*'

What The Cat Thinks of the Dog

Anon

I am not altogether sure whether I like the Dog or merely tolerate him. It puzzles me to say just what I do, in a manner, like about my house companion. For a certainty, his manners are very distressing, and they evoke my most hearty disapproval. I cannot abide those rude volcanic barking fits of his. Often, when lying snugly tail-enfolded by the gently warming kitchen stove, lost in a comfortable dreamless doze – how delicious this semi-Nirvana of the senses! – I would suddenly be startled into undesired wakefulness by my friend's frenzied howls. You'd think he had wanted to call my attention to a mouse recently entrapped or, at least, to the arrival of the butcher with a fat quarter of lamb wherefrom one might expect the carving of good cheer for him and me. But no! nine times out of ten it would be some uninteresting urchin whom he had caught sight of through the window, and who was sauntering a block away with an insolent swagger that could not but arouse my profound contempt. I sometimes find it far from easy to keep my temper in such circumstances and to refrain from wishing him and his urchin a watery grave the next time they betake themselves to the river for swimming and diving sports. Yet I must not judge him harshly. An unkind nature has granted him a most unmusical, a most nerve-shattering voice, incapable of the least culture.

I take much exception also to the ungentle and ungraceful manner in which he swings his tail, or rather flips it back and forth and jerks it up and down, for one can hardly talk of swinging where no smooth delicately rounded curves are perceptible. How inferior, both by heredity and by training, is the Dog's handling of his tail to that of the Cat! How little he understands the art of curving and waving and uncurving the tail in the nicely nuanced rhythms and exquisitely designed patterns that are so familiar to ourselves! If the aerial artistry of the Cat's tail may be fitly compared to the beautifully rounded brushwork of our Chinese laundryman when, as I have incidentally observed him more than once, he prepares his stack of wash tickets, the tail movements of the Dog remind me of nothing so much as the ugly zigzagging and unsymmetrical lines that my master's little boy produces, squeakingly, on his slate in his vain attempts to draw a locomotive (at least I gather, from various remarks that I have overhead, that this is what he has in mind). No, there is not the slightest reason to allow for an aesthetic strain in my friend's psychology. Frankly, I do not believe he knows the difference between an Impressionist masterpiece and a billboard daub. Nothing, further, can be more absurd than the frequency with which the Dog's rapid and angular tail movements are executed. No sooner does the master, or his little boy, or the mistress, or even the garbage man appear, than this tail that I speak of is set furiously wagging and swishing, often at the cost of a cup or plate which may happen to be within reach of its tufted point. I wonder that they tolerate him in the kitchen at all. I shall never forget the time that, excited beyond control at the unexpected return of the master from a fishing excursion, he scampered about madly and lashed his tail from side to side with the utmost fury. Well accustomed by this time to his vulgar ways I paid little attention to the hubbub but continued quietly lapping up my saucer of milk, when I was suddenly stunned by a powerful swish of the Dog's milk-spattered tail against my face. Angered beyond expression, both by the Dog's extreme rudeness and by the almost total loss of a savory meal, I was about to scratch out his eyes, but the evident unwillingness of the maid to suffer retaliatory measures, and the reflection on my part that the Dog's conduct, reprehensible as it was, had not been dictated by any unfriendly feeling for myself, prevented a scrimmage. It was a well, for nothing pains me more than to part company with my dignity, even if only for a moment.

In view of so many just grounds for complaint – and there are many that I might add – it puzzles me, I repeat, to say just what I like about the Dog. Can it be that, living as we do, under the same roof, and thus forced by circumstance to put up with each other for better or for worse, we have become habituated to a common lot, and learned to ignore the numerous divergencies of taste and philosophy? From a strictly scientific standpoint, this is an excellent explanation of our mutual forebearance, but I am afraid that sincerity prevents me from accepting it as a completely satisfying solution of the problem. How comes it that, when the Dog, in company with his master, has absented himself from the house for a period of more than usual length, as once for a week's hunting jaunt, I find myself getting jittery and morose, as though there were something missing to complete my usual feeling of contentment? And how comes it that last year, when the Dog's right forefoot was caught in the door, and he set up a caterwauling (excuse the Hibernicism) that made him a frightful nuisance for the rest of the day, I, who would ordinarily have been the first to resent such a noise, as evidencing a deplorable lack of vocal self-control and taste, did on the contrary feel no small amount of sympathy for the suffering wretch? I imagine that there was something about the tilt of my tail and the glance in my eye that communicated my compassion to the Dog, for the next day he seemed a trifle more considerate of my preferences than had been his wont. I construed this as a species of thankfulness on his part. (Yet I would not lay too great stress on this; he may merely have had an attack of the blues, as a result of his recent misadventure.) And how comes it, farther, that I felt considerably nettled the other day when the neighbor's boy kicked the Dog three times in succession? Prudence, to be sure, prevented my taking up an active defence of my friend, but I certainly felt at least an indefinite impulse in that direction.

Such incidents seem to argue a genuine vein of fellow feeling, of sympathy, of the Dog, though, I must insist, this sympathy never degenerates into a maudlin sentimentality. After all is said and done, there is never entirely absent a grain of contempt from my estimate of a mere dog, even of the Dog of the House. It is enough to admit that there is commingled with this contempt a certain something of more benevolent hue, a something which I must leave it to others to explain.

The Cat

Mary E. Wilkins Freeman

The snow was falling, and the Cat's fur was stiffly pointed with it, but he was imperturbable. He sat crouched, ready for the death-spring, as he had sat for hours. It was night – but that made no difference – all times were as one to the Cat when he was in wait for prey. Then, too, he was under no constraint of human will, for he was living alone that winter. Nowhere in the world was any voice calling him; on no hearth was there a waiting dish. He was quite free except for his own desires, which tyrannized over him when unsatisfied as now.

The Cat was very hungry – almost famished, in fact. For days the weather had been very bitter, and all the feebler wild things which were his prey by inheritance, the born serfs to his family, had kept, for the most part, in their burrows and nests, and the Cat's long hunt had availed him nothing. But he waited with the inconceivable patience and persistency of his race; besides, he was certain. The Cat was a creature of absolute convictions, and his faith in his deductions never wavered.

The Rabbit had gone in there between those low-hung pine boughs. Now her little doorway had before it a shaggy curtain of snow, but in there she was. The Cat had seen her enter, so like a swift grey shadow that even his sharp and practised eyes had glanced back for the substance following, and then she was gone. So he sat down and waited; and he waited still in the white night, listening angrily to the north wind starting in the upper heights of the mountains with distant screams, then swelling into an awful crescendo of rage, and swooping down with furious white wings of snow like a flock of fierce eagles into the valleys and ravines.

The Cat was on the side of a mountain, on a wooded terrace. Above him a few feet away towered the rock ascent as steep as the wall of a cathedral. The Cat had never climbed it – trees were the ladders to his heights of life. He had often looked with wonder at the rock, and miauled bitterly and resentfully as man does in the face of a forbidding Providence. At his left was the sheer precipice. Behind him, with a short stretch of woody growth between, was the frozen perpendicular wall of a mountain stream. Before him was the way to his home. When the Rabbit came out she was trapped; her little cloven feet could not scale such unbroken steeps. So that Cat waited.

The place in which he was, looked like a maelstrom of the wood. The tangle of trees and bushes clinging to the mountainside with a stern clutch of roots, the prostrate trunks and branches, the vines embracing everything with strong knots and coils of growth, had a curious effect, as of things which had whirled for ages in a current of raging water, only it was not water, but wind, which had disposed everything in circling lines of yielding to its fiercest points of onset.

And now over all this whirl of wood and rock and dead trunks and branches and vines descended the snow. It blew down like smoke over the rock-crest above; it stood in a gyrating column like some death-wraith of nature, on the level, then it broke over the edge of the precipice; and the Cat cowered before the fierce backward set of it. It was as if ice needles pricked his skin through his beautiful thick fur, but he never faltered and never once cried. He had nothing to gain from crying, and everything to lose; the Rabbit would hear him cry, and know he was waiting.

It grew darker and darker, with a strange white smother, instead of the natural blackness of night. It was a night of storm and death superadded to the night of nature. The mountains were all hidden, wrapped about, overawed, and tumultuously overborne by it; but in the midst of it waited, quite unconquered, this little, unswerving, living patience and power under a little coat of grey fur.

A fiercer blast swept over the rock, spun on one mighty foot of whirlwind athwart the level, then was over the precipice.

Then the Cat saw two eyes luminous with terror, frantic with the impulse of flight; he saw a little, quivering, dilating nose, he saw two pointing ears, and he kept still, with every one of his fine nerves and muscles strained like wires. Then the Rabbit was out – there was one long line of incarnate flight and terror - and the Cat had her.

Then the Cat went home, trailing his prey through the snow.

The Cat lived in the house which his master had built, as rudely as a child's block-house, but stanchly enough. The snow was heavy on the low slant of its roof, but it would not settle under it. The two windows and the door were made fast, but the Cat knew a way in. Up a pine-tree, behind the house he scuttled, though it was hard work with his heavy Rabbit, and was in his little window under the eaves, then down through the trap to the room below, and on his master's bed with a spring and a great cry of triumph, Rabbit and all. But his master was not there; he had been gone since early fall, and it was now February. He would not return until spring, for he was an old man, and the cruel cold of the mountains clutched at his vitals like a Panther, and he had gone to the village to winter. The cat had known for a long time that his master was gone, but his reasoning was always sequential and circuitous; always for him what had been would be; and the more easily for marvellous waiting powers, so he always came home expecting to find his master.

When he saw that he was still gone, he dragged the Rabbit off the rude couch which was the bed to the floor, put one little paw on the carcass to keep it steady, and began gnawing with head to one side to bring his strongest teeth to bear.

It was darker in the house than it had been in the wood, and the cold was as deadly, though not so fierce. If the Cat had not received his fur coat unquestioningly of Providence, he would have been thankful that he had it. It was a mottled grey, white on the face and breast, and thick as fur could grow.

The wind drove the snow on the windows with such force that it rattled like sleet, and the house trembled a little. Then all at once the Cat heard a noise and stopped gnawing his Rabbit, and listened, his shining green eyes fixed upon a window. Then he heard a hoarse shout, a halloo of despair and entreaty; but he knew it was not his master come home, and he waited, one paw still on the Rabbit. Then the halloo came again, and then the Cat answered. He said all that was essential quite plainly to his own comprehension. There was in his cry of response, inquiry, information, warning, terror, and finally, the offer of comradeship; but the man outside did not hear him, because of the howling of the storm.

Then there was a great battering pound at the door, then another, and another. The Cat dragged his Rabbit under the bed. The blows came thicker and faster. It was a weak arm which gave them, but it was nerved by desperation. Finally the lock yielded, and the stranger came in. Then the Cat, peering from under the bed, blinked with a sudden light, and his green eyes narrowed. The stranger struck a match and looked about. The Cat saw a face wild and blue with hunger and cold, and a man who looked poorer and older than his poor old master, who was an outcast among men for his poverty and lowly mystery of antecedents; and he heard a muttered, unintelligible voicing of distress from the harsh piteous mouth. There was in it both profanity and prayer, but the Cat knew nothing of that.

The stranger braced the door which he had forced, got some wood from the stock in the corner, and kindled a fire in the old stove as quickly as his half-frozen hands would allow. He shook so pitiably as he worked that the Cat under the bed felt the tremor of it. Then the man, who was small and feeble, and marked with the scars of suffering which he had pulled down upon his own head, sat down in one of the old chairs and crouched over the fire as if it were his one love and desire of his soul, holding out his yellow hands like yellow claws, and he groaned. The Cat came out from under the bed and leaped up on his lap with the Rabbit. The man gave a great shout and start of terror, and sprang, and the Cat slid clawing to the floor, and the Rabbit fell inertly, and the man leaned, gasping with fright, and ghastly, against the wall. The Cat grabbed the Rabbit by the slack of its neck and dragged it to the man's feet. Then he raised his shrill, insistent cry, he arched his back high, his tail was a splendid waving plume. He rubbed against the man's feet, which were bursting out of their torn shoes.

The man pushed the Cat away, gently enough, and began searching about the little cabin. He even climbed painfully the ladder to the loft, lit a match, and peered up in the darkness with straining eyes. He feared lest there might be a man, since there was a Cat. His experience with men had not been pleasant, and neither had the experience of men been pleasant with him. He was an old wandering Ishmael among his kind; he had stumbled upon the house of a brother, and the brother was not at home, and he was glad.

He returned to the Cat and stooped stiffly and stroked his back, which the animal arched like the spring of a bow.

Then he took up the Rabbit and looked at it eagerly by the fire-light. His jaws worked. He could almost have devoured it raw. He fumbled – the Cat close at his heels – around some rude shelves and a table, and found, with a grunt of self-gratulation, a lamp with oil in it. That he lighted; then he found a frying-pan and a knife, and skinned the Rabbit, and prepared it for cooking, the Cat always at his feet.

When the odour of the cooking flesh filled the cabin, both the man and the Cat looked wolfish. The man turned the Rabbit with one hand, and stooped to pat the Cat with the other. The Cat thought him a fine man. He loved him with all his heart, though he had known him such a short time, and though the man had a face both pitiful and sharply set at variance with the best of things.

It was a face with the grimy grizzle of age upon it, with fever hollows in the cheeks, and the memories of wrong in the dim eyes, but the Cat accepted the man unquestioningly and loved him. When the Rabbit was half cooked, neither the man nor the Cat could wait any longer. The man took it from the fire, divided it exactly in halves, gave the Cat one, and took the other himself. Then they ate.

Then the man blew out the light, called the Cat to him, got on the bed, drew up the ragged coverings, and fell asleep with the Cat in his bosom.

The man was the Cat's guest all the rest of the winter, and winter is long in the mountains. The rightful owner of the little hut did not return until May. All that time the Cat toiled hard, and he grew rather thin himself, for he shared everything except Mice with his guest; and sometimes game was wary, and the fruit of patience of days was very little for two. The man was ill and weak, however, and unable to eat much, which was fortunate, since he could not hunt for himself. All day long he lay on the bed, or else crouched over the fire. It was a good thing that fire-wood was ready at hand for the picking up, not a stone's-throw from the door, for that he had to attend to himself.

The Cat foraged tirelessly. Sometimes he was gone for days together, and at first the man used to be terrified, thinking he would never return; then he would hear the familiar cry at the door, and stumble to his feet and let him in. Then the two would dine together, sharing equally; then the Cat would rest and purr, and finally sleep in the man's arms.

Towards spring the game grew plentiful; more wild little quarry were tempted out of their homes, in search of love as well as food. One day the Cat had luck – a Rabbit, a Partridge, and a Mouse. He could not carry them all at once, but finally he had them together at the house door. Then he cried, but no one answered. All the mountain streams were loosened and the air was full of the gurgle of many waters, occasionally pierced by a bird whistle. The trees rustled with a new sound to the spring wind; there was a flush of rose and gold-green on the breasting surface of a distant mountain seen through an opening in the wood. The tips of the bushes were swollen and glistening red, and now and then there was a flower; but the Cat had nothing to do with flowers. He stood beside his booty at the house door, and cried and cried with his insistent triumph and complaint and pleading, but no one came to let him in. Then the Cat left his little treasures at the door, and went around to the back of the house to the pine tree, and was up the trunk with a wild scramble, and in through his little window, and down through the trap to the room; and the man was gone.

The Cat cried again – that cry of the animal for human companionship which is one of the sad notes of the world; he looked in all the corners; he sprang to the chair at the window and looked out; but no one came. The man was gone and he never came again.

The Cat ate his Mouse on the turf beside the house; the Rabbit and the Partridge he carried painfully into the house, but the man did not come to share them. Finally, in the course of a day or two, he ate them up himself; then he slept a long time on the bed, and when he waked the man was not there.

Then the Cat went forth to his hunting grounds again, and

came home at night with a plump bird, reasoning with his tireless persistency in expectancy that the man would be there; and there was a light in the window, and when he cried, his old master opened the door and let him in.

His master had strong comradeship with the Cat, but not affection. He never patted him like that gentler outcast, but he had a pride in him and an anxiety for his welfare, though he had left him alone all winter without scruple. He feared lest some misfortune might have come to the Cat, though he was so large of his kind, and a mighty hunter. Therefore, when he saw him at the door in all the glory of his glossy winter coat, his white breast and face shining like snow in the sun, his own face lit up with welcome, and the Cat embraced his feet with his sinuous body vibrant with rejoicing purrs.

The Cat had his bird to himself, for his master had his own supper already cooking on the stove. After supper the Cat's master took his pipe, and sought a small store of tobacco which he had left in his hut over winter. He had thought often of it; that and the Cat seemed something to come home to in the spring. But the tobacco was gone; not a dust left. The man swore a little in a grim monotone, which made the profanity lose its customary effect. He had been, and was, a hard drinker; he had knocked about the world until the marks of its sharp corners were on his very soul, which was thereby calloused, until his very sensibility to loss was dulled. He was a very old man.

He searched for the tobacco with a sort of dull combativeness of persistency; then he stared with stupid wonder around the room. Suddenly many features struck him as being changed. Another stove-lid was broken; an old piece of carpet was tacked up over a window to keep out the cold; his firewood was gone. He looked and there was no oil left in his can. He looked at the coverings on his bed; he took them up, and again he made that strange remonstrant noise in his throat. Then he looked again for his tobacco.

Finally he gave it up. He sat down beside the fire, for May in the mountains is cold; he held his empty pipe in his mouth, his rough forehead knitted, and he and the Cat looked at each other across that impassable barrier of silence which has been set between man and beast from the creation of the world.

On the Death of a Cat

A friend of mine aged ten years and a half

Who shall tell the lady's grief
When her Cat was past relief?
Who shall number the hot tears
Shed o'er her, belov'd for many years?
Who shall say the dark dismay
Which her dying caused that day?

Come, ye Muses, one and all,
Come obedient to my call:
Come and mourn with tuneful breath
Each one for a separate death;
And, while you in numbers sigh,
I will sing her elegy.

Of a noble race she came,
And Grimalkin was her name,
Young and old full many a mouse
Felt the prowess of her house;
Weak and strong full many a rat
Cowered beneath her crushing pat;
And the birds around the place
Shrank from her too close embrace,
But one night, reft of her strength,
She laid down and died at length:
Lay a kitten by her side
In whose life the mother died,

Spare her line and lineage,
Guard her kitten's tender age
And that kitten's name as wide
Shall be known as hers that died.
And whoever passes by
The poor grave where Puss doth lie,
Softly, softly let him tread,
Nor disturb her narrow bed.

CHRISTINA ROSSETTI

Dick Baker's Cat

Mark Twain

One of my comrades there – another of those victims of eighteen years of unrequited toil and blighted hopes – was one of the gentlest spirits that ever bore its patient cross in a weary exile; grave and simple Dick Baker, pocket miner of Dead-Horse Gulch. He was forty-six, gray as a rat, earnest, thoughtful, slenderly educated, slouchily dressed, and clay-soiled, but his heart was finer metal than any gold his shovel ever brought to light – than any, indeed, that ever was mined or minted.

Whenever he was out of luck and a little downhearted, he would fall to mourning over the loss of a wonderful cat he used to own (for where women and children are not, men of kindly impulses take up with pets, for they must love something). And he always spoke of the strange sagacity of that cat with the air of a man who believed in his secret heart that there was something human about it – maybe even supernatural.

I heard him talking about this animal once. He said: 'Gentlemen, I used to have a cat here, by the name of Tom Quartz, which you'd 'a' took an interest in, I reckon – most anybody would. I had him here eight year – and he was the remarkablest cat I ever see. He was a large gray one of the Tom specie, an' he had more hard, natchral sense than any man in this camp – 'n' a *power* of dignity – he wouldn't let the Gov'ner of Californy be familiar with him. He never ketched a rat in his life – 'peared to be above it. He never cared for nothing but mining. He knowed more about mining, that cat did, than any man I ever, ever see. You couldn't tell *him* noth'n' 'bout placer-diggin's – 'n' as for pocket mining, why he was just born for it. He would dig out after me an' Jim when we went over the hills prospect'n', and he would trot along behind us for as much as five mile, if we went so fur. An' he had the best judgement about mining ground – why, you never see anything like it. When we went to work, he'd scatter a glance round, 'n' if he didn't think much of the indications, he would give a look as much as to say, "Well, I'll have to get you to excuse *me*" – 'n' without another word he'd hyste his nose in the air 'n' shove for home. But if the ground suited him, he would lay low 'n' keep dark till the first pan was washed, 'n' he would sidle up 'n' take a look, an' if there was about six or seven grains of gold *he* was satisfied – he didn't want no better prospect 'n' that – 'n' then he would lay down on our coats and snore like a steamboat till we'd struck the pocket, an' then get up 'n' superintend. He was nearly lightnin' on superintending.

Well by an' by, up comes this yer quartz excitement. Everybody was into it – everybody was pick'n' 'n' blast'n' instead of shovelin' dirt on the hillside – everybody was putt'n' down a shaft instead of scrapin' the surface. Noth'n' would do Jim, but *we* must tackle the ledges, too, 'n' so we did. We commenced putt'n' down a shaft, 'n' Tom Quartz he begin to wonder what in the dickens it was all about. He hadn't ever seen any mining like that before, 'n' he was all upset, as you may say – he couldn't come to a right understanding of it no way – it was too many for *him*. He was down on it too, you bet you – he was down on it powerful – 'n' always appeared to consider it the cussedest foolishness out. But that cat, you know, was *always* agin' newfangled arrangements – somehow he could never abide 'em. *You* know how it is with old habits. But by and by Tom Quartz begin to git sort of reconciled a little though he never *could* altogether understand that eternal sinkin' of a shaft an' never pannin' out anything. At last he got to comin' down in the shaft hisself, to try to cipher it out. An' when he'd git the blues, 'n' feel kid o' scruffy, 'n' aggravated 'n' disgusted – knowin' as he did, that the bills was runnin' up all the time an' we warn't makin' a cent – he would curl up on a gunnysack in the corner an' go to sleep. Well, one day when the shaft was down about eight foot, the rock got so hard that we had to put in a blast – the first blast'n' we'd ever done since Tom Quartz was born. An' then we lit the fuse 'n' clumb out 'n' got off 'bout fifty yards -'n' forgot 'n' left Tom Quartz sound asleep on the gunnysack. In 'bout a minute we seen a puff of smoke bust up out of the hole, 'n' then everything let go with an awful crash, 'n' about four million tons of rocks 'n' dirt 'n' smoke 'n' splinters shot up 'bout a mile an' a half into the air, an' by George, right in the dead center of it was old Tom Quartz a-goin' end over end, an' a-snortin' an' a-sneezin', an' a-clawin' an' a-reach'n' for things like all possessed. But is warn't no use, you know, it warn't no use. An' that was the last we see of *him* for about two minutes 'n' a half, an' then all of a sudden it begin to rain rocks and rubbage an' directly he come down ker-whoop about ten foot off f'm where we stood. Well, I reckon he was p'r'aps the orneriest-lookin' beast you ever see. One ear was sot back on his neck, 'n' his tail was stove up, 'n' his eye-winkers was singed off, 'n' he was all blacked up with powder an' smoke, an' all sloppy with mud 'n' slush f'm one end to the other. Well, sir, it warn't no use to try to apologize – we couldn't say a word. He took a sort of disgusted look at himself, 'n' then he looked at us – an' it was exactly the same as if he had said – "Gents, maybe *you* think it's smart to take advantage of a cat that ain't had no experience of quartz minin', but *I* think different" – an' then he turned on his heel 'n' marched off home without ever saying another word.

That was jest his style. An' maybe you won't believe it, but after that you never see a cat so prejudiced agin' quartz mining as what he was. An' by an' by when he *did* get to goin' down in the shaft agin', you'd 'a' been astonished at his sagacity. The minute we'd tetch off a blast 'n' the fuse'd begin to sizzle, he'd give a look as much as to say, "Well, I'll have to git you to excuse *me*," an' it was surpris'n' the way he'd shin out of that hole 'n' go f'r a tree. Sagacity? It ain't no name for it. 'Twas inspiration!'

I said, 'Well, Mr Baker, his prejudice against quartz mining *was* remarkable, considering how he came by it. Couldn't you ever cure him of it?'

'*Cure him!* No! When Tom Quartz was sot once, he was *always* sot – and you might 'a' blowed him up as much as three million times 'n' you'd never 'a' broken him of his cussed prejudice agin' quartz mining.'

Hannibal

Anatole France

'Guardian, just guess what I have in my handkerchief.'

'Judging from appearances, Jeanne, I should say flowers.'

'Oh no – not flowers. Look!'

I look, and I see a little gray head poking itself out of the handkerchief. It is the head of a little gray cat. The handkerchief opens; the animal leaps down upon the carpet, shakes itself, pricks up first one ear and then the other, and begins to examine with due caution the locality and the inhabitants thereof.

Thérèse, out of breath, with her basket on her arm, suddenly makes her appearance in time to take an objective part in this examination, which does not appear to result altogether in her favour; for the young cat moves slowly away from her, without, however, venturing near my legs, or approaching Jeanne, who displays extraordinary volubility in the use of caressing appellations. Thérèse, whose chief fault is her inability to hide her feelings, thereupon vehemently reproaches Mademoiselle for bringing home a cat that she did not know anything about. Jeanne, in order to justify herself, tells the whole story. While she was passing with Thérèse before a drug-tore, she saw the clerk kick a little cat into the street. The cat, astonished and frightened, seemed to be asking itself whether to remain in the street where it was being terrified and knocked about by the people passing by, or whether to go back into the drug-store even at the risk of being kicked out a second time. Jeanne thought it was in a very critical position, and understood its hesitation. It looked so stupid; and she knew it looked stupid only because it could not decide what to do. So she took it up in her arms. And as it had not been able to obtain any rest either in-doors or out-of-doors, it allowed her to hold it. Then she stroked and petted it to keep it from being afraid, and boldly went to the drug-clerk and said,

'If you don't like that animal, you mustn't beat it; you must give it to me.'

'Take it,' said the drug-clerk.

. . .' Now here!' adds Jeanne, by way of conclusion; and then she changes her voice again to a flute-tone in order to say all kinds of sweet things to the cat.

'He is horribly thin,' I observe, looking at the wretched animal; – 'moreover, he is horribly ugly.' Jeanne thinks he is not ugly at all, but she acknowledges that he looks even more stupid than he lookcd at first: this time she thinks it not indecision, but surprise, which gives that unfortunate aspect to his countenance. She asks us to imagine ourselves in his place; – then we are obliged to acknowledge that he cannot possibly understand what has happened to him. And then we all burst out laughing in the face of the poor little beast, which maintains the most comical look of gravity. Jeanne wants to take him up; but he hides himself under the table, and cannot even be tempted to come out by the lure of a saucer of milk.

We all turn our backs and promise not to look; when we inspect the saucer again, we find it empty.

'Jeanne,' I observe, 'your *protegé* has a decidedly tristful aspect of countenance; he is of a sly and suspicious disposition; I trust he is not going to commit in the City of Books any such misdemeanours as might render it necessary for us to send him back to his drug-store. In the meantime we must give him a name. Suppose we call him"Don Gris de Gouttière"; but perhaps that is too long. "Pill," "Drug," or "Castor oil" would be short enough, and would further serve to recall his early condition in life. What do you think about it?'

'"Pill" would not sound bad,' answers Jeanne, 'but it would be very unkind to give him a name which would be always reminding him of the misery from which we saved him. It would be making him pay too dearly for our hospitality. Let us be more generous, and give him a pretty name, in hopes that he is going to deserve it. See how he looks at us! He knows that we are talking about him. And now that he is no longer unhappy, he is beginning to look a great deal less stupid. I am not joking! Un-happiness does make people look stupid, – I am perfectly sure it does.'

'Well, Jeanne, if you like, we will call your *protegé* Hannibal. The appropriateness of that name does not seem to strike you at once. But the Angora cat who preceded him here as an inmate of the City of Books, and to whom I was in the habit of telling all my secrets – for he was a very wise and discreet person – used to be called Hamilcar. It is natural that this name should succeed Hamilcar.'

We all agreed upon this point.

'Hannibal!' cried Jeanne, 'come here!'

Hannibal, greatly frightened by the strange sonority of his own name, ran to hide himself under a bookcase in an orifice so small that a rat could not have squeezed himself into it.

A nice way of doing credit to so great a name!

Cat's Company

Michael Joseph

I have rarely been without a cat. Even in France during the war I contrived to keep a cat most of the time. One of my trench pets was a jolly black and white kitten, christened Scissors by the mess cook, whose company he regularly patronised. Scissors, whose glossy black fur was ornamented by a neat white waistcoat, was a great favourite and knew his way about the whole of the sector. He used to follow us up the poppy-lined communication trenches and along the front line. Only a narrow strip of No-man's-land separated us from the German front line and Scissors had a playful but dangerous habit of leaping gracefully on to the parapet and picking his way delicately along the broken ground, through the wire and over the massed sand-bags, keeping pace with my orderly and myself as we made our cautious way below along the zig-zag of the front line. It must have been perfectly obvious to the 'enemy' that Scissors was accompanying his officer on his morning round – indeed, one fine August morning we distinctly heard a laugh and a shout in guttural German from beyond the wire – but that part of the line was then known to both armies as 'peaceful' and no sniper or bomb-thrower tried his skill on the furry target.

Scissors was wounded before we left the Arras sector by a stray fragment of shrapnel. It was, luckily, a flesh wound only, and when he got used to the little bandage I tied round his leg he became quite proud of it and displayed it to all and sundry; a habit which nearly got me into trouble with the Brigade Major, who, evidently disapproving of trench pets in general and bandaged kittens in particular, snorted at Scissors in an apoplectic kind of way which caused me great alarm. I knew that snort! I remember hastily asking a random question about gas masks (which happened to be his particular hobby) and the crisis passed.

Thanks chiefly to a lavish diet of bully beef, which he adored (to the derisive amusement of the men in my machine-gun section) Scissors grew fat and fast. But he never forsook his nightly habit of rat-hunting. Rats in their thousands infested the trenches and dug-outs and gave Scissors plenty of scope. That most of them were larger than Scissors did not in the least deter him. Scissors discovered early in his life that a cornered rat will show fight and he was bitten several times in his nightly encounters. I can see him now, as the flare of the Very lights used to reveal him, streaking along the trench boards in pursuit of a grey rat larger than himself. Scissors hunted for love of the chase; he never attempted to eat his victims. What sensible cat would, with unlimited bully beef at his disposal?

Poor Scissors! He was 'missing' when the division moved to another part of the line, and there was no time to search for him. I have often wondered what became of him. Somehow I cannot picture him as a casualty. I prefer to believe that he made friends with one of the officers or men who relieved us, or that he wandered across No-man's-land into the German line. My batman was horrified, I remember, at the mere suggestion, but I never had any qualms. If Scissors could survive the wrath of our Brigade Major he was safe enough with the Bavarians across the way.

When I was invalided home from France I adopted a wistful-looking tabby – or rather she adopted me – and contrary to all the rules and regulations installed her in my hut in camp. For some obscure reason I can no longer remember she was called Lillywhite. Lillywhite (which my camp batman invariably abbreviated to Lilly) was a very intelligent cat. She understood perfectly well that cats were not officially allowed in army huts; and when, as occasionally happened, some senior officer made a tour of inspection of the officers' quarters – this usually occurred during our absence – Lillywhite would promptly disappear through the open top of the window and lie low until the sound of strange boots and spurs had died away. Beaver (my batman) was very proud of this accomplishment of Lillywhite's. 'That's a knowing ca-at, sir,' he used to say in his broad Lancashire accent.

Lillywhite was also adept at extracting condensed milk out of tins. A small hole punctured in the top of the tin sufficed for my purposes, and Lillywhite soon learned to roll the tin over, some-times with disastrous results to blankets and boots, and cause a steady stream of thick, sticky juice to flow by pressure of paws on the side of the tin. Beaver was always catching her at it. But then he used to call her by more names than 'knowing ca-at.'

It was Lillywhite's insatiable appetite that eventually separated us. To be truthful, she deserted me in favour of the sergeants' mess close by, and although she sometimes condescended to pay me a visit, always looking hungry and wistful (how deceptive was the hussy's appearance! – she traded on it, I am sure), our re-lationship was not the same. I have always attributed her deser-tion to the bits of raw rabbit for which she rapidly acquired a taste at the door of the sergeants' mess.

For some months after the war I was without a cat of my own. This sad state of affairs was remedied as soon as I was able to find a London flat which permitted a cat – or cats – (the plural is justi-fied as you will presently realise) to share my tenancy. As it turned out, the flat was as ideal for cats as it was thoroughly un-comfortable for humans. It was situated on an invisible line which separated a fashionable neighbourhood from a - well, unfashion-able is a charitable description of the slum which lay to the east of the house. It was an old, queer building, and the uncomfortable peculiarity of my flat was that all the rooms led from one to the other in a straight line. Outside there was a narrow strip of 'gar-den,' in which nothing ever grew on account of a high brick wall which successfully obscured the sun. This 'garden' came to be called the 'Strut' and a happy playground it proved to be for Dudley and the Dudley family.

Dudley, a present to me from my favourite aunt, was a little ball of orange fluff, with tiny white paws and a pedigree as long as Piccadilly, which was lost in the post. Under the mistaken im-pression that she was a gentleman cat, I christened her Dudley, on account of her aristocratic manners. But it presently became manifest that Dudley was no gentleman. And so, like Dickens, whose cat William was rechristened Williamina, we had to call her Lady Dudley. That is to say, we made valiant but futile efforts to give her the additional title, for after a week or so the household reverted to Dudley with the occasional variation of Dudley-Duff.

From the days of her kittenhood it was plain that she would grow into a distinguished cat. On the small side, she was lithe and graceful as a young panther, and correspondingly strong, as many a neighbouring cat and dog subsequently discovered.

The 'Strut' captured her fancy from the first. As soon as she was old enough to compass the distance she would spring gracefully through the air from the kitchen windowsill on to the top of the brick wall and there sit sunning herself in splendid isolation. Her tenancy of the wall was, however, promptly disputed by an old grey patriarch of a cat who appeared one morning and stalked along the top of the wall, fur bristling, towards the immobile Dudley.

I happened to be looking out of my bedroom window and thus had an excellent view of the subsequent proceedings. The weather-beaten grey was clearly a veteran. One ear was decidedly smaller, and unnaturally so, than the other; and his fur bore unmistakable traces of recent combat. Dudley, on the other hand, apart from a doorstep skirmish or two, was an untried recruit. There was no time for me to go to her rescue, for the battle began almost instantly. And Dudley began it.

Without warning she advanced swiftly to the attack. Her paw flashed out with lightning speed and an infuriated gasp from the old grey paid tribute to the accuracy of her aim. Instantly following up this advantage with a whirlwind onslaught – all I saw was a streak of orange launch itself at the intruder – she gave the grey no time to recover. Spitting rage, he lost his balance and slithered off the wall down to the flower-beds on the other side. Dudley looked serenely in my direction, resumed her former position in the most sun-favoured place on the wall, idly licked her paws and – dozed off to sleep!

That was the beginning of Dudley's fighting career. She was not a quarrelsome cat and never, to my knowledge, fought except to defend herself or her kittens, but when she did have occasion to fight she made a thorough job of it. In the house she was always good-tempered to the point of being placid and used to let the babies play with her as they liked – and everyone knows that no self-respecting human baby can resist a pussycat's tail.

Dudley was an uncommonly intelligent cat. She was voiceless except for a very faint squeak which she managed to produce if really agitated about something. This inability to 'miaow' had its practical disadvantages. For instance, she could not audibly attract attention if she were by chance locked out. But she soon learned how to gain admittance.

As I have said, the rooms in my flat led from one to the other, the sequence being, drawing-room, dining-room, then a sort of ante-room into which a bathroom had been built, kitchen, bedroom, dressing-room, bedroom. All these rooms, except the bathroom, had windows looking out on to the 'Strut.' If, as frequently happened, Dudley came home late and found the door shut she would jump on each windowsill in turn, until she came to the room I was in. Then sitting upright, she would beat a tattoo on the window pane *with her outstretched claws.* She knew that the thump of a padded paw was not enough. Almost invariably she chose the room I was in, but if I happened to be out, she went on a tour of investigation, finally tapping at the window most likely to be opened for her. Most of my servants have been fond of cats (they have to be!) and Dudley usually had no difficulty in getting in *via* the kitchen, but she never patronised the kitchen window if she disapproved, as she sometimes did, of its occupants.

The bathroom had two doors, one leading into the little ante-room which separated it from the main passage of the flat and another which opened on to the 'Strut.' This outside door was usually bolted on the inside but in the summer it was often left open or merely latched. Dudley soon learned that if the latch were pressed down, the door would open: that is, if it were not bolted on the inside. It was difficult for her to manipulate the latch because it was just out of her reach when she stood upright and the nearest windowsill was too far away to enable her to operate it from a higher level. So she had to jump up at it. To make it more complicated, there were two or three stone steps outside the door; which meant that she had to take a standing jump from the narrow top step. But I never saw her miss her aim. Invariably her small white paw fell neatly on the lever and depressed it. When the door was bolted this naturally had no effect and Dudley appeared to understand perfectly that no amount of playing with the latch would open the door, for she would always give it up immediately as a bad job.

Dudley was an undemonstrative cat. Most people she ignored completely. How I remember her look of disdain and the haughty tilt of her head if well-meaning strangers affronted her, however coaxingly, with the words 'Puss, puss!' When food was in the offing she answered a call immediately but she rarely answered to her name on other occasions. Most decidedly she was not a sociable cat. If she wanted to go out (and she often did) she would ask to be released, but made it clear she was not asking favours. She just demanded that doors or windows should be opened and if by chance anyone delayed her she would frown (it is the only word that describes her expression) and lash her tail with ladylike annoyance. But she never lost her temper. That would not have been *comme il faut* for a well-bred cat.

I should like to be able to say that Dudley reserved all her love for me. Actually, I had very little of it. She displayed signs of affection for other members of the family when she was in the mood but I was seldom favoured. Her attitude towards me was one of gentle toleration. She may have loved me. I wonder . . .

One of her few friends was an old man who had a wooden leg and sold matches. His 'pitch' was near the house and Dudley used often to visit him. This old man, who was by way of being a friend of mine, used to stand by a brick wall beside a wired-in window, underneath which was a narrow ledge. On this he laid out in cardboard trays his stock of matches, shoe-laces and studs. Dudley was not a pavement cat (when she had to walk along it I was always reminded of a lady of fashion picking her way fastidiously through a common market-place) and she soon took to installing herself on the ledge, the old man considerately moving his stock to make room for her. There she would sit for hours, looking out over her friend's shoulder at the passers-by. In this way she became a well-known local character and familiarly greeted as 'Ginger' by small boys.

Talking to the old man one day, I discovered Dudley's lapse from gentility. He told me that punctually every Saturday night Dudley presented herself on his ledge. He admitted with engaging candour that he was particularly glad to see her then, for it was the busiest night of the week and Dudley improved his 'custom.' People, he said, would often spend a copper or two because of the cat. The reason for Dudley's Saturday-night appearances, however, was not altruistic. The old man went on to tell me that every Saturday night the 'girls' and 'lads' bought fried fish at the fish-and-chips shop round the corner, and as by the time they passed his place of business the first edge of their appetite had worn off it had become customary for one or two of the more generously disposed to offer Dudley a piece of fish. Lady Dudley eating fried fish on a Saturday night! She, who would turn up her patrician nose at home if breast of chicken were not to her liking! It was her one fall from grace.

The old man refused to call her Dudley. He obviously thought I was a little wrong in the head to have given so queer a name to a cat who patently had to be called Ginger. To the uninitiated – and especially the low-born Londoner – all orange cats are 'ginger.' I have heard them referred to as yellow cats and sandy cats and marmalade cats by superior persons, but the voice of the people proclaims them ginger.

When we left the flat Dudley did not forget her friend of the wooden leg. Or it may have been the lure of the fried fish! At any rate she used to visit him at irregular intervals. The first time she appeared he packed up his stock and stumped all the way to my new house about a mile away, carrying her in his arms. He was afraid she had lost her way, and refused to accept any reward. I think he was as fond of Dudley as she was of him.

When Dudley had kittens she surprised me by proving herself a devoted mother. Her supercilious manner at once disappeared. She purred contentedly most of the day, and was as proud of her babies as any ordinary cat might be. Indeed, she became almost human. (I mean that figuratively.) For so independent and reserved a cat her devotion to her kittens was remarkable. She never tired of displaying them for our approval. Dudley was a great success as a mother and evidently enjoyed the experience, to judge by the frequent regularity with which she subsequently repeated it.

Her kittens were much admired. Dudley herself was more aristocratic-looking than beautiful, but her offspring, while they inherited their mother's quality, were for the most part uncommonly attractive. Ginnaboi, one of my best-loved cats, was her first-born. Minna Minna Mowbray came much later. Meestah and a kitten who was christened 'The Wu' for some odd reason completed the first litter.

'The Wu' was an odd cat for whom I had no special liking. He was tortoiseshell and white with a long tail and no manners. He was greedy and very vain. Meestah was a beauty, with a soft, curiously marked bronze coat and the most placid of tempers. If she was not especially intelligent she made up for it by excessive affection, which was a welcome contrast to Dudley's detachment.

Ginnaboi was my favourite. He was a half-Persian orange, handsome and most lovable. From his kitten days he seemed to realise that I had singled him out for affection and his response was as eager as it was gratifying. With the exception of my Siamese Charles O'Malley, he was the only cat I have ever had who followed me about, jumped on my knee when I sat down, curled up under the eiderdown on my bed and came regularly to greet me when I opened the front door. I could not have resisted his blandishments if I had wanted to.

His favourite position was lying half-asleep on my chest. I encouraged him to do this when he was a kitten, and he never forsook the habit. He used to lie facing me, his eyes blinking lazily out of his doze and his claws gently thrusting in and out of my dressing-gown. This claw-exercising habit, common to most cats when they are pleased, we used to call 'carding.' It was hard on my dressing-gown but I did not mind.

Ginnaoboi's fur was long and I regret to say he did not take care of it. In truth, he was a lazy cat, although I liked him none the less for that. He cleaned himself irregularly and never thoroughly. His sister Meestah – they were devoted to each other - used to wash him even when he was grown up and ought to have known better. He thoroughly approved of this proceeding and made no bones about letting Meestah perform his toilet. It was a sad day for Ginnaboi when Meestah in her turn had kittens, for then he had shamefacedly to attend to his own ablutions.

It was soon after this that his coat became matted. I had been away from home and was horrified on my return to find Ginnaboi looking more like a sweep than a self-respecting cat. He was so delighted to see me again that I could not scold him. Instead, I took him out into the 'Strut' for a good brushing to begin with.

Then I discovered the condition of his fur. Every day for a week I spent at least an hour patiently unravelling his matted fur with a comb. It was in such a bad state that the more difficult lumps had to be cut with scissors. Throughout the proceedings Ginnaboi lay placidly on his back, purring with pleasure. Yet he strongly disliked other people even stroking him.

Although majestically beautiful, he was a delicate and particularly sensitive cat. He had no use for strangers and shrank from their attempts to caress him. With his magnificent ruff, big amber eyes, curving white whiskers, and huge plume of a tail which matched his long, vividly orange coat in its richness of colour, he was a strikingly handsome cat. In Dudley's presence he always behaved like a shy, awkward and overgrown boy and it was amusing to watch him with his mother. She looked on him as a big booby, which by her exacting standards I dare say he was. He carefully avoided other tom cats after he had disgracefully been put to flight by an aggressive tabby neighbour much smaller than himself. I am sure that Dudley regarded his conduct as a blot on the otherwise honourable family escutcheon.

As cats go, Ginnaboi was neither brave nor intelligent. He liked food and sleeping in the sun above all things. He inherited from Dudley a fastidious palate, would not eat unless he were really hungry, refused milk unless it were warmed for him, caught neither mice nor birds (his jaw instinctively moved at the sight of a bird but, so far as I know, he never made an attempt to catch one) and rejected such feline luxuries as cream and cod's head.

I used sometimes to tease him, and he hated it. If I made fun of his furry 'trousers' when his back was turned he never failed to pretend annoyance by turning round and sweeping his bushy tail from side to side. I can see him now, his blunt little nose wrinkled and his eyes blinking at me with the pretence of displeasure. He was a lovable cat and my best friend in those days.

I remember Pansy, one of Dudley's later kittens, particularly well because of a rather amusing episode. Pansy was a brightly coloured tortoiseshell of mischievous disposition who disorganised the whole household by staying out at night when she was little more than a kitten. Where she went I shall never know, but it must have been a place where dirt abounded. It was a very dirty and bedraggled Pansy who was found on the doorstep with the early morning milk. Dudley strongly disapproved of the bad company and late hours her daughter was keeping and scolded her in the best maternal tradition. But Pansy took no notice and went to sleep off the effect of her dissipations.

But one morning Pansy did not return. The day went by without any sign of the truant. There was consternation in the house, for Pansy was a great favourite. The next morning we were still Pansy-less. So I hurried round to a printer's and ordered a quantity of those bills headed by '10/- Reward' in heavy, black type. I described Pansy in detail. The printer kept his word and delivered the leaflets that evening, when I hastily proceeded to paste them up in every possible place in the neighbourhood.

We did not have to wait long for results. Late that night there was a peal at the bell. Going to the door myself, I was confronted by a very dirty urchin whom the prospect of earning ten shillings had apparently reduced to incoherence. But it transpired he was out of breath, having run all the way to the house from the timber-yard where he had seen the truant Pansy. I did not wait to get my hat or explain where I was going but set out at once with my small escort, who informed me I would have to hurry or the night watchman might be asleep and unable to let us in. 'He allus goes to sleep 'bout this time,' said the dirty small boy. 'Too much beer, that's wot it is.'

I will draw a veil, as the old-fashioned novelists used to say, over the rest of the evening's performance, or rather I will confine myself to the bare facts. The night watchman was surly and succumbed only to liberal largesse. I bruised my shins in several places stumbling over piles of wood in the dark and the small boy angrily accused me of not knowing my own cat when we eventually discovered a mangy tabby coiled up asleep on top of a stack of timber.

The next morning the fun began. Writing in retrospect I use the word 'fun' but it was not so funny at the time. I have already mentioned our proximity to a slum neighbourhood. From this quarter emerged at intervals, a procession of dirty and expectant children, carrying cats alleged to tally with the description of Pansy. Dazzled by the prospect of ten whole shillings reward, the entire youthful population had, it seemed, organised themselves into search parties for the missing cat (it was holiday time) and any unfortunate animal bearing the slightest resemblance to my lost Pansy was forthwith seized and dragged to our doorstep.

It was only at the end of a day spent for the most part in opening the front door and repudiating the cats submitted that I realised my mistake. The first arrival had no doubt been genuinely mistaken for Pansy and the youngster who brought the animal was so disappointed that I had naturally rewarded him for his trouble. I also distributed largesse – in decreasing amounts - to those who followed. It was only when I finally lost patience and stopped the donations that the appearance of strange cats on my doorstep significantly ceased.

As for Pansy, she turned up a few days later of her own accord, so filthy as to be almost unrecognisable and with a faraway look in her eye which I will not attempt to interpret.

The Sending of Dana Da

Rudyard Kipling

'When the Devil rides on your chest remember the low-caste man
Native Proverb'

Once upon a time, some people in India made a new Heaven and a new Earth out of broken teacups, a missing brooch or two, and a hairbrush. These were hidden under bushes, or stuffed into holes in the hillside, and an entire Civil Service of subordinate Gods used to find or mend them again; and every one said: 'There are more things in Heaven and Earth than are dreamt of in our philosophy.' Several other things happeed also, but the Religion never seemed to get much beyond its manifestations; though it added an air-line postal service and orchestral effects in order to keep abreast of the times and choke off competition.

This Religion was too elastic for ordinary use. It stretched itself and embraced pieces of everything that the medicine-men of all ages have manufactured. It approved of and stole from Freemasonry; looted the Latter-day Rosicrucians of half their pet words; took any fragments of Egyptian philosophy that it found in the *Encyclopaedia Britannica*; annexed as many of the Vedas as had been translated into French or English, and talked of all the rest; built in the German versions of what is left of the Zend Avesta; encouraged White, Grey, and Black Magic, including spiritualism, palmistry, fortune-telling by cards, hot chestnuts, double-kernelled nuts, and tallow droppings; would have adopted Voodoo and Obeah had it known anything about them, and showed itself, in every way, one of the most accommodating arrangements that had ever been invented since the birth of the Sea.

When it was in thorough working order, with all the machinery, down to the subscriptions, complete, Dana Da came from nowhere, with nothing in his hands, and wrote a chapter in its history which has hitherto been unpublished. He said that his first name was Dana, and his second was Da. Now, setting aside Dana of the *New York Sun*, Dana is a Bhil name, and Da fits no native of India unless you accept the Bengali Dé as the original spelling. Da is Lap or Finnish; and Dana Da was neither Finn, Chin, Bhil, Bengali, Lap, Nair, Gond, Romany, Magh, Bokhariot, Kurd, Armenian, Levantine, Jew, Persian, Punjabi, Madrasi, Parsee, nor anything else known to ethnologists. He was simply Dana Da, and declined to give further information. For the sake of brevity and as roughly indicating his origin, he was called 'The Native'. He might have been the original Old Man of the Mountains, who is said to be the only authorised Head of the Tea-cup Creed. Some people said that he was; but Dana Da used to smile and deny any connection with the cult, explaining that he was an 'Independent Experimenter'.

As I have said, he came from nowhere, with his hands behind his back, and studied the Creed for three weeks, sitting at the feet of those best competent to explain its mysteries. Then he laughed aloud and went away, but the laugh might have been either of devotion or derision.

When he returned he was without money, but his pride was unabated. He declared that he knew more about the Things in Heaven and Earth than those who taught him, and for this contumacy was abandoned altogether.

His next appearance in public life was at a big cantonment in Upper India, and he was then telling fortunes with the help of three leaden dice, a very dirty old cloth, and a little tin box of opium pills. He told better fortunes when he was allowed half a bottle of whisky; but the things which he invented on the opium were quite worth the money. He was in reduced circumstances. Among other people's he told the fortune of an Englishman who had once been interested in the Simla Creed, but who, later on, had married and forgotten all his old knowledge in the study of babies and things. The Englishman allowed Dana Da to tell a fortune for charity's sake, and gave him five rupees, a dinner, and some old clothes. When he had eaten, Dana Da professed gratitude, and asked if there were anything he could do for his host – in the esoteric line.

'Is there any one that you love?' said Dana Da. The Englishman loved his wife, but had no desire to drag her name into the conversation. He therefore shook his head.

'Is there anyone that you hate?' said Dana Da. The Englishman said that there were several men whom he hated deeply.

'Very good,' said Dana Da, upon whom the whisky and the opium were beginning to tell. 'Only give me their names, and I will despatch a Sending to them and kill them.'

Now a Sending is a horrible arrangement, first invented, they say, in Iceland. It is a Thing sent by a wizard, and may take any form, but, most generally, wanders about the land in the shape of a little purple cloud till it find the Sendee, and him it kills by changing into the form of a horse, or a cat, or a man without a face. It is not strictly a native patent, though *chamars* of the skin and hide castes can, if irritated, despatch a Sending which sits on the breast of their enemy by night and nearly kills him. Very few natives care to irritate *chamars* for this reason.

'Let me despatch a Sending,' said Dana Da. 'I am nearly dead now with want, and drink, and opium; but I should like to kill a man before I die. I can send a Sending anywhere you choose, and in any form except in the shape of a man.'

The Englishman had no friends that he wished to kill, but partly to soothe Dana Da, whose eyes were rolling, and partly to see what would be done, he asked whether a modified Sending could not be arranged for – such a Sending as should make a man's life a burden to him, and yet do him no harm. If this were possible, he notifies his willingness to give Dana Da ten rupees for the job.

'I am not what I was once,' said Dana Da, 'and I must take the money because I am poor. To what Englishman shall I send it?'

'Send a Sending to Lone Sahib,' said the Englishman, naming a man who had been most bitter in rebuking him for his apostasy from the Tea-cup Creed. Dana Da laughed and nodded.

'I could have chosen no better man myself,' said he 'I will see that he find the Sending about his path and about his bed.'

He lay down on the hearth-rug, turned up the whites of his eyes, shivered all over, and began to snort. This was Magic, or Opium, or the Sending, or all three. When he opened his eyes he vowed that the Sending had started upon the war-path, and was at that moment flying up to the town where Lone Sahib lived.

'Give me my ten rupees,' said Dana Da wearily, 'and write a letter to Lone Sahib, telling him, and all who believe with him, that you and a friend are using a power greater than theirs. They will see that you are speaking the truth.'

He departed unsteadily, with the promise of some more rupees if anything came of the Sending.

The Englishman sent a letter to Lone Sahib, couched in what he remembered of the terminology of the Creed. He wrote: 'I also, in the days of what you held to be my back-sliding have obtained Enlightenment, and with Enlightenment has come Power.' Then he grew so deeply mysterious that the recipient of the letter could make neither head nor tail of it, and was proportionately impressed; for he fancied that his friend had become a 'fifth-rounder'. When a man is a 'fifth-rounder' he can do more than Slade and Houdini combined.

Lone Sahib read the letter in five different fashions, and was beginning a sixth interpretation when his bearer dashed in with the news that there was a cat on the bed. Now if there was one thing that Lone Sahib hated more than another, it was a cat. He scolded the bearer for not turning it out of the house. The bearer said that he was afraid. All the doors of the bedroom had been shut throughout the morning, and no *real* cat could possibly have entered the room. He would prefer not to meddle with the creature.

Lone Sahib entered the room gingerly, and there, on the pillow of his bed, sprawled and whimpered a wee white kitten; not a jumpsome, frisky little beast, but a slug-like crawler with its eyes barely opened and its paws lacking strength or direction – a kitten that ought to have been in a basket with its mamma. Lone Sahib caught it by the scruff of its neck, handed it over to the sweeper to be drowned, and fined the bearer four annas.

That evening, as he was reading in his room, he fancied that he saw something moving about on the hearth-rug, outside the circle of light from his reading-lamp. When the thing began to myowl he realized that it was a kitten – a wee white kitten, nearly blind and very miserable. He was seriously angry, and spoke bitterly to his bearer, who said that there was no kitten in the room when he brought in the lamps, and *real* kittens of tender age generally had mother-cats in attendance.

'If the Presence will go out into the veranda and listen,' said the bearer, 'he will hear no cats. How, therefore, can the kittens on the bed and the kitten on the hearth-rug be real kittens?'

Lone Sahib went out to listen, and the bearer followed him, but there was no sound of any one mewing for her children. He returned to his room, having hurled the kitten down the hillside, and wrote out the incidents of the day for the benfit of his co-religionists. Those people were so absolutely free from superstition that they ascribed anything a little out of common to Agencies. As it was their business to know all about the Agencies, they were on terms of almost indecent familiarity with Manifestations of every kind. Their letters dropped from the ceiling – unstamped – and Spirits used to squatter up and down their staircases all night; but they had never come into contact with kittens. Lone Sahib wrote out the facts, noting the hour and the minute, as every Physical Observer is bound to do, and appending the Englishman's letter, because it was the most mysterious document and might have had a bearing upon anything in this world or the next. An outsider would have translated all the tangle thus: 'Look out! You laughed at me once, and now I am going to make you sit up.'

Lone Sahib's co-religionists found that meaning in it; but their translation was refined and full of four-syllable words. They held a sederunt, and were filled with tremulous joy, for, in spite of their familiarity with all the other worlds and cycles, they had a very human awe of things sent from Ghostland. They met in Lone Sahib's room in shrouded and sepulchral gloom, and their conclave was broken up by a clinking among the photo-frames on the mantelpiece. A wee white kitten, nearly blind, was looping and writhing itself between the clock and the candlesticks. That stopped all investigations or doubtings. Here was the Manifestation in the flesh. It was, so far as could be seen, devoid of purpose, but it was a Manifestation of undoubted authenticity.

They drafted a Round Robin to the Englishman, the backslider of old days, adjuring him in the interests of the Creed to explain whether there was any connection between the embodiment of some Egyptian God or other (I have forgotten the name) and his communication. They called the kitten Ra, or Thoth, or Tum, or something; and when Lone Sahib confessed that the first one had, at his most misguided instance, been drowned by the sweeper, they said consolingly that in his next life he would be a 'bounder', and not even a 'rounder' of the lowest grade. These words may not be quite correct, but they accurately express the sense of the house.

When the Englishman received the Round Robin – it came by post – he was startled and bewildered. He sent into the bazar for Dana Da, who read the letter and laughed. 'That is my Sending,' said he. 'I told you I would work well. Now give me another ten rupees.'

'But what in the world is this gibberish about Egyptian Gods?' asked the Englishman.

'Cats,' said Dana Da with a hiccough, for he had discovered the Englishman's whisky-bottle. 'Cats, and cats, and cats! Never was such a Sending. A hundred of cats. Now give me ten more rupees and write as I dictate.'

Dana Da's letter was a curiosity. It bore the Englishman's signature, and hinted at cats – at a Sending of Cats. The mere words on paper were creepy and uncanny to behold.

'What have you done, though?' said the Englishman. 'I am as much in the dark as ever. Do you mean to say that you can actually send this absurd Sending you talk about?'

In a little time they will all be at my feet and yours, and I – oh, glory! – will be drugged or drunk all day long.'

Dana Da knew his people.

When a man who hates cats wakes up in the morning and finds a little squirming kitten on his breast, or puts his hand into his ulster-pocket and finds a little half-dead kitten where his gloves should be, or opens his trunk and finds a vile kitten among his dress-shirts, or goes for a long ride with his mackintosh strapped on his saddle-bow and shakes a little squawking kitten from its folds when he opens it, or goes out to dinner and finds a little blind kitten under his chair, or stays at home and finds a writhing kitten under the quilt, or wriggling among his boots, or hanging, head downwards, in his tobacco-jar, or being mangled by his terrier in the veranda – when such a man finds one kitten, neither more nor less, once a day in a place where no kitten rightly could or should be, he is naturally upset. When he dare not murder his daily trove because he believes it to be a Manifestation, an Emissary, an Embodiment, and half-a-dozen other things all out of the regular course of nature, he is more than upset. He is acutally distressed. Some of Lone Sahib's co-religionists thought that he was a highly-favoured individual; but many said that if he had treated the first kitten with proper respect – as suited a Thoth-Ra-Tum-Sennacherib Embodiment – all this trouble would have been averted. They compared him to the Ancient Mariner, but none the less they were proud of him and proud of the Englishman who had sent the Manifestation. They did not call it a Sending because Icelandic magic was not in their programme.

After sixteen kittens, that is to say, after one fortnight, for there were three kittens on the first day to impress the fact of the Sending, the whole camp was uplifted by a letter – it came flying through a window – from the Old Man of the Mountains – the Head of the Creed – explaining the Manifestation in the most beautiful language and soaking up all the credit for himself. The Englishman, said the letter, was not there at all. He was a back-slider without Power or Asceticism who could not even raise a table by force of volition, much less project an army of kittens through space. The entire arrangement, said the letter, was strictly orthodox, worked and sanctioned by the highest Authorities within the pale of the Creed. There was great joy at this, for some of the weaker brethren, seeing that an outsider who had been working on independent lines could create kittens, whereas their own rulers had never gone beyond crockery – and broken at best – were showing a desire to break line on their own trail. In fact, there was the promise of a schism. A second Round Robin was drafted to the Englishman, beginning: 'O Scoffer,' and ending with a selection of curses from the Rites of Mizraim and Memphis, and the Commination of Jugana, who was a 'fifth-rounder' upon whose name an upstart 'third-rounder' once traded. A papal excommunication is a *billet-doux* compared with the Commination of Jugana. The Englishman had been proved, under hand and seal of the Old Man of the Mountains, to have appropriated Virtue and pretended to have Power which, in reality, belonged only to the Supreme Head. Naturally the Round Robin did not spare him.

He handed the letter to Dana Da to translate into decent English. The effect on Dana Da was curious. At first he was furiously angry, and then he laughed for five minutes.

'I had thought,' he said, 'that they would have come to me. In another week I would have shown that I sent the Sending, and they would have discrowned the Old Man of the Mountains who has sent this Sending of mine. Do you do nothing. The time has come for me to act. Write as I dictate, and I will put them to shame. But give me ten more rupees.'

At Dana Da's dictation the Englishman wrote nothing less than a formal challenge to the Old Man of the Mountains. It wound up: 'And if this Manifestation be from your hand, then let it go forward; but if it be from my hand, I will that the Sending shall cease in two days' time. On that day there shall be twelve kittens and thenceforward none at all. The people shall judge between us.' This was signed by Dana Da, who added pentacles and pentagrams, and a *crux ansata*, and half-a-dozen *swastikas*, and a Triple Tau to his name, just to show that he was all he laid claim to be.

The challenge was read out to the gentlemen and ladies, and they remembered then that Dana Da had laughed at them some years ago. It was officially announced that the Old Man of the Mountains would treat the matter with contempt; Dana Da being an Independent Investigator without a single 'round' at the back of him. But this did not soothe his people. They wanted to see a fight. They were very human for all their spirituality. Lone Sahib, who was really being worn out with kittens, submitted meekly to his fate. He felt that he was being 'kittened to prove the power of Dana Da', as the poet says.

When the stated day dawned the shower of kittens began. Some were white and some were tabby, and all were about the same loathsome age. Three were on his hearth-rug, three in his bathroom, and the other six turned up at intervals among the visitors who came to see the prophecy break down. Never was a more satisfactory Sending. On the next day there were no kittens, and next day and all the other days were kittenless and quiet. The people murmured and looked to the Old Man of the Mountains for an explanation. A letter, written on a palm-leaf, dropped from the ceiling, but every one except Lone Sahib felt that letters were not what the occasion demanded. There should have been cats, there should have been cats – full-grown ones. The letter proved conclusively that there had been a hitch in the Psychic Current which, colliding with a Dual Identity, had interfered with the Percipient Activity all along the main line. The kittens were still going on, but owing to some failure in the Developing Fluid, they were not materialized. The air was thick with letters for a few days afterwards. Unseen hands played Glück and Beethoven on finger-bowls and clock-shades; but all men felt that Psychic Life was a mockery without materialized kittens. Even Lone Sahib shouted with the majority on his head. Dana Da's letters were very insulting, and if he had then offered to lead a new departure, there is no knowing what might have happened.

But Dana Da was dying of whisky and opium in the Englishman's godown, and had small heart for honours.

'They had been put to shame,' said he. 'Never was such a Sending. It has killed me.'

'Nonsense!' said the Englishman. 'You are going to die, Dana Da, and that sort of stuff must be left behind. I'll admit that you have made some queer things come about. Tell me honestly, now, how was it done?'

'Give me ten more rupees,' said Dana Da faintly, 'and if I die before I spend them, bury them with me.' The silver was counted out while Dana Da was fighting with Death. His hand closed upon the money and he smiled a grim smile.

'Bend low,' he whispered. The Englishman bent.

'*Bunnia* – Mission school – expelled – *box wallah* [pedler] – Ceylon pearl-merchant – all mine English education – out-casted, and made up name Dana Da – England with American thought-reading man and – and – you gave me ten rupees several times – I gave the Sahib's bearer two-eight a month for cats – little, little cats. I wrote – and he put them about – very clever man. Very few kittens now in the bazar. Ask Lone Sahib's sweeper wife.'

So saying, Dana Da gasped and passed away into a land where, if all be true, there are no materializations and the making of new creeds is discouraged.

But consider the gorgeous simplicity of it all!

Dogs and Cats

Alexandre Dumas

It is admitted that the dog has intelligence, a heart and perhaps a soul, likewise it is agreed that the cat is a traitor, deceiver, thief, an egotist, an ingrate. How many have we not heard say: 'Oh, I cannot abide a cat! It is an animal that loves not its master; it is attached only to the house; one must keep it under lock and key. I had one once, for I was in the country and there were mice. The cook had the imprudence to leave upon the table a poulet that she had just purchased; the cat carried it off, no morsel of it was ever seen after. Since that day I have said: "I will have no cat."' Its reputation is detestable, the fact cannot be disguised, and one must acknowledge that the cat does nothing to modify the opinion in which it is held. It is entirely unpopular, but it cares as little about this as it does about the Grand Turk. Must I confess it to you? It is for this that I love it, for in this world one can remain indifferent to things the most serious – if there are serious things, and this one knows only at the end of his life; but he cannot evade the question of dogs and cats. There is always a moment when he must declare himself. Well, then! I love cats! Ah! the times they have said to me:

'What, you love cats?'

'Yes!'

'Do you not like dogs better?'

'No, I love cats much more.'

'That is extraordinary.'

I prefer certainly to have neither cat nor dog, but were I forced to live with one of these two individuals, I would choose the cat. It has for me the manners essential to social relations. At first, in its early youth, it possesses all the graces, all the suppleness, all the unexpectedness by which the most exacting, artistic fancy can be amused! It is adroit, it always knows where it is. Prudent unto caution, it goes everywhere, it examines without soiling, breaking nothing; it is in itself a warmth and a caress; it has not a snout, but a mouth – and what a mouth! It steals the mutton as does the dog, but, unlike the latter, makes no delight of carrion; it is discreet and of fastidious cleanliness, which might be well imitated by a number of its detractors. It washes its face, and in so doing foretells the weather into the bargain. One can entertain the idea of putting a ribbon around its neck, never a collar; it cannot be enslaved. It permits no modifications in its race; it lends itself to no combinations that industry could attempt. The cat reflects, this is obvious, contrary to the dog, a lackbrain whose rabies is his crowning idiocy. In short, the cat is a dignified, proud, disdainful animal that hides its love affairs in the shadows, almost within the clouds, upon the roofs, in the vicinity of the night-working students. It defies advances, tolerates no insults, it abandons the house in which it is not treated according to its merits; in short, the cat is truly an aristocrat in type and origin, whereas the dog is and ever will be naught but a vulgar parvenu by dint of complaisance.

The sole argument at all plausible against the cat is that it destroys the birds, the nightingales as well as the sparrows. If the dog does not as much it is because he is too clumsy and stupid. He runs also after the birds, but barking, the birds escape him, and he stays behind completely dumfounded, open-mouthed and with astonished tail. He makes up for it upon the partridges and rabbits, after two years' submission to the strong collar in order to learn his art, and it is not for himself, but for the hunter, that he goes in quest of game. The imbecile! He persecutes the animals, an animal himself, for the profit of the man who beats him. At least, when the cat catches a bird she has an excuse; it is to eat it herself. Why would that authorize man to slander her? Let men regard one another! They will see in their race, as in that of cats, those who have claws and have no other preoccupation but to destroy those who have wings.

Three little kittens

Three little kittens,
They lost their mittens,
And they began to cry,
'Oh mother dear, we sadly fear
That we have lost our mittens.'

'What! Lost your mittens,
You naughty kittens!
Then you shall have no pie.
Mee-ow, mee-ow, mee-ow.
No, you shall have no pie.'

The three little kittens,
They found their mittens,
And they began to cry,
'Oh, mother dear, see here, see here
For we have found our mittens.'

'What! Found your mittens,
You silly kittens!
Then you shall have some pie.
Purr-r, purr-r, purr-r,
Oh, let us have some pie.'

Three little kittens,
Put on their mittens,
And soon ate up their pie;

'Oh, mother dear, we greatly fear
That we have soiled our mittens.'

What! Soiled your mittens,
You naughty kittens.'
Then they began to sigh,
'Mee-ow, mee-ow, mee-ow.'
Then they began to sigh.

The three little kittens,
They washed their mittens,
And hung them out to dry.
'Oh, mother dear, do you not hear,
That we have washed our mittens?'

'What! Washed your mittens?
You're good little kittens.
But I smell a rat close by!
Hush! Hush! Hush!
I smell a rat close by.'

ANON

Calvin, The Cat

Charles Dudley Warner

Calvin is dead. His life, long to him, but short for the rest of us, was not marked by startling adventures, but his character was so uncommon and his qualities were so worthy of imitation that I have been asked by those who personally knew him to set down my recollections of his career.

His origin and ancestry were shrouded in mystery; even his age was a matter of pure conjecture. Although he was of the Maltese race, I have reason to suppose that he was American by birth as he certainly was in sympathy. Calvin was given to me eight years ago by Mrs Stowe, but she knew nothing of his age or origin. He walked into her house one day out of the great unknown and became at once at home, as if he had been always a friend of the family. He appeared to have artistic and literary tastes, and it was as if he had inquired at the door if that was the residence of the author of *Uncle Tom's Cabin*, and, upon being assured that it was, had decided to dwell there. This is, of course, fanciful, for his antecedents were wholly unknown, but in his time he could hardly have been in any household where he would not have heard *Uncle Tom's Cabin* talked about. When he came to Mrs Stowe, he was as large as he ever was, and apparently as old as he ever became. Yet there was in him no appearance of age; he was in the happy maturity of all his powers, and you would rather have said in that maturity he had found the secret of perpetual youth. And it was as difficult to believe that he would ever be aged as it was to imagine that he had ever been in immature youth. There was in him a mysterious perpetuity.

After some years, when Mrs Stowe made her winter home in

Florida, Calvin came to live with us. From the first moment, he fell into the ways of the house and assumed a recognized position in the family – I say recognized, because after he became known he was always inquired for by visitors, and in the letters to the other members of the family he always received a message. Although the least obtrusive of beings, his individuality always made itself felt.

His personal appearance had much to do with this, for he was of royal mold, and had an air of high breeding. He was large, but he had nothing of the fat grossness of the celebrated Angora family; though powerful, he was exquisitely proportioned, and as graceful in every movement as a young leopard. When he stood up to open a door – he opened all the doors with old-fashioned latches – he was portentously tall, and when he stretched on the rug before the fire he seemed too long for this world – as indeed he was. His coat was the finest and softest I have ever seen, a shade of quiet Maltese; and from his throat downward, underneath, to the white tips of his feet, he wore the whitest and most delicate ermine; and no person was ever more fastidiously neat. In his finely formed head you saw something of his aristocratic character; the ears were small and cleanly cut, there was a tinge of pink in the nostrils, his face was handsome, and the expression of his countenance exceedingly intelligent – I should call it even a sweet expression if the term were not inconsistent with his look of alertness and sagacity.

It is difficult to convey a just idea of his gaiety in connection with his dignity and gravity, which his name expressed. As we know nothing of his family, of course it will be understood that Calvin was his Christian name. He had times of relaxation into utter playfulness, delighting in a ball of yarn, catching sportively at stray ribbons when his mistress was at her toilet, and pursuing his own tail, with hilarity, for lack of anything better. He could amuse himself by the hour, and he did not care for children; perhaps something in his past was present to his memory. He had absolutely no bad habits, and his disposition was perfect. I never saw him exactly angry, though I have seen his tail grow to an enormous size when a strange cat appeared upon his lawn. He disliked cats, evidently regarding them as feline and treacherous, and he had no association with them. Occasionally there would be heard a night concert in the shrubbery. Calvin would ask to have the door opened, and then you would hear a rush and a 'Pestzt,' and the concert would explode, and Calvin would quietly come and resume his seat on the hearth. There was no trace of anger in his manner, but he wouldn't have any of that about the house. He had the rare virtue of magnanimity. Although he had fixed notions about his own rights, and extraordinary persistency in getting them, he never showed temper at a repulse; he simple and firmly persisted till he had what he wanted. His diet was one point; his idea was that of the scholars about dictionaries – to 'get the best.' He knew as well as anyone what was in the house, and would refuse beef if turkey was to be had; and if there oysters, he would wait over the turkey to see if the oysters would not be forthcoming. And yet he was not a gross gourmand; he would eat bread if he saw me eating it, and thought he was not being imposed on. His habits of feeding, also, were refined; he never used a knife, and he would put up his hand and draw the fork down to his mouth as gracefully as a grown person. Unless necessity compelled, he would not eat in the kitchen, but insisted upon his meals in the dining room, and would wait patiently, unless a stranger were present; and then he was sure to importune the visitor, hoping that the latter was ignorant of the rule of the house, and would give him something. They used to say that he preferred as his tablecloth on the floor a certain well-known Church journal; but this was said by an Episcopalian. So far as I know, he had no religious prejudices, except that he did not like the association with Romanists. He tolerated the servants, because they belonged to the house, and would sometimes linger by the kitchen stove; but the moment visitors came in he arose, opened the door, and marched into the drawing room. Yet he enjoyed the company of his equals, and never withdrew, no matter how many callers – whom he recognized as of his society – might come into the drawing room. Calvin was fond of company, but he wanted to choose it; and I have no doubt that his was an aristocratic fastidiousness rather than one of faith. It was so with most people.

The intelligence of Calvin was something phenomenal, in his rank of life. He established a method of communicating his wants, and even some of his sentiments; and he could help himself in many things. There was a furnace register in a retired room, where he used to go when he wished to be alone, that he always opened when he desired more heat; but never shut, any more than he shut the door after himself. He could do almost everything but speak, and you would declare sometimes that you could see a pathetic longing to do that in his intelligent face. I have no desire to overdraw his qualities, but if there was one thing in him more noticeable than another, it was his fondness for nature. He could content himself for hours at a low window, looking into the ravine and at the great trees, noting the smallest stir there; he delighted above all things, to accompany me walking about the garden, hearing the birds, getting the smell of the fresh earth, and rejoicing in the sunshine. He followed me and gamboled like a dog, rolling over on the turf and exhibiting his delight in a hundred ways. If I worked, he sat and watched me, or looked off over the bank, and kept his ear open to the twitter in the cherry trees. When it stormed, he was sure to sit at the window, keenly watching the rain or the snow, glancing up and down at its falling; and a winter tempest always delighted him. I think he was genuinely fond of birds, but, so far as I know, he usually confined himself to one a day; he never killed, as some sportsmen do, for the sake of killing, but only as civilized people do – from necessity. He was intimate with the flying squirrels who dwelt in the chestnut trees – too intimate, for almost every day in the summer he would bring in one, until he nearly discouraged them. He was, indeed, a superb hunter, and would have been a devastating one if his bump of destructiveness had not been offset by a bump of moderation. There was very little of the brutality of the lower animals about him; I don't think he enjoyed rats for themselves, but he knew his business, and for the first few months of his residence with us he waged an awful campaign against the horde, and after that his simple presence was sufficient to deter them from coming on the premises. Mice amused him, but he usually considered them too small game to be taken seriously; I have seen him play for an hour with a mouse, and then let him go with a royal condescension. In this whole matter 'getting a living,' Calvin was a great contrast to the rapacity of the age in which he lived.

I hesitate to speak of his capacity for friendship and the

affectionateness of his nature, for I know from his own reserve that he would care to have it much talked about. We understood each other perfectly, but we never made any fuss about it; when I spoke his name and snapped my fingers, he came to me; when I returned home at night, he was pretty sure to be waiting for me near the gate, and would rise and saunter along the walk, as if his being there were purely accidental – so shy was he commonly of showing feeling; and when I opened the door he never rushed in, like a cat, but loitered, and lounged, as if he had had no intention of going in, but he would condescend to. And yet, the fact was, he knew dinner was ready, and he was bound to be there. He kept the run of dinnertime. It happened sometimes, during our absence in the summer, that dinner would be early, and Calvin, walking about the grounds, missed it and came in late. But he never made a mistake the second day. There was one thing he never did – he never rushed through an open doorway. He never forgot his dignity. If he had asked to have the door opened, and was eager to go out, he always went deliberately; I can see him now, standing on the sill, looking about at the sky as if he was thinking whether it were worthwhile to take an umbrella, until he was near having his tail shut in.

His friendship was rather constant than demonstrative. When we returned from an absence of nearly two years. Calvin welcomed us with evident pleasure, but showed his satisfaction rather by tranquil happiness than by fuming about. He had the faculty of making us glad to get home. It was his constancy that was so attractive. He liked companionship, but he wouldn't be petted, or fussed over, or sit in anyone's lap a moment; he always extricated himself from such familiarity with dignity and with no show of temper. If there was any petting to be done, however, he chose to do it. Often he would sit looking at me, and then, moved by a delicate affection, come and pull at my coat and sleeve until he could touch my face with his nose, and then go away contented. He had a habit of coming to my study in the morning, sitting quietly by my side or on the table for hours, watching the pen run over the paper, occasionally swinging his tail round for a blotter, and then going to sleep among the papers by the inkstand. Or, more rarely, he would watch the writing from a perch on my shoulder. Writing always interested him, and, until he understood it, he wanted to hold the pen.

He always held himself in a kind of reserve with his friend, as if he had said, 'Let us respect our personality, and not make a "mess" of friendship.' He saw, with Emerson, the risk of degrading it to trivial conveniency. 'Why insist on rash personal relations with your friends? Leave this touching and clawing.' Yet I would not give an unfair notion of his aloofness, his fine sense of the sacredness of the me and the not-me. And, at the risk of not being believed, I will relate an incident, which was often repeated. Calvin had the practice of passing a portion of the night in the contemplation of its beauties, and would come into our chamber over the roof of the conservatory through the open window, summer and winter, and go to sleep at the foot of my bed. He would do this always exactly in this way; he never was content to stay in the chamber if we compelled him to go upstairs and through the door. He had the obstinacy of General Grant. But this is by the way. In the morning he performed his toilet and went down to breakfast with the rest of the family. Now, when the mistress was absent from home, and at no other time, Calvin would come in the morning, when the bell rang, to the head of the bed, put up his feet and look into my face, follow me about when I rose, 'assist' at the dressing, and in many purring ways show his fondness, as if he had plainly said, 'I know that she has gone away, but I am here.' Such was Calvin in rare moments.

He had his limitations. Whatever passion he had for nature, he had no conception of art. There was sent to him once a fine and very expressive cat's head in bronze, by Frémiet. I placed it on the floor. He regarded it intently, approached it cautiously and crouchingly, touched it with his nose, perceived the fraud, turned away abruptly, and never would notice it afterward. On the whole, his life was not only a successful one, but a happy one. He never had but one fear, so far as I know: he had a mortal and a reasonable terror of plumbers. He would never stay in the house when they were here. No coaxing could quiet him. Of course, he didn't share our fear about their charges, but he must have had some dreadful experience with them in that portion of his life which is unknown to us. A plumber was to him the devil, and I have no doubt that, in his scheme, plumbers were foreordained to do him mischief.

In speaking of his worth, it has never occurred to me to estimate Calvin by the worldly standard. I know that it is customary now, when anyone dies, to ask how much he was worth, and that no obituary in the newspapers is considered complete without such an estimate. The plumbers in our house were one day overheard to say that, 'They say that *she* says that *he* says that he wouldn't take a hundred dollars for him.' It is unnecessary to say that I never made such a remark, and that, so far as Calvin was concerned, there was no purchase in money.

As I look back upon it, Calvin's life seems to me a fortunate one, for it was natural and unforced. He ate when he was hungry, slept when he was sleepy, and enjoyed existence to the very tips of his toes and the end of his expressive and slow-moving tail. He delighted to roam about the garden, and stroll among the trees, and to lie on the green grass and luxuriate in all the sweet influences of summer. You could never accuse him of idleness, and yet he knew the secret of repose. The poet who wrote so prettily of him that his little life was rounded with a sleep, understated his felicity; it was founded with a good many. His conscience never seemed to interfere with his slumbers. In fact, he had good habits and a contented mind. I can see him now walk in at the study door, sit down by my chair, bring his tail artistically about his feet, and look up at me with unspeakable happiness in his handsome face. I often thought that he felt the dumb limitation which denied him the power of language. But since he was denied speech, he scorned the inarticulate mouthings of the lower animals. The vulgar mewing and yowling of the cat species was beneath him; he sometimes uttered a sort of articulate and well-bred ejaculation when he wished to call attention to something that he considered remarkable or to some want of his, but he never went whining about. He would sit for hours at a closed window, when he desired to enter, without a murmur, and when it was opened he never admitted that he had been impatient by bolting in. Though speech he had not, and the unpleasant kind of utterance given to his race he would not use, he had a mighty power of purr to express his measureless content with congenial society. There was in him a musical organ with stops of varied power and expression, upon which I have no doubt he could have performed Scarlatti's celebrated cat's fugue.

Whether Calvin died of old age, or was carried off by one of the diseases incident to youth, it is impossible to say; for his departure was as quiet as his advent was mysterious. I only know that he appeared to us in this world in his perfect stature and beauty, and that after a time, like Lohengrin, he withdrew. In his illness there was nothing more to be regretted than in all his blameless life. I suppose there never was an illness that had more dignity and sweetness and resignation in it. It came on gradually, in a kind of listlessness and want of appetite. An alarming symptom was his preference for the warmth of a furnace register to the lively sparkle of the open wood fire. Whatever pain he suffered, he bore it in silence, and seemed only anxious not to obtrude his malady. We tempted him with the delicacies of the season, but it soon became impossible for him to eat, and for two weeks he ate or drank scarcely anything. Sometimes he made an effort to take something, but it was evident that he made the effort to please us. The neighbors – and I am convinced that the advice of neighbors is never good for anything – suggested catnip. He wouldn't even smell it. We had the attendance of an amateur practitioner of medicine, whose real office was the cure of souls, but nothing touched his case. He took what was offered, but it was with the air of one to whom the time for pellets was past. He sat or lay day after day almost motionless, never once making a display of those vulgar convulsions or contortions of pain which are so disagreeable to society. His favorite place was on the brightest spot of a Smyrna rug by the conservatory, where the sunlight fell and he could hear the fountain play. If we went to him and exhibited our interest in his condition, he always purred in recognition of our sympathy. And when I spoke his name, he looked up with an expression that said, 'I understand it, old fellow, but it's no use.' He was to all who came to visit him a model of calmness and patience in affliction.

I was absent from home at the last, but heard by daily postal card of his failing condition; and never again saw him alive. One sunny morning he rose from his rug, went into the conservatory (he was very thin then), walked around it deliberately, looking at all the plants he knew, and then went to the bay window in the dining room, and stood a long time looking out upon the little field, now brown and sere, and toward the garden, where perhaps the happiest hours of his life had been spent. It was a last look. He turned and walked away, laid himself down upon the bright spot in the rug, and quietly died.

It is not too much to say that a little shock went through the neighborhood when it was known that Calvin was dead, so marked with his individuality; and his friends, one after another, came in to see him. There was no sentimental nonsense about his obsequies; it was felt that any parade would have been distasteful to him. John, who acted as undertaker, prepared a candlebox for him, and I believe assumed a professional decorum; but there may have been the usual levity underneath, for I heard that he remarked in the kitchen that it was the 'driest wake he ever attended.' Everybody, however, felt a fondness for Calvin, and regarded him with a certain respect. Between him and Bertha there existed a great friendship, and she apprehended his nature; she used to say that sometimes she was afraid of him, he looked at her so intelligently; she was never certain that he was what he appeared to be.

When I returned, they had laid Calvin on a table in an upper chamber by an open window. It was February. He reposed in a candlebox, lined about the edge with evergreen, and at his head stood a little wineglass with flowers. He lay with his head tucked down in his arms – a favorite position of his before the fire – as if asleep in the comfort of his soft and exquisite fur. It was the involuntary exclamation of those who saw him, 'How natural he looks!' As for myself, I said nothing. John buried him under the twin hawthorn trees – one white and the other pink – in a spot where Calvin was fond of lying and listening to the hum of summer insects and the twitter of birds.

Perhaps I have failed to make appear the individuality of character that was so evident to those who knew him. At any rate, I have set down nothing concerning him but the literal truth. He was always a mystery. I did not know whence he came; I do not know whither he has gone. I would not weave one spray of falsehood in the wreath I lay upon his grave.

Why is there Enmity Between the Cat and the Dog?

From the Hebrew Alphabet of Ben Sira

When the cat was created it became the companion of the dog. They hunted together and ate together of the prey. It so happened at one time that two or three days passed and they had not got anything to eat. The dog said to the cat, 'Why are we sitting here ahungered? Go to Adam and sit in his house and be fed there, and we will go after the creeping things and reptiles and will feed upon them, and we shall both be kept alive.' The cat then replied to the dog, 'Let it be so, but we must take an oath that we will not go both together to one master.' He replied, 'Thou hast spoken well.' There and then they both took an oath, and the cat went to the house of Adam, where she found mice, which she caught and ate: the rest ran away from her. When Adam saw what had happened, he said, 'A great salvation has God sent me.'

Then he took the cat into his house and fed it and gave it to drink.

The dog went to the wolf and said unto him, 'Let me come and spend the night with thee.' He replied, 'Very well.' Both went to a cave to sleep there. In the night the dog heard the footsteps of the various animals, so he woke the wolf and told him, 'I heard the steps of thieves.' The wolf replied, 'Go out to them and drive them away.'

The beasts turned upon him to kill him. The dog fled away and went to the ape, but the ape drove him away. Then he went to the sheep. The sheep received him and allowed him to sleep there. He heard the noise of feet and he said to the sheep, 'I hear the footsteps of robbers.' The sheep replied, 'Go out.' The dog went out and began to bark. The wolves said, 'Surely sheep are there.' So they went thither and ate the sheep.

The dog fled away and went from place to place trying to find some shelter, but could not find any. At last he came to Adam, who took him in and allowed him to sleep there. In the middle of the night the dog said to Adam, 'I hear the noise of footsteps.' Adam rose at once, took his spear, and going out with the dog drove the wild beasts away and returned home with the dog. Then Adam said to the dog, 'Come into my house, dwell with me, eat of my food and drink of my water.' And the dog went with him. When the cat heard the voice of the dog she came out to him and said, 'Why dost thou come thither to my place?' And he replied, 'Adam has brought me hither.' Adam said to the cat, 'Why dost thou quarrel with him? I have brought him in, for I found him clever and full of courage. Thou needst not grieve, thou shalt be kept also as before.' The cat replied, 'My Lord, he is a thief, is it right to dwell in one place with a thief?' And the cat went on to say to the dog, 'Why hast thou broken thy oath?' He replied, 'I will not enter thy dwelling place, I will not eat of anything that belongs to thee, I will not cause thee the least harm.' But the cat did not listen and began to quarrel.

When the dog saw this, he went away from the house of Adam, and going to that of Seth, dwelt there. And the dog tried all the time to make peace with the cat, but it was all in vain. In that state they have remained to this very day, in constant enmity, for the children follow the example of their forebears; as the proverb has it, sheep follow sheep.

The Musion

from *Workes of Armorie,* by Bossewell, 1572

The beaste is called a Musion, for that he is enimie to Myse, and Rattes. And he is called a Catte of the Greekes because he is slye, and wittie: for that he seeth so shaepely, that he overcommeth darkness of the nighte, by the shyninge lyghte of his eyne. In shape of body he is like unto a Leoparde, and hath a greate mouth. He dothe delighte that he enjoyeth his libertie: and in his youthe he is swifte, plyante, and merye. Hemaketh a rufull noyse, and a gastefull, when one profereth to fighte with an other. He is a cruell beaste, when he is wilde, and falleth his ownne feete from moste highe places: and oneth is hurte therewith. When he hathe a fayre skinne (he is, as it were, prowde thereof), and then he goeth faste aboute to be seene.

Feline Instinct

Bernard Perez

Mitis and Riquet are two tom-cats saved from a litter of five; their mother is an Angora, slate-coloured, with the neck, breast, and tips of the paws white. Mitis has a large head and limbs, and a coat which promises to be Angora and the same colour as his mother's, a white muzzle, and white underneath his eyes, while his lips and the tip of his nose are bright pink. Riquet's body and tail are black, with grey marks; his head, which is smaller than his brother's, is grey, with zebra-like bands of black crossing longitudinally and laterally; two white streaks branch out from the upper end of the nose, and on the forehead two curved lines, starting from the corners of his eyes, surround a disc of black and grey.

No sooner has their mother licked them over than they set off whining and seeking for her teats. I made some observations of their movements on the first and second days; but as I am afraid of not recording them with sufficient accuracy from memory, I will begin with the third day, when I took to writing down my observations.

12th May. – They are perpetually moving about, even when sucking and sleeping. Sleep overtakes them in the act of sucking, and then, according to what position they were in at the moment, they either remain ensconced in their mother's silky breast, or fall over with open mouths into some graceful attitude. The little gluttons, Riquet especially, who seems to be delicately organised, are often troubled with hiccoughs, reminding one of young children who have sucked too copiously. It is curious to watch them when searching for a teat, turning their heads abruptly from right to left, and left to right, pushing now with their foreheads, now with their muzzles; tumbling and jumping one over the other, sliding between their mother's legs, trying to suck no matter what part of her body; and finally, when they have settled down to their meal, resembling leeches, whose whole activity is concentrated on the work of suction, and who, as soon as they have thoroughly gorged themselves, let go their hold and fall back into *inertia*.

Whenever their sensibility is unpleasantly excited, as, for instance, if their mother leans on them too heavily, or leaves them alone, or performs their toilet too roughly, they give vent to monotonous – I had almost said monosyllabic – plaints; sounds which can scarcely be called *mias*, still less *miaows*; they are best described as trembling *mi-i-is*. They also emit these plaintive sounds when they have been searching long for a teat without finding one, or if they annoy each other during the laborious search; or if I take them up too quickly, or turn them over in the palm of my hand to examine them. If I set them up in my hand in a standing position, they will remain motionless for a few seconds, as if enjoying the warmth of my hand; but very soon again they begin clamouring with loud whines for their home in the mother's warm, soft stomach, which is at once their shelter and their dining-room, the familiar, and perhaps the loved, theatre of their nascent activity.

13th May. – This morning Mitis appeared to be ill. He was languid, did not whine when I took him up, and made no attempt at sucking; he had an attack of hiccoughs, accompanied by shiverings all over his body, which made me anxious. It only lasted an hour, however: there may have been some temporary cause of indisposition; or perhaps excessive sucking, or a very great need of sleep, had reduced him to a semi-inert mass.

Riquet's head is prettier than it was yesterday; the white spot has increased in size, the grey marks have spread and grown lighter, and the head and neck are rather larger; but Mitis has still by far the finest carriage.

Twelve o'clock. – The two leeches have been operating for twenty minutes without desisting. They are now brimful of milk, and settling themselves down, no matter where – one on the mother's stomach, the other on her paws; no sooner have they placed themselves than they fall asleep.

Two o'clock. – They have no fixed position for sucking; any does that comes first.

When the mother leaves them alone for a moment they turn in rapid gyrations round and round, over and under each other, delighting in the mutual contact of their bodies and the warmth which it engenders. If the mother remains absent for some minutes, they end by falling asleep one over the other in the shape of a cross. If I lift up the top one, the other soon begins to whine: they are not accustomed to solitude, and it produces a painful impression of cold. Very young animals are easily chilled, and sometimes die of cold in a temperature which is not very low. This is owing to the smallness of their bodies and the feebleness of their respiratory organs.

Between four and five o'clock Riquet seemed to me very lively. He was searching for a teat which he could not find, and for ten minutes he crossed backwards and forwards over his brother's body, giving him frequent slaps with his paws.

Riquet's nose is a pink-brown, but tending to red-brown.

This evening (ten o'clock) I showed the mother a saucer full of milk; she left her kittens to go and drink it, and afterwards she took a turn at a plate of porridge; her absence lasted barely five minutes. The kittens, during this time, went through their usual manoeuvres: Riquet turned three times running round his brother; the latter, who is more indolent, or perhaps has more need of sleep, stretched himself out full length on his side. Riquet, however, cannot rest till he has found what he is searching for – viz., the body of his mother. He is still in a state of agitation when the cat comes back, raises herself with her front-paws on the edge of the box, and drops quietly down by the side of her little ones without touching them. Instantly they start up, raising their little wagging heads; they know that their mother is there – the slight noise she made in getting into the box, and the movement she imparted to it, are associated in their memory with the idea of her presence.

The mother's first care is to see to their toilet, and she proceeds to turn them over with two or three strokes of her tongue, and then operates on them with the same natural instrument. Both have their turn; and at the end of the operation, which seems to worry them, they whine considerably, though not at all loud. A few minutes after, the melodious snoring of the mother informs me that the whole family is at rest. I take a peep at them: the mother is laid on her left side, describing a large and elegant curve; Mitis, half on his hind-paws, half on his stomach, is stretched across Riquet, and both are sleeping, or sucking – perhaps doing both at the same time.

14th May. – My kittens seem to grow as I watch them, especially Mitis's head, neck, and back; he is a massive heavy kitten, but his forehead is broad and high: he will probably be an intelligent cat; his leonine chin, large and well developed, indicates energy and goodness. He begins to show more vivacity than during the earlier days; when he encounters his brother in searching for a teat, or if the latter disputes with him the one he has got hold of, he deals out at him rapid strokes with his paw, which remind one of a dog swimming. His mother has just been performing his toilet in the manner aforesaid, and has no doubt kept him longer at it than he liked; he shows his displeasure by striking out his hind paws, one of which knocks against his ear, and uttering two or three impatient *mis*.

These very occasional and but slightly emphasised cries are the only ones which Riquet – even the brisk and lively Riquet – gives out, even when I take him in my hand. . . .

. . . *15th May.* – Today I held Riquet on my hand for three minutes. I was smoking a cigar; the little creature stretched out its neck, poked its nose up in the air, and sniffed with a persistent little noise. A sparrow, whose cage was hung up over us, frightened at my smoking-cap, began to fly round the cage and beat at it with its wings. At the sound of this noise Riquet was seized with a sudden fit of trembling, which made him squat down precipitately in my hand. Movements of this kind are reflex ones, the production of which is associated in the organism with certain auditory impressions; but the animal is necessarily more or less conscious of them, or will soon be so. From five minutes' observation I have thus learnt that Riquet is sensible to strong smells, and that he already goes through the consecutive movements of sentiment and fear.

Riquet's head is visibly changing to silver-grey; the marks on his back are also assuming this shade.

I took Mitis in my hands, stretched them out and drew them up again. He does not seem to know quite what to make of it; he attempts a few steps, feels about uncertainly with his head, and comes in contact with my coat smelling of the cigar; he appears to be scenting my coat, but not with so much noise and vivacity as Riquet does. He waggles his head about, feels about with his paws, and tries to suck my coat and my hands; he is evidently out of his element and unhappy. The mother calls to him from the bottom of the box; this causes him to turn his head quickly in the direction from which the sound comes (what a number of movements or ideas associated in the intelligence and organism of a little animal four days old!); he starts off again, making a step forward, then drawing back, turning to the right and to the left, with a waddling movement. I give him back to his mother.

I thought I noticed once again this evening that the light of my lamp, when held near the kittens' box, caused rather lively excitation of their eyelids, although these were closed. The light must pass through these thin coverings and startle the retinas. The kittens were agitated during a few seconds; they raised and shook their heads, then lowered them and hid them in the maternal bosom.

The noise of carriages, the sound of my voice, the twittering of the sparrow, the movements imparted to the box by my hand – all throw them into the same kind of agitation. These movements may be coupled with the movements, unconscious no doubt, but determined by external causes, which are observed in the young. *16th May.* – Mitis' tail is thickening at the root; the hair of its head and neck is close and silky; he will no doubt turn out a considerable fraction of an Angora . . .

. . . This evening Mitis, having escaped from the constraint in which his mother holds him to perform his toilet, half *plantigrade* half *gastéropode*, dragged himself slowly, though as fast as he was able, along his mother's paws, and at last nestled down in the soft fur of her stomach. While in this position his head, rolling like that of a drunken man, knocked against the head of Riquet, who was in the act of sucking. Instantly Mitis lifts a paw and brings it down on his brother's head. The latter holds on, as he is very comfortably spread out on the bottom of the box, and is sucking a teat placed lower down. A second attempt of Mitis' fails equally. He then performs rapid movements with his head, searching vigorously for his cup, but not finding it. The mother then places a paw on his back, and his centre of gravity being thus better established, he at last accomplishes his object. Here we have several actions which are no doubt in some degree conscious, but which come chiefly under the head of automatism: the scent which helps in the search for the teat, the instinct to dispute the ground with another who is discovered to be sucking, the movements of intentional repulsion, of struggle, of combativeness. What an admirable machine for sensation sentiment, volition, activity, and consciousness, is a young animal only just born!

17th May. – I have observed – or think I have observed – in Mitis, the more indolent of the two brothers, the first symptoms of playfulness: lying on his back with his mouth half open, he twiddles his four paws with an air of satisfaction, and as if seeking to touch some one or something. It is eight o'clock in the evening, the window is open, the sparrow is singing with all its might in its cage, we are talking and laughing close to the cat's box. Do all these noises in some way excite the sensoriums of the two *repus* kittens? The fact is, that they have been in a state of agitation for more than a quarter of an hour, travelling one over the other and walking over their mother's stomach, paws, and head. Mitis, the heavier of the two and soonest tired out, was the first to return to the teat. Riquet's return to the maternal breast has been a long and roundabout journey from one corner of the box to the other, and round and round his mother.

At nine o'clock I went to look at them with the light. This threw them into dreadful consternation. I observe in them both something like intentions to bite, while rolling each other over, they keep their mouths open, and snap instead of sucking when they come in contact with any part of each other's bodies; but it is all mechanical. Here we have an increase of activity produced by an accession of powers and temporary over-excitement.

18th May. – They are lying asleep on their sides, facing each other, with their fore-paws half stretched out against the hind ones. Riquet's sleep is much disturbed; his mouth touches one of his brother's paws, which he instantly begins to suck. Is this a mechanical or unconscious action? Is he not possibly dreaming? After four or five attempts at sucking he lets go the paw, and sleeps on tranquilly for four minutes; but the noise of a carriage passing in the street, and perhaps the consequent vibration of the floor and the bottom of the box, causes violent trembling in his lips, paws, and tail.

The mother gets back in the box; and the kittens, instantly awake and erect, utter three or four *mis* to welcome the joyful return.

In settling herself down the mother leans rather heavily on Riquet; the latter, who used formerly to extricate himself mechanically, and who already knows from experience the inconvenience of such a position, moves off brusquely, goes further away than he would have done formerly, and Mitis, on the lookout for a teat, hears close to him the noise of his brother's sucking. He pommels his head with his hind-paws, rolls up against him, striking out with his fore-paws, and knocks him over with the weight of his body; he is now in possession of the teat which his brother had first tried, and, finding it as good as the one he was sucking before, he sticks to it.

18th May. – Mitis was trying to worry Riquet who was busy sucking. I hold out my hand to make a barrier between the two; Mitis pushes it back with his paw, but soon perceives the difference between the two bodies which he is pushing against, gives over his excitement, and looks out for another teat. No doubt in this case there was no comparative perception of difference, but different sensations producing different muscular actions; that is all, I imagine, but this is nevertheless the germ of veritable comparison.

19th May. – Both the eyes of both kittens are about to open; the eyelids seem slightly slit, and are covered with an oozy film. At the external corner of Mitis' right eye there is a little round opening disclosing a pale blue speck of eyeball, the size of a pin's head. At the internal commissure of the left eye there is also a round opening, but much smaller,and showing no eye-ball through it. Riquet's right eye is also opening slightly; the edges of the left eyelids are stopped up by a yellowish discharge.

I fancied that Mitis was playing in the box; I tumbled him over on his back, tickled his stomach, and stroked his head; he struck out his paws without attempting to pick himself up; this was evidently a more or less conscious attempt at play. His mother came to lick him in this attitude, and he performed with his fore-paws as previously. Riquet, too, shows a tendency to play, but not of such a pronounced nature.

21st May. – Riquet's left eye is beginning to open at the inside corner.

I took them both up on my hand, and waved my fingers in front of their partially opened eyes; but I did not observe any movement from which I could infer the power of distinguishing objects.

Mitis, placed close to his mother's head, nibbles at it and plays with his paws on her nose; the mother does not approve of this amusement; she lays a paw on her son's neck and teaches him respect; soon he escapes from her grasp, and begins searching for a teat.

Some streaks of fawn-colour have mixed with the zebra-like black and grey on Riquet's neck: he is now quadri-coloured.

Mitis is seated on my hand. I kiss him on the head, three times running, making a slight noise with my lips; he shakes his head twice. This is an habitual movement of the mother cat when one kisses or strokes her head and it displeases, or if she is occupied with something else.

When I pass my hand in front of their heads, at about four *centimètres* distance, they make a movement with the head and wink their eyes; I am not sure whether this means that they see, though their eyes have been more or less open since yesterday evening.

They have not yet begun to purr.

22nd May. – I went up to the box towards twelve o'clock. Riquet's left eye, the light blue colour of which I can see, seems to perceive me, but it must be very indistinctly. I wave my hand at ten *centimètres* from his eyes, and it is only the noise I make and the disturbance of the air that cause him to make any movement.

Both Mitis's eyes are almost entirely open; I hold my finger near his nose without touching it, I wave it from right to left and left to right, and I fancy I perceive in the eyes – in the eyes more than in the head – a slight tendency to move in the direction of my movements.

23rd May, 7pm – Their movements are less trembling, quicker, and fierce not only because of increased strength and exercise, but because intention, directed by eyesight, is beginning to operate

. . .

. . . I placed Mitis on a foot-warmer, the contact with which produced two or three nervous tremblings, somewhat similar to slight shiverings; he seemed pleased, however, and stretched himself out on the warm surface, with his eyes half-closed, as if going to sleep. Afterwards I placed Riquet there; he went through the same trembling movements, but then proceeded with an inspection with his muzzle – scenting or feeling, I do not know which, the article on which he had been deposited. He then gently stretched out a paw and laid himself down flat, the contact with the warm surface inducing sleep, by reason of the familiar associations between the like sensation of warmth experienced on his mother's breast and the instinctive need of sleep.

When they trot about in their box, some of their movements appear to be directed by sight.

Their ears have lengthened perceptibly during the last two days, and so have their tails.

When any one walks about the room, if they are not asleep or sucking, they begin frisking about immediately.

The mother, whom I sent to take a little exercise in the courtyard, has been absent for half an hour. Mitis is asleep; Riquet, lying with his head on his brother's neck, was awakened by the sound of my footsteps, all the more easily roused no doubt because he was hungry, and because his mother had been absent so long. I stroke his head with my finger, and he puts on a smiling look. I make a little noise with my lips to rouse the sparrow, and this noise pleases Riquet, who listens with the same smiling countenance.

They now attempt to climb higher; they do not knock their noses so frequently against the partitions of the box, they certainly direct their paws at certain points determined by their vision; eyes, noses, and paws now operate in concert on the teats or any other objects that come across their way; for they do not go much in search of objects as yet. Their field of vision does not stretch very far; what they see is matter of chance and accident rather than of real intention. If I wish to attract their attention by waving my hand, I must not hold it further than fifteen *centimètres* from their eyes. I must go very close to them before they appear to distinguish my person. I am not sure that they see the whole of it; I rather think that only certain portions are visible to them, –

amongst others my nose, because it stands out in relief, and my eyes, because they reflect the light vividly.

24th May, 9 pm – The orbits of their eyes seem to me rather more expanded than this morning, possibly because the light makes their pupils contract. I placed a candle on a chair by the side of their box; the light evidently annoyed them, but it stimulated them to exercise their limbs. Mitis, after having promenaded and struggled about in a corner of the box, and grown accustomed to the lively sensations on his retina, directs his steps towards the most brightly-lighted point of the box. A band of light falls full on the upper part of the partition on the side facing me. Mitis, and Riquet after him, – more from imitation than personal excitement, – tries to climb up this luminous board; he does not succeed, but the attraction continues undiminished. I thought involuntarily of the plants which struggle up walls to reach the light.

Mitis, still somewhat disconcerted – though much less so than at first – when he looks directly at light, retires into a corner, and tired, no doubt, with the exercise he has just been taking, places himself, or rather falls back, on his mother's tail. I take him up gently, and set him in front of his mother's stomach, and by the side of Riquet, who had just finished his gambols also, and was sucking. Then began a scuffle, the front paws working away perceptibly like the *battoirs* of a washerwoman. I come to the rescue, placing my hand between them, and this calms them down; they favour me, however, with a few ridiculous little taps. Mitis, meanwhile, has taken possession of the contested teat, and celebrates his victory by the first *purr* that to my knowledge he has produced.

Riquet is now in a great state of agitation; he is lying in the dark, behind his mother's back, and close to the side of the box facing me. I hold my finger to him; he lifts himself up and leans his head slowly forward to touch or scent my finger. He can now distinguish people, but more by touch, scent, or hearing than by sight, the latter sense being very imperfectly developed and little exercised. When I make a slight noise with my lips the little creature starts and jumps about, but does not lift up his eyes to my face, which he has seen close to him, has looked at with attention, but which he is very imperfectly acquainted with, and does not accurately localise with respect to my hand and my body.

Riquet is close to his mother's head. He has stretched a paw over her neck, and is looking at some part or other of her head, I don't know which, while playing gently with his little paw. Here we see an intelligent development of affection; he now leaves his mother in a more conscious way; his visual and tactile perceptions are becoming coordinated, are amplifying his knowledge, and giving strength and precision to his sentiments.

I stretch out my finger to Mitis, who is still lying on the spot where I found him at first. In return, either from curiosity, or from instinctive impulse and movement, he holds out his little paw, which seems to enjoy the grasp of my finger, and sticks to it.

25th May. – I place my kittens, one after the other, in the hollow of my hand. Mitis squealed when I lifted him out of the box, and during the three minutes that I kept them in my hand they both seemed almost indifferent. The instant, however, that I put them back in the box they seemed quite delighted to get back again, or else they were stimulated to play by the various sensations – muscular, visual, tactile, and thermal – which I had occasioned them. Standing and walking about on my hand had stimulated Mitis to an extraordinary display of strength. In his desire for prolonged exercise, and no doubt also wishing to renew the vivid sensations of light he had just experienced, he set to work to climb up the perpendicular wall of his dwelling, making all the time a great noise of scratching. All movement produces sensations; and all sensations produce movements.

26th May. – They both play with their paws and their muzzles, but frequently, as if by chance, only without very marked intention, and with very uncertain movements.

I seem already to distinguish in them two different characters. If one can go by appearances, Mitis will be gentle, patient, rather indolent and lazy, prudent and good-natured; Riquet, on the contrary, lively, petulant, irritable, playful, and audacious. Noise and contact seem to excite him more than his brother. But both of them are very affectionate towards their mother, or perhaps I should say very appreciative of the pleasure of being with her, of seeing, hearing, and touching her, and not only of sucking from her.

I hold Mitis up to the edge of the box; he evinces a desire to get back to his mother, but does not know how to manage it. His muscles have not yet acquired the habit of responding to this particular psycho-motive stimulus; he crawls up to where my hand ends, advances first one paw, then another, and finds only empty space; he then stretches out his neck, and two or three times running makes an attempt with his paws at the movements which are the precursors of the act of jumping. He would like to jump down, but cannot do so; instinctive intention is here in advance of the adaptiveness or the strength of the muscular apparatus fitted to execute it. He retreats frightened and discouraged, and whines for help.

Riquet placed in the same position, goes through almost the same movements, but he is able to do more; he has managed to seize hold (chance perhaps assisting him) of the edge of the box, he sticks to it, leans over without letting go, and would have got down, or rather tumbled down, into the box, if I had let him.

27th May. Every day they get to know me better. Now, after I have taken them in my hands, or stroked their head, neck, or lips, they go back to their box quite excited; they walk about in it faster than before, snap at each other and strike out their paws with much more spirit. Play has now become a matter of experience with them, and grows day by day a little more complicated; they seem to be aware of their growth in strength and skill, and to derive pleasure from it. Today, for the first time, Riquet scratched the piece of stuff on the bottom of the box, and he did it with playful gestures and an expression of delight; first he stretched out one paw, then the other, with his claws turned out, and, being pleased with the noise produced by drawing back his claws, he renewed the operation twice, but no more. It will be necessary to go through the same experience two or three times more, in order to fix the idea of this game in his little head.

They have already tried several times running (either by accident or with a vague idea of ascending) to hold on to, or climb up, the sides of the box; if they were not slippery, or were covered with a cloth, I think they would have strength enough to lift themselves up to the edge.

They lift their head and paws as high as they can, in order to see better. All the inside of the box seems to be sufficiently well known to them, but all the same they are constantly making experiments in it, either by touch, sight, hearing, scent, and even taste; for they frequently lick the board, and try to suck the cloth at the bottom. They would no doubt gladly extend the area of their experiences, but I shall leave them habitually in the box until they are able to get out of it by themselves; they can get quite enough exercise in it, and they have enough air and light, and I think the prolongation of this calm, happy, retired existence makes them more gentle. The mother prefers their being in the box, and I am of the same opinion, though not perhaps for the same reasons. They would become too independent if allowed to follow their caprices, and exposed to the dangers of adventure, instead of being accustomed to the restraint of the hand which they love and which *humanises* them. I want them to become so thoroughly accustomed to my hand, that, when they receive their freedom, they will still recognise it from a distance, and come to it at my will. My hand is a very precious instrument of preservation and education for them.

28th May. When, standing close to the box, I take Mitis in my hands, he looks at the box, bends his head, stretches out his paws, and shows a considerable desire to get down, but without making any effort towards this end. I hold him a little lower down, at a few *centimètres* from his mother and he no longer hesitates but lets himself glide down to her, his movements, however, only turning out a success thanks to my assistance. Can it be that he had (what Tiedemann does not even allow his fourteen-months-old child to have possessed) a vague perception of distance, of empty and inhabited space, anterior to personal experience? 'He had not yet any idea of the falling of bodies from a height, or of the difference between empty and inhabited space. On the 14th October he still wanted to precipitate himself from heights, and several times he let his biscuit fall to the ground when intending to dip it in his cup.'

The kittens endeavour to climb along the sides of the box, but their idea of height (perhaps an instinctive idea) is not sufficiently determined; they seem quite astounded at not reaching the goal with the first stroke. At the same time I may be mistaken in my observations; perhaps they went up these four or five *centimètres* mechanically, because in walking along horizontally they found under their paws the surface of the partition which may have seemed a natural continuation of their road. Perhaps they have no wish to get up to the edge of the box.

28th May. – The grey spots on Riquet's back are now almost as large as the black ones.

The eyes of both kittens are getting less and less blue; they are assuming an indistinct colour, between dirty grey and light brown. Their expression is frank and sympathetic; they seem to direct their looks consciously and voluntarily.

Riquet is looking at me with an expression of pleasure, seated upright, with his paws lifted languidly. I hold my finger near him, and he extends his left paw. I stroke the left side of his head, and he leans the part which I caress on my finger, as a full-grown cat would do, and rubs himself two or three times running against my finger. These are *invented* movements – I mean movements furnished all of a sudden by the stimulus of hereditary virtualities, and which seem to astonish the young animal as well as to please him; it is thus that we see automatic movements at one moment coming under the control of consciousness, and the next escaping from it, refined, simplified, adapted, and perfected. Life invents but few new movements; but there are many, no doubt, ready to appear if the influences of surroundings permitted it.

29th May. – They are learning more and more to exercise their muscles and perfect their movements; they are daily acquiring fresh powers and *adaptations*, and in their games with each other and their mother they show intention and pleasure; they are learning more and more to distinguish people; if any one presents a finger to them, they always hold out their nose, or else a paw; this seems to have become a reflex action with them. They also appear to localise certain sensations which are in some sort artificial. I touch the tip of Mitis' left paw, (he has been sucking, and instantly turns his head in the direction of his paw; but this is perhaps because he has seen my hand, and the muscular sensation associated with this visual sensation may have determined his movement alone and almost automatically. I vary the experiment, however, and pass my finger two or three times running across his neck; he raises his head and looks behind him, as if understanding where I had touched him. However this may be, I should not like to affirm in him the faculty of localisation of sensations, which would be the result of certain anterior *adaptations*.

The mother is engaged on the toilet of Mitis, who neither looks pleased or displeased; he makes a sound which is neither a cry of pain, or the whining of complaint or anger; if he is giving expression to a mental condition well defined to himself, I cannot guess at it. It is a tremulous noise which might be represented by the following letters: *m r r r i m r . . .*

2nd June. – Riquet's ears grow more than those of Mitis. The hair of the latter has ceased to grow, and his tail is scarcely more bushy than his brother's. He will not be more of an Angora than Riquet, in spite of the long silky hair, which during the first days grew so abundantly on his neck, stomach, and thighs.

Riquet has become more patient, and Mitis more lively during the last few days. It would be very presumptuous to pretend to found precise indications as to the futures on observations taken during the first days; hypothesis itself must maintain the most scrupulous reserve, especially as regards predictions concerning intelligence and character. A cat which appears very intelligent at the age of one or two months, often shows very mediocre intelligence when a year or two old, and *vice versâ*. As to the colour and nature of the hair, six weeks must have elapsed before one can give any certain opinion as to the real shade that it will be, and as to its flexibility, abundance, brilliancy, and waviness. As for the ears I have often erred in my predictions. . . . which are scarcely perceptible at birth; and during the first eight or ten days, will sometimes grow to a disproportionate length afterwards. With regard to the paws and the tail, half a *decimètre's* length at the moment of birth indicates undoubtedly an appreciable length later on. One can also determine on the first day the future firmness of the muscles and bones by the relative resistance of these little velvety lumps when held in the hand. A strong voice, which is more especially the appendage of male kittens, indicates at any rate good lungs.

Mitis, who is so gentle, has more flattened ears than Riquet; the latter's stand up more like those of foxes and wolves. The little complementary *pavilion* . . . which is attached to both edges of the ear, slightly towards the bottom, and which in man is designated by a slight rudimentary excrescence, is beginning to appear in both my kittens.

They are now well advanced in the art of play; they fence well with their paws, lick each other, and tumble and roll each other over. Riquet, who has some difficulty in standing upright on his legs, has attempted a jump. They try to bite each other at play, specially aiming at each other's paws. Often by mistake they seize their own paws with their teeth and gnaw at them; but they are not long in finding out their error.

I place them on the ground. They tremble, seem frightened, or rather astonished, or undecided, and make a few uncertain movements. One of them perceives the mother at a distance of about a *mètre*, looking at them from under a chair. He goes straight up to her, but very slowly, and with a great deal of waddling; all of a sudden he stops. He has heard his brother's voice, the latter having whined on my touching him to rouse him out of his persistent immovability; he turns his head in our direction, distinguishes me, turns straight round, and comes up to me with much greater rapidity and assurance than he has shown in going to his mother. The reason for this is, that the road to me was shorter and surer, and the stimulus to traverse it greater, owing to the larger proportions of my body. I place them back in the box, and they begin playing again with zest. The one who had only moved feebly on the floor, walks, and even jumps, much better this morning. This little outing seems to have stimulated him to an effort which he had not made before. In like manner we sometimes note progress in young children from day to day.

They can now climb up to the middle of the box.

A board, a few *centimètres* wide, is nailed to the top of the box, and covers about a fourth part of it. Mitis looks at it with longing eyes; he makes up his mind, draws himself up as erect as he can, stretches up his paws to the partition and within five *centimètres* of the upper plank; he is longing to make an upward leap, and finally he ventures on it; but his heavy abdomen and his weak legs play him false, and he rolls over ignominiously. In like manner a young child, not yet firm on his legs, leaving the support of the chair to venture a step alone, falls in a soft heap on the floor.

4th June. – They play more and more with my finger, bite at it and lick it. They seem to look at all objects more attentively, and more sympathetically at their mother and me.

When they are playing about under their mother, one sees only a confusion of white paws, pink noses, shining eyes, and whisking tails. I have put them on my bed. They walk much better there than in the box, and infinitely better than on the floor; they studied everything in this new locality, walking, climbing up and down, sliding and rolling about. Riquet, having reached the edge of the bed, would have fallen over if I had not held him back. His more circumspect brother, finding himself in the same situation, leant his head over for a moment, and then, as if defying a danger more or less realised, turned round and precipitated himself at the other side of the bed.

11th June. – They frisk and bound about, and catch at all objects indiscriminately with their claws to try and climb. They look into each other's eyes as if trying to discover the expression of sentiments and ideas. This may proceed from astonishment and curiosity, and the delight of the ever new impressions which the movement of the eyes cannot fail to produce in them. But must it not also be partly the result of an hereditary predisposition of their organisation, which leads them to seek in the eyes for the meaning which they express? We know that adult animals, as well as man, are endowed with this tendency which proceeds from instinct rather than individual experience.

Partly from imitation of their mother and sister, partly from the teaching of their instinct, they went off one day to a certain out-of-the-way spot, where was placed a pan full of ashes, the object of which does not require to be explained. Observing this, I carried them from time to time to this pan. The smell proceeding from it was in itself sufficient to excite them to satisfy their needs. Three or four such experiences sufficed to associate with the idea of this smell the idea of the pan, of the place where it was, and of the need to be satisfied. I do not say that this habit of cleanliness, so quickly acquired, may not as quickly be lost, by means of new associations taking the place of the first. There is no doubt, however, that if the people would make it a rule to watch over the formation of habits in cats during the first weeks (and probably also in other animals and in children), it would not afterwards be necessary to have recourse to a system of barbarous, and often useless measures, in order to obtain from them by violence that which nature will manage alone with but very slight assistance.

The shutters are closed on account of the extreme heat, so that the room is in semi-darkness, and all the objects in it steeped in mysterious shadow. Riquet, frisking about at a little distance from the box, sees a footstool at about a *mètre's* distance. This object, with its four feet and their shadows would easily produce in my mind the illusion of some mysterious animal. This, however, cannot be the case with the kitten, unless we suppose in it a mental confusion of the inanimate with the animate, that is to say, the animalisation of the inanimate. My opinion is that the surprise, and presently, too, the terror which Riquet manifests, and which keeps him transfixed to the spot, have their origin rather in a certain indeterminate tendency to fear in the presence of all sudden and unusual impressions. Such an apparition would have had no effect whatever on him a few days ago; but today it is so much out of harmony with his now numerous experiences, that it contradicts and jars against all his familiar habits. This is, in my mind, the sole cause of his terror. However, it may be, he draws himself up on his small paws, bristles his tail, humps up his back, and without either retreating or advancing, sways right and left in the same attitude. I make a movement; this noise brings his paroxysm of fear to a crisis, and he gives expression to it by a fretful *fû*; he then turns round and goes off as fast as his legs will carry him, the first way that comes, which happens to be to the side of the bed.

12th June. – They are attracted by the noise which I make in crumpling paper, in scratching the wall, or tapping a piece of furniture; but metallic sounds, if soft, do not have the same effect on them; the noise of objects being knocked, dull heavy sounds, or the noise of sharp voices, astonish them and make them prick up their ears, but not lift their paws. They take pleasure, however, in all the noises which they make themselves, provided they are not too reverberating, or caused by the displacement or fall of some large object. The loudest voice that I can put on pleases them almost as much as the little playful tones I generally address them in; they also delight in the strings of articulated consonants, which I repeat to them; but they do not like whistling, although they are not so much annoyed by it as is their mother, who comes up to me and rubs her head under my chin and over my mouth, and gives me little taps on my lips with her paw directly she hears me whistling. What specially delights them are the dry sounds which their claws make on wood, linen, paper, the straw seats of chairs, and the covering of the bed.

Mitis has drunk some milk this morning for the first time. I put the tip of my finger, moistened with this fluid, under his nose, and he licked it several times running. Enticed by the smell, he dipped his nose into a cup of milk, but did not know how to set about drinking; up came the mother and took his place, as if the milk was her rightful property. She generally tries to take away from her little ones anything fresh, when it is first given to them, perhaps out of maternal precaution, not thinking them strong enough to digest anything but her milk. As she laps in a great hurry, she always spills a certain quantity of milk round the saucer. I place Mitis in front of what had been spilled, and whether by chance, or because he was incited by the smell, he fell to licking and cleaned it all up. A quarter of an hour later he drank out of the cup, very awkwardly however, and very little, plunging his nose so far into the milk as to make him sneeze.

Riquet, to whom the same advances were made, licked the tip of my finger, but did not touch the milk in the cup. He is less strong than Mitis, and possibly less precocious in this respect.

When I came back into the room after an absence of even half an hour, the mother raises herself on her paws, as if moved by a spring, and her two satellites with her, – all at the same instant and with the same movement.

They still continue to be very fond of us, and not to be startled by strangers.

I have tried to make Riquet drink: I put his nose into the milk, and he then dipped his paw in himself and licked it, but would not lap. He went so far as to approach the cup with his nose and just touch it with his lips, but he then started off again.

He is now under the chimney, sniffing and then scratching the ashes, which, as his movements indicate, remind him of his ashpan. If I once or twice tolerated an infraction of my rule, the habits of cleanliness so easily formed in him would perhaps be hopelessly lost; this is why I hasten to carry him to his pan.

At 3 o'clock we repeated with Riquet the experiment which had failed in the morning; we smeared his nose with milk. He then licked it, and afterwards put his nose in the cup, and drank a good teaspoonful.

This morning they are more vigorous and nimble than yesterday, and they have been disporting themselves on my bed for more than an hour, whilst their mother and elder sister were engaged, by way of recreation, in snatching tufts of hair from each other's coats, in scratching and throttling each other. The mother gives a cry to indicate that this sport has reached its limits. Mitis has tumbled off the bed with affright, uttering a plaintive cry.

A ludicrous incident very nearly parted me from my two little pets. An old laundress, whose sight is very feeble, as well as her mind, shut them up in her bundle of linen, on which they had been playing whilst she was counting it. I gave them up for lost, having searched for them everywhere, even in my boots. Three hours later they were brought back to me safe and sound. This is what had happened: on opening the bundle, out walked a kitten (Mitis) who seemed very much surprised, he was put in a basket with a cup of milk beside him; the other was only found an hour later, to the great astonishment of the laundress, squatting under a cupboard and showing nothing but the tip of his nose. He refused all manner of consolation, and would not touch the milk, in spite of the example of Mitis who did not wait to be pressed.

As soon as they were safe back with me they both ate some bread soaked in milk.

The mother was very much dejected by their absence. When, after calling them in vain with her most caressing voice, and making pretence to play to entice them to come to her, she became convinced of their absence, she filled my rooms with agonised screams. She then begged to be let out to look for them in the courtyard, but soon came in again and began screaming and hunting about as before. She came up to me and got up on my knees, looked me fixedly in the eyes, and then curled herself up on the bed where the kittens often slept with her. Her eyes went beyond the expression of profound despair; her eyelids quivered, a slight moisture covered the eyeballs, and at the inside corners there was the appearance of tears. There is no doubt that cats cry.

I have several times noticed, but in a specially distinct manner today, on lifting them away from any place where they are comfortable, an instinctive, or perhaps intentional, tendency to lean either with the stomach or the paws, in order to remain fixed to the spot. An analogous movement may be noticed in young children, when one tries to take them out of the arms of some one they are fond of. I might no doubt have observed this fact in my kittens long ago.

I was holding Mitis in my hands, and I lifted him near to his mother and Riquet; he made a precipitate movement to get down to them, instinct urging him to spring – and that all the more since he is now stronger; – but his experience and his strength not sufficing to enable him to adapt his efforts to the distance he has to cross. Thus it is that falling from the bed often means in his case a bad attempt at jumping down. It is also possible that it is the example of his mother and big sister, as much as his increased strength, which suggests these somewhat impulsive bounds, which moreover belong to the organic habits of the species. The little unfledged bird also falls from its nest, when attempting a premature flight.

Nothing in the shape of food comes amiss to Riquet: soup, meat, potatoes, pease, lard – he snaps at, and devours whatever he comes across and whatever is offered him; but one must beware of the little glutton's sharp claws. Mitis takes his food more gently.

18th June. – Riquet is playing with me on the sofa. A sole is placed on the table. The smell of the fish excites and puzzles him, for he does not know whence it comes; he travels over me in all directions, trying to follow the scent, and is soon perched up on my left shoulder, which is tolerably close to the table; he works towards the table, and I stoop my shoulder to let him slide on to it. He rubs his nose first against a spoon and then against a glass; the plate containing the sole is only a *decimètre* from the glass, but as he does not know that a plate contains food, and that it is from there that the savoury smell proceeds, he does not direct his steps towards it. Finally, however, he finds himself in front of the plate, puts his four paws on it, and instantly disposes himself to eat the whole fish. I instantly carry him off. What a small number of experiencs he will need (two or three only I have determined) in order to adapt to actual practice these judgements and movements which unite instinctively with certain sensations! We call this *reasoning* in man, and, nevertheless, it closely resembles a piece of subjective mechanism, which is blind at starting, and which adapts itself to objective representations with such promptitude, that consciousness seems to follow, not to precede, its operations.

Whilst I was at my breakfast they climbed up my legs, and I had the weakness to let them stay for a moment on the table. They invaded my plate, Mitis going so far as to bite into the fish, and Riquet licking and gnawing the edge of the plate; the smell of the fish is so penetrating that he confuses it with the plate. Moreover, he has no idea of *containing* and being *contained*. Soon he comes across a mouthful of fish which I have prepared for him: he flattens himself out on the plate, and eats with courageous and deliberate precipitation, inclining his head now to the left, now to the right, sometimes closing his eyes from delight, but oftenest keeping them open and fixed attentively on the plate, – one would say he was afraid of losing his precious morsel; and here we see a result of the preservative instinct which he has received from his ancestors.

Mitis has got into a round earthen pan, and from association of impressions tries to satisfy a need which he would not otherwise have felt. The vessel, however, being small, and his movements causing it to totter, he jumped out and ran off to his own pan. *20th June.* – Mitis suddenly springs from the table to the floor, first feeling his mother with the end of his paw, and then passing over her without touching her: is it a personal or a social motive which makes him act thus? Does he wish to avoid walking on ground that is not firm, or is he trying not to her his mother? In like manner will a horse, on the point of trampling a live body, hastily withdraw his foot.

They have been playing for a long time on my bed; before I go to sleep I shall carry them to their own bedroom, to their mother who awaits them somewhat sadly. They came back into my room as soon as I did myself. I sit down in front of my table, they climb up along my legs, and I determine to place them back on my bed. Twenty minutes later I reinstate them a second time in their domicile, but they do not stay there two minutes. I had just got into bed again when back they come, spring at the bedcover, the chairs, the wall, with a noise of scratching and rustling which excites them to continue their difficult ascent; at the end of two minutes the siege is accomplished, and I am seized upon, trodden over, scratched and gnawed. I cannot be master in my own room except by shutting the door, at which, however, they come and scratch, but without much persistence.

So there they are, now pretty well masters of their movements, taking headers to get down from the bed to the chair, from the chair to the floor, climbing up along the curtains and the tapestry, and even attempting to climb the furniture and polished objects. A few more days and their mode of descending will be less like tumbling, their ascents less like scrambling: they will spring and they will bound, and will be real individual cats.

Hey Diddle Diddle

Hey diddle, diddle,
The cat and the fiddle,
The cow jumped over the moon;
The little dog laughed
To see such sport,
And the dish ran away with the spoon.

ANON

The Cat That Walked By Himself

Rudyard Kipling

Hear and attend and listen; for this befell and behappened and became and was, O my Best Beloved, when the Tame animals were wild. The Dog was wild, and the Horse was wild, and the Cow was wild, and the Sheep was wild, and the Pig was wild – as wild as wild could be – and they walked in the Wet Wild Woods by their wild lones. But the wildest of all the wild animals was the Cat. He walked by himself, and all places were alike to him.

Of course the Man was wild too. He was dreadfully wild. He didn't even begin to be tame till he met the Woman, and she told him that she did not like living in his wild ways. She picked out a nice dry Cave, instead of a heap of wet leaves, to lie down in; and she strewed clean sand on the floor; and she lit a nice fire of wood at the back of the Cave; and she hung a dried wild-horse skin, tail-down, across the opening of the Cave; and she said, 'Wipe your feet, dear, when you come in, and now we'll keep house.'

That night, Best Beloved, they ate wild sheep roasted on the hot stones, and flavoured with wild garlic and wild pepper; and wild duck stuffed with wild rice and wild fenugreek and wild coriander; and marrow-bones of wild oxen; and wild cherries, and wild grenadillas. Then the Man went to sleep in front of the fire ever so happy; but the Woman sat up, combing her hair. She took the bone of the shoulder of mutton – the big fat blade-bone – and she looked at the wonderful marks on it, and she threw more wood on the fire, and she made a Magic. She made the First Singing Magic in the world.

Out in the Wet Wild Woods all the wild animals gathered together where they could see the light of the fire a long way off, and they wondered what it meant.

Then Wild Horse stamped with his wild food and said, 'O my Friends and O my Enemies, why have the Man and the Woman made that great light in that great Cave, and what harm will it do us?'

Wild Dog lifted up his wild nose and smelled the smell of the roast mutton, and said 'I will go up and see and look, and say; for I think it is good. Cat, come with me.'

'Nenni!' said the Cat. 'I am the Cat who walks by himself, and all places are alike to me. I will not come.'

'Then we can never be friends again,' said Wild Dog, and he trotted off to the Cave. But when he had gone a little way the Cat said to himself, 'All places are alike to me. Why should I not go too and see and look and come away at my own liking?' So he slipped after Wild Dog softly, very softly, and hid himself where he could hear everything.

When Wild Dog reached the mouth of the Cave he lifted up the dried horse-skin with his nose and sniffed the beautiful smell of the roast mutton, and the Woman, looking at the blade-bone, heard him, and laughed, and said, 'Here comes the first. Wild Thing out of the Wild Woods, what do you want?'

Wild Dog said, 'O my Enemy and Wife of my Enemy, what is this that smells so good in the Wild Woods?'

Then the Woman picked up a roasted mutton-bone and threw it to Wild Dog, and said, 'Wild Thing out of the Wild Woods, taste and try.' Wild Dog gnawed the bone, and it was more delicious than anything he had ever tasted, and he said, 'O my Enemy and Wife of my Enemy, give me another.'

The Woman said, 'Wild Thing out of the Wild Woods, help my Man to hunt through the day and guard this Cave at night, and I will give you as many roast bones as you need.'

'Ah!' said the Cat, listening. 'This is a very wise Woman, but she is not so wise as I am.'

Wild Dog crawled into the Cave and laid his head on the Woman's lap, and said, 'O my Friend and Wife of my Friend, I will help your Man to hunt through the day, and at night I will guard your Cave.'

'Ah!' said the Cat, listening. 'That is a very foolish Dog.' And he went back through the Wet Wild Woods waving his wild tail, and walking by his wild lone. But he never told anybody.

When the Man waked up he said, 'What is Wild Dog doing here?' And the Woman said, 'His name is not Wild Dog any more, but the First Friend, because he will be our friend for always and always and always. Take him with you when you go hunting.'

Next night the Woman cut great green armfuls of fresh grass from the water-meadows, and dried it before the fire, so that it smelt like new-mown hay, and she sat at the mouth of the Cave and plaited a halter out of horse-hide, and she looked at the shoulder-of-mutton bone – at the big broad blade-bone – and she made a Magic. She made the Second Singing Magic in the world.

Out in the Wild Woods all the animals wondered what had happened to Wild Dog, and at last Wild Horse stamped with his foot and said, 'I will go and see and say why Wild Dog has not returned. Cat, come with me.'

'Nenni!' said the Cat. 'I am the Cat who walks by himself, and all places are alike to me. I will not come.' But all the same he followed Wild Horse softly, very softly, and hid himself where he could hear everything.

When the Woman heard Wild Horse tripping and stumbling on his long mane, she laughed and said, 'Here comes the second. Wild Thing out of the Wild Woods, what do you want?'

Wild Horse said, 'O my Enemy and Wife of my Enemy, where is Wild Dog?'

The Woman laughed, and picked up the blade-bone and looked at it, and said, 'Wild Thing out of the Wild Woods, you did not come here for Wild Dog, but for the sake of this good grass.'

And Wild Horse, tripping and stumbling on his long mane, said, 'That is true; give it to me to eat.'

The Woman said, 'Wild Thing out of the Wild Woods, bend your wild head and wear what I give you, and you shall eat the wonderful grass three times a day.'

'Ah!' said the Cat, listening. This is a clever Woman, but she is not so clever as I am.'

Wild Horse bent his wild head, and the Woman slipped the plaited-hide halter over it, and Wild Horse breathed on the Woman's feet and said, 'O my Mistress, and Wife of my Master, I will be your servant for the sake of the wonderful grass.'

'Ah!' said the Cat, listening. 'That is a very foolish Horse.' And he went back through the Wet Wild Woods, waving his wild tail and walking by his wild lone. But he never told anybody.

When the Man and the Dog came back from hunting, the Man said, 'What is Wild Horse doing here?' And the Woman said, 'His name is not Wild Horse any more, but the First Servant, because he will carry us from place to place for always and always and always. Ride on his back when you go hunting.

Next day, holding her wild head high that her wild horn should not catch in the wild trees, Wild Cow came up to the Cave, and the Cat followed, and hid himself just the same as before, and everything happened just the same as before; and the Cat said the same things as before; and when Wild Cow had promised to give her milk to the Woman every day in exchange for the wonderful grass, the Cat went back through the Wet Wild Woods waving his wild tail and walking by his wild lone, just the same as before. But he never told anybody. And when the Man and the Horse and the Dog came home from hunting and asked the same questions same as before, the Woman said, 'Her name is not Wild Cow any more, but the Giver of Good Food. She will give us the warm white milk for always and always and always, and I will take care of her while you and the First Friend and the First Servant go hunting.'

Next day the Cat waited to see if any other Wild Thing would go up to the Cave, but no one moved in the Wet Wild Woods, so the Cat walked there by himself; and he saw the Woman milking the cow, and he saw the light of the fire in the Cave, and he smelt the smell of the warm white milk.

Cat said, 'O my Enemy and Wife of my Enemy, where did Wild Cow go?'

The Woman laughed and said, 'Wild Thing out of the Wild Woods, go back to the Woods again, for I have braided my hair, and I have put away the magic blade-bone, and we have no more need of either friends or servants in our Cave.'

Cat said, 'I am not a friend, and I am not a servant. I am the Cat who walks by himself, and I wish to come into your Cave.'

Woman said, 'Then why did you not come with First Friend on the first night?'

Cat grew very angry and said, 'Has Wild Dog told tales of me?'

Then the Woman laughed and said, 'You are the Cat who walks by himself, and all places are alike to you. You are neither a friend nor a servant. You have said it yourself. Go away and walk by yourself in all places alike.'

Then Cat pretended to be sorry and said, 'Must I never come into the Cave?' Must I never sit by the warm fire? Must I never drink the warm white milk? You are very wise and very beautiful. You should not be cruel even to a Cat.'

Woman said. 'I knew I was wise, but I did not know I was beautiful. So I will make a bargain with you. If ever I say one word in your praise, you may come into the Cave.'

'And if you say two words in my praise?' said the Cat.

'I never shall,' said the Woman, 'but if I say two words in your praise, you may sit by the fire in the Cave.'

'And if you say three words?' said the Cat.

'I never shall,' said the Woman, 'but if I say three words in your praise, you may drink the warm white milk three times a day for always and always and always.'

Then the Cat arched his back and said, 'Now let the curtain at the mouth of the Cave, and the Fire at the back of the Cave, and the Milk-pots that stand beside the Fire, remember what my Enemy and the Wife of my Enemy has said.' And he went away through the Wet Wild Woods waving his wild tail and walking by his wild lone.

That night when the Man and the Horse and the Dog came home from hunting, the Woman did not tell of the bargain that she had made with Cat, because she was afraid that they might not like it.

Cat went far and far away and hid himself in the Wet Wild Woods by his wild lone for a long time till the Woman forgot all about him. Only the Bat – the little upside-down Bat that hung inside the Cave knew where Cat hid; and every evening Bat would fly to Cat with news of what was happening.

One evening Bat said, 'There is a Baby in the Cave. He is new and pink and fat and small, and the Woman is very fond of him.'

'Ah,' said the Cat, listening. 'But what is the Baby fond of?'

'He is fond of things that are soft and tickle,' said the Bat. 'He is fond of warm things to hold in his arms when he goes to sleep. He is fond of being played with. He is fond of all those things.'

'Ah,' said the Cat, listening. 'Then my time has come.'

Next night Cat walked through the Wet Wild Woods and hid very near the Cave till morning-time, and Man and Dog and Horse went hunting. The Woman was busy cooking that morning, and the Baby cried and interrupted. So she carried him outside the Cave and gave him a handful of pebbles to play with. But still the Baby cried.

Then the Cat put out his paddy paw and patted the baby on the cheek, and it cooed; and the Cat rubbed against its fat knees and tickled it under its fat chin with his tail. And the Baby laughed; and the Woman heard him and smiled.

Then the Bat – the little upside-down Bat – that hung in the mouth of the Cave said, 'O my Hostess and Wife of my Host and Mother of my Host's Son, a Wild Thing from the Wild Woods is most beautifully playing with your Baby.'

'A blessing on that Wild Thing whoever he may be,' said the Woman, straightening her back, 'for I was a busy woman this morning and he has done me a service.'

That very minute and second, Best Beloved, the dried horse-skin Curtain that was stretched tail-down at the mouth of the Cave fell down – *whoosh!* – because it remembered the bargain she had made with the Cat; and when the Woman went to pick it up – lo and behold! the Cat was sitting quite comfy inside the Cave.

'O my Enemy and Wife of My Enemy and Mother of my Enemy,' said the Cat, 'it is I: for you have spoken a word in my praise, and now I can sit within the Cave for always and always and always. But still I am the Cat who walks by himself, and all places are alike to me.'

The Woman was very angry, and shut her lips tight and took up her spinning-wheel and began to spin.

But the Baby cried because the Cat had gone away, and the Woman could not hush it, for it struggled and kicked and grew black in the face.

'O my Enemy and Wife of my Enemy and Mother of my Enemy,' said the Cat, 'take a strand of the thread that you are spinning and tie it to your spindle-whorl and drag it along the floor, and I will show you a Magic that shall make your Baby laugh as loudly as he is now crying.'

'I will do so,' said the Woman, 'because I am at my wits' end;

but I will not thank you for it.'

She tied the thread to the little clay spindle-whorl and drew it across the floor, and the Cat ran after it and patted it with his paws and rolled head over heels, and tossed it backwards over his shoulder and chased it between his hind legs and pretended to lose it, and pounced down upon it again, till the Baby laughed as loudly as it had been crying, and scrambled after the Cat and frolicked all over the Cave till it grew tired and settled down to sleep with the Cat in its arms.

'Now,' said Cat, 'I will sing the Baby a song that shall keep him asleep for an hour.' And he began to purr, loud and low, low and loud, till the Baby fell fast asleep. The Woman smiled as she looked down upon the two of them, and said, 'That was wonderfully done. No question but you are very clever, O Cat.'

That very minute and second, Best Beloved, the smoke of the Fire at the back of the Cave came down in clouds from the roof – *puff!* – because it remembered the bargain she had made with the Cat; and when it had cleared away – lo and behold! – the Cat was sitting quite comfy close to the fire.

'O my Enemy and Wife of my Enemy and Mother of my Enemy,' said the Cat, 'it is I: for you have spoken a second word in my praise, and now I can sit by the warm fire at the back of the Cave for always and always and always. But still I am the Cat who walks by himself, and all places are alike to me.'

'Then the Woman was very, very angry, and let down her hair and put more wood on the fire and brought out the broad bladebone of the shoulder of mutton and began to make a Magic that should prevent her from saying a third word in praise of the Cat. It was not a Singing Magic, Best Beloved, it was a Still Magic; and by and by the Cave grew so still that a little wee-wee mouse crept out of a corner and ran across the floor.

'O my Enemy and Wife of my Enemy and Mother of my Enemy,' said the Cat, 'is that mouse part of your Magic?'

'Ouh! Chee! No indeed! said the Woman, and she dropped the blade-bone and jumped upon the footstool in front of the fire and braided up her hair very quick for fear that the mouse should run up it.

'Ah,' said the Cat, watching, 'Then the mouse will do me no harm if I eat it?'

'No,' said the Woman, braiding up her hair, 'eat it quickly and I will ever be grateful to you.'

Cat made one jump and caught the little mouse, and the Woman said, 'A hundred thanks. Even the First Friend is not quick enough to catch little mice as you have done. You must be very wise.'

That very minute and second, O Best Beloved, the Milk-pot that stood by the fire cracked in two pieces – *ffft!* – because it re-membered the bargain she had made with the Cat; and when the Woman jumped down from the footstool – lo and behold! – the Cat was lapping up the warm white milk that lay in one of the broken pieces.

'O my Enemy and Wife of my Enemy and Mother of my Enemy,' said the Cat, 'it is I: for you have spoken three words in my praise, and now I can drink the warm white milk three times a day for always and always and always.But *still* I am the Cat who walks by himself, and all places are alike to me.'

Then the Woman laughed and set the Cat a bowl of the warm white milk and said, 'O Cat, you are as clever as a man, but re-member that your bargain was not made with the Man or the Dog, and I do not know what they will do when they come home.'

'What is that to me?' said the Cat. 'If I have my place in the Cave by the fire and my warm white milk three times a day I do not care what the Man or the Dog can do.'

That evening when the Man and the Dog came into the Cave, the Woman told them all the story of the bargain, while the Cat sat by the fire and smiled. Then the Man said, 'Yes, but he has not made a bargain with *me* or with all proper Men after me.' Then he took of his two leather boots and he took up his little stone axe (that makes three) and he fetched a piece of wood and a hatchet (that is five altogether), and he set them out in a row and he said, 'Now we will make *our* bargain. If you do not catch mice when you are in the Cave for always and always and always, I will throw these five things at you whenever I see you, and so shall all proper Men do after me.'

'Ah!' said the Woman, listening. 'This is a very clever Cat, but he is not so clever as my Man.'

The Cat counted the five things (and they looked very knobby) and he said, 'I will catch mice when I am in the Cave for always and always and always; but *still* I am the Cat who walks by himself, and all places are alike to me.'

'Not when I am near,' said the Man. 'If you had not said that last I would have put all these things away for always and always and always; but now I am going to throw my two boots and my little stone axe (that makes three) at you whenever I meet you. And so shall all proper Men do after me!'

Then the Dog said, 'Wait a minute. He has not made a bargain with *me* or with all proper Dogs after me.' And he showed his teeth and said, ' If you are not kind to the Baby while I am in the Cave for always and always and always, I will hunt you till I catch you, and when I catch you I will bite you. And so shall all proper Dogs do after me.'

'Ah!' said the Woman listening. 'This is a very clever Cat, but he is not so clever as the Dog.

Cat counted the Dog's teeth (and they looked very pointed) and he said, 'I will be kind to the Baby while I am in the Cave, as long as he does not pull my tail too hard, for always and always and always. But *still* I am the Cat who walks by himself, and all places are alike to me.'

'Not when I am near,' said the Dog. 'If you had not said that last I would have shut my mouth for always and always and always; but *now* I am going to hunt you up a tree whenever I meet you. And so shall all proper Dogs do after me.'

Then the Man threw this two boots and his little stone axe (that makes three) at the Cat, and the Cat ran out of the Cave and the Dog chased him up a tree; and from that day to this, Best Beloved, three proper Men out of five will always throw things at a Cat whenever they meet him, and all proper Dogs will chase him up a tree. But the Cat keeps his side of the bargain too. He will kill mice, and he will be kind to Babies when he is in the house, just as long as they do not pull his tail too hard. But when he has done that, and between times, and when the moon gets up and night comes, he is the Cat that walks by himself, and all places are alike to him. Then he goes out to the Wet Wild Woods or up the Wet Wild Trees or on the Wet Wild Roofs, waving his wild tail and walking by his wild lone.

The Cat and the Robin

She sights a bird, she chuckles,
She flattens, then she crawls,
She runs without the look of feet,
Her eyes increase to balls.

Her jaws stir, twitching, hungry,
Her teeth can hardly stand,
She leaps – but robin leaps the first!
Ah, pussy of the sand

The hopes so juicy ripening
You almost bathed your tongue
When bliss disclosed a hundred wings
And fled with every one!

EMILY DICKINSON

The Undoing of Morning Glory Adolphus

N. Margaret Campbell

Morning Glory Adolphus is our oldest and most sedate cat. He has his own hunting preserves in a wooded ravine at the back of our house, and woe to the cat or dog who invades it. In his early youth he won an enviable reputation as a hunter of big game, and he had his own method of securing due recognition for his exploits. Whenever he captures a rabbit, a squirrel, a water-rat, or a snake, he hunts until he finds his mistress and lays the tribute proudly at her feet. This determination to be cited for bravery and prowess becomes a trifle embarrassing at times, especially when he drags a five-foot snake into the music-room and lets it wriggle on the rug to the horror and confusion of guests. But whatever the hazards, Adolphus is not to be thwarted of due publicity for his skill. If he were a man, he would be accompanied on all of his hunting-trips by a press-agent, and would have luncheon with the editors of all the sporting journals upon his return. As it is, without even a correspondence course in advertising, Adolphus manages quite well.

For the study of majestic dignity, tinged on occasions with lofty disdain, interpreters of muscular expression would do well to seek out Adolphus. He walks the highway without haste or concern for his personal survival in the midst of tooting automobiles and charging dogs. When a strange dog appears and mistakes Adolphus for an ordinary cat who may be chased for the sport of the thing, it is the custom of Adolphus to slow his pace somewhat and stretch out in the path of the oncoming enemy, assuming the pose and the expression of the sphinx. He is the graven image of repose and perfect muscular control. Only his slumbrous amber eyes burn unblinkingly, never leaving the enraged countenance of his enemy, who bears down upon him with exposed fangs and hackles erect. When the assault is too ferocious to be in good taste even among dogs, accompanied by hysterical yapping and snapping, Adolphus has been known to yawn in the face of his assailant, quite deliberately and very politely, as a gentleman of good breeding might when bored by an excessive display of emotion. Usually the dog mysteriously halts within a foot or so of those calm yellow eyes and describes a semi-circle within the range of those twin fires, filling the air with defiant taunts that gradually die away to foolish whimpering as he begins an undignified withdrawal, while Adolphus winks solemnly and stares past his cowering foe into a mysterious space undesecrated by blustering dogs.

A few dogs there have been who have failed to halt at the hypnotic command of those yellow eyes. Then there came a lightning-flash of fur through the air, and Adolphus landed neatly on his victim's neck, his great claws beginning to rip with businesslike precision through the soft ears and forehead of the terrified dog. Perhaps the rumour of these encounters spread among the canine population of our neighbourhood, for it is never counted against the reputation of any dog as a fighter if he makes a wide detour of the regions frequented by Adolphus.

For years the rule of Adolphus among the cats of his own household had been undisputed. Then came Silver Paws, a handsome young rogue whose satiny coat was beautiful with broken silver and blue lights. There was no question about it, Silver Paws had a way with the ladies. While Adolphus still looked upon him as a frolicsome kitten whose sense of humour was unbalanced by a proper sense of dignity, he artfully won all hearts and easily became the centre of attraction wherever he appeared. It was plainly disgusting to Adolphus to see the way the conceited young thing arched his back expectantly whenever a human hand came near enough to caress him.

If Adolphus had had the small mind of a punster, he might have observed, after the cynical manner of others who have lost their place in the public affections to an unworthy rival, that the glory was passing out of his name. But he was never one to surrender without a struggle. He went to his nightly hunt with cold murder in his heart and a high resolve to force the spotlight back upon himself. Daily he laid at the feet of his mistress older and wilder rabbits, fierce-eyed rats, and longer snakes. All to no purpose. He even played the heroic role of the deliverer when his hated rival was treed by the grocer's dog. He simply walked calmly up to the tree where the dog was dancing wildly under the limb where the trembling Silver Paws clung, and the dog suddenly remembered that he really ought to catch up to the grocer's wagon and it wasn't much fun to bark at a silly kitten, anyway! When the frightened Silver Paws slid down the tree, Adolphus walked up to him with the self-righteous air of a benevolent gentleman who has rescued a lost soul not because the soul deserved it, but because he himself was made that way. This magnanimous act gave Adolphus a momentary advantage over his rival, but the fickle attentions of the household were soon centred upon the handsome young charmer again. Then Adolphus took to sitting about the house, gazing solemnly past the spot where Silver Paws was receiving the choicest bits of meat with many endearing words, and smoothing his whiskers with a reflective paw.

It was about this time that Silver Paws, to the consternation of the household, disappeared. A search was instituted in the neighbourhood, but he was gone without a trace, just as though he had been whisked away on a magic broom. Mournfully we gathered up the playthings he had left scattered over the house – a bit of fur on a string, a bright-coloured ball, some dried beans that rattled in the pod when batted about by a velvet paw – and of these remembrances we made a heap in his favourite rocking-chair. 'He'll want them if he ever comes back,' we said.

A remarkable change had come over Morning Glory Adolphus. We had long honoured him as a craft hunter and first rate fighting-man, but we had judged him to be somewhat lacking in sentiment, a trifle indifferent and unresponsive, as was natural enough in one who had achieved no small amount of fame. What was our astonishment to find that he had become, overnight, warmly demonstrative in his affections and sympathetically desirous of turning our thoughts from useless brooding over the lost one. It was really touching to see the way he followed us about the house, sitting at our feet to sing with rapturous abandon wherever we happened to pause. Forgotten were the joys of the chase, the pleasant pastime of disciplining unmannerly dogs. For three whole days he gave himself up wholly to the business of love-making. If we attempted to ignore him, he threw himself at our feet and lay on his back at our mercy, as one who would say that he bared his faithful heart that we might kill him if we could not love him. He walked about the house with the proudly possessive air of a haughty ruler who has returned to his domains after an enforced absence, and he curled up blissfully on the cushions where his late rival had been accustomed to take his ease. Once we found him stretched contemptuously over the playthings that lay in a little heap in the rocking-chair. It must have been a bumpy sort of bed, but Adolphus looked happy and comfortable.

Suspicion instantly seized upon his mistress. 'Adolphus,' she said sternly, 'I believe you know what has become of our beautiful Silver Paws!' The accused rose stiffly to his full height, regarded her with the gravely innocent expression of an outraged deacon, and then, turning his back deliberately upon her, gave himself up again to the slumbers of the just.

But the suspicions of the household were not laid. 'Adolphus is trying too hard to be good,' they argued. 'It is not natural. There must be something on his conscience!' For this was Adolphus's way of raising a smoke-screen, as it were, to hide his evil deeds. They had observed this in the past. It was all very humiliating to a proud soul like Adolphus, and he showed his resentment by stalking out of the house and letting the screen-door slam behind him after the manner of any offended male.

The household followed him from afar. He walked straight to the ravine, where he was accustomed to hunt, and stood peering intently down into it over the edge of a cliff, his ears pricked forward, every line of him expressing gloating satisfaction, from his agitated whiskers to the top of his quivering tail. It was hard to believe that he was the same kindly creature who had been making affectionate advances to us a few hours before. As we drew near we could hear a faint crying, pleading and pitiful, and down among the bushes we discovered our lost Silver Paws, too weak from loss of food to stand, and rather battered from the rough treatment he had received from his jailor.

The moment that Adolphus saw us looking into the ravine he withdrew in disgust, for he knew that his game was up. With lofty scorn he watched us gather up his banished rival, revive him with warm milk, caress and comfort him. With what dire threats had Adolphus kept his captive down in the ravine, within sound of our voices, all the long hours while he wooed us at his leisure, and what spell had he cast over him that the hungry kitten had not dared to come at our call?

While we rejoiced and scolded, the grocer's dog was observed coming round the corner of the house. He had grown bold during those days of weakness when Adolphus had been courting the ladies. But one look into the amber eyes of Adolphus, and he was off with a shriek, for he could see that the fighter was once more the master of his emotions.

The Boy Who Drew Cats

Ambrose Bierce

A long, long time ago, in a small country village in Japan, there lived a poor farmer and his wife, who were very good people. They had a number of children, and found it very hard to feed them all. The elder son was strong enough when only fourteen years old to help his father; and the little girls learned to help their mother almost as soon as they could walk.

But the youngest child, a little boy, did not seem to be fit for hard work. He was very clever, – cleverer than all his brothers and sisters; but he was quite weak and small, and people said he could never grow very big. So his parents thought it would be better for him to become a priest than to become a farmer. They took him with them to the village temple one day, and asked the good old priest who lived there, if he would have their little boy for his acolyte, and teach him all that a priest ought to know.

The old man spoke kindly to the lad, and asked him some hard questions. So clever were the answers that the priest agreed to take the little fellow into the temple as an acolyte, and to educate him for the priesthood.

The boy learned quickly what the old priest told him, and was very obedient in most things. But he had one fault. He liked to draw cats during study hours, and to draw cats even where cats ought not to have been drawn at all.

Whenever he found himself alone, he drew cats. He drew them on the margins of the priest's books, and on all the screens of the temple, and on the walls, and on the pillars. Several times the priest told him this was not right; but he did not stop drawing cats. He drew them because he could not really help it. He had what is called 'the genius of an *artist*,' and just for that reason he was not quite fit to be an acolyte; – a good acolyte should study books.

One day after he had drawn some very clever pictures of cats upon a paper screen, the old priest said to him severely: 'My boy, you must go away from this temple at once. You will never make a good priest, but perhaps you will become a great artist. Now let me give you a last piece of advice, and be sure you never forget it. *Avoid large places at night; – keep to small!*'

The boy did not know what the priest meant by saying, '*Avoid large places; – keep to small.*' He thought and thought, while he was tying up his little bundle of clothes to go away; but he could not understand those words, and he was afraid to speak to the priest any more, except to say goodbye.

He left the temple very sorrowfully, and began to wonder what he should do. If he went straight home he felt sure his father would punish him for having been disobedient to the priest: so he was afraid to go home. All at once he remembered that at the next village, twelve miles away, there was a very big temple. He had heard there were several priests at that temple; and he made up his mind to go to them and ask them to take him for their acolyte.

Now that big temple was closed up, but the boy did not know this fact. The reason it had been closed up was that a goblin had frightened the priests away, and had taken possession of the place. Some brave warriors had afterwards gone to the temple at night to kill the goblin; but they had never been seen alive again. Nobody had ever told these things to the boy; – so he walked all the way to the villge hoping to be kindly treated by the priests.

When he got to the village it was already dark, and all the people were in bed; but he saw the big temple on a hill at the other end of the principal street, and he saw there was a light in the temple. People who tell the story say the goblin used to make that light, in order to tempt lonely travellers to ask for shelter. The boy went at once to the temple, and knocked. There was no sound inside. He knocked and knocked again; but still nobody came. At last he pushed gently at the door, and was quite glad to find that it had not been fastened. So he went in, and saw a lamp burning, – but no priest.

He thought some priest would be sure to come very soon, and

he sat down and waited. Then he noticed that everything in the temple was grey with dust, and thickly spun over with cobwebs. So he thought to himself that the priests would certainly like to have an acolyte, to keep the place clean. He wondered why they had allowed everything to get so dusty. What most pleased him, however, were some big white screens, good to paint cats upon. Though he was tired, he looked at once for a writing box, and found one, and ground some ink, and began to paint cats.

He painted a great many cats upon the screens; and then he began to feel very, very sleepy. He was just on the point of lying down to sleep beside one of the screens, when he suddenly remembered the words, *'Avoid large places; – keep to small!'*

The temple was very large; he was all alone; and as he thought of these words, – though he could not quite understand them – he began to feel for the first time a little afraid; and he resolved to look for a *small place* in which to sleep. He found a little cabinet, with a sliding door, and went into it, and shut himself up. Then he lay down and fell fast asleep.

Very late in the night he was awakened by a most terrible noise, – a noise of fighting and screaming. It was so dreadful that he was afraid even to look through a chink of the little cabinet: he lay very still, holding his breath for fright.

The light that had been in the temple went out; but the awful sounds continued, and became more awful, and all the temple shook. After a long time silence came; but the boy was still afraid to move. He did not move until the light of the morning sun shone into the cabinet through the chinks of the little door.

Then he got out of his hiding-place very cautiously, and looked about. The first thing he saw was that all the floor of the temple was covered with blood. And then he saw, lying dead in the middle of it, an enormous, monstrous rat, – a goblin-rat, – bigger than a cow!

But who or what could have killed it? There was no man or other creature to be seen. Suddenly the boy observed that the mouths of all the cats he had drawn the night before, were red and wet with blood. Then he knew that the goblin had been killed by the cats which he had drawn. And then also, for the first time, he understood why the wise old priest had said to him, *'Avoid large places at night' – keep to small.'*

Afterwards that boy became a famous artist. Some of the cats which he drew are still shown to travellers in Japan.

The Cat Painter

Anon, from The Penny Magazine, 1834

The subject of this paper, Gottfried Mind, was a very remarkable man, with one pursuit – almost with only one idea. In the exercise of the one talent which he possessed, he was highly distinguished. In most other things, his power was not superior to that of ordinary men; in many respects, it was inferior. He was a painter of cats; and, with the exception of bears, which he occasionally delineated, he appeared to think that all other subjects, however beautiful, were unworthy of his notice. The following account is drawn from the *Biographie Universelle* and the *Biographie des Contemporains*.

This remarkable person was born at Berne, in Switzerland, in the year 1768. His father, who survived him, was a native of Hungary, but had settled at Berne, where he exercised the trade of a joiner. As Gottfried manifested a taste for drawing, his father placed him with Frudenberger, a clever artist; but who, neglecting or not perceiving Mind's talent for design, employed him in colouring his *Sketches of Helvetic Customs*. For several years after the death of his master, he remained with the widow; and appeared to have been kept so constantly to his work that, if he possessed the inclination, so little time was allowed him for the cultivation of his mind, that he was scarcely able to write his own name. Nevertheless, he sometimes contrived to steal a few moments from his manual labour to design children in their gambols and disputes; and he soon learned to group his figures very successfully, in the manner of Frudenberger. We are not informed how his attention was first directed to the study of bears and cats, to which he became devoted with remarkable exclusiveness, earnestness, and zeal, without which the most gifted can seldom attain the objects they pursue. The truth and excellence with which Mind represented these two species of animals were without precedent; and his drawings of cats, especially, were so admirable as to entitle him to the honourable, but rather awkward, title of 'the Raphael of Cats,' by which he was distinguished. No painter before him had ever succeeded in representing, with so much of nature and spirit, the mingled humility and fierceness, suavity and cunning, which the appearance of this animal presents, or the grace of its various postures in action or repose. Kittens he particularly delighted to represent. He varied, to infinity, their fine attitudes whilst at play around the mother; and represented their gambols with inimitable effect. Each of his cats, too, had an individual character and expression, and was, in fact, a portrait, which seemed animated: the very fur appeared so soft and silky as to tempt a caressing stroke from the spectator. In time, the merit of Mind's performance came to be so well understood that travellers made it a point to visit him, and to obtain, if possible, his drawings, which even sovereigns sought for, and amateurs treasured carefully in their portfolios. But it does not appear that popularity had any effect on him, either for good or evil, or in any degree modified his simple tastes and habits of life. His attachment was unbounded to the living animals he delighted to represent. Mind and his cats were inseparable. Minette, his favourite cat, was always near him when at work; and he seemed to carry on a sort of conversation with her by gestures and by words. Sometimes this cat occupied his lap, while two or three kittens were perched on each shoulder, or reposed in the hollow formed at the back of his neck, while sitting in a stooping posture at his table. Mind would remain for hours together in this posture without stirring, for fear of disturbing the beloved companions of his solitude, whose complacent purring seemed to him an ample compensation for the inconvenience. Not at any time what is called a good-humoured man, he was particularly surly if disturbed by visitors when thus situated.

Symptoms of madness having been manifested among the cats of Berne in the year 1809, the magistrates gave orders for their destruction. Mind exhibited the greatest distress when he heard of this cruel mandate. He cherished his dear Minette in secret; but

his sorrow for the death of 800 cats immolated to the public safety
was inexpressible, nor was he ever completely consoled . . . he
amused the long evenings of the ensuing winter in cutting chestnuts into the miniature figures of bears and cats. These fine trifles
were executed with such astonishing address, that, notwithstanding his dexterity, he was unable to supply the demand for
them. But, being mostly employed as ornaments for the mantelpiece, they were soon attacked by worms, and there is scarcely
reason to expect that any specimens of Mind's talents in this line
now exist.

The Cat's Pilgrimage

James Anthony Froude

'It is all very fine,' said the Cat, yawning, and stretching herself against the fender, 'but it is rather a bore; I don't see the use of it.' She raised herself, and arranging her tail into a ring, and seating herself in the middle of it, with her forepaws in a straight line from her shoulders, at right angles to the hearth rug, she looked pensively at the fire. 'It is very odd,' she went on: 'there is my poor Tom; he is gone. I saw him stretched out in the yard. I spoke to him, and he took no notice of me. He won't, I suppose, ever any more, for they put him under the earth. Nice fellow he was. It is wonderful how little one cares about it. So many jolly evenings we spent together; and now I seem to get on quite as well without him. I wonder what has become of him; and my last children, too, what has become of them? What are we here for? I would ask the men, only they are so conceited and stupid they can't understand what we say. I hear them droning away, teaching their little ones every day; telling them to be good, and to do what they are bid, and all that. Nobody ever tells me to do any thing; if they do I don't do it, and I am very good. I wonder whether I should be any better if I minded more. I'll ask the Dog.'

'Dog,' said she, to a little fat spaniel coiled up on a mat like a lady's muff with a head and tail stuck on to it, 'Dog, what do you make of it all?'

The Dog faintly opened his languid eyes, looked sleepily at the Cat for a moment, and dropped them again.

'Dog,' she said, 'I want to talk to you; don't go to sleep. Can't you answer a civil question?'

'Don't bother me,' said the Dog, 'I am tired. I stood on my hind legs ten minutes this morning before I could get my breakfast, and it hasn't agreed with me.'

'Who told you to do it?' said the Cat.

'Why, the lady I have to take care of me,' replied the Dog.

'Do you feel any better for it, Dog, after you have been standing on your legs?' asked she.

'Hav'n't I told you, you stupid Cat, that it hasn't agreed with me; let me go to sleep and don't plague me.'

'But I mean,' persisted the Cat, 'do you feel improved, as the men call it? They tell their children that if they do what they are told they will improve, and grow good and great. Do you feel good and great?'

'What do I know?' said the Dog. 'I eat my breakfast and am happy. Let me alone.'

'Do you never think, O Dog without a soul! Do you never wonder what dogs are, and what this world is?'

The Dog stretched himself, and rolled his eyes lazily round the room. 'I conceive,' he said, 'that the world is for dogs, and men and women are put into it to take care of dogs; women to take care of little dogs, like me, and men for the big dogs like those in the yard – and cats,' he continued, 'are to know their place, and not to be troublesome.'

'They beat you sometimes,' said the Cat. 'Why do they do that? They never beat me.'

'If they forget their places, and beat me,' snarled the Dog, I bite them, and they don't do it again. I should like to bite you, too, you nasty Cat; you have woke me up.'

'There may be truth in what you say,' said the Cat, calmly; 'but I think your view is limited. If you listened like me you would hear the men say it was all made for them, and you and I were made to amuse them.'

'They don't dare to say so,' said the Dog.

'They do indeed,' said the Cat. 'I hear many things which you lose by sleeping so much. They think I am asleep, and so they are not afraid to talk before me; but my ears are open when my eyes are shut.'

'You surprise me,' said the Dog. 'I never listen to them, except when I take notice of them, and then they never talk of any thing except of me.'

'I could tell you a thing or two about yourself which you don't know,' said the Cat. 'You have never heard, I dare say, that once upon a time your fathers lived in a temple, and that people prayed to them.'

'Prayed? What is that?'

'Why, they went on their knees to you to ask you to give them good things, just as you stand on your toes to them now to ask for your breakfast. You don't know either that you have got one of those bright things we see up in the air at night called after you.'

'Well, it is just what I said,' answered the Dog. 'I told you it was all made for us. They never did any thing of that sort for you?'

'Didn't they? Why, there was a whole city where the people did nothing else, and as soon as we got stiff and couldn't move about any more, instead of being put under the ground like poor Tom, we used to be stuffed full of all sorts of nice things, and kept better than we were when we were alive.'

'You are a very wise Cat,' answered her companion; 'but what good is it knowing all this?'

'Why, don't you see,' said she, 'they don't do it any more. We are going down in the world, we are, and that is why living on in this way is such an unsatisfactory sort of thing. I don't mean to complain for myself, and you needn't, Dog; we have a quiet life of it; but a quiet life is not the thing, and if there is nothing to be done except sleep and eat, and eat and sleep, why, as I said before, I don't see the use of it. There is more in it than that; there was once, and there will be again, and I sha'n't be happy till I find it out. It is a shame, dog, I say. The men have been here only a few thousand years, and we – why, we have been here hundreds of thousands; if we are older, we ought to be wiser; I'll go and ask the creatures in the woods.'

'You'll learn from the men,' said the Dog.

'They are stupid, and they don't know what I say to them; besides, they are so conceited they care for nothing except themselves. No, I shall try what I can do in the woods. I'd as soon go after poor Tom as stay living any longer like this.'

'And where is poor Tom?' yawned the Dog.

'That is just one of the things I want to know,' answered she. 'Poor Tom is lying under the yard, or the skin of him, but whether that is the whole I don't feel so sure. They didn't think so in the city I told you about. It is a beautiful day, Dog; you won't take a trot out with me?' she added, wistfully.

'Who -I?' said the Dog. 'Not quite.'

'You may get so wise,' said she.

'Wisdom is good,' said the Dog; 'but so is the hearthrug, thank you!'

'But you may be free,' said she.

'I shall have to hunt for my own dinner,' said he.

'But, Dog, they may pray to you again,' said she.

'But I sha'n't have a softer mat to sleep on, Cat, and as I am rather delicate, that is a consideration.'

So the Dog wouldn't go, and the Cat set off by herself to learn how to be happy, and to be all that a Cat could be. It was a fine sunny morning. She determined to try the meadow first, and, after an hour or two, if she had not succeeded, then go off to the wood. A Blackbird was piping away on a thornbush as if his heart was running over with happiness. The Cat had breakfasted, and so was able to listen without any mixture of feeling. She didn't sneak. She walked boldly up under the bush, and the bird, seeing she had no bad purpose, sat still and sang on.

'Good morning, Blackbird; you seem to be enjoying yourself this fine day.'

'Good morning, Cat.'

'Blackbird, it is an odd question, perhaps – what ought one to do to be as happy as you?'

'Do your duty, Cat.'

'But what is my duty, Blackbird?'

'Take care of your little ones, Cat.'

'I hav'n't any,' said she.

'Then sing to your mate,' said the bird.

'Tom is dead,' said she.

'Poor Cat!' said the bird. 'Then sing over his grave. If your song is sad, you will find your heart grow lighter for it.'

'Mercy!' thought the Cat. 'I could do a little singing with a living lover, but I never heard of singing for a dead one. But you see, bird, it isn't Cats' nature. When I am cross, I mew. When I am pleased, I purr; but I must be pleased first. I can't purr myself into happiness.'

'I am afraid there is something the matter with your heart, my Cat. It wants warming; good-bye.'

The Blackbird flew away. The Cat looked sadly after him. 'He thinks I am like him; and he doesn't know that a Cat is a Cat,' said she. 'As it happens now, I feel a great deal for a Cat. If I hadn't got a heart I shouldn't be unhappy. I won't be angry. I'll try that great fat fellow.'

The Ox lay placidly chewing, with content beaming out of his eyes and playing on his mouth.

'Ox,' she said, 'what is the way to be happy?'

'Do your duty,' said the Ox.

'Bother,' said the Cat; 'duty again! What is it, Ox?'

'Get your dinner,' said the Ox.

'But it is got for me, Ox; and I have nothing to do but to eat it.'

'Well, eat it, then, like me.'

'So I do; but I am not happy for all that.'

'Then you are a very wicked, ungrateful Cat.' The Ox munched away. A Bee buzzed into a buttercup under the Cat's nose.

'I beg your pardon,' said the Cat; 'It isn't curiosity – what are you doing?'

'Doing my duty; don't stop me, Cat.'

'But, Bee, what is your duty?'

'Making honey,' said the Bee.

'I wish I could make honey,' sighed the Cat.

'Do you mean to say you can't?' said the Bee. 'How stupid you must be. What do you do, then?'

'I do nothing, Bee. I can't get anything to do.'

'You won't get any thing to do, you mean, you lazy Cat! You are a good-for-nothing drone. Do you know what we do to our drones? We kill them; and that is all they are fit for. Good morning to you.'

'Well, I am sure,' said the Cat, 'they are treating me civilly; I had better have stopped at home at this rate. Stroke my whiskers! Heartless! wicked! good-for-nothing! stupid! and only fit to be killed! This is a pleasant beginning, anyhow. I must look for some wiser creatures than these are. What shall I do? I know. I know where I will go.'

It was in the middle of the wood. The bush was very dark, but she found him by his wonderful eye. Presently, as she got used to the light, she distinguished a sloping roll of feathers, a rounded breast, surmounted by a round head, set close to the body, without an inch of neck intervening. 'How wise he looks!' she said; 'what a brain! what a forehead! His head is not long, but what an expanse! and what a depth of earnestness!' The Owl sloped his head a little on one side; the Cat slanted hers upon the other. The Owl set it straight again, the Cat did the same. They stood looking in this way for some minutes; at last, in a whispering voice, the Owl said, 'What are you who presume to look into my repose? Pass on upon your way, and carry elsewhere those prying eyes.'

'O wonderful Owl,' said the Cat, ' you are wise, and I want to be wise; and I am come to you to teach me.'

A film floated backwards and forwards over the Owl's eyes; it was his way of showing that he was pleased.

'I have heard in our schoolroom,' went on the cat, 'that you sat on the shoulder of Pallas, and she told you all about it.'

'And what would you know, O my daughter?' said the Owl.

'Every thing,' said the Cat, 'every thing. First of all, how to be happy.'

'Mice content you not, my child, even as they content not me,' said the Owl. 'It is good.'

'Mice, indeed!' said the Cat; 'no, Parlor Cats don't eat mice. I have better than mice, and no trouble to get it; but I want something more.'

'The body's meat is provided. You would now fill your soul.'

'I want to improve,' said the Cat. 'I want something to do. I want to find out what the creatures call my duty.'

'You would learn how to employ those happy hours of your leisure – rather how to make them happy by a worthy use. Meditate, O Cat! meditate! meditate!'

'That is the very thing,' said she. 'Meditate! that is what I like above all things. Only I want to know how: I want something to meditate about. Tell me Owl, and I will bless you every hour of the day as I sit by the parlor fire.'

'I will tell you,' answered the Owl, 'what I have been thinking of ever since the moon changed. You shall take it home with you and think about it too; and the next full moon you shall come again to me; we will compare our conclusions.'

'Delightful! delightful!' said the Cat. 'What is it? I will try this minute.'

'From the beginning,' replied the Owl, 'our race have been considering which first existed, the Owl or the egg. The Owl comes from the egg, but likewise the egg from the Owl.'

'Mercy!' said the Cat.

'From sunrise to sunset I ponder on it, O Cat! When I reflect on the beauty of the complete Owl, I think that must have been first, as the cause is greater than the effect. When I remember my own childhood, I incline the other way.'

'Well, how are we to find out?' said the Cat.

'Find out!' said the Owl. 'We can never find out. The beauty of the question is, that its solution is impossible. What would become of all our delightful reasonings, O unwise Cat! if we were so unhappy as to know?'

'But what in the world is the good of thinking about it, if you can't, O Owl?'

'My child, that is a foolish question. It is good, in order that the thoughts on these things may stimulate wonder. It is in wonder that the Owl is great.'

'Then you don't know any thing at all,' said the cat. 'What did you sit on Pallas' shoulder for? You must have gone to sleep.'

'Your tone is overflippant, Cat, for philosophy. The highest of all knowledge is to know that we know nothing.'

The Cat made two great arches with her back and her tail.

'Bless the mother that laid you,' said she. 'You were dropped by mistake in a goose nest. You won't do. I don't know much, but I am not such a creature as you, anyhow. A great white thing!'

She straightened her body, stuck her tail up on end, and marched off with much dignity. But, though she respected herself rather more than before, she was not on the way to the end of her difficulties. She tried all the creatures she met without advancing a step. They had all the old story, 'Do your duty.' But each had its own, and no one could tell her what hers was. Only one point they all agreed upon – the duty of getting their dinner when they were hungry. The day wore on, and she began to think she would like hers. Her meals came so regularly at home that she scarcely knew what hunger was; but now the sensation came over her very palpably, and she experienced quite new emotions as the hares and rabbits skipped about her, or as she spied a bird upon a tree. For a moment she thought she would go back and eat the Owl – he was the most useless creature she had seen; but on second thought she didn't fancy he would be nice; besides that, his claws were sharp and his beak too. Presently, however, as she sauntered down the path, she came on a little open patch of green, in the middle of which a fine fat Rabbit was sitting. There was no escape. The path ended there, and the bushes were so thick on each side that he couldn't get away except through her paws.

'Really,' said the Cat, 'I don't wish to be troublesome; I wouldn't do it if I could help it; but I am very hungry, I am afraid I must eat you. It is very unpleasant, I assure you, to me as well as to you.'

The poor rabbit begged for mercy.

'Well,' said she, 'I think it is hard; I do really – and, if the law could be altered, I should be the first to welcome it. But what can a Cat do? You eat the grass; I eat you. But, Rabbit, I wish you would do me a favor.'

'Any thing to save my life,' said the Rabbit.

'It is not exactly that,' said the Cat; 'but I haven't been used to killing my own dinner, and it is disagreeable. Couldn't you die? I shall hurt you dreadfully if I kill you.'

'Oh!' said the Rabbit, 'you are a kind Cat; I see it in your eyes, and your whiskers don't curl like those of the cats in the woods. I am sure you will spare me.'

'But, Rabbit, it is a question of principle. I have to do my duty; And the only duty I have, as far as I can make out, is to get my dinner.'

'If you kill me, Cat, to do your duty, I sha'n't be able to do mine.'

It was a doubtful point, and the Cat was new to casuistry. 'What is your duty?' said she.

'I have seven little ones at home – seven little ones, and they will all die without me. Pray let me go.'

'What! do you take care of your children?' said the Cat. 'How interesting! I should like to see that; take me.'

'Oh! you would eat them, you would,' said the Rabbit. 'No! better eat me than them, No. No.'

'Well, well,' said the Cat, 'I don't know; I suppose I couldn't answer for myself. I don't think I am right, for duty is pleasant, and it is very unpleasant to be so hungry; but I suppose you must go. You seem a good Rabbit. Are you happy, Rabbit?'

'Happy! O dear beautiful Cat! If you spare me to my poor babies!'

'Pooh, pooh!' said the Cat, peevishly; 'I don't want fine speeches; I meant whether you thought it worth while to be alive! Of course you do! It don't matter. Go, and keep out of my way;' for, if I don't get my dinner, you may not get off another time. Get along, Rabbit.'

It was a great day in the Fox's cave. The eldest cub had the night before brought home his first goose, and they were just sitting down to it as the Cat came by.

'Ah, my young lady! what, you in the woods? Bad feeding at home, eh? Come out to hunt for yourself?'

The goose smelt excellent; the Cat couldn't help a wistful look. She was only come, she said, to pay her respects to her wild friends.

'Just in time,' said the Fox. 'Sit down and take a bit of dinner; I see you want it. Make room, you cubs; place a seat for the lady.'

'Why, thank you,' said the Cat, 'yes; I acknowledge it is not unwelcome. Pray, don't disturb yourselves, young Foxes. I am hungry. I met a rabbit on my way here. I was going to eat him, but he talked so prettily I let him go.'

The cubs looked up from their plates, and burst out laughing.

'For shame, young rascals!' said their father. 'Where are your manners? Mind your dinner, and don't be rude.'

'Fox,' she said, when it was over, and the cubs had gone to play, 'you are very clever. The other creatures are all stupid.' The Fox bowed. 'Your family were always clever,' she continued. 'I have heard about them in the books they use in our schoolroom. It is many years since your ancestor stole the crow's dinner.'

'Don't say stole, Cat; it is not pretty. Obtained by superior ability.'

'I beg your pardon,' said the Cat; 'it is all living with those men. That is not the point. Well, but I want to know whether you are any wiser or any better than Foxes were then?'

'Really,' said the Fox, 'I am what Nature made me. I don't know. I am proud of my ancestors, and do my best to keep up the credit of the family.'

'Well, but Fox, I mean do you improve? do I? Do any of you? The men are always talking about doing their duty, and that, they say, is the way to improve, and to be happy. And as I was not happy, I thought that had, perhaps, something to do with it, so I came out to talk to the creatures. They also had the old chant – duty, duty, duty; but none of them could tell me what mine was, or whether I had any.'

The Fox smiled. 'Another leaf out of your schoolroom,' said he. 'Can't they tell you there?'

'Indeed,' she said, 'they are very absurd. They say a great deal about themselves, but they only speak disrespectfully of us. If such creatures as they can do their duty, and improve, and be happy, why can't we?'

'They say they do, do they?' said the Fox. 'What do they say of me?'

The Cat hesitated.

'Don't be afraid of hurting my feelings, Cat. Out with it.'

'They do all justice to your abilities, Fox,' said she; 'but your morality, they say, is not high. They say you are a rogue.'

'Morality!' said the Fox. 'Very moral and good they are. And you really believe all that? What do they mean by calling me a rogue?'

'They mean you take whatever you can get, without caring whether it is just or not.'

'My dear Cat, it is very well for a man, if he can't bear his own face, to paint a pretty one on a panel and call it a looking-glass; but you don't mean that it takes *you* in?'

'Teach me,' said the Cat. 'I fear I am weak.'

'Who get justice from the men unless they can force it? Ask the sheep that are cut into mutton. Ask the horses that draw their ploughs. I don't mean it is wrong of the men to do as they do; but they needn't lie about it.'

'You surprise me,' said the Cat.

'My good Cat, there is but one law in the world. The weakest go to the wall. The men are sharper-witted than the creatures, and so they get the better of them and use them. They may call it just if they like; but when a tiger eats a man, I guess he has just as much justice on his side as the man when he eats a sheep.'

'And that is the whole of it,' said the Cat. 'Well, it is very sad. What do you do with yourself?'

'My duty, to be sure,' said the Fox; 'use my wits and enjoy myself. My dear friend, you and I are on the lucky side. We eat and are not eaten.'

'Except by the hounds now and then,' said the Cat.

'Yes; by brutes that forget their nature, and sell their freedom to the man,' said the Fox, bitterly. 'In the mean time my wits have kept my skin whole hitherto, and I bless Nature for making me a Fox and not a goose.'

'And are you happy, Fox?'

'Happy! Yes, of course. So would you be if you would do like me, and use your wits. My good Cat, I should be as miserable as you if I found my geese every day at the cave's mouth. I have to hunt for them; cheat those old fat farmers, and bring out what there is inside me; and then I am happy – of course I am. And then, Cat, think of my feelings as a father last night, when my dear boy comes home with the very young gosling which was marked for the Michaelmas dinner! Old Reineke himself wasn't more than a match for that young Fox at his years. You know our epic?'

'A little of it, Fox. They don't read it in our schoolroom. They say it is not moral; but I have heard pieces of it. I hope it is not all quite true.'

'Pack of stuff! it is the only true book that ever was written. If it is not, it ought to be. Why, that book is the law of the world – *la carrière aux talents* – and writing it was the honestest thing ever done by a man. That fellow knew a thing or two, and wasn't ashamed of himself when he did know. They are all like him, too, if they would only say so. There never was one of them yet who wasn't more ashamed of being called ugly than of being called a rogue, and being called stupid than of being called naughty.'

'It has a roguish end, this life of yours, if you keep clear of the hounds, Fox,' said the Cat.

'What! a rope in the yard! Well, it must end some day; and when the farmer catches me I shall be getting old, and my brains will be taking leave of me; so the sooner I go the better, that I may disgrace myself the less. Better be jolly while it lasts, than sit mewing out your life and grumbling at it as a bore.'

'Well,' said the Cat, 'I am very much obliged to you. I suppose I may even get home again. I shall not find a wiser friend than you, and perhaps I shall not find another good-natured enough to give me so good a dinner. But it is very sad.'

'Think of what I have said,' answered the Fox. 'I'll call at your house some night; you will take me a walk round the yard, and then I'll show you.'

'Not quite,' thought the Cat, as she trotted off; 'one good turn deserves another, that is true; and you have given me a good dinner. But they have given me many at home, and I mean to take a few more of them; so I think you mustn't go round our yard.'

The next morning, when the Dog came down to breakfast, he found his old friend sitting in her usual place on the hearth-rug.

'Oh! so you have come back,' said he. 'How d'ye do? You don't look as if you had had a very pleasant journey.'

'I have learnt something,' said the Cat. 'Knowledge is never pleasant.'

'Then it is better to be without it,' said the Dog.

'Especially, better to be without knowing how to stand on one's hind legs, Dog,' said the Cat; 'still, you see, you are proud of it; but I have learnt a great deal, Dog. They won't worship you any more, and it is better for you; you wouldn't be any happier. What did you do yesterday?'

'Indeed,' said the Dog, 'I hardly remember. I slept after you went away. In the afternoon I took a drive in the carriage. Then I had my dinner. My maid washed me and put me to bed. There is a difference between you and me; you have to wash yourself and put yourself to bed.'

'And you really don't find it a bore, living like this? Wouldn't you like something to do? Wouldn't you like some children to play with? The Fox seemed to find it very pleasant.'

'Children indeed!' said the Dog, 'when I have got men and women. Children are well enough for foxes and wild creatures; refined dogs know better; and, for doing – can't I stand on my toes? can't I dance? at least, couldn't I before I was so fat?'

'Ah! I see every body likes what he was bred to,' sighed the

Cat. 'I was bred to do nothing, and I must like that. Train the cat as the cat should go, and the cat will be happy and ask no questions. Never seek for impossibilities, Dog. That is the secret.'

'And you have spent a day in the woods to learn that,' said he. 'I could have taught you that. Why, Cat, one day when you were sitting scratching your nose before the fire, I thought you looked so pretty that I should have liked to marry you; but I knew I couldn't, so I didn't make myself miserable.'

The Cat looked at him with her odd green eyes. 'I never wished to marry you, Dog; I shouldn't have presumed. But it was wise of you not to fret about it. But, listen to me, Dog – listen. I met many creatures in the wood, all sorts of creatures, beasts and birds. They were all happy; they didn't find it a bore. They went about their work, and did it, and enjoyed it, and yet none of them had the same story to tell. Some did one thing, some another; and, except the Fox, each had got a sort of notion of doing its duty. The Fox was a rogue; he said he was; but yet he was not unhappy. His conscience never troubled him. Your work is standing on your toes, and you are happy. I have none, and that is why I am unhappy. When I came to think about it, I found every creature out in the wood had to get its own living. I tried to get mine, but I didn't like it, because I wasn't used to it; and as for knowing, the Fox, who didn't care to know any thing except how to cheat greater fools than himself, was the cleverest fellow I came across. Oh! the Owl, Dog – you should have heard the Owl. But I came to this, that it was no use trying to know, and the only way to be jolly was to go about one's own business like a decent Cat. Cats' business seems to be killing rabbits and suchlike; and it is not the pleasantest possible; so the sooner one is bred to it the better. As for me, that have been bred to do nothing, why, as I said before, I must try to like that; but I consider myself an unfortunate Cat.'

'So don't I consider myself an unfortunate Dog,' said her companion.

'Very likely you do not,' said the Cat.

By this time their breakfast was come in. The cat ate hers, the dog did penance for his; and if one might judge by the purring on the hearthrug, the Cat, if not the happiest of the two, at least was not exceedingly miserable.

Verses on a Cat

I

A Cat in distress,
Nothing more, nor less;
Good folks, I must faithfully tell ye,
As I am a sinner,
It waits for some dinner
To stuff out its own little belly.

II

You would not easily guess
All the modes of distress
Which torture the tenants of earth;
And the various evils,
Which like so many devils,
Attend the poor souls from their birth.

III

Some a living require,
And others desire
An old fellow out of the way;
And which is the best
I leave to be guessed,
For I cannot pretend to say.

IV

One wants society,
Another variety,

Others a tranquil life;
  Some want food,
  Others, as good,
Only want a wife.

V
But this poor little cat
Only wanted a rat,
To stuff out its own little maw;
  And it were as good
  Some people had such food,
To make them *hold their jaw!*

PERCY BYSSHE SHELLEY

Of some amiable Cats, and Cats that have been good Mothers.

C. H. Ross

To lead a 'Cat and Dog life' means a good deal of scratching and biting; but dogs and Cats have been known to get on very amiably before now.

There was a Cat which had formed a very warm friendship with a large Newfoundland dog: she continually caressed him – advanced in all haste when he came home, with her tail erect, and rubbed her head against him, purring with delight. When he lay before the kitchen fire, she used him as a bed, pulling up and settling his hair with her claws to make it comfortable. As soon as she had arranged it to her liking, she lay down upon him, and fell asleep. The dog bore this combing of his locks with patient placidity, turning his head towards her during the operation, and sometimes gently licked her.

Pincher and Puss were sworn friends. Puss had a young family, with whom Pincher was on visiting terms. The nursery was at the top of the house. One day there was a storm; Puss was upstairs with the babies, and Pincher was in the parlour. Pincher evidently was disturbed by the thunder. Presently Puss came downstairs mewing, went straight to Pincher, rubbed her cheek against his, and touched him gently with her paw, and then walked to the door, and, looking back, mewed, as though asking him go with her. But Pincher was himself sorely afraid, and could render no assistance. Puss grew desperate, and having renewed her application with increased energy, but without success, at last left the room, mewing piteously, while Pincher sat, with a guilty face, evidently knowing his conduct was selfish. A lady, who had watched this scene, went out to look after the Cat, when the animal, mewing, led the way to a bedroom on the first floor, from under a wardrobe in which a small voice was heard crying. Puss had brought one of her babies downstairs, and was racked with anxiety respecting its welfare while she fetched the others. It was as clear as possible she wanted Pincher to lend a paw – that is to say, look after this isolated infant while she brought down the rest. The lady took up the kitten in her arms, and accompanied Puss upstairs, then moved the little bed from the window, through which the lightning had been flashing so vividly as to alarm Puss for the safety of her family. She remained with the Cat until the storm had subsided, and all was calm. On the following morning, the lady was much surprised to find Puss waiting for her outside her bedroom door, and she went with her downstairs to breakfast, sat by her side, and caressed her in every possible way. Puss had always been in the habit of going down with the lady of the house, but on this occasion she had resisted all her mistress's coaxing to leave the other lady's door, and would not go away until she made her appearance. She remained till breakfast was over, then went upstairs to her family. She had never done this before, and never did it again. She had shown her gratitude for the lady's care of her little ones, and her duty was done.

A gentleman, residing in Sussex, had a Cat which showed the greatest attachment for a young blackbird, which was given to her by a stable-boy for food a day or two after she had been deprived of her kittens. She tended it with the greatest care; they became inseparable companions, and no mother could show a greater fondness for her offspring than she did for the bird.

This incongruity of attachment in animals will generally be found to arise either from the feelings of natural affection which the mother is possessed of, or else from that love of sociability, and dislike of being alone, which is possessed, more or less, by every created being.

A Horse and Cat were great friends, and the latter generally slept in the manger. When the horse was about to be fed, he always took up the Cat gently by the skin of the neck, and dropped her into the next stall, that she might not be in his way while he was feeding. At other times, he was pleased to have her near him.

Mr Bingley tells of a friend of his who had a Cat and Dog that were always fighting. At last the dog conquered, and the Cat was driven away; but the servant, whose sweetheart the dog disturbed, poisoned him, and his body was carried lifeless into the courtyard. The Cat, from a neighbouring roof, was observed to watch the motions of several persons who went up to look at him, and when all had retired, he descended and crept cautiously towards the body, then patted it with his paw. Apparently satisfied that the dog's day was over, Puss re-entered the house and washed his face before the fire.

The Reverend Gilbert White, in his amusing book, tells of a boy, who having taken three little young squirrels in their nest or 'dray,' put these small creatures under the care of a Cat that had lately lost her kittens, and found that she nursed and suckled them with the same assiduity and affection as if they were her own offspring. This circumstance, to some extent, corroborates the stories told of deserted children being nurtured by female beasts of prey who had lost their young, of the truth of which some authors have seriously vouched. Many people went to see the little squirrels suckled by the Cat, and the foster mother became jealous of her charge, and fearing for their safety, hid them over the ceiling, where one died. This circumstance proves her affection for the fondlings, and that she supposed them to be her young. In like fashion hens, when they have hatched ducklings, are as attached to them as though they were their own chickens.

The Owl and the Pussy-Cat

I.

.The Owl and the Pussy-Cat went to sea
  In a beautiful pea-green boat,
They took some honey, and plenty of money,
  Wrapped up in a five-pound note.
The Owl looked up to the stars above,
  And sang to a small guitar,
'O lovely Pussy! O Pussy, my love,
  'What a beautiful Pussy you are,
    'You are,
    'You are!
'What a beautiful Pussy you are!'

II.

Pussy said to the Owl, 'You elegant fowl!
  'How charmingly sweet you sing!
'O let us be married! too long we have tarried:
  'But what shall we do for a ring?'
They sailed away for a year and a day,
  To the land where the Bong-tree grows,
And there in a wood a Piggy-wig stood,
  With a ring at the end of his nose,
    His nose,
    His nose,
  With a ring at the end of his nose.

III.

'Dear Pig, are you willing to sell for one shilling
  'Your ring?' Said the Piggy, 'I will.'
So they took it away, and were married next day
  By the Turkey who lives on the hill.
They dined on mince, and slices of quince,
  Which they ate with a runcible spoon;
And hand in hand, on the edge of the sand,
  They danced by the light of the moon,
    The moon,
    The moon,
  They danced by the light of the moon.

EDWARD LEAR

The Theatre Cat

John S. Lopez

I came across the serious student, late one morning, stretching his lank form along an area railing, a sprig of withered green held absently between two fingers, and a huge tortoise-shell cat rubbing expectantly against his legs.

'Have you become a Dick Whittington of the Drama?' I asked.

'Precisely', he said; 'a surfeit of talking plays makes me seek guidance of the dumb animals. There are theatre cats. Why? The answer may disclose unsuspected phases of the dramatic art. I shall begin investigation with a bribe – this catnip.' Whereupon he dropped the green spray, which the cat immediately seized and disappeared down the area-way.

We followed, and found ourselves upon the stage at Wallack's. There was to be a benefit matinée, and stage hands from several other theatres had come to handle their scenery. They had stopped for lunch, and were lounging picturesquely about a jumble of trunks and props piled at one side of the stage. The Student singled out a grizzled veteran.

'Why is there a cat attached to every theatre?' he asked, respectfully.

The old man extricated his teeth from an enormous sandwich and swallowed meditatively.

'Well, sometimes they're actors', began the old man. 'I knew a cat – '

'You mean old Salt!' broke in a Wallack stage hand. 'He began as an actor. They wanted a cat in a show called "The Salt of the Earth", and we had to furnish some props. Used to send boys out to steal 'em, and I guess we got a dozen and lost 'em before Salt was brought in and liked it enough to stick. He's an old-timer now; been around here ten or twelve years and is part of the place. He has the run of the theatre, and most every patron knows him. Never caused a bit of trouble; he's as wise as they come.'

'Speakin' of wise cats; they've got to be trained to – ' began the veteran again deliberately, laying down his sandwich.

'Yes,' interrupted the Wallack man; 'you've got to get 'em young. We had a cat, called Reds, down at the old house, afterward the Star. We found her one day way up in the fly gallery. She was a kitten with her eyes just opened. The mystery always was how she got there. But she grew to be a wise one – '

'Yes, they've got to be brought up in the business,' a man from Daly's broke in. 'There's old black Tom over at our house; he must be fifteen if he's a day. The Governor used to stand in the gallery doorway near Thirtieth Street and wait for a Broadway car most every night late after the show. One night in a snowstorm a poor little kitten rubs against Mr Daly's legs. He opened up the theatre again and put it in his own office. Tom's too wise now to go on the stage – '

'Speakin' of cats goin' on the stage – ' began the veteran again, hopefully.

'That's what', spoke up a quiet-looking man, enthusiastically; 'they got to be trained up from infancy. We got an old cat at the Belasco who has the proper notion of bringing up her kittens. We always find them first in Box B, the boss's private box; and we can't keep her out of there. It's funny, after the kittens can walk, to see the mother lead them back on the stage and march them around from one side to the other. It's a fact; she'll do it for hours, and never let them get outside the scenery. If they try to, she thumps them.'

'Now, our old Tom', said the man from Daly's, 'knows enough to keep off when there's anything doing; but he knows what the stage is for all right. Often after the show, if he catches a rat or mouse, he brings it right out on the stage under the gas jet and gives a performance with it, because he knows I'm up in the gallery closing up and will see him.'

'I'll tell you how a cat can get to understand about acting', began the veteran determinedly, but the Wallack man seized the cue:

'That's another reason why these ordinary cats cause trouble around a theatre; they ain't got the real understanding of the stage, like old Salt.'

'He appreciates drama, then?' gasped the student, hopefully.

'Sure!' asseverated the Wallack man, sweeping a defiant glance over the group. 'Salt knows more about shows than all the actors and critics in New York rolled together. You've seen him camping in the private boxes? Well, he's not there to show off, like most people in 'em. No, sir; he's there to keep tabs from the front and see that things go right.'

'Regular stage-manager', remarked the man from Daly's, *sotto voce*, with a comprehensive wink. The Wallack man heard him.

'Better'n some around here', he said, pointedly. 'Why, if I believed in this transformation of souls, I'd think Jim Wallack or some of the oldtime real ones was squatted in Salt's body. By watching that cat we can always tell whether a new show will make good. Sometimes in the middle of the first act he'll get up and leave the box, and then I never knew it to fail that the show falls down. Sometimes he'll stay longer; and when *he* sits to the finish, the piece is worth seeing'.

The man from Daly's laughed superciliously, and the other turned on him.

'Think I'm a nature-faker, do you? Well, ask anybody around this theatre; and most every actor that's played the house is wise to it. There was a comedian had an experience here with a musical show he won't forget. It had one good act in it, which Salt stops to see every night. The comedian has a song in it which was usually the hit of the show – but not always. Whenever Salt gets up and leaves, the song goes bad.

'He begins bringin' in all kinds of popular cat grub, but it don't make any difference to Salt. By and by, every show, there's a bunch of us in the wings, waiting to see what the cat will do. Then we begin to notice that the comedian actually sings his song to Salt. Sometimes the cat'll rest comfortable to the finish, and the song is sure to go fine. But sometimes, half through, you'll see Salt get up and hump his back and yawn; and then its pathetic to watch the comedian throw in the expression and gestures and work hard to make the cat change its mind. Sometimes he succeeds, but usually not; at which times he loses his nerve and finishes so bad that it's sure to be a frost.

'I hear the manager explain to him, one night, that if he didn't pay any attention to Salt, he would be able always to do the song the same. He offers to have Salt kept out of the private boxes, but Mr Comedian won't hear to it; says it would the worst kind of bad luck.'

'There should be more such cats as correctives of musical comedy', mused the Student. 'Did the actor finally improve?'

'Well', explained the Wallack man, 'the comedian hadn't been in good health, anyhow, and after a while he had to go to a sanitarium to rest up his brains.'

The veteran assured himself elaborately that there was a pause.

'Speakin' of cat's brains', he began, 'you've got to figure on mice or – '

'Yes,' cut in a man from the Empire, 'we had a blow-out when I was props down at the old Lyceum Theatre. There were three white mice belonged to one of the principal actresses. She was kissing and hugging them all the time. Had bows of blue baby ribbon on their necks and kept them in a padded brass bird cage in her dressing room. Says I to her, very respectful, she'd better be careful as our old cat, Adolph, was strictly on his job.

'"Why, how ridiculous," she says, with a laugh, "the dear little things are white mice."

'I tell her straight that in the matter of vermin, Adolph is colour blind. I'm thinking, but she won't listen. I ain't worried over the mice's health, but I want to hold my job, and I know I'll be blamed if there's an accident. So I keep Adolph penned up.

'Well, one afternoon when she's on, I notice her door open a little, and see Adolph come out lookin' satisfied and lickin' his chops. I got sense enough to put the fancy cage back in place and straighten things up a bit before she comes off.

'By the time I'm sent for, I've been doing some thinking, and I says, 'The mice simply got out to have a little look around. When they get hungry they'll come back; sure to before the show tonight.'

'What I do is to send the prop boy over to buy three mice that'll match up. Say, it worked fine! Only trouble was tying new bows on their necks; worked an hour before the boy says let it go any old way, as mice out on a bat would sure have their trimmings mussed. The new mice was a bit nervous at bein' welcomed home with kisses, but she blamed that and the ribbon to their wandering off and maybe gettin' into bad company.'

'It's most always pets that cause trouble with the theatre cats', spoke up the veteran, cautiously bent on being heard.

'But a cat may be mighty useful when it gets a home-feeling in a theatre – '

'That's right', said another at his elbow. 'I'll tell you what happened down at the Academy one night when we were putting on a big production of *Ingomar*. The star had a pet cat that she called Vivien or something – one of these with a fluffy tail and bushy face like a chrysanthemum. Well, she gets one peep at our tough old house-cat, John L, and she can't have Vivien associating with him. I tie up John L, and he's mighty sore. Vivien has the run of the place and is in everybody's way.

'Well, it's during the act where there's a big arched gate. The star is leaning against it and spieling some soft stuff with half lights, when all of a sudden I hear a low yowl that sounds familiar. She hears it too, and gets nervous. It's near, but I can't figure where, till I happen to glance up at the arch, which is a big one stretching three deep on one side and backed with heavy scantling. On top I see John L pointing my way, crouched and waving his tail. Between me and him is Vivien facing him. John L has chewed his rope and is on the warpath. He's a wise one, and knew who's to blame for his bein' tied up.

'He gives another yowl, so I get in the entrance and hiss at him. He always used to mind me. Then I wave at him to blow off, but he must have thought I meant to set him on. Whew! There's a yowl and a screech that stops the show, and before the star has time to get away, down come the cats at her feet, spitting and rolling around so fast they look like one ball of fur with legs stickin' out all over.

'We sent John L away till the show was gone. But even when he came back, judgin' from his looks, Vivien wasn't such a rotten scrapper if she was high-class.'

'Cats is important to a theatre, and they know it', spoke the veteran who had been waiting impatiently. 'Why, if we hadn't had a cat once – '

'You can't blame 'em for being jealous of their job', spoke up another man. 'Theatre cats, when they stake out a soft claim, won't allow any buttin' in. Of course, though, they know what they're there for and will make allowances, like an old cat we got up at the Broadway. Except when there's a mouse show on, he wouldn't let another cat hardly pass the stage door.'

'What's a mouse show – one with trained mice?' asked the Student.

'No, no', explained the Broadway man, impatiently; 'one that has props and stuff that draws mice and rats – more'n one cat can handle satisfactory. Well, in such cases our cat will stand for others being brought in, though he never gets friendly. But as fast as the mice get diminished, he'll run the cats out, one at a time, till there is only one left, and then he finishes it off in a big battle.'

A gleam of deadly determination had been growing in the veteran's eye. He leaned forward and said, distinctly, significantly:

'There was a cat I knew became a big star by accident.'

He paused and glared challengingly around at the others as if to say, 'Now, does that remind any of you of anything?' Assured at last by utter silence, he went on:

'There was a play on in a house where I worked; it had a pretty good cast, but every one was nervous because it didn't measure up strong in lines and situations. On the opening night there's a crowded house, but the first act is a sad sketch. We know the second will be worse, because, barring a lot of quiet talk-talk, there's nothing in it but a swell setting with a fine open fire place and real gas logs down left.

'It's a cold sleety night, and Peter, our house-cat, has been out visiting. He comes in while the act is on and walks down off side. He looks across and sees the logs burning, and naturally they appeal to him. First thing you know he starts over the stage with a dignified actor walk, and proceeds to make his toilet right down in front of the blaze.

'Say, the homelike effect is great! The two stars don't notice it and go right on. I'm looking for the house to throw a laugh, but instead of that, a few moments later, there's a burst of applause that almost knocks us silly. Luckily it's 'most time for curtain and we hurry it a bit. But the hand keeps growing stronger and out go the stars and take several bows. Then we hear 'em out front calling, "The cat; bring out the cat!" The manager gets wise quick and

has the leading lady carry out Pete. Whew! You ought to of heard
the cheering and stamping.

'Next day the papers were enthusiastic about "the wonderful
piece of realism", and said the cat is the best actor in the cast and
has made a success of what would have been a sure frost.'

'Of course you kept Pete in the play', said the Student.

'We did', said the veteran reminiscently. 'Luckily next day was
Sunday, so an early rehearsal is called to break Pete in on that
scene. The log-fire is set going, and Pete is carried down and his
head pointed from the opposite entrance. But it's no go. He just
turns and sneaks for the prop room. The boss thinks of a plan to
open everything up and chill off the stage so that the heat will
attract Pete. But it don't work; and, anyway, the ladies say they'll
quit if they have to take chances of getting pneumonia.

'Then we put something to eat in front of the fire. Pete has been
starved all day, and he'll chase over and grab a piece of meat and
blow. Tying the meat on a string and pulling it through a hole
don't do, because he sets up a crying and tries to claw his way
after it through the scenery.

'It's about ten o'clock at night with everybody exhausted and
sore, when the property-boy dopes out the way. He's a bright
kid, and knew a thing or two about cat nature. Says he:

' "No cat ain't damn fool enough to let itself be trained to do
extra work. Lookin' after mice and rats is Pete's job, and we got to
make him do the stunt along them lines."

'The manager is down and out; he says go ahead and try anything. So the kid produces a trap with two mice in it he had set for
his and Pete's amusement. Pete is immediately very much lit up,
and if we hold him off side and set the cage by the fireplace, he
makes a beeline across. Then the kid cuts a little hole in one
corner of the fireplace and sticks one of the mice's heads out from
behind just far enough for Pete to see but not reach. After he gets
on to the game, he'll sneak across the stage and camp in front of
the fire and just sit there quiet, watchin' and wavin' his tail, same
as any cat on the trail. After that, by keeping him hungry and
always pushin' out a mouse when the curtain drops, we manage
to pull through a season of ten weeks with only one mishap.'

'What was that?' asked the Student.

'Well', said the veteran, 'one night the boy who is holding the mouse lets it slip. It jumps by Peter and reaches where the leading lady is sobbing out some tender lines. Pete is right behind and makes a beautiful merry-go-round chase circling her skirts. The audience thinks it's great; and, by gum, the manager was fool enough to figure if we could possibly repeat it.'

'Did you try?' asked the Student.

'Not on your life', said the veteran. 'The leading lady said she'd quit on the spot if they ever pulled a rehearsal.'

How a Cat Played Robinson Crusoe

Charles G.D. Roberts

The island was a mere sandbank off the low, flat coast. Not a tree broke its bleak levels – not even a shrub. But the long, gritty stalks of the marsh grass clothed it everywhere above tide-mark; and a tiny rivulet of sweet water, flowing from a spring at its centre, drew a ribbon of inland herbage and tenderer green across the harsh and sombre yellow grey of the grass. Few would have chosen the island as a place to live, yet at its seaward end, where the changing tides were never still, stood a spacious, one-storied, wide-verandaed cottage, with a low shed behind it. The virtue of this lone plot of sand was coolness. When the neighbour mainland would be sweltering day and night alike under a breathless heat, out here on the island there was always a cool wind blowing. Therefore a wise city dweller had appropriated the sea waif and built his summer home thereon, where the tonic airs might bring back the rose to the pale cheeks of his children.

The family came to the island toward the end of June. In the first week of September they went away, leaving every door and window of house and shed securely shuttered, bolted or barred against the winter's storms. A roomy boat, rowed by two fishermen, carried them across the half mile of racing tides that separated them from the mainland. The elders of the household were not sorry to get back to the world of men, after two months of mere wind, and sun, and waves, and waving grass tops. But the children went with tear-stained faces. They were leaving behind them their favourite pet, the accustomed comrade of their migrations, a handsome, moon-faced cat, striped like a tiger. The animal had mysteriously disappeared two days before, vanishing from the face of the island without leaving a trace behind. The only reasonable explanation seemed to be that she had been snapped up by a passing eagle. The cat, meanwhile, was a fast prisoner at the other end of the island, hidden beneath a broken barrel and some hundred-weight of drifted sand.

The old barrel, with the staves battered out of one side, had stood, half buried, on the crest of a sand ridge raised by a long prevailing wind. Under its lee the cat had found a sheltered hollow, full of sun, where she had been wont to lie curled up for hours at a time, basking and sleeping. Meanwhile the sand had been steadily piling itself higher and higher behind the unstable barrier. At last it had piled too high; and suddenly, before a stronger gust, the barrel had come toppling over beneath a mass of sand, burying the sleeping cat out of sight and light. But at the same time the sound half of the barrel had formed a safe roof to her prison, and she was neither crushed nor smothered. When the children in their anxious search all over the island chanced upon the mound of fine, white sand they gave it but one careless look. They could not hear the faint cries that came, at intervals, from the close darkness within. So they went away sorrowfully, little dreaming that their friend was imprisoned almost beneath their feet.

For three days the prisoner kept up her appeals for help. On the third day the wind changed and presently blew up a gale. In a few hours it had uncovered the barrel. At one corner a tiny spot of light appeared.

Eagerly the cat stuck her paw through the hole. When she withdrew it again the hole was much enlarged. She took the hint and fell to scratching. At first her efforts were rather aimless; but presently, whether by good luck or quick sagacity, she learned to make her scratching more effective. The opening rapidly enlarged, and at last she was able to squeeze her way out.

The wind was tearing madly across the island, filled with flying sand. The seas hurled themselves trampling up the beach, with the uproar of a bombardment. The grasses lay bowed flat in long quivering ranks. Over the turmoil the sun stared down from a deep, unclouded blue. The cat, when first she met the full force of the gale, was fairly blown off her feet. As soon as she could recover herself she crouched low and darted into the grasses for shelter. But there was little shelter there, the long stalks being held down almost level. Through their lashed lines, however, she sped straight before the gale, making for the cottage at the other end of the island, where she would find, as she fondly imagined, not only food and shelter but also loving comfort to make her forget her terrors.

Still and desolate in the bright sunshine and the tearing wind, the house frightened her. She could not understand the tight-closed shutters, the blind, unresponding doors that would no longer open to her anxious appeal. The wind swept her savagely across the naked veranda. Climbing with difficulty to the dining-room windowsill, where so often she had been let in, she clung there a few moments and yowled heartbrokenly. Then, in a sudden panic, she jumped down and ran to the shed. That, too, was closed. Never before had she seen the shed doors closed, and she could not understand it. Cautiously she crept around the foundations – but those had been built honestly: there was no such thing as getting in that way. On every side it was nothing but a blank, forbidding face that the old familiar house confronted her with.

The cat had always been so coddled and pampered by the children that she had had no need to forage for herself; but, fortunately for her, she had learned to hunt the marsh mice and grass sparrows for amusement. so now, being ravenous from her long fast under the sand, she slunk mournfully away from the deserted house and crept along under the lee of a sand ridge to a little grassy hollow which she knew. Here the gale caught only the tops of the grasses; and here, in the warmth and comparative calm, the furry little marsh folk, mice and shrews, were going about their business undisturbed.

The cat, quick and stealthy, soon caught one and eased her hunger. She caught several. And then, making her way back to the house, she spent hours in heartsick prowling around it and around, sniffing and peering, yowling piteously on the threshold and windowsill; and every now and then being blown ignominiously across the smooth, naked expanse of the veranda floor. At last, hopelessly discouraged, she curled herself up beneath the children's window and went to sleep.

In spite of her loneliness and grief the life of the island prisoner during the next two or three weeks was by no means one of hardship. Besides her abundant food of birds and mice she quickly learned to catch tiny fish in the mouth of the rivulet, where salt water and fresh water met. It was an exciting game, and she became expert at dashing the grey tom-cod and blue-and-silver sand-lance far up the slope with a sweep of her armed paw. But when the equinoctial storms roared down upon the island, with furious rain, and low, black clouds torn to shreds, then life became more difficult for her. Game all took to cover, where it was hard to find. It was difficult to get around in the drenched and lashing grass; and, moreover, she loathed wet. Most of the time she went hungry, sitting sullen and desolate under the lee of the house, glaring out defiantly at the rush and battling tumult of the waves.

The storm lasted nearly ten days before it blew itself clean out. On the eighth day the abandoned wreck of a small Nova Scotia schooner drove ashore, battered out of all likeness to a ship. But hulk as it was it had passengers of a sort. A horde of rats got through the surf and scurried into the hiding of the grass roots. They promptly made themselves at home, burrowing under the grass and beneath old, half-buried timbers, and carrying panic into the ranks of the mice and shrews.

When the storm was over the cat had a decided surprise in her first long hunting expedition. Something had rustled the grass heavily and she trailed it, expecting a particularly large, fat marsh mouse. When she pounced and alighted upon an immense old ship's rat, many-voyaged and many-battled, she got badly bitten. Such an experience had never before fallen to her lot. At first she felt so injured that she was on the point of backing out and running away. Then her latent pugnacity awoke, and the fire of far-off ancestors. She flung herself into the fight with a rage that took no accounting of the wounds she got; and the struggle was soon over. Her wounds, faithfully licked, quickly healed themselves in that clean and tonic air; and after that, having learned how to handle such big game, she no more got bitten.

During the first full moon after her abandonment – the first week in October – the island was visited by still weather with sharp night frosts. The cat discovered then that it was most exciting to hunt by night and do her sleeping in the daytime. She found that now, under the strange whiteness of the moon, all her game was astir – except the birds, which had fled to the mainland during the storm, gathering for the southward flight. The blanched grasses, she found, were now everywhere a-rustle; and everywhere dim little shapes went darting with thin squeaks across ghostly-white sands. Also she made the acquaintance of a new bird, which she regarded at first uneasily and then with vengeful wrath. This was the brown marsh owl, which came over from the mainland to do some autumn mouse hunting. There were two pairs of these big, downy-winged, round-eyed hunters, and they did not know there was a cat on the island.

The cat, spying one of them as it swooped soundlessly hither and thither over the silvered grass tops, crouched with flattened ears. With its wide spread of wing it looked bigger than herself; and the great round face, with hooked beak and wild, staring eyes, appeared extremely formidable. However, she was no coward; and presently, though not without reasonable caution, she went about her hunting. Suddenly the owl caught a partial glimpse of her in the grass – probably of her ears or head. He swooped; and at the same instant she sprang upward to meet the assault, spitting and growling harshly and striking with unsheathed claws. With a frantic flapping of his great wings the owl checked himself and drew back into the air, just escaping the clutch of those indignant claws. After that the marsh owls were careful to give her a wide berth. They realized that the black-striped animal with the quick spring and the clutching claws was not to be interfered with. They percevied that she was some relation to that ferocious prowler, the lynx.

In spite of all this hunting, however, the furry life of the marsh grass was so teeming, so inexhaustible, that the depredations of cat, rats and owls were powerless to make more than a passing impression upon it. So the hunting and the merry-making went on side by side under the indifferent moon.

As the winter deepened – with bursts of sharp cold and changing winds that forced the cat to be continually changing her refuge – she grew more and more unhappy. She felt her homelessness keenly. Nowhere on the whole island could she find a nook where she might feel secure from both wind and rain. As for the old barrel, the first cause of her misfortunes, there was no help in that. The winds had long ago turned it completely over, open to the sky, then drifted it full of sand and reburied it. And in any case the cat would have been afraid to go near it again. So it came about that she alone of all the island dwellers had no shelter to turn to when the real winter arrived, with snows that smothered the grass tops out of sight, and frosts that lined the shore with grinding ice cakes. The rats had their holes under the buried fragments of wreckage; the mice and shrews had their deep, warm tunnels; the owls had nests in hollow trees far away in the forests of the mainland. But the cat, shivering and frightened, could do nothing but crouch against the blind walls of the unrelenting house and let the snow whirl itself and pile itself about her.

And now, in her misery, she found her food cut off. The mice ran secure in their hidden runways, where the grass roots on each side of them gave them easy and abundant provender. The rats, too, were out of sight – digging burrows themselves in the soft snow in the hope of intercepting some of the tunnels of the mice, and now and then snapping up an unwary passer-by. The ice fringe, crumbling and heaving under the ruthless tide, put an end to her fishing. She would have tried to capture one of the formidable owls in her hunger, but the owls no longer came to the island. They would return, no doubt, later in the season when the snow had hardened and the mice had begun to come out and play on the surface. But for the present they were following an easier chase in the deeps of the upland forest.

When the snow stopped falling and the sun came out again there fell such keen cold as the cat had never felt before. The day, as it chanced, was Christmas; and if the cat had had any idea as to the calendar she would certainly have marked the day in her memory as it was an eventful one for her. Starving as she was she could not sleep, but kept ceaselessly on the prowl. This was fortunate, for had she gone to sleep without any more shelter than the wall of the house she would never have wakened again. In her restlessness she wandered to the farther side of the island where, in a somewhat sheltered and sunny recess of the shore facing the mainland, she found a patch of bare sand, free of ice cakes and just uncovered by the tide. Opening upon this recess were the tiny entrances to several of the mouse tunnels.

Close beside one of these holes in the snow the cat crouched, quiveringly intent. For ten minutes or more she waited, never so much as twitching a whisker. At last a mouse thrust out its little pointed head. Not daring to give it time to change its mind or take alarm, she pounced. The mouse, glimpsing the doom ere it fell, doubled back upon itself in the narrow runway. Hardly realizing what she did in her desperation the cat plunged head and shoulders into the snow, reaching blindly after the vanished prize. By great good luck she caught it.

It was her first meal in four bitter days. The children had always tried to share with her their Christmas cheer and enthusiasm, and had usually succeeded in interesting her by an agreeable lavishness in the matter of cream; but never before had she found a Christmas feast so good.

Now she had learned a lesson. Being naturally clever and her wits sharpened by her fierce necessities, she had grasped the idea that it was possible to follow her prey a little way into the snow. She had not realized that the snow was so penetrable. She had quite wiped out the door of this particular runway; so she went and crouched beside a similar one, but here she had to wait a long time before an adventurous mouse came to peer out. But this time she showed that she had grasped her lesson. It was straight at the side of the entrance that she pounced, where instinct told her that the body of the mouse would be. One outstretched paw thus cut off the quarry's retreat. Her tactics were completely successful; and as her head went plunging into the fluffy whiteness she felt the prize between her paws.

Her hunger now fairly appeased, she found herself immensely excited over this new fashion of hunting. Often before had she waited at mouse holes, but never had she found it possible to break down the walls and invade the holes themselves. It was a thrilling idea. As she crept toward another hole a mouse scurried swiftly up the sand and darted into it. The cat, too late to catch him before he disappeared, tried to follow him. Scratching clumsily but hopefully she succeeded in forcing the full length of her body into the snow. She found no sign of the fugitive, which was by this time racing in safety down some dim transverse tunnel. Her eyes, mouth, whiskers and fur full of the powdery white particles, she backed out, much disappointed. But in that moment she had realized that it was much warmer in there beneath the snow than out in the stinging air. It was a second and vitally important lesson; and though she was probably unconscious of having learned it she instinctively put the new lore into practice a little while later.

Having succeeded in catching yet another mouse for which her appetite made no immediate demand, she carried it back to the house and laid it down in tribute on the veranda steps while she meowed and stared hopefully at the desolate, snow-draped door. Getting no response she carried the mouse down with her to the hollow behind the drift which had been caused by the bulging front of the bay-window on the end of the house. Here she curled herself up forlornly, thinking to have a wink of sleep.

But the still cold was too searching. She looked at the sloping wall of snow beside her and cautiously thrust her paw into it. It was very soft and light. It seemed to offer practically no resistance. She pawed away in an awkward fashion till she had scooped out a sort of tiny cave. Gently she pushed herself into it, pressing back the snow on every side till she had room to turn around.

Then turn around she did several times, as dogs do in getting their beds arranged to their liking. In this process she not only packed down the snow beneath her, but she also rounded out for herself a snug chamber with a comparatively narrow doorway. From this snowy retreat she gazed forth with a solemn air of possession; then she went to sleep with a sense of comfort, of 'homeyness', such as she had never before felt since the disappearance of her friends.

Having thus conquered misfortune and won herself the freedom of the winter wild, her life though strenuous was no longer one of any terrible hardship. With patience at the mouse holes she could catch enough to eat; and in her snowy den she slept warm and secure. In a little while, when a crust had formed over the surface, the mice took to coming out at night and holding revels on the snow. Then the owls, too, came back; and the cat, having tried to catch one, got sharply bitten and clawed before she realized the propriety of letting it go. After this experience she decided that owls, on the whole, were meant to be let alone. But for all that she found it fine hunting, out there on the bleak, unfenced, white reaches of the snow.

Thus, mistress of the situaation, she found the winter slipping by without further serious trials. Only once, toward the end of January, did Fate send her another bad quarter of an hour. On the heels of a peculiarly bitter cold snap a huge white owl from the Arctic Barrens came one night to the island. The cat, taking observations from the corner of the veranda, caught sight of him. One look was enough to assure her that this was a very different kind of visitor from the brown marsh owls. She slipped inconspicuously down into her burrow; and until the great white owl went away, some twenty-four hours later, she kept herself discreetly out of sight.

When spring came back to the island, with the nightly shrill chorus of fluting frogs in the shallow, sedgy pools and the young grass alive with nesting birds, the prisoner's life became almost luxurious in its easy abundance. But now she was once more homeless, since her snug den had vanished with the snow. This did not much matter to her, however, for the weather grew warmer and more tranquil day by day; and moreover, she herself, in being forced back upon her instincts, had learned to be as contented as a tramp. Nevertheless, with all her capacity for learning and adapting herself she had not forgotten anything. So when, one day in June, a crowded boat came over from the mainland, and children's voices, clamouring across the grass tops, broke the desolate silence of the island, the cat heard and sprang up out of her sleep on the veranda steps.

For one second she stood, listening intently. Then, almost as a dog would have done, and as few of her supercilious tribe ever condescend to do, she went racing across to the landing place – to be snatched up into the arms of four happy children at once, and to have her fine fur ruffled to a state which it would cost her an hour's assiduous toilet to put in order.

Little White King

Marguerite Steen

He walks on small pink pads of silence through a world of still and moving shapes: a world loaded with wonder to his eyes which are the blue of the sky on early summer mornings. His coat is the white of a choirboy's surplice at the Easter mass, and, deep within the frail pink petals of his ears, lies a shade of blue that tones with his eyes. Though barely four months old, and motherless, he is immaculate.

During brief periods between dusk and dark he is tossed by incalculable gaieties, but for the most part he is grave; even serious. He bends his intelligence to the solution of a problem of which he has only just become aware.

He has seen himself.

He used to be foolish about the looking-glass, seeking that other white kitten behind it. Now he knows the kitten is himself. He looks briefly upon his beauty and dismisses it. He is beginning to grow up, and to accept the burden of living.

Shadows – of grasses, of leaves, of branches – are intangible; but there are objects he can get his claws into, he can scratch, or bite. Some he is not supposed to touch: he feels a tap, or he is picked up sharply from behind. He is learning not to do certain things – along the road of harsh experience.

Siamese cats are notorious for turning out their children as from a finishing school. My only Siamese, Thebaw, kennel-bred and therefore unused to domesticity, was impeccable, from the moment he arrived from a thirty-six hour railway journey, at my Lakeland cottage. The scores of cats and kittens who grew up under my North Country roof were educated by their parents in the ways of human society, and gave no trouble to anyone in the house.

How did one begin to educate a kitten, of ambiguous breeding, separated from his mother, *and stone deaf*?

Taking all that into consideration, he was very good. The old baking tin filled with earth struck him, to begin with, as an excellent playground; he did not at all gather its significance. He had to be pushed into corners and his attention drawn with a smart tap to his indiscretions. He might have been spared many such indignities if he had been able to hear; for, in my experience with both cats and dogs, the disciplinary power of the human voice is more effective than physical punishment.

So for several weeks he flung the earth in his tin lightheartedly over the floor, he batted it about the freshly polished linoleum. He chose a corner of the dining-room, or close to the radiators, for the performance of his functions, and, having performed them, returned to frolic in his tin: which, as it was his favourite playground, he naturally, with the instinctive fastidiousness of his race, wanted to keep clean. But eventually light dawned. Caught, by good luck, *in flagrante delicto*, and firmly pushed, and held down, on the tin, he got the idea, and sinned no more.

It was more difficult, when the rains and winds ceased, to woo him from the tin to the out of doors, and I cannot think how, with all my cat experience, I came to be such an unimaginative fool. I suppose the problem had never presented itself: those tough, North Country kittens of mine were chased out, hail, rain or snow, by their parents, to their latrine under the valerian shrubs along the garden wall, where, unless in times of storm, the soil was dry and dusty and soft to little paws.

Day after day, with desperate patience, I picked up the white morsel and pinned it down – always in the same place – on the border, at the roots of the periwinkles. Although his instinct was to make his little hole, his tender paw made no impression on the heavy Berkshire loam, so I had to help him. In due course, he was to be trusted. But when Michael Joseph told me - what must have occured to anyone but an idiot – that what I ought to have done was to take his tin out, with garden soil gradually taking the place of the dried earth to which he was accustomed, in it, until he effected the transfer of his own accord – 'was my face red!' After all these years, I had still things to learn about cats.

(While on this subject of hygiene, I cannot resist referring to my cat Castlerosse, who, brought back to town for a few hours between two visits to the country, and finding himself in a fifth-floor apartment with no access to the open spaces to which he was accustomed, made straight for the toilet, of which he availed himself with the aplomb of a human being.)

At about this time, Le Petit Roi developed acrobatic gifts out of all proportion to his size and age. Nothing, apparently, but suction accounted for an uncanny power of propelling himself from the floor to a table top. He was too small to leap it, and his claws too soft to act as leverage up the shiny legs of chairs or tables. I tried, but never once succeeded in catching him at it. If I was about, he mewed hypocritically to be lifted up. If for a moment I went out of the room, leaving him on the floor, sure as little apples, when I returned, there he was, conducting his toilette in the middle of the table. Useless to attempt to spy on him through the door jamb; some infallible cat instinct warned him of observation, and he would settle, disgruntled, his paws tucked under his chest, on a corner of the carpet.

There are cat addicts who, justifying themselves by the cleanliness of cats, have no objection to their parading themselves on tables where food is prepared. Cat-lover and cat-keeper from childhood, I shudder with disgust at the sight of a cat stropping itself on a loaf presently to be served at the meal; I loathe the idea of its hairs knitting themselves into my toast – and it is, moreover, a complete fallacy, that *all* cats are fastidious.

He had therefore to learn that he must not get on tables, and this was a matter of some smart slaps and, when these failed to produce the desired effect, of rough handling, which he disliked more than the soon-over tap on the nose or rap on the tip of his tail. This particular discipline was complicated by the fact that he was allowed on my work-table where he could toy with pens and pencils, bite rubbers and sweep paper clips on to the floor. But, having been thrown off the kitchen table three or four times, having been rough-housed when he climbed on the dining-table, licked the butter and sniffed pensively at the salt - he worked it out in his own small brain. Kitchen and dining-room were soon immune from his intrusions; my work-room, by tacit agreement, was his privileged playground. He must have grasped, eventually, that the prohibition had to do, not with elevation but with food; for he would bound lightly and without misgiving on the little pie-crust tables in the parlour, on a card table, on a dresser, cabinet or chest, waving his tail with proud assurance of righteousness.

Another trial of the cat-lover is the 'claw-sharpening' habit, which is invariably directed towards the more precious or valuable articles of furniture. Before the war there used to be a thing called the 'Kitty-post,' claimed by its inventors to divert any cat's attention from the brocades, the velvets, satins or damasks of the average drawing-room.

Not many people, I imagine, realize that when a cat attacks their treasured upholstery, it is not 'sharpening,' but cleaning, its claws. A cat's claws are not only its hunting weapons, its weapons of defence; it uses them for innumerable purposes and they quickly get dirty, which causes it discomfort. You do not sharpen a knife on woven material; you use it to remove stains, or to polish.

I soon discovered that Le Petit Roi's claw-cleaning was a sign of boredom, or of mental inquietude – precisely as human beings bite their nails. He was not being paid sufficient attention. Or he had been given nothing to play with. He indulged it quite deliberately, as a protest against being ignored. Trail a cord, bounce a ping-pong ball, devote five minutes to his entertainment, and he would settle, good as gold, into peaceful contemplation, under the valance of one of the parlour chairs. Too long enclosed in my bedroom, he would vent his annoyance on my dressing stool; it only meant he was bored, and wanted to go out. There was as little point in punishing him as there would have been in punishing a child who scribbles on the wall, because he has not been given a drawing block or a blackboard to scrawl upon. With no other outlet for his energy, he set about his manicure; surely a laudable occupation in itself? – if unfortunate for the furniture.

The question of obedience to the call was out, in the case of a little deaf cat. It loaded one with anxieties. At the bottom of the lane was the main road, with its lethal traffic which, unhappily, fascinated him. He would cross the road, to curl up on a bench under the elms, or to sit on the opposite bank, watching the cars, the lorries, the buses go by. Between five and six came, in an endless stream, the buses with the workers from what is locally known as 'The Atom' – the Harwell research station. We always managed, when tea-time was over, to catch him and imprison him – to his fury – in the house. He could have watched them just as well from his own garden, but crossing the road gave him a sense of independence. It was useless to call, when he went trotting down the lane; unless to attempt to impose on him the discipline which kept the Black One within the safety zone.

But he was very good. When I, or his true love, Alice, went down to collect him, he came trotting politely, head and tail in the air, inviting us to gather him into our arms. If he could have heard, he would probably have been the most obedient cat in the world. If he could have heard . . .

The Tom Cat

At MIDNIGHT in the alley
   A Tom-cat comes to wail,
And he chants the hate of a million years
   As he swings his snaky tail.

Malevolent, bony, brindled,
   Tiger and devil and bard,
His eyes are coals from middle of Hell
   And his heart is black and hard.

He twists and crouches and capers
   And bares his curved sharp claws,
And he sings to the stars of the jungle nights
   Ere cities were, or laws.

Beast from a world primeval,
   He and his leaping clan,
When the blotched red moon leers over the roofs
   Give voice to their scorn of man.

He will lie on a rug tomorrow
   And lick his silky fur,
And veil the brute in his yellow eyes
   And play he's tame and purr.

But at midnight in the alley
  He will crouch again and wail,
And beat the time for his demon's song
  With the swing of his demon's tail.

DON MARQUIS

The Cat And Cupid

Arnold Bennett

I

The secret history of the Ebag marriage is now printed for the first time. The Ebag family, who prefer their name to be accented on the first syllable, once almost ruled Oldcastle, which is a clean and conceited borough, with long historical traditions, on the very edge of the industrial, democratic and unclean Five Towns. The Ebag family still lives in the grateful memory of Oldcastle, for no family ever did more to preserve the celebrated Oldcastilian superiority in social, moral and religious matters over the vulgar Five Towns. The episodes leading to the Ebag marriage could only have happened in Oldcastle. By which I mean merely that they could not have happened in any of the Five Towns. In the Five Towns that sort of thing does not occur. I don't know why, but it doesn't. The people are too deeply interested in football, starting prices, rates, public parks, sliding scales, excursions to Blackpool, and municipal shindies, to concern themselves with organists as such. In the Five Towns an organist may be a sanitary inspector or an auctioneer on Mondays. In Oldcastle an organist is an organist, recognized as such in the streets. No one ever heard of an organist in the Five Towns being taken up and petted by a couple of old ladies. But this may occur at Oldcastle. It, in fact, did.

The scandalous circumstances which led to the disappearance from the Oldcastle scene of Mr Skerritt, the original organist of St Placid, have no relation to the present narrative, which opens when the ladies Ebag began to seek for a new organist. The new church of St Placid owed its magnificent existence to the Ebag family. The apse had been given entirely by old Caiaphas Ebag (ex-M.P., now a paralytic sufferer) at a cost of twelve thousand pounds; and his was the original idea of building the church. When, owing to the decline of the working man's interest in beer, and one or two other things, Caiaphas lost nearly the whole of his fortune, which had been gained by honest labour in mighty speculations, he rather regretted the church; he would have preferred twelve thousand in cash to a view of the apse from his bedroom window; but he was man enough never to complain. He lived, after his misfortunes, in a comparatively small house with his two daughters, Mrs Ebag and Miss Ebag. These two ladies are the heroines of the tale.

Mrs Ebag had married her cousin, who had died. She possessed about six hundred a year of her own. She was two years older than her sister, Miss Ebag, a spinster. Miss Ebag was two years younger than Mrs Ebag. No further information as to their respective ages ever leaked out. Miss Ebag had a little money of her own from her deceased mother, and Caiaphas had the wreck of his riches. The total income of the household was not far short of a thousand a year, but of this quite two hundred a year was absorbed by young Edith Ebag, Mrs Ebag's step-daughter (for Mrs Ebag had been her husband's second choice). Edith, who was notorious as a silly chit and spent most of her time in London and other absurd places, formed no part of the household, though she visited it occasionally. The household consisted of old Caiaphas, bedridden, and his two daughters and Goldie. Goldie was the tomcat, so termed by reason of his splendid tawniness. Goldie had more to do with the Ebag marriage than anyone or anything, except the weathercock on the top of the house. This may sound queer, but is as naught to the queerness about to be unfolded.

II

It cannot be considered unnatural that Mrs and Miss Ebag, with the assistance of the vicar, should have managed the affairs of the church. People nicknamed them 'the churchwardens,' which was not quite nice, having regard to the fact that their sole aim was the truest welfare of the church. They and the vicar, in a friendly and effusive way, hated each other. Sometimes they got the better of the vicar, and, less often, he got the better of them. In the choice of a new organist they won. Their candidate was Mr Carl Ullman, the artistic orphan.

Mr Carl Ullman is the hero of the tale. The son of one of those German designers of earthenware who at intervals come and settle in the Five Towns for the purpose of explaining fully to the inhabitants how inferior England is to Germany, he had an English mother, and he himself was violently English. He spoke English like an Englishman and German like an Englishman. He could paint, model in clay, and play three musical instruments, including the organ. His one failing was that he could never earn enough to live on. It seemed as if he was always being drawn by an invisible string towards the workhouse door. Now and then he made half a sovereign extra by deputizing on the organ. In such manner had he been introduced to the Ebag ladies. His romantic and gloomy appearance had attracted them, with the result that they had asked him to lunch after the service, and he had remained with them till the evening service. During the visit they had learnt that his grandfather had been Court Councillor in the Kingdom of Saxony. Afterwards they often said to each other how ideal it would be if only Mr Skerritt might be removed and Carl Ullman take his place. And when Mr Skerritt actually was removed, by his own wickedness, they regarded it as almost an answer to prayer, and successfully employed their powerful interest on behalf of Carl. The salary was a hundred a year. Not once in his life had Carl earned a hundred pounds in a single year. For him the situation meant opulence. He accepted it, but calmly, gloomily. Romantic gloom was his joy in life. He said with deep melancholy that he was sure he could not find a convenient lodging in Oldcastle. And the ladies Ebag then said that he must really come and spend a few days with them and Goldie and papa until he was 'suited.' He said that he hated to plant himself on people, and yielded to the request. The ladies Ebag fussed around his dark-eyed and tranquil pessimism, and both of them instantly grew younger – a curious but authentic phenomenon. They adored his playing, and they were enchanted to discover that his notions about hymn tunes agreed with theirs, and by consequence disagreed with the vicar's. In the first week or two they scored off the vicar five times, and the advantage of having your organist in your own house grew very apparent. They were also greatly impressed by his gentleness with Goldie and by his intelligent interest in serious questions.

One day Miss Ebag said timidly to her sister: 'It's just six months today.'

'What do you mean, sister?' asked Mrs Ebag, self-consciously.

'Since Mr Ullman came.'

'So it is!' said Mrs Ebag, who was just as well aware of the date as the spinster was aware of it.

They said no more. The position was the least bit delicate. Carl had found no lodging. He did not offer to go. They did not want him to go. He did not offer to pay. And really he cost them nothing except laundry, whisky and fussing. How could they suggest that he should pay? He lived amidst them like a beautiful mystery, and all were seemingly content. Carl was probably saving the whole of his salary, for he never bought clothes and he did not smoke. The ladies Ebag simply did what they liked about hymn-tunes.

III

You would have thought that no outsider would find a word to say, and you would have been mistaken. The fact that Mrs Ebag was two years older than Miss and Miss two years younger than Mrs Ebag; the fact that old Caiaphas was, for strong reasons, always in the house; the fact that the ladies were notorious cat-idolaters; the fact that the reputation of the Ebag family was and had ever been spotless; the fact that the Ebag family had given the apse and practically created the entire church; all these facts added together did not prevent the outsider from finding a word to say.

At first words were not said; but looks were looked, and coughs were coughed. Then someone, strolling into the church of a morning while Carl Ullman was practising, saw Miss Ebag sitting in silent ecstasy in a corner. And a few mornings later the same someone, whose curiosity had been excited, veritably saw Mrs Ebag in the organ-loft with Carl Ullman, but no sign of Miss Ebag. It was at this juncture that words began to be said.

Words! Not complete sentences! The sentences were never finished. 'Of course, it's no affair of mine, but – ' 'I wonder that people like the Ebags should – ' 'Not that I should ever dream of hinting that – ' 'First one and then the other – well!' 'I'm sure that if either Mrs or Miss Ebag had the slightest idea they'd at once – ' And so on. Intangible gossamer criticism, floating in the air!

IV

One evening – it was precisely the first of June – when a thunderstorm was blowing up from the south-west, and scattering the smoke of the Five Towns to the four corners of the world, and making the weathercock of the house of the Ebags creak, the ladies Ebag and Carl Ullman sat together as usual in the drawing-room. The French window was open, but banged to at intervals. Carl Ullman had played the piano and the ladies Ebag – Mrs Ebag, somewhat comfortably stout and Miss Ebag spare – were talking very well and sensibly about the influence of music on character. They invariably chose such subjects for conversation. Carl was chiefly silent, but now and then, after a sip of whisky, he would say 'Yes' with impressiveness and stare gloomily out of the darkening window. The ladies Ebag had a remarkable example of the influence of music on character in the person of Edith Ebag. It appeared that Edith would never play anything but waltzes – Waldteufel's for choice – and that the foolish frivolity of her flya-way character was a direct consequence of this habit. Carl felt sadly glad, after hearing the description of Edith's carryings-on, that Edith had chosen to live far away.

And then the conversation languished and died with the daylight, and a certain self-consciousness obscured the social atmosphere. For a vague rumour of the chatter of the town had penetrated the house, and the ladies Ebag, though they scorned chatter, were affected by it; Carl Ullman, too. It had the customary effect of such chatter; it fixed the thoughts of those chatted about on matters which perhaps would not otherwise have occupied their attention.

The ladies Ebag said to themselves: 'We are no longer aged nineteen. We are moreover living with our father. If he is bedridden, what then? This gossip connecting our names with that of Mr Ullman is worse than baseless; it is preposterous. We assert positively that we have no designs of any kind on Mr Ullman.'

Nevertheless, by dint of thinking about that gossip, the naked idea of a marriage with Mr Ullman soon ceased to shock them. They could gaze at it without going into hysterics.

As for Carl, he often meditated upon his own age, which might have been anything between thirty and forty-five, and upon the mysterious ages of the ladies, and upon their goodness, their charm, their seriousness, their intelligence and their sympathy with himself.

Hence the self-consciousness in the gloaming.

To create a diversion Miss Ebag walked primly to the window and cried:

'Goldie! Goldie!'

It was Goldie's bedtime. In summer he always strolled into the garden after dinner, and he nearly always sensibly responded to the call when his bed-hour sounded. No one would have dreamed of retiring until Goldie was safely ensconced in his large basket under the stairs.

'Naughty Goldie!' Miss Ebag said, comprehensively, to the garden.

She went into the garden to search, and Mrs Ebag followed her, and Carl Ullman followed Mrs Ebag. And they searched without result, until it was black night and the threatening storm at last fell. The vision of Goldie out in that storm desolated the ladies, and Carl Ullman displayed the nicest feeling. At length the rain drove them in and they stood in the drawing-room with anxious faces, while two servants, under directions from Carl, searched the house for Goldie.

'If you pleas'm.' stammered the housemaid, rushing rather unconventionally into the drawing-droom, 'cook says she thinks Goldie must be on the roof, in the vane.'

'On the roof in the vane?' exclaimed Mrs Ebag, pale. 'In the vane?'

'Yes'm.'

'Whatever do you mean, Sarah?' asked Miss Ebag, even paler.

The ladies Ebag were utterly convinced that Goldie was not like other cats, that he never went on the roof, that he never had any wish to do anything that was not in the strictest sense gentlemanly and correct. And if by chance he did go on the roof, it was merely to examine the roof itself, or to enjoy the view therefrom out of gentlemanly curiosity. So that this reference to the roof shocked them. The night did not favour the theory of view-gazing.

'Cook says she heard the weather-vane creaking ever since she went upstairs after dinner, and now it's stopped; and she can hear Goldie a-myowling like anything.'

'Is cook in her attic?' asked Mrs Ebag.

'Yes'm.'

'Ask her to come out. Mr Ullman, will you be so very good as to come upstairs and investigate?'

Cook, enveloped in a cloak, stood out on the second landing, while Mr Ullman and the ladies invaded her chamber. The noise of myowling was terrible. Mr Ullman opened the dormer window, and the rain burst in, together with a fury of myowling. But he did not care. It lightened and thundered. But he did not care. He procured a chair of cook's and put it under the window and stood on it, with his back to the window, and twisted forth his body so that he could spy up the roof. The ladies protested that he would be wet through, but he paid no heed to them.

Then his head, dripping, returned into the room.

'I've just seen by a flash of lightning,' he said in a voice of emotion. 'The poor animal has got his tail fast in the socket of the weather-vane. He must have been whisking it about up there, and the vane turned and caught it. The vane is jammed.'

'How dreadful!' said Mrs Ebag. 'Whatever can be done?'

'He'll be dead before morning,' sobbed Miss Ebag.

'I shall climb up the roof and release him,' said Carl Ullman, gravely.

They forbade him to do so. Then they implored him to refrain. But he was adamant. And in their supplications there was a note of insincerity, for their hearts bled for Goldie, and, further, they were not altogether unwilling that Carl should prove himself a hero. And so, amid apprehensive feminine cries of the acuteness of his danger, Carl crawled out of the window and faced the thunder, the lightning, the rain, the slippery roof, and the maddened cat. A group of three servants were huddled outside the attic door.

In the attic the ladies could hear his movements on the roof, moving higher and higher. The suspense was extreme. Then there was silence; even the myowling had ceased. Then a clap of thunder; and then, after that, a terrific clatter on the roof, a bounding downwards as of a great stone, a curse, a horrid pause, and finally a terrific smashing of foliage and cracking of wood.

Mrs Ebag sprang to the window.

'It's all right,' came a calm, gloomy voice from below. 'I fell into the rhododendrons, and Goldie followed me. I'm not hurt, thank goodness! Just my luck!'

A bell rang imperiously. It was the paralytic's bell. He had been disturbed by these unaccustomed phenomena.

'Sister, do go to father at once, said Mrs Ebag, as they both hastened downstairs in a state of emotion, assuredly unique in their lives.

V

Mrs Ebag met Carl and the cat as they dripped into the gas-lit drawing-room. They presented a surprising spectacle, and they were doing damage to the Persian carpet at the rate of about five shillings a second; but that Carl, and the beloved creature for whom he had dared so much, were equally unhurt appeared to be indubitable. Of course, it was a mircale. It could not be regarded as other than a miracle. Mrs Ebag gave vent to an exclamation in which were mingled pity, pride, admiration and solicitude, and then remained, as it were spellbound. The cat escaped from those protecting arms and fled away. Instead of following Goldie, Mrs Ebag continued to gaze at the hero.

'How can I thank you!' she whispered.

'What for?' asked Carl, with laconic gloom.

'For having saved my darling!' said Mrs Ebag. And there was passion in her voice.

'Oh!' said Carl. 'It was nothing!'

'Nothing?' Mrs Ebag repeated after him, with melting eyes, as if to imply that, instead of being nothing, it was everything; as if to imply that his deed must rank hereafter with the most splendid deeds of antiquity; as if to imply that the whole affair was beyond words to utter or gratitude to repay.

And in fact Carl himself was moved. You cannot fall from the roof of a two-story house into a very high-class rhododendron bush, carrying a prize cat in your arms, without being a bit shaken. And Carl was a bit shaken, not merely physically, but morally and spiritually. He could not deny to himself that he had after all done something rather wondrous, which ought to be celebrated in sounding verse. He felt that he was in an atmosphere far removed from the commonplace.

He dripped steadily on to the carpet.

'You know how dear my cat was to me,' proceeded Mrs Ebag. 'And you risked your life to spare me the pain of his suffering, perhaps his death. How thankful I am that I insisted on having those rhododendrons planted just where they are – fifteen years ago! I never anticipated – '

She stopped. Tears came into her dowager eyes. It was obvious that she worshipped him. She was so absorbed in his heroism that she had no thought even for his dampness. As Carl's eyes met hers she seemed to him to grow younger. And there came into his mind all the rumour that had vaguely reached him coupling their names together; and also his early dreams of love and passion and a marriage that would be one long honeymoon. And he saw how absurd had been those early dreams. He saw that the best chance of a felicitous marriage lay in a union of mature and serious persons, animated by grave interests and lofty ideals. Yes, she was older than he. But not much, not much! Not more than - how many years? And he remembered surprising her rapt glance that very evening as she watched him playing the piano. What had romance to do with age? Romance could occur at any age. It was occurring now. Her soft eyes, her portly form, exuded romance. And had not the renowned Beaconsfield espoused a lady appreciably older than himself, and did not those espousals achieve the ideal of bliss? In the act of saving the cat he had not been definitely aware that it was so particularly the cat of the household. But now, influenced by her attitude and her shining reverence, he actually did begin to persuade himself that an uncontrollable instinctive desire to please her and win her for his own had moved him to undertake the perilous passage of the sloping roof.

In short, the idle chatter of the town was about to be justified. In another moment he might have dripped into her generous arms . . . had not Miss Ebag swept into the drawing-room!

'Gracious!' gasped Miss Ebag. 'The poor dear thing will have pneumonia. Sister, you know his chest is not strong. Dear Mr Ullman, please, please, do go and – er – change.'

He did the discreet thing and went to bed, hot whisky following him on a tray carried by the housemaid.

VI

The next morning the slightly unusual happened. It was the custom for Carl Ullman to breakfast alone, while reading *The Staffordshire Signal*. The ladies Ebag breakfasted mysteriously in bed. But on this morning Carl found Miss Ebag before him in the breakfast-room. She prosecuted minute inquiries as to his health and nerves. She went out with him to regard the rhododendron bushes, and shuddered at the sight of the ruin which had saved him. She said, following famous philosophers, that Chance was merely the name we give to the effect of laws which we cannot understand. And, upon this high level of conversation, she poured forth his coffee and passed his toast.

It was a lovely morning after the tempest.

Goldie, all newly combed, and looking as though he had never seen a roof, strolled pompously into the room with tail unfurled. Miss Ebag picked the animal up and kissed it passionately.

'Darling!' she murmured, not exactly to Mr Ullman, nor yet exactly to the cat. Then she glanced effulgently at Carl and said, 'When I think that you risked your precious life, in that awful storm, to save my poor Goldie? . . . You must have guessed how dear he was to me? . . . No, really, Mr Ullman, I cannot thank you properly! I can't express my – '

Her eyes were moist.

Although not young, she was two years younger. Her age was two years less. The touch of man had never profaned her. No masculine kiss had ever rested on that cheek, that mouth. And Carl felt that he might be the first to cull the flower that had so long waited. He did not see, just then, the hollow beneath her chin, the two lines of sinew that, bounding a depression, disappeared beneath her collarette. He saw only her soul. He guessed that she would be more malleable than the widow, and he was sure that she was not in a position, as the widow was, to make comparisons between husbands. Certainly there appeared to be some confusion as to the proprietorship of this cat. Certainly he could not have saved the cat's life for love of two different persons. But that was beside the point. The essential thing was that he began to be glad that he had decided nothing definite about the widow on the previous evening.

'Darling!' said she again, with a new access of passion, kissing Goldie, but darting a glance at Carl.

He might have put to her the momentous question, between two bites of buttered toast, had not Mrs Ebag, at the precise instant, swum amply into the room.

'Sister! You up!' exclaimed Miss Ebag.

'And you, sister!' retorted Mrs Ebag.

VII

It is impossible to divine what might have occurred for the delectation of the very ancient borough of Oldcastle if that frivolous piece of goods, Edith, had not taken it into her head to run down from London for a few days, on the plea that London was too ridiculously hot. She was a pretty girl, with fluffy honey-coloured hair and about thirty white frocks. And she seemed to be quite as silly as her staid stepmother and her prim step-aunt had said. She transformed the careful order of the house into a wild disorder, and left a novel or so lying on the drawing-room table between her stepmother's *Contemporary Review* and her step-aunt's *History of European Morals*. Her taste in music was candidly and brazenly bad. It was a fact, as her elders had stated, that she played nothing but waltzes. What was worse, she compelled Carl Ullman to perform waltzes. And one day she burst into the drawing-room when Carl was alone there, with a roll under her luscious arm, and said:

'What do you think I've found at Barrowfoot's?'

'I don't know,' said Carl, gloomily smiling, and then smiling without gloom.

'Waldteufel's waltzes arranged for four hands. You must play them with me at once.'

And he did. It was a sad spectacle to see the organist of St Placid's galloping through a series of dances with the empty-headed Edith.

The worst was, he liked it. He knew that he ought to prefer the high intellectual plane, the severe artistic tastes, of the elderly sisters. But he did not. He was amazed to discover that frivolity appealed more powerfully to his secret soul. He was also amazed to discover that his gloom was leaving him. This vanishing of gloom gave him strange sensations, akin to the sensations of a man who, after having worn gaiters into middle-age, abandons them.

After the Waldteufel she began to tell him all about herself; how she went slumming in the East End, and how jolly it was. And how she helped in the Bloomsbury Settlement, and how jolly that was. And, later, she said:

'You must have thought it very odd of me, Mr Ullman, not thanking you for so bravely rescuing my poor cat; but the truth is I never heard of it till today. I can't say how grateful I am. I should have loved to see you doing it.'

'Is Goldie your cat?' he feebly inquired.

'Why, of course?' she said. 'Didn't you know? Of course you did! Goldie always belonged to me. Grandpa bought him for me. But I couldn't do with him in London, so I always leave him here for them to take care of. He adores me. He never forgets me. He'll come to me before anyone. You must have noticed that. I can't say how grateful I am! It was perfectly marvellous of you! I can't help laughing, though, whenever I think what a state mother and auntie must have been in that night!'

Strictly speaking, they hadn't a cent between them, except his hundred a year. But he married her hair and she married his melancholy eyes; and she was content to settle in Oldcastle, where there are almost no slums. And her stepmother was forced by Edith to make the hundred up to four hundred. This was rather hard on Mrs Ebag. Thus it fell out that Mrs Ebag remained a widow, and that Miss Ebag continues a flower unculled. However, gossip was stifled.

In his appointed time, and in the fulness of years, Goldie died, and was mourned. And by none was he more sincerely mourned than by the aged bedridden Caiaphas.

'I miss my cat, I can tell ye!' said old Caiaphas pettishly to Carl, who was sitting by his couch. 'He knew his master, Goldie did! Edith did her best to steal him from me when you married and set up house. A nice thing considering I bought him and he never belonged to anybody but me! Ay! I shall never have another cat like that cat.'

And this is the whole truth of the affair.

Why The Cat Sleeps Indoors And The Dog Outside

African Folktale

There once lived a barren woman who wanted nothing more than a son. She sought out one of her gods and asked him for one, and he, pitying her, promised to grant her wish.

Her son was duly born and grew rapidly into a youth, for he was a special child. She loved him dearly and all but forgot the god's warning that he would one day put her into debt. When the boy was playing outside the house one day he suddenly asked her for gold dust with which to buy some salt. Loving him as she did she could refuse him nothing, so in spite of her misgivings he was soon on his way with the money.

He had not gone far when he met a man with a dog. As soon as he saw it, he knew he must have that dog whatever its cost. The man refused to part with the animal, but when he saw all the gold dust that was offered him for it he finally agreed to sell it. When the boy reached home with his purchase his mother realized that her fears had not been for nothing.

This did not keep her from giving her son more gold a second and a third time. The second time it bought a cat, the third time a pigeon. There could be no fourth time because there no longer was any money, so the boy, dog, cat, and pigeon stayed close to home.

The pigeon said to the boy one day, 'Take me home to my village. There I am a chief and the people will gladly give you a reward for my return. I was accidentally caught when I was making a journey, and since you rescued me I want to repay you.'

The youth did not believe this story, but he finally agreed to take the pigeon to his home. There his people hailed him with joy as their long-lost chief. They could not thank their chief's rescuer enough and showered him with gifts, one of which was a magic ring which would give its owner whatever he desired.

Through the ring's magic the boy was soon chief of a village of his own. Naturally everyone was very curious about his sudden good fortune, and it wasn't long before his best friend succeeded in finding out the reason for it. Craving the ring for himself, he soon managed to steal it and set up his own village which was far finer than that of the ring's true owner.

The boy visited a god to find out who had stolen the ring and how he could regain it. When he heard the answer he went home and called his dog and cat to him.

'You can now repay me for having bought you,' he said. 'My ring has been stolen from me and only you two can get it back. There is one difficulty. The thief has learned that you are being sent to recover the ring. To stop you he has placed drugged meat along your way. When you come to this meat leave it untouched and continue on your journey.'

The dog taunted the cat, saying that she would be unable to resist the meat, but when they reached it on their journey it turned out otherwise. The dog complained to the cat that he had a stomach-ache and could go no farther. She replied that they couldn't delay and went on alone. When she was out of sight the dog raced over to the meat and devoured it, but when he tried to get up and follow the cat he found that he couldn't.

The cat, in the meantime, had reached the room where the ring lay in a box. Knowing she could not get it from the box by herself she caught a mouse, and when the mouse begged for its life she told it she would spare it in return for the ring. Then, tying a string around it, she let it go. The mouse ran to the box and in a short time had gnawed a hole in it. Picking up the ring in its mouth it raced back to the cat. Without a second glance at the mouse she seized the ring and started for home.

She met the dog at the same place where she had left him and saw that the meat was gone. The dog said that he had no idea what had happened to it but that the cat had better give him the ring when they got to the river they must cross before reaching home. He told her that if she kept it she would certainly lose it, because the river was now in flood and she had to walk across its bottom to get to the other side, whereas he could swim.

The cat decided that he was right and gave him the ring. When they reached the river she crossed it at once, but the dog became tired halfway across and had to take a deep breath. When he did, the ring fell from his mouth and was swallowed by a large fish swimming near by.

When he got to shore the cat asked the dog for the ring and he had to tell her what had happened. She ran into the water, caught the fish, and forced it to cough up the ring. With it once again in her possession the dog begged the cat not to tell their master what had happened. The cat said nothing, but when they reached home she related everything – how the dog had eaten the drugged meat and then had lost the ring. Everyone who heard this became very angry with the dog and praised the cat.

And so it is that to this day you will find the cat sleeping in the best place in the house and eating the best food, while the dog must sleep outside in the dead ashes of the fire and take many beatings.

The Fat Cat

Q. Patrick

The marines found her when they finally captured the old mission house at Fufa. After two days of relentless pounding, they hadn't expected to find anything alive there – least of all a fat cat.

And she was a very fat cat, sandy as a Scotsman, with enormous agate eyes and a fat amiable face. She sat there on the mat – or rather what was left of the mat – in front of what had been the mission porch, licking her paws as placidly as if the shell-blasted jungle were a summer lawn in New Jersey.

One of the men, remembering his childhood primer, quoted: 'The fat cat sat on the mat.'

The other men laughed; not that the remark was really funny, but laughter broke the tension and expressed their relief at having at last reached their objective, after two days of bitter fighting.

The fat cat, still sitting on the mat, smiled at them, as if to show she didn't mind the joke being on her. Then she saw Corporal Randy Jones, and for some reason known only to herself ran toward him as though he were her long-lost master. With a refrigerator purr, she weaved in and out of his muddy legs.

Everyone laughed again as Randy picked her up and pushed his ugly face against the sleek fur. It was funny to see any living thing show a preference for the dour, solitary Randy.

A sergeant flicked his fingers. 'Kitty. Come here. We'll make you B Company mascot.'

But the cat, perched on Randy's shoulder like a queen on her throne, merely smiled down majestically as much as to say: 'You can be my subjects if you like. But this is my man – my royal consort.'

And never for a second did she swerve from her devotion. She lived with Randy, slept with him, ate only food provided by him. almost every man in Company B tried to seduce her with caresses and morsels of canned ration, but all advances were met with a yawn of contempt.

For Randy this new love was ecstasy. He guarded her with the possessive tenderness of a mother. He combed her fur sleek; he almost starved himself to maintain her fatness. And all the time there was a strange wonder in him. The homeliest and ungainliest of ten in a West Virginia mining family, he had never before aroused affection in man or woman. No one had counted for him until the fat cat.

Randy's felicity, however, was short-lived. In a few days B Company was selected to carry out a flanking movement to surprise and possibly capture the enemy's headquarters, known to be twenty miles away through dense, sniper-infested jungle. The going would be rugged. Each man would carry his own supply of food and water, and sleep in foxholes with no support from the base.

The C.O. was definite about the fat cat: the stricken Randy was informed that the presence of a cat would seriously endanger the safety of the whole company. If it were seen following him, it would be shot on sight. Just before their scheduled departure, Randy carried the fat cat over to the mess of Company H, where she was enthusiastically received by an equally fat cook. Randy could not bring himself to look back at the reproachful stare which he knew would be in the cat's agate eyes.

But all through that first day of perilous jungle travel, the thought of the cat's stare haunted him, and he was prey to all the heartache of parting; in leaving the cat, he had left behind wife, mother, and child.

Darkness, like an immense black parachute, had descended hours ago on the jungle, when Randy was awakened from exhausted sleep. Something soft and warm was brushing his cheek; and his foxhole resounded to a symphony of purring. He stretched out an incredulous hand, but this was no dream. Real and solid, the cat was curled in a contented ball at his shoulder.

His first rush of pleasure was chilled as he remembered his

C.O.'s words. The cat, spurning the blandishments of H Company's cuisine, had followed him through miles of treacherous jungle, only to face death the moment daylight revealed her presence. Randy was in an agony of uncertainty. To carry her back to the base would be desertion. To beat and drive her away was beyond the power of his simple nature.

The cat nuzzled his face again and breathed a mournful meow. She was hungry, of course, after her desperate trek. Suddenly Randy saw what he must do. If he could bring himself not to feed her, hunger would surely drive her back to the sanctuary of the cook.

She meowed again. He shushed her and gave her a half-hearted slap. 'Ain't got nothing for you, honey. Scram. Go home. Scat.'

To his mingled pleasure and disappointment, she leaped silently out of the foxhole. When morning came there was no sign of her.

As B Company inched its furtive advance through the dense undergrowth, Randy felt the visit from the cat must have been a dream. But on the third night it came again. It brushed against his cheek and daintily took his ear in its teeth. When it meowed, the sound was still soft and cautious, but held a pitiful quaver of beseechment which cut through Randy like a Japanese bayonet.

On its first visit, Randy had not seen the cat, but tonight some impulse made him reach for his flashlight. Holding it carefully downward, he turned it on. What he saw was the ultimate ordeal. The fat cat was fat no longer. Her body sagged; her sleek fur was matted and mud-stained, her paws torn and bloody. but it was the eyes, blinking up at him, that were the worst. There was no hint of reproach in them, only an expression of infinite trust and pleading.

Forgetting everything but those eyes, Randy tugged out one of his few remaining cans of ration. At the sight of it, the cat weakly licked its lips. Randy moved to open the can. Then the realization that he would be signing the cat's death warrant surged over him. And, because the pent-up emotion in him had to have some outlet, it turned into unreasoning anger against this animal whose suffering had become more than he could bear. 'Scat,' he hissed. But the cat did not move.

He lashed out at her with the heavy flashlight. For a second she lay motionless under the blow. Then with a little moan she fled.

The next night she did not come back and Randy did not sleep.

On the fifth day they reached really dangerous territory. Randy and another marine, Joe were sent forward to scout for the Japanese command headquarters. Suddenly, weaving through the jungle, they came upon it.

A profound silence hung over the glade, with its two hastily erected shacks. Peering through the dense foliage, they saw traces of recent evacuation – waste paper scattered on the grass, a pile of fresh garbage, a Japanese army shirt flapping on a tree. Outside one of the shacks, under an awning, stretched a rough table strewn with the remains of a meal. 'They must have got wind of us and scrammed,' breathed Joe.

Randy edged forward – then froze as something stirred in the long grasses near the door of the first shack. As he watched, the once fat cat hobbled out into the sunlight.

A sense of heightened danger warred with Randy's pride that she had not abandoned him. Stiff with suspense, he watched it disappear into the shack. Soon it padded out.

'No Japs,' said Joe. 'That cat'd have raised 'em sure as shooting.'

He started boldly into the glade. 'Hey, Randy, there's a whole chicken on that table. Chicken's going to taste good after K rations.'

He broke off, for the cat had seen the chicken too, and with pitiful clumsiness had leaped on to the table. With an angry yell Joe stooped for a rock and threw it.

Indignation blazed in Randy. He'd starved and spurned the cat, and yet she'd followed him with blind devotion. The chicken, surely should be her reward. In his slow, simple mind it seemed the most important thing in the world for his beloved to have her fair share of the booty.

The cat, seeing the rock coming, lumbered off the table, just in time, for the rock struck the chicken squarely, knocking it off its plate.

Randy leaped into the clearing. As he did so, a deafening explosion made him drop to the ground. A few seconds later, when he raised himself, there was no table, no shack, nothing but a blazing wreckage of wood.

Dazedly he heard Joe's voice: 'Booby trap under that chicken. Gee, if that cat hadn't jumped for it, I wouldn't have hurled the rock; we'd have grabbed it ourselves – and we'd be in heaven now.' His voice dropped to an awed whisper. 'That cat, I guess it's blown to hell. . . . But it saved our lives.' Randy couldn't speak. There was a constriction in his throat. He lay there, feeling more desolate than he'd ever felt in his life before.

Then from behind came a contented purr.

He spun round. Freakishly, the explosion had hurled a crude rush mat out of the shack. It had come to rest on the grass behind him.

And, seated serenely on the mat, the cat was smiling at him.

The Cat and the Fox

The cat and fox, when saints were all the rage,
    Together went on pilgrimage.
    Arch hypocrites and swindlers, they,
      By sleight of face and sleight of paw,
      Regardless both of right and law,
Contrived expenses to repay,
    By eating many a fowl and cheese,
    And other tricks as bad as these.
    Disputing served them to beguile
    The road of many a weary mile.
    Disputing! but for this resort,
    The world would go to sleep, in short.
    Our pilgrims, as a thing of course,
    Disputed till their throats were hoarse.
      Then, dropping to a lower tone,
    They talk'd of this, and talk'd of that,
    Till Renard whisper'd to the cat,
      'You think yourself a knowing one:
    How many cunning tricks have you?
    For I've a hundred, old and new,
    All ready in my haversack.'
    The cat replied, 'I do not lack,
      Though with but one provided;
    And, truth to honour, for that matter,
    I hold it than a thousand better.'
      In fresh dispute they sided;
    And loudly were they at it, when

Approach'd a mob of dogs and men.
'Now,' said the cat, 'your tricks ransack,
And put your cunning brains to rack,
One life to save; I'll show you mine –
A trick, you see, for saving nine.'
With that, she climb'd a lofty pine.
The fox his hundred ruses tried,
   And yet no safety found.
A hundred times he falsified
   The nose of every hound. –
Was here, and there, and everywhere,
   Above, and under ground;
But yet to stop he did not dare,
Pent in a hole, it was no joke,
To meet the terriers or the smoke.
So, leaping into upper air,
He met two dogs, that choked him there.

Expedients may be too many,
Consuming time to choose and try.
   On one, but that as good as any,
'Tis best in danger to rely.

LA FONTAINE

Some Clever Cats

C. H. Ross

It is difficult, but by no means impossible, to teach a Cat tricks. I myself had a favourite Cat, lately dead, which performed a variety of amusing feats, though I must own that it was extremely coquettish, and nine times out of ten refused to exhibit before a visitor, invited specially to witness the little comedy. Many Cats, without teaching, learn droll tricks.

Doctor Smellie tells of a Cat that had learned to lift the latch of a door; and other tales have been related of Cats that have been taught to ring a bell by hanging to the bell rope; and this anecdote is related by the illustrious Sam Slick, of Slickville. It occurred, several times, that his servant entered the library without having been summoned by his master, and in all cases the domestic was quite sure he had heard the bell. Great wonderment was caused by this, and the servant began to suspect that the house was haunted. It was, at length, noticed that on all these mysterious occasions the Cat entered with the servant. She was, therefore, watched, and it was soon perceived that whenever she found the library door closed against her, she jumped on to the window-sill, and thence sprang at the bell. This feat was exhibited to several of the clockmaker's friends, for the Cat when shut out of the room, would at once resort to this mode of obtaining admission.

My third story is a time-honoured one that almost every person who has written about Cats has related. There was once upon a time, a monastery, a Cat, and a dinner-bell. Every day at a certain hour the bell was rung, and the monks and the Cat had their meal together. There however came a time when, during the bell ring-ing, the Cat happened to be locked in a room at the other end of the building. Some hours afterwards she was released, and ran straight to the refectory, to find, alas! nothing but bare tables to welcome her. Presently the monks were astonished by a loud summons from the dinner-bell. Had the cook, in his absence of mind, prepared another dinner? Some of them hurried to the spot, where they found the Cat swinging on the bell-rope. She had learnt from experience that there never was any dinner without a bell ringing; and by force of reasoning, no doubt, had come to the conclusion that the dinner would be sure to come if she only rang loud enough.

But that story is not half so wonderful as another, about an Angora Cat belonging to a Carthusian monastery at Paris. This ingenious animal discovered that, when a certain bell rang, the cook left the kitchen to answer it, leaving the monks' dinners, portioned out in plates, unprotected. The plan the Cat adopted was to ring the bell, the handle of which hung outside the kitchen by the side of the window, to leap through the window, and back again when she had secured one of the portions. This little manoeuvre she carried on for some weeks before the perpetrator of the robbery was discovered; and there is no saying, during this lapse of time, how many innocent persons were unjustly suspected. Who shall say, indeed, but that the head of the establishment did not, as in the great Jackdaw case, call for his candle, his bell, and his book, and in holy anger, in pious grief, solemnly curse that rascally thief, as, you remember, the Cardinal cursed the Jackdaw:

'He cursed him at board, he cursed him in bed,
From the sole of his foot to the crown of his head;
He cursed him in eating, he cursed him in drinking,
He cursed him in coughing, in sneezing, in winking;
He cursed him in sitting, in standing, in lying;
He cursed him in walking, in riding, in flying;
He cursed him in living, he cursed him in dying; –
Never was heard such a terrible curse!
　　But what gave rise
　　To no little surprise,
Nobody seemed one penny the worse!'

When, however, they found out that Pussy was the wrong-doer, and, unlike the Jackdaw, had grown fat upon her misdeeds, they did not hang her, as you might suppose, though I have no doubt that course was suggested; on the contrary, they allowed her to pursue her nefarious career, and charged visitors a small fee to be allowed to see her do it. Out of evil sometimes may come good; but one would hardly think that the best way of making a person's fortune was to rob him.

Cats have been frequently known to do their best to protect the property of their masters, as well as dogs. A man who was imprisoned for a burglary, in America, stated after his conviction, that he and two others broke into the house of a gentleman, near Harlem. While they were in the act of plundering it, a large black Cat flew at one of the robbers, and fixed her claws on each side of his face. He added, that he never saw a man so frightened in his life; and that in his alarm, he made such an outcry, that they had to beat a precipitate retreat, to avoid detection.

A lady in Liverpool had a favourite Cat. She never returned home, after a short absence, without being joyfully received by it. One Sunday, however, on returning from church, she was surprised to find that Pussy did not receive her as usual, and its continued absence made her a little uneasy. The servants were all appealed to, but none could account for the circumstance. The lady, therefore, made a strict search for her feline friend, and descending to the lower storey, was surprised to hear her cries of 'Puss' answered by the mewing of a Cat, the sounds proceeding from the wine cellar, which had been properly locked and the key placed in safe custody. As the Cat was in the parlour when the lady left for chuch, it was unnecessary to consult a 'wise man' to ascertain that the servants had clandestine means of getting into the wine cellar, and that they had forgotten, when they themselves returned, to request pussy, also, to withdraw. The contents of the cellar, from that time forward, did not disappear as quickly as they had been doing for some time previously.

A woman was murdered at Lyons, and when the body was found weltering in blood, a large white Cat was seen mounted on the cornice of a cupboard. He sat motionless, his eyes fixed on the corpse, and his attitude and looks expressing horror and affright. Next morning, he was still found there; and when the room was filled by the officers of justice, neither the clattering of the soldiers' arms nor the loud conversation frightened him away. As soon, however, as the suspected persons were brought in, his eyes glared with fury, and his hair bristled. He darted into the middle of the room, where he stopped for a moment to gaze on them, and then fled precipitately. The faces of the assassins showed, for the first time, signs of guilt: they were afterwards brought to trial, condemned, and, before execution, confessed.

In September, 1850, the mistress of a public house in the Commercial Road, London, going late at night into the tap-room, found her Cat in a state of great excitement. It would not suffer itself to be stroked, but ran wildly, to and fro, between its mistress and the chimney-piece, mewing loudly. The landlady alarmed, summoned assistance, and presently a robber was discovered up the chimney. Upon his trial it was proved that he had robbed several public-houses, by remaining last in the tap-room, and concealing himself in a similar manner.

An old maiden lady, rich and miserly, had, in the latter years of her life, placed all her affections upon a Cat she called 'Minny,' for which she had made a fine bed-place in the wainscot, over a closet in the parlour, where she kept the animal's provisions. The food in question was stowed away in a drawer, and under the drawer which served as Minny's safe, was another, very artfully concealed, and closing with a spring. To the latter the Cat had often seen its mistress pay lengthened visits. When the old lady died, her heirs came to live in the house, and Minny being no longer fed with the same regularity, was often hungry, and would then go and scratch at the drawer where its food had been kept. The drawer being at length opened, some pieces of meat were found within in a mummified state. These having been given to the Cat, failed to console her, and she scratched harder than ever at the secret drawer underneath; and Minny's new masters, in course of time understanding what she meant, broke it open, and found twenty small canvas bags of guineas snugly packed up within. My authority does not say how Minny fared after this little discovery. Let us hope she was allowed her old sleeping-place, and got her food with tolerable regularity. But there is no knowing.

Cats are very fond of creeping into out-of-the-way holes and corners, and, sometimes, pay dearly for so doing.

Once when repairing the organ in Westminster Abbey, a dried Cat was found in one of the large recumbent wooden pipes, which had been out of tune for some time. In one of the rooms at the Foreign Office, some years ago, there was, for a long time, a very disagreeable smell, which was supposed to arise from the drains. At length some heavy volumes being taken down from a shelf, the body of a dried Cat was found behind them. The unfortunate animal had been shut up by accident, and starved to death, a prisoner, like the heroine of the 'Oak Chest.'

Mrs Loudon, in her book of *Domestic Pets*, tells several amusing stories. Her mother, the writer says, had a servant who disliked Cats very much, and in particular a large black Cat, which she was in the habit of beating, whenever she could do so unobserved. The Cat disliked and feared the girl exceedingly; however, one day, when her enemy was carrying some dishes downstairs into the kitchen, and had both her hands full, the Cat flew at her and scratched her hands and face severely.

A strange Cat had two kittens in a stable belonging to the house, and one day, pitying its wretched condition, Mrs Loudon ordered her some milk. A large Tom Cat, attached to the establishment, watched the proceeding very attentively, and while the Cat was lapping, went to the stable, brought out one of the kittens in his mouth, and placed it beside the saucer, and then fetched the other, looking up into the lady's face, and mewing when he had done so, as much as to say, 'You have fed the mother, so you may as well feed the children,' which was done; and it should be added, for the credit of Tom's character, that he never attempted to touch the milk himself.

But the best story is this:- Mrs Loudon had a Cat which had unfortunately hurt its leg. During the whole time the leg was bad, that lady constantly gave it milk; but, at last, she found out that, though the Cat had become quite well, yet whenever it saw her, it used to walk lame and hold up its paw, as though it were painful to put it to the ground.

A favourite Cat, much petted by her mistress, was one day struck by a servant. She resented the injury so much that she refused to eat anything which he gave her. Day after day he handed her dinner to her, but she sat in sulky indignation, though she eagerly ate the food as soon as it was offered to her by any other person. Her resentment continued, undimnished, for upwards of six weeks.

The same Cat, having been offended by the housemaid, watched three days before she found a favourable opportunity for retaliation. The housemaid was on her knees, washing the passage, when the Cat went up to her and scratched her arm, to show her that no one should illuse her with impunity. It is, however, but fair to record her good qualities as well as her bad ones. If her resentment was strong, her attachment was equally so, and she took a singular mode of showing it. All the tit-bits she could steal from the pantry, and all the dainty mice she could catch, she invariably brought and laid at her mistress's feet. She has been known to bring a mouse to her door in the middle of the night, and mew till it was opened, when she would present it to her mistress. After doing this she was quiet and contented.

Just before the earthquake at Messina, a merchant of that town noticed that his Cats were scratching at the door of his room, in a state of great excitement. He opened the door for them, and they flew down-stairs and began to scratch more violently still at the street-door. Filled with wonder, the master let them out and followed them through the town out of the gates, and into the fields beyond, but, even then, they seemed half mad with fright, and scratched and tore at the grass. Very shortly the first shock of the earthquake was felt, and many houses (the merchant's among them) came thundering in ruins to the ground.

A family in Callander had in their possession a favourite Tom Cat, which had, upon several occasions, exhibited more than ordinary sagacity. One day, Tom made off with a piece of beef, and the servant followed him cautiously, with the intention of catching, and administering to him a little wholesome correction. To her amazement, she saw the Cat go to a corner of the yard where she knew a rat-hole existed, and lay the beef down by the side of it. Leaving the beef there, he hid himself a short distance off, and watched until a rat made its appearance. Tom's tail then began to wag, and just as the rat was moving away with the bait, he sprang upon, and killed it.

It one day occured to M de la Croix that he ought to try an experiment upon a Cat with an air pump. The necessity for her torture was not, however, so apparent to the intended victim of science as to the scientific experimenter. Therefore, when she found the air growing scarce, and discovered how it was being exhausted, she stopped up the valve with her paw. Then M de la Croix let the air run back, and Pussy took away her paw, but as soon as he began to pump, she again stopped up the hole. This baffled the man of science, and there is no knowing what valuable discovery might have been made, had not his feline friend been so very unaccommodating.

Dr Careri, in his *Voyage round the World*, in 1695, says, that a person, in order to punish a mischievous monkey, placed upon the fire a cocoa nut, and then hid himself, to see how the monkey would take it from the fire without burning his paws. The cunning creature looked about, and seeing a Cat by the fireside, held her head in his mouth, and with her paws took off the nut, which he then threw into water to cool, and ate it.

Cats have always been famous for the wonderful manner in which they have found their way back to their old home, when they have been taken from it, and for this reason alone, have often been accused of loving only the house and not its inmates. It is more probable though, I should think, that the animal returns to the place because its associations there have been happy, and, in the confusion and strangeness of the new house, it cannot comprehend that its old friends have come with it. For instance, I have known a Cat when taken away from a house, return to it, and going from room to room, mew pitifully, in search of the former inmates. When taken away a second time, the new place having in the meantime been set straight, it found nothing to frighten it there, and returned no more to its old house.

I knew a person who was in the habit of moving about a great deal, and hiring furnished houses, who had a Cat called Sandy, on account of his colour, which he found in the first instance, in a sort of half-wild state, on Hampstead Heath, mostly living up a tree. It had been left behind by the people who had last occupied the house, and locked out by the landlady. It was about nine or ten years old, and goodness knows how many dwelling places it may have had; with its new friends, I know of five or six changes, and am told that it always made itself perfectly at home in half an hour after entering a new house. It was taken from place to place in a hamper, and the lid being raised would put out its head and sniff the air in the drollest manner. Getting out very cautiously, it would then make a tour of the premises, and inspect the furniture; at the end of about half an hour it washed its face and seemed settled.

A lady residing in Glasgow had a handsome Cat sent to her from Edinburgh: it was conveyed to her in a close basket in a carriage. The animal was carefully watched for two months; but having produced a pair of young ones at the end of that time, she was left to her own discretion, which she very soon employed in disappearing with both her kittens. The lady at Glasgow wrote to her friend at Edinburgh, deploring her loss, and the Cat was supposed to have formed some new attachment. About a fortnight, however, after her disappearance from Glasgow, her well-known mew was heard at the street-door of her Edinburgh mistress; and there she was with both her kittens, they in the best state, but she, herself, very thin. It is clear that she could carry only one kitten at a time. The distance from Glasgow to Edinburgh is forty-four miles, so that if she brought one kitten part of the way, and then went back for the other, and thus conveyed them alternately, she must have travelled 120 miles at least. She, also, must have journeyed only during the night, and must have resorted to many other precautions for the safety of her young.

Mr Lord relates a story of a Cat living with some friends of his in a house on an island. The family changed residence, and the Cat was sewn up in a hamper and taken round to the other side of the island in a boat. The island was sparsely inhabited, timbered, and there were but few paths cut to traverse it by, and yet the Cat found its way during the night back again to its old residence. There could have been no scent of foot-prints, neither was there any road or path to guide it.

Another Cat was conveyed from its home in Jamaica to a place five miles distant, and during the time of its transport was sown up closely in a bag. Between the two places were two rivers, one of them about eighty feet broad, deep, and running strong; the other wider and more rapid. The Cat must have swum these rivers, as there were no bridges; but in spite of all obstacles, she made her way back to the house from which she had been taken.

In 1819 a favourite Tabby belonging to a shipmaster was left on shore, by accident, while his vessel sailed from the harbour of Aberdour, Fifeshire, which is about half a mile from the village. The vessel was a month absent, and on her return, to the astonishment of the shipmaster, Puss came on board with a fine stout kitten in her mouth, apparently about three weeks old, and went directly down into the cabin. Two others of her young ones were afterwards caught, quite wild, in a neighbouring wood, where she must have remained with them until the return of the ship. The shipmaster did not allow her, again, to go on shore, otherwise it is probable she would have brought all her family on board. It was very remarkable, because vessels were daily going in and out of the harbour, none of which she ever thought of visiting till the one she had left returned.

In a parish in Norfolk, not six miles from the town of Bungay, lived a clergyman, who, having a Cat, sentenced it to transportation for life because it had committed certain depredations on his larder. But the worthy gentleman found it far easier to pronounce the sentence than to carry it into execution. Poor Puss was first taken to Bungay, but had hardly got there when she escaped, and was soon at home again. Her morals, however, had in no way improved, and a felonious abstraction of butcher's meat immediately occurred. This time the master determined to send the hardened culprit away to a distance, which, as he expressed it, 'she would not walk in a hurry.' He accordingly gave her (generous man) to a person living at Fakenham, distant at least forty miles. The man called for her in the morning, and carried her off in a bag, that she might not know by what road he went. Vain hope! She knew well enough the way home, as he found to his cost, for directly the house-door was opened the next morning, she rushed out and he saw no more of her. The night after a faint mewing was heard outside the minister's dwelling, but not being so rare an occurence no attention was paid to it. However, on opening the door next morning, there lay the very Cat which he thought was forty miles away, her feet all cut and blistered, from the hardness of the road, and her silky fur all clotted and matted together with dust and dirt. She had her reward; however her thievish propensities might annoy him, the worthy vicar resolved never again to send her away from the house she loved so well, and exerted herself so nobly to regain.

The Rev. Mr Wood furnishes some curious particulars of two commercial Cats of his acquaintance, which he very comically describes:-

'I will tell you,' says he, 'something about our Mincing Lane Cats. Their home was in the cellar, and their habits and surroundings, as you may imagine, from the locality, were decidedly commercial. We had one cunning old black fellow, whose wisdom was acquired by sad experience. In early youth, he must have been very careless; he then was always getting in the way of the men and the wine cases, and frequent were the disasters he suffered through coming into collision with moving bodies. His ribs had often been fractured, and when nature repaired them, she must have handed them over to the care of her 'prentice hand,' for the work was done in rather a rough and knotty manner. This battered and suffering Pussy was at last assisted by a younger hero, which, profiting by the teachings of his senior, managed to avoid the scrapes which had tortured the one who was self-educated. These two Cats, Junior and Senior, appeared to swear (Cats will swear) eternal friendship at first sight. An interchange of good offices was at once established. Senior taught Junior to avoid men's feet and wine cases in motion, and pointed out the favourite hunting grounds, while Junior offered to his Mentor the aid of his activity and physical prowess.

Senior had a cultivated and epicurean taste for mice, though he was too old to catch them; he therefore entered into a solemn league and covenant with the junior to this effect: – It was agreed between the two contracting powers, that Junior should devote his energies to catching mice for the benefit of Senior, who, in consideration of such service, was to relinquish his claim to a certain daily allowance of Cat's meat in favour of Junior. This courteous compact was actually and seriously carried out. It was an amusing and touching spectacle, to behold young Pussy gravely laying at the feet of his elder the contents of his game bag; on the other hand, Senior, true to his bargain, licking his jaws and watching Junior steadily consuming a double allowance of Cat's meat.

Senior had the rare talent of being able to carry a bottle of champagne from one end of the cellar to the other, perhaps a distance of a hundred and fifty feet. The performance was managed in this wise. You gently and lovingly approached the Cat as if you did not mean to perpetrate anything wicked; having gained his confidence by fondly stroking his back, you suddenly seized his tail, and by that member raised the animal bodily from the ground – his fore feet sprawling in the air ready to catch hold of any object within reach. You then quickly brought the bottle of wine to the seizing point; Pussy clutched the object with a kind of despairing grip. By means of the aforesaid tail, you carefully carried pussy, bottle and all, from one part of the cellar to the other. Pussy, however, soon became disgusted with this manoeuvre, and whenever he saw a friend with a bottle of champagne looming, he used to beat a precipitate retreat.

The reverend gentleman before quoted, had at one time in his possession a marvellously clever little Cat, which he called 'Pret,' and concerning which he relates a host of anecdotes; from them are culled the following: –

Pret knew but one fear, and had but few hates. The booming sound of thunder smote her with terror, and she most cordially hated grinding organs and singular costumes. At the sound of a thunderclap poor Pret would fly to her mistress for succour, trembling in every limb. If the dreaded sound occurred in the night or early morning, Pret would leap on the bed and crawl under the clothes as far as the very foot. If the thunder came on by day, Pret would climb on her mistress's knees, put her paws round her neck and hide her face between them with deliberation.

She disliked music of all kinds, but bore a special antipathy to barrel organs; probably because the costume of the organ-grinder was as unpleasing to her eyes, as his doleful sounds were to her ears. But her indignation reached the highest bounds at the sight of a Greenwich pensioner accoutred in those grotesque habiliments with which the crippled defenders of their country are forced to invest their battered frames. It was the first time that so uncouth an apparition had presented itself to her eyes, and her anger seemed only equalled by her astonishment. She got on the window-sill, and there chafed and growled with a sound resembling the miniature roar of a lion. When thus excited she used to present a strange appearance, owing to a crest or ridge of hair which then erected itself on her back, and extended from the top of her head to the root of her tail, which latter member was marvellously expanded. Gentle as she was in her ordinary demeanour, Pret was a terrible Cat when she saw cause, and was undaunted by size or numbers.

She had a curious habit of catching mice by the very tips of their tails, and of carrying the poor little animals about the house, dangling miserably from her jaws. Apparently her object in so doing was to present her prey uninjured to her mistress, who she evidently supposed would enjoy a game with a mouse as well as herself, for like human beings she judged the characters of others by her own. This strange custom of tail-bearing was carried into the privacy of her own family, and caused rather ludicrous results. When Pret became a mother, and desired to transport her kittens from one place to another, she followed her acquired habit of porterage, and tried to carry her kittens about by the tips of their tails. As might be supposed, they objected to this mode of conveyance, and sticking their claws in the carpet, held firmly to the ground, mewing piteously, while their mother was tugging at their tails. It was absolutely necessary to release the kittens from their painful position, and to teach Pret how a kitten ought to be carried. After a while, she seemed to comprehend the state of things, and ever afterwards carried her offspring by the nape of the neck. At one time, when she was yet in her kittenhood, another kitten lived in the same house, and very much annoyed Pret, by coming into the room and eating the meat that had been laid out for herself. However, Pret soon got over the difficulty, by going to the plate as soon as it was placed at her accustomed spot, picking out all the large pieces of meat and hiding them under the table. She then sat down quietly, placing herself sentry over her hidden treasure, while the intruding Cat entered the room, walked up to the plate, and finished the little scraps of meat that Pret had thought fit to leave. After the obnoxious individual had left the room, Pret brought her concealed treasures from their hiding-place and consumed them with deliberation.

Clever as Pret was, she sometimes displayed a most unexpected simplicity of character. After the fashion of the Cat tribe, she delighted in covering up the remainder of her food with any substance that seemed most convenient. She was accustomed, after taking her meals, to fetch a piece of paper and lay it over the saucer, or to put her paw in her mistress's pocket and extract her handkerchief for the same purpose. This little performance showed some depth of reasoning in the creature, but she would sometimes act in a manner totally opposed to rational actions. Paper or handkerchief failing, she has been often seen, after partly finishing her meal, to fetch one of her kittens and to lay it over the plate for the purpose of covering up the remaining food. When kitten, paper, and handkerchief were all wanting, she did her best to scratch up the carpet and lay the fragments over the plate. She has been known, in her anxiety to find a covering for the superabundant food, to drag a tablecloth from its proper locality, and to cause a sad demolition of the superincumbent fragile ware. Please to remember that I have the above upon Mr Wood's authority, not my own.

Regarding the attachment of Cats to places, the following remarks of the late Rev. Caesar Otway, in his lecture on the 'Intellectuality of Domestic Animals' before the Royal Zoological Society of Ireland, some years ago, deserve attention. 'Of Cats,' he says, 'time does not allow me to say much, but this I must affirm, that they are misrepresented, and often the victims of prejudice. It is strictly maintained that they have little or no affection for *persons*, and that their partialities are confined to *places*. I have known many instances of the reverse. When leaving, about fifteen years ago, a glebe-house to remove into Dublin, the Cat that was a favourite with me, and with my children, was left behind, in our hurry. On seeing strange faces come into the house, she instantly left it, and took up her abode in the top of a large cabbage stalk, whose head had been cut off, but which retained a sufficient number of leaves to protect poor Puss from the weather. In this position she remained and nothing could induce her to leave it, until I sent a special messenger to bring her to my house in town. At present I have a Cat that follows my housekeeper up and down like a Dog; every morning she comes up at daybreak in winter to the door of the room in which the maid servants sleep, and there she mews until they get up.'

I think I ought to conclude my chapter of Clever Cats with this story, which, though old, is funny: – There was a lady of Potsdam, living with her little children, one of whom, while at play, ran a splinter into her foot, causing her to scream violently. The elder sister was asleep at the time, but awakened by the child's cries, and while just in the act of getting up to quiet it, observed a favourite Cat, with whom the children were wont to play, and which was of a remarkably gentle disposition, leave its seat by the fire, go to the crying baby, and give her a smart blow on the cheek with one of her paws; after which, Puss walked back with the greatest composure and gravity to her place, as if satisfied with her own conduct, and with the hope of being able to go on with her nap undisturbed.

Childhood of Miss Churt

F. R. Buckley

Miss Churt – British, like everyone else aboard the Malvern - sat on the storm sill of the galley and with glazed eyes surveyed the North Atlantic.

Miss Churt was meditating sombrely on the rump steak the cook had given her. 'Eat it up, Kitty; good!' the cook had said, and Miss Churt had followed the suggestion.

Now – although the steak had been delicious – Miss Churt was experiencing certain qualms; a sensation, as of cannon balls in the midriff, has assailed her . . .

Miss Churt decided that she would get a little fresh air and drop in on her friend Mr Wharton.

She dropped from her perch and, with tail at its meridian height, walked unsteadily toward the cuddy stairway.

The Malvern was moving unsteadily also, and likewise because of the heavy feeling in the midriff; caused not by cannon balls but by much more modern munitions of war. Never on very cordial terms with her rudder, she had now been be-shelled and be-packing-cased and be-airplane-parted until she would just as soon go anywhere as anywhere else, and was constantly trying to do so.

In a room on the boat deck, the first officer and the chief engineer were discussing this phenomenon and others related to the comfort and well-being of the ship's company. Mr McIvor, who was naturally the engineer, had joined in New York and was absorbing pessimism from Mr Wharton.

'He's a kind of mixed product of the flu and the board room', said the first mate, alluding to his captain. 'He's – well, you saw him.'

'I saw *something*', said Mr McIvor, cautiously.

'That'd be him. Chairman's nephew; on the beach for years; war come along – old Stokes gets flu – hand o' Providence – an' here I am sayin' "Aye, aye, sir!" to *that*. If he'd got eyelashes I wouldn't mind so much, but – '

Mr McIvor nodded, and his unclean pipe said, 'Cluck, cluck.'

'Have any trouble comin' over?'

'Subs you mean? Naw. Hello, sweetheart! Hello! Come to see Poppa?'

Mr McIvor, thunderstruck, made an instinctive motion to smooth his hair, but it was only Miss Churt. Mr Wharton went over, picked her up out of the aperture of the hooked door and before sitting down again on his berth spread a month-old newspaper carefully on the carpet. The page uppermost bore a picture of Lady Somebody's wedding to Captain Gossakes-Whosis of the guards; Mr Wharton, bending with Miss Churt sprawled over his palm, surveyed orange blossoms, smiles, teeth, tonsils and the arch of swords with a nitric eye.

'There, sweetheart', he said, putting Miss Churt down on them.

'You a married mon?' asked Mr McIvor.

'Nah. But I *will* be. That's her.'

The engineer rolled an eye at the picture on the bureau.

'Nice gurrul.'

'You said it. Canon Hobson an' all. Speakin' of cannon, have you seen our 4.7 on the poop deck?'

'To my grief. But what's this?, said Mr McIvor, whose intake of personal news was disproportionate to his output, 'aboot a cannon? The young leddy's no got a smash on um?'

'On old Hobson? Not *that* kind,' said Mr Wharton; and his look made Mr McIvor wonder whether he should have asked. 'Fact is – that's a good little sweetheart! Come to Poppa! 'At's a girlie!'

'Ye seem fond o' yon kitten.'

'I'm mad about her. and she's just wild about Harry, aren't you, pet?'

Miss Churt licked a gnarled and knotted hand. It tasted something like the rump steak, flavoured with tar, salt, tobacco and Mallinson's Wonder Ointment for superficial cuts and bruises. . . .

'Then whaur *does* this canon come in?'

'All the girls round our way in Liverpool are mad about him. See – he had us all in Sunday school; children's choral guild, he called it; us boys got away after we'd been confirmed, of course, but you can believe it or not, I've never been the swearer I ought to have.'

'I noticed that when we was warpin' into the stream'. said Mr McIvor. 'I thocht maybe ye was a nance.'

A sudden squeezing of Miss Churt's ribs evoked a mew.

'Did I hurt ums bellah?' asked Mr Wharton. 'Dere Snuzzle down, a good girlie; such a full ickle tummy . . . Ho, you did, hah?'

'Until we met', said Mr McIvor in haste. 'But – he canna be a young mon, this parson?'

'Canon', said Mr Wharton. 'Naw, an' he's no beauty neither. But he's the bee's knees so far's Annie's concerned, an' she's goin' to be married by him or nobody, so so far it's been nobody - an' now they go an' put this pink-whiskered nincompoop in over my head – '

'What's it matter who morries ye? It takes no longer than havin' a tooth out.'

'Ho, doesn't it? That's where *you* drop your tow. Old Hobson's strong for the ritual an all that; and that means veils an' orange flowers for Annie an' a top hat an' tails for me.'

'But not in wartime!'

'How do *you* know?'

'I'd go', said Mr McIvor after reflection, 'an' see the old mon an' say "Fush" to um.'

'You would *not*', said Mr Wharton darkly, 'not if you saw him. He's only five foot six, but I've seen him sober, an' askin' for coffee. He's got one o' those kissers you carve out o' granite with a road drill. Looks something like you.'

The chief engineer considered this judicially, and put his glass down.

'Awheel', he said, rising. 'It's the wull o' Allah, I suppawse, that some us should be married an' hae bairns, while ithers lovish their possions on tobby cots. Guid nicht, Mr Wharton.'

In the doorway he turned to see the burst of this Glaswegian bomb. Miss Churt, who had been awakened by something that felt like an earth tremor, blinked at him and went to sleep again.

'We've naval ratings aboard to work yon gun?' McIvor asked, to cover his more morbid curiosity.

'We have', said Mr Wharton, 'an' if anybody asks you who's in command o' that gun, it's me. Naval reserve.'

'You bein' in turn commanded by Captain Timbs. Weel – guid nicht.'

'You heard about that timber ship gettin' torpedoed?' Wharton asked.

'No. What was that?'

'Oh, just that they thought she mightn't have sunk properly, an' be derelict hereabouts. Timbs has been radioin' everybody bar Churchill an' President Roosevelt, but nobody's seen her. Dark night, too. Well – pleasant dreams.'

A certain pensiveness marked Mr McIvor's departure but the first mate seemed to feel better.

He extracted Miss Churt gently from the land of nod, held her up with forelegs dangling, treated her to a gigantic smile and kissed her unhygienically on the nose.

'Azza booful girlie!' said Mr Wharton. 'You like Poppa go home to his other girl an' get married, please, an' zen you have lovely house an' garden to scratch in?'

Miss Churt was exceedingly drowsy; moreover that rump steak seemed still to be clogging her articulation. She opened her pink mouth, but no sound issued.

'I'll bet you', said Mr Wharton. 'And that reminds me – '

He had just risen to pick up the newspaper with the wedding on it when from for'ard, out of the starry dark, there came a thunderous crash.

The Malvern stopped in her tracks like a dowager smitten in the breadbasket.

Simultaneously, the lights went out.

It was, of course, that derelict, floating bottom up at what the French so prettily call the flower of the water, or, in Anglo-Saxon sea talk, awash.

Having accomplished the destiny given her by those heavenly lights overhead – Neptune afflicted by Mars, perhaps; who knows? - and buckled the Malvern's blunt bows backward like the bellows of a concertina, the timber ship rolled, spewed a few hundred thousand board feet from a new gash and sank; while down behind the forepeak of the Malvern, Mr Wharton and a number of nearly naked shipmates strove to save their tub from doing likewise.

It was a question of strengthening a bulkhead, and strengthening bulkheads is uneasy work in the pitch dark.

It was an hour before Mr McIvor and his horde got the uprooted dynamo going again; and then what was revealed by hand lights led into the hold was the reverse of encouraging.

Not only was the bulkhead spouting water through the holes of deracinated rivets; it was bulging bodily and visibly inward, so that it was obvious that no time remained for carpenter work and fancy shoring.

Mr Wharton's eyes, under a mop of embattled hair, shuttled desperately about the hold. The port and starboard sides were solid-packed with minor munitions, forming admirable buttresses for the wings of the forward wall. But in the midst stood two cases that had taxed the stevedores; they were large and heavy enough to have contained whippet tanks, and the Malvern's notorious instability had caused them to be stowed well aft of the bulkhead.

The space between was filled with this and that, in packets weighing mere hundreds of pounds.

'Get that junk out o' the way!' roared Mr Wharton. 'C'mon, boys!'

He himself was about to seize a crate when the third mate grabbed his shoulder.

'I say – Wharton – '

'The hell you do. Muck in an' shift something. I'm going' to shove these locomotives up, or whatever they are'.

'Listen! The Old Man's in a sweat of funk – sendin' out SOS till the ether's got clots in it – '

'To hell with him!'

'An' now he's getting ready to abandon ship.'

Mr Wharton disposed of his current crate and dashed forward to cut the key case out of a jam. Somehow or other his shirt had disintegrated, and his trousers consisted of but a breechclout and one leg, but still he was not swearing.

Canon Hobson, at that moment asleep in far-off Liverpool, his craglike nose in a soft pillow made for him by a parishioner, would have been gratified could he have known.

'What are you goin' to do?' demanded the third officer. 'He's got all the ship's papers ready, an' he says his duty's to his men, an' unless we get help by dawn he's gonna take to the boats.'

'If you don't get outa my dog-rammed way we won't be afloat till dawn,' said Mr Wharton. 'Hey – '

'But you got to stop him!'

'An' risk my ticket – mutiny? No, sir; I obey – get that stuff movin', you bunch of lobsters! Come along aft here, you knob-eyed slackers – want me to shove this myself? You Fawdry – you Wilson – '

A cleared space now lay between the bulkhead and the first tank, which, of course, was not really a tank, it just felt like one. Anyway, the problem was to get it up to that bulkhead – and the other one up behind it, if possible. And the bulkhead was re-marking, in the language of tortured steel, that it would be damned if it was going to wait for such support much longer.

'You can't shift 'em', said the third mate weakly, 'an' if you do, you'll shove her bow down an' we'll slide.'

'Like the Tornado at Coney Island', gasped Mr Wharton, grinning. '"Down went McGinty" – ready, boys? Line up, get your shoulders against it. It's shove or grow gills! Now – one -two – '

The case didn't move.

'The Old Man says – ' gasped the third mate.

'Give us a chantey', grunted one of the men; and Mr Wharton obliged. It might almost be said that out of the fullness of the heart the mouth spoke. It could hardly be called singing, and the verbiage was bald and incomplete; yet in topicality, direction and – yes – the passion of love denied, Mr Wharton's chantey might have claimed kinship with the romaunts of the troubadours. 'Ca-a-a-ptain T-i-i-mbs', he emitted in a wavering roar, 'is the son of a – *heave!*'

The men had had their leave stopped in Staten Island.

'Ca-a-a-ptain T-i-i-mbs', they agreed fulsomely, 'is the son of a *heave!*'

The case budged.

'Ca-a-a-ptain Timbs – *heave!*',

It moved six inches.

' – son of a *heave!*'

Six inches more.

Up on the bridge, the subject of the chantey was talking to three naval ratings, who seemed not to like him. They were the men responsible for the 4.7 aft, and they seemed to be suffering from the spirit of Nelson, or Collingwood or somebody.

All they did about it, though, was to say they didn't think -

'You don't have to think!' said Captain Timbs.

'You're not our officer, sir,' said the Senior rating.

'You're under my orders! If I say to abandon ship, we'll abandon ship!'

This made it the turn of the junior rating.

'Aye, aye, sir', he said. 'If you say so.'

Captain Timbs swallowed a large and visible lump in the throat. 'That's the order,' he said. 'Soon's it's dawn. We're ripped wide open.'

'Roughish sea, sir', said the senior rating impassively.

'I've got a Swedish freighter on the radio – she'll be here by then, standing by. Who the hell are you, questioning my orders?'

'Nobody, sir', said the second rating.

'Get to hell out!'

'Aye, aye, sir', said the third; and out they went.

What they said as they went below is nobody's business; such low speculations about the sums payable by governments to bereaved ship owners; so much plain, vulgar swearing. One may, however, make extracts to the extent that the senior remarked that dawn was breaking already; the second said that the old gal felt like taking the high dive, at that; while the junior, peering aft, remarked sentimentally that anyhow she'd go down with her flag up and her gun shotted.

'Might go an' fire her off for once', he said.

'Might go down an' give Wharton a hand', said his senior severely; and so they did.

Some time later, Miss Churt, whose rump steak had filled slumber with dreams of gigantic rats chasing her down unending alleyways, awoke with a start and a bad taste in her mouth.

She yawned and decided that a little fresh air, again, would do her good. Jumping down from the settee, she found that the floor was not exactly where he had left it – it sloped downward now, and before she could correct her stance her for'ard legs had given way and she had rolled into a corner.

Picking herself thence, and reaching the door-sill, she rolled forth in search of company. It was light, so she gave the yawn and stretch by which cats thank God for each night spent in shelter – but something appeared to be wrong.

Where was everybody, to start with?

And why wasn't the deck vibrating as it always had, except just before and after mother left? And then the cargo winches had been working, with a roar that set one's ears back; now there was stillness – and behold! as one crossed behind the charthouse the bulwark of boats was gone and the wind smote one unimpeded.

Just some ropes trailing . . .

Miss Churt walked forward a few more paces and sat down, like the treble clef in a musical stave. Far in the misty distance she could see a ship standing still; and as for the Malvern's boats, they were on the water – swimming, actually, and swimming away from her.

And in one of them, along with three naval ratings and some other able-bodied gentlemen who disapproved of Captain Timbs and were saying so, Mr Wharton was at this identical moment remembering that he had left Miss Churt aboard.

'Noah's nails!' he ejaculated; and Canon Hobson, still sleeping, smiled in his distant dreams. 'Why – '

The oars lifted.

'Forgot something, sir?' asked the senior rating.

'Forgotten something?' said Mr Wharton. 'I've left my cat behind!'

From the bow of the boat came an imperfectly stifled chuckle.

'You laugh at me and I'll put a head on you,' said the first officer; and silence redescended on the ocean.

'Want to go back, sir?'

'I – think I will,' said Mr Wharton. 'If we're to save our dirty hides when there's no need to, I don't see why a poor dumb animal should suffer. Unless these gentlemen object? Pull stab-bud, back port! Come on, you bunch of tailors!'

'Captain's boat's stopped rowin', sir', said the bow oar.

'Ne'er mind', said Mr Wharton, 'we can rat just as well in ten minutes' time. An' that Swede can wait. Some expensive nephew for – c'mon, put some beef into it!'

A distant hail came over the water – which, by the way, was now astonishingly calm.

'I'll just swarm up the falls an' be back in a jiffy', said Mr Wharton – not knowing that a mile the other side of the Malvern the sea, hidden from him by the wallowing bulk of that ship, was just being broken by the conning tower of a submarine.

Her commander, a pleasant enough fellow named Koenig, usually resident in Munich, Glocknergasse No.8, had heard the frantic distress signals wirelessed by Captain Timbs and had wondered if perchance they might portend something in his line of business. There was, he knew, a temporary scarcity of destroyers in this area, but the event was turning out better than his hopes. Through the periscope he had watched the crew abandoning ship, and, when the Malvern failed to slide precipitately out of sight, had commented soul-ticklingly to his men on the unsea-to-dare-worthiness of British sailors.

That this was no Q-ship he was well assured, both by the presence of the Swedish ship and the perilous trim of the Malvern itself. So it was his intent to combine business with pleasure by letting the fleeing crew watch him use their vessel for target practice. He thought he would use percussion fuse and blow the funnel out of her first.

As the submarine came awash her gun crew tumbled up, ran for'ard and proceeded to clear their gun.

And simultaneously, the longing gaze of Miss Churt was gratified by the spectacle of Mr Wharton, shaggier than ever. Miss Churt liked shagginess, it gave one more corners to nestle in.

Her master, landing on the boat deck from the falls, didn't seem as cheery as usual; something seemed to be bothering him; he didn't smile.

But Miss Churt knew how to remedy that. When anybody looked sad, she ran away, and Mr Wharton ran after her and picked her up and called her a little devil and corrected himself and said 'weevil' and kissed her on the end of the nose.

Miss Churt therefore ran away now, skidding slightly because of the slant of the deck; her ears cocked for the sound of beloved footsteps pursuing.

And here they came.

But here came something else.

Something terrible. A long, increasing noise, coming out of the middle of a distant thump, boring into her ears – so terrifying – and then – a vast flash of light, taking up the whole world and tearing it to pieces, shaking her stomach so the steak didn't matter any more. . . .

Mr Wharton, rushing from behind the wireless house, paused a moment.

He saw a very large scorched hole in the boat deck planking, around which he had to pick his way.

While thus engaged, he saw Captain Koenig's submarine, lying perhaps three quarters of a mile off.

But what he was looking for was a small ball of soiled fur; and this he found, very limp, just for'ard of the bridge deck ladder. The curious thing is that Captain Koenig also adored cats, and had three at home in the Glocknergasse.

But that's war.

Mr Wharton took up in his very large hand what war had left of Miss Churt, and he laid the other hand over cursed Captain Koenig and his superiors and inferiors and her like the lid of a little coffin; and then raised both his arms and, still holding the limp form in his right hand, all his works in a voice that almost carried the distance.

Indeed – in St. Mary's Rectory, Canon Hobson awoke with a start; looked at his bedside clock and found it was 5.25; rolled over – but somehow was disinclined to go to sleep again.

'You bloody, sneaking *bloody* butcher!' Mr Wharton was now shouting; and there came a sudden crack in his voice. 'My little – '

A voice spoke from just behind him. It had not seemed quite proper to the naval ratings that their officer should go aboard without escort, so they had swarmed up the falls also and here they were. The voice was the voice of the senior rating, as was proper.

'How about giving 'em a packet, sir?' he inquired.

Mr Wharton had forgotten the 4.7 gun aft. Now he remembered and gave a perfect snarl of assent.

The body of Miss Churt he crammed into the side pocket of his coat; and then down the ladder he went, and after him came the ratings.

They had to descend another ladder and cross the aft well-deck and then climb the poop; and it was now that Captain Koenig saw them.

With a welter of ow sounds and a swamp of terminations in ch, he directed his men to shift target and give Wharton *et al* a packet; so that the question resolved itself roughly into one of who should give whom a packet first.

The U-boat, being in the groove, got her shot off the earlier; but the hastily altered aim was high and the shell went to miss the Swedish ship by no more than half a mile. (Memorandum of March 27, 1940, paragraph 2.)

Meantime, the senior rating had done various manipulations of various things; and now, with a nod of the head, he expressed himself satisfied. Quite unnecessarily, he looked at Mr Wharton, opened his mouth and was just about to ask if he should open fire when the officer (not a regular navy man, of course) shoved him aside, seized the firing lever and got the shot off himself.

It was just luck, blind luck, for all concerned; but the fact remains that that unconventional, almost illegitimate, shell flew as through a tube to the barrel of the U-boat's gun, bent it, zoomed thereof without touching Captain Koenig or his men, and smote the lip of the conning tower, where it exploded with the abandon peculiar to high explosive.

Nobody was hurt, save Seaman Albrecht Otto of Bremen (deafness and scratches) – but the conning tower was impossible to close. That meant no submersion –
And on the southern sky line there had appeared, and was approaching, a smudge of smoke, which betokened destroyers. The ratings pointed this out to one another.

Meanwhile Mr Wharton, at the other rail, was expressing his completely berserk opinion of Captain Timbs and all men who would take to boats leaving cats on perfectly sound ships full of badly needed munitions.

This expression, in addition to blistering (if the third officer may be believed) the paint on the thwarts of Lifeboat No. 1, left Mr Wharton rather exhausted. And softened in mood.

He put his hand into his pocket and pulled out the mortal envelope of Miss Churt. The bluish eyes were closed, the furry head rolled on the neck, and all her whiskers had been singed away.

'You want us to come back, sir?' came a hail from the boats.

'You can go to hell!' roared Mr Wharton; so they started towards him.

But a voice pitched to carry a quarter of a mile is tremendous at close range.

Miss Churt vibrated in every cell.

Her stomach began to trouble her again. There was a familiar smell in her nostrils, seeping past the stench of burned whiskers - tobacco, tar and Mallinson's –

She opened her eyes and said: 'Mew!'

For all that it was wartime, the parish church of St Mary's was properly decorated for this wedding; though in view of the circumstances, Canon Hobson had consented to relax the clothing rules so far as the bridegroom was concerned.

Miss Woollard, however, was in the prescribed raiment even down to the seventy-ninth orange blossom; albeit inclined, apparently, to take nervous bites out of her veil. She was more nervous than brides usually are; more nervous even than seemed warranted by the fact that her bridegroom had three best men – the senior, junior and middle naval ratings, all with medals but one degree inferior to that which had been bestowed on Mr Wharton.

The cause of this uneasiness came to light when Canon Hobson, opening his prayer book, first glanced, then looked, then stared at the bridegroom's right-hand coat pocket.

It should perhaps be mentioned here that in addition to a granite face and an extraordinarily soft heart, the reverend gentleman was equipped with eyes that seemed to have been chipped out of adamant and grounded to fine points.

He furled the prayer book and spoke in a low, dazed voice.

'Henry', he said, while the congregation craned, 'that cannot be a cat you have in your coat pocket? Not a *cat*?'

This was rather an exaggeration of the status of Miss Churt, who was six weeks old that day and had just put her shell-shaven face out for a little air. But the general proposition was undeniable.

'Yes', said Mr Wharton. 'It is.'

'He *would* bring it – he *would* – I said – ' quavered the bride; but Canon Hobson paid no attention to her, though she began to sob.

Meeting the bluish eyes of Miss Churt, however, his adamantine orbs underwent a peculiar process. First they flickered from the condemning stare; then, as it were, they liquefied, so that their penetrative qualities became nil.

He spoke:

'Am I to assume that – this – is some kind of mascot? Connected perhaps with the recent -? What has happened to her whiskers?'

'I'll tell you about it in the vestry', said Mr Wharton; and meeting the canon's gaze, mourned for the misjudgments of his youth.

Canon Hobson nodded; opened the book which he had closed on a probationary thumb, and cleared his throat.

'Dearly beloved', he proclaimed, 'we are gathered together – '

Miss Churt could not quite identify all the smells (largely lilies) or sounds (mostly Canon Hobson) that were going on.

They were interesting, and she had a vague idea that something of the same general purport might be her personal concern one day.

But not now.

Not for a long time yet.

And meantime she had had enough air.

She withdrew her head from the atmosphere of St Mary's into the warm tweediness of Mr Wharton's pocket and composed herself to sleep.

Ming's Biggest Prey

Patricia Highsmith

Ming was resting comfortably on the foot of his mistress's bunk, when the man picked him up by the back of the neck, stuck him out on the deck and closed the cabin door. Ming's blue eyes widened in shock and brief anger, then nearly closed again because of the brilliant sunlight. It was not the first time Ming had been thrust out of the cabin rudely, and Ming realized that the man did it when his mistress, Elaine, was not looking.

The sailboat now offered no shelter from the sun, but Ming was not yet too warm. He leapt easily to the cabin roof and stepped on to the coil of rope just behind the mast. Ming liked the rope coil as a couch, because he could see everything from the height, the cup shape of the rope protected him from strong breezes, and also minimized the swaying and sudden changes of angle of the *White Lark*, since it was more or less the centre point. But just now the sail had been taken down, because Elaine and the man had eaten lunch, and often they had a siesta afterward, during which time, Ming knew, that man didn't like him in the cabin. Lunchtime was all right. In fact, Ming had just lunched on delicious grilled fish and a bit of lobster. Now, lying in a relaxed curve on the coil of rope, Ming opened his mouth in a great yawn, then with his slant eyes almost closed against the strong sunlight, gazed at the beige hills and the white and pink houses and hotels that circled the bay of Acapulco. Between the *White Lark* and the shore where people plashed inaudibly, the sun twinkled on the water's surface like thousands of tiny electric lights going on and off. A water-skier went by, skimming up white spray behind him. Such activity! Ming half dozed, feeling the heat of the sun sink into his fur.

Ming was from New York, and he considered Acapulco a great improvement over his environment in the first weeks of his life. He remembered a sunless box with straw on the bottom, three or four other kittens in with him, and a window behind which giant forms paused for a few moments, tried to catch his attention by tapping, then passed on. He did not remember his mother at all. One day a young woman who smelled of something pleasant came into the place and took him away – away from the ugly, frightening smell of dogs, of medicine and parrot dung. Then they went on what Ming now knew was an aeroplane. He was quite used to aeroplanes now and rather liked them. On aeroplane's he sat on Elaine's lap, or slept on her lap, and there were always titbits to eat if he was hungry.

Elaine spent much of the day in a shop in Acapulco, where dresses and slacks and bathing suits hung on all the walls. This place smelled clean and fresh, there were flowers in pots and in boxes out front, and the floor was of cool blue and white tiles. Ming had perfect freedom to wander out into the patio behind the shop, or to sleep in his basket in a corner. There was more sunlight in front of the shop, but mischievous boys often tried to grab him if he sat in front, and Ming could never relax there.

Ming liked best lying in the sun with his mistress on one of the long canvas chairs on their terrace at home. What Ming did not like were the people she sometimes invited to their house, people who spent the night, people by the score who stayed up very late eating and drinking, playing the gramophone or the piano – people who separated him from Elaine. People who stepped on his toes, people who sometimes picked him up from behind before he could do anything about it, so that he had to squirm and fight to get free, people who stroked him roughly, people who closed a door somewhere, locking him in. *People!* Ming detested people. In all the world, he liked only Elaine. Elaine loved him and understood.

Especially this man called Teddie Ming detested now. Teddie was around all the time lately. Ming did not like the way Teddie looked at him, when Elaine was not watching. And sometimes Teddie, when Elaine was not near, muttered something which Ming knew was a threat. Or a command to leave the room. Ming took it calmly. Dignity was to be preserved. Besides, wasn't his mistress on his side? The man was the intruder. When Elaine was watching, the man sometimes pretended a fondness for him, but Ming always moved gracefully but unmistakably in another direction.

Ming's nap was interrupted by the sound of the cabin door opening. He heard Elaine and the man laughing and talking. The big red-orange sun was near the horizon.

'Ming!' Elaine came over to him. 'Aren't you getting *cooked*, darling? I thought you were *in*!'

'So did I!' said Teddie.

Ming purred as he always did when he was awakened. She picked him up gently, cradled him in her arms, and took him below in the suddenly cool shade of the cabin. She was talking to the man, and not in a gentle tone. She set Ming down in front of his dish of water, and though he was not thirsty, he drank a little to please her. Ming did feel addled by the heat, and he staggered a little.

Elaine took a wet towel and wiped Ming's face, his ears and his four paws. Then she laid him gently on the bunk that smelled of Elaine's perfume but also of the man whom Ming detested.

Now his mistress and the man were quarrelling, Ming could tell from the tone. Elaine was staying with Ming, sitting on the edge of the bunk. Ming at last heard the splash that meant Teddie had dived into the water. Ming hoped he stayed there, hoped he drowned, hoped he never came back. Elaine wet a bathtowel in the aluminium sink, wrung it out, spread it on the bunk, and lifted Ming on to it. She brought water, and now Ming was thirsty, and drank. She left him to sleep again while she washed and put away the dishes. These were comfortable sounds Ming liked to hear.

But soon there was another *plash* and *plpp*, Teddie's wet feet on the deck, and Ming was awake again.

The tone of quarrelling recommenced. Elaine went up the few steps on to the deck. Ming, tense, but with his chin still resting on the moistened bathtowel, kept his eyes on the cabin door. It was Teddie's feet that he heard descending. Ming lifted his head slightly, aware that there was no exit behind him, that he was trapped in the cabin. The man paused with a towel in his hands staring at Ming.

Ming relaxed completely, as he might do preparatory to a yawn, and this caused his eyes to cross. Ming then let his tongue slide a little way out of his mouth. The man started to say something, looked as if he wanted to hurl the wadded towel at Ming, but he wavered, whatever he had been going to say never got out of his mouth, and he threw the towel in the sink, then bent to wash his face. It was not the first time Ming had let his tongue slide out at Teddie. Lots of people laughed when Ming did this, if they were people at a party, for instance, and Ming rather enjoyed that. But Ming sensed that Teddie took it as a hostile gesture of some kind, which was why Ming did it deliberately to Teddie, whereas among other people, if was often an accident when Ming's tongue slid out.

The quarrelling continued. Elaine made coffee. Ming began to feel better, and went on deck again, because the sun had now set. Elaine had started the motor, and they were gliding slowly towards the shore. Ming caught the song of birds, the odd screams, like shrill phrases, of certain birds that cried only at sunset. Ming looked forward to the adobe house on the cliff that was his and his mistress's home. He knew that the reason she did not leave him at home (where he would have been more comfortable) when she went on the boat, was because she was afraid that people might trap him, even kill him. Ming understood. People had tried to grab him from almost under Elaine's eyes. Once he had been suddenly hauled away in a cloth bag and, though fighting as hard as he could, he was not sure he would have been able to get out if Elaine had not hit the boy herself and grabbed the bag from him.

Ming had intended to jump up on the cabin roof again but, after glancing at it, he decided to save his strength, so he crouched on the warm, gently sloping deck with his feet tucked in, and gazed at the approaching shore. Now he could hear guitar music from the beach. The voices of his mistress and the man had come to a halt. For a few moments, the loudest sound was the *chug-chug-chug* of the boat's motor. Then Ming heard the man's bare feet climbing the cabin steps. Ming did not turn his head to look at him, but his ears twitched back a little, involuntarily. Ming looked at the water just the distance of a short leap in front of him and below him. Strangely, there was no sound from the man behind him. The hair on Ming's neck prickled, and Ming glanced over his right shoulder.

In that instant, the man bent forward and rushed at Ming with his arms outspread.

Ming was on his feet at once, darting straight towards the man, which was the only direction of safety on the rail-less deck, and the man swung his left arm and cuffed Ming in the chest. Ming went flying backwards, claws scraping the deck, but his hind legs went over the edge. Ming clung with his front feet to the sleek wood which gave him little hold, while his hind legs worked to heave him up, worked at the side of the boat which sloped to Ming's disadvantage.

The man advanced to shove a foot against Ming's paws, but Elaine came up the cabin steps just then.

'What's happening? *Ming!*'

Ming's strong hind legs were getting him on to the deck little by little. The man had knelt as if to lend a hand. Elaine had fallen on her knees also, and had Ming by the back of the neck now.

Ming relaxed, hunched on the deck. His tail was wet.

'He fell overboard!' Teddie said. 'It's true, he's groggy. Just lurched over and fell when the boat gave a dip!'

'It's the sun. Poor *Ming!*' Elaine held the cat against her breast, and carried him into the cabin. 'Teddie – could you steer?'

The man came down to the cabin. Elaine had Ming on the bunk and was talking to him softly. Ming's heart was still beating fast. He was alert against the man at the wheel, even though Elaine was with him. Ming was aware that they had entered a little cove where they always went before getting off the boat.

Here were the friends and allies of Teddie, whom Ming detested by association, although these were merely Mexican boys. Two or three boys in shorts called 'Señor Teddie!' and offered a hand to Elaine to climb on to the dock, took the rope attached to the front of the boat, offered to carry '*Ming! – Ming!*' Ming leapt on to the dock himself and crouched, waiting for Elaine, ready to dart away from any other hand that might reach for him. And there were several brown hands making a rush for him, so that Ming had to keep jumping aside. There were laughs, yelps, stomps of bare feet on wooden boards. But there was also the reassuring voice of Elaine warning them off. Ming knew she was busy carrying off the plastic satchels, locking the cabin door. Teddie with the aid of one of the Mexican boys was stretching the canvas over the cabin now. And Elaine's sandalled feet were beside Ming. Ming followed her as she walked away. A boy took the things Elaine was carrying, then she picked Ming up.

They got into the big car without a roof that belonged to Teddie, and drove up the winding road towards Elaine's and Ming's house. One of the boys was driving. Now the tone in which Elaine and Teddie were speaking was calmer, softer. The man laughed. Ming sat tensely on his mistress's lap. He could feel her concern for him in the way she stroked him and touched the back of his neck. The man reached out to put his fingers on Ming's back, and Ming gave a low growl that rose and fell and rumbled deep in his throat.

'Well, well,' said the man, pretending to be amused, and took his hand away.

Elaine's voice had stopped in the middle of something she was saying. Ming was tired, and wanted nothing more than to take a nap on the big bed at home. The bed was covered with a red and white striped blanket of thin wool.

Hardly had Ming thought of this, when he found himself in the cool, fragrant atmosphere of his own home, being lowered gently on to the bed with the soft woollen cover. His mistress kissed his cheek, and said something with the word hungry in it. Ming understood, at any rate. He was to tell her when he was hungry.

Ming dozed, and awakened at the sound of voices on the terrace a couple of yards away, past the open glass doors. Now it was dark. Ming could see one end of the table, and could tell from the quality of the light that there were candles on the table. Concha, the servant who slept in the house, was clearing the table. Ming heard her voices, then the voices of Elaine and the man. Ming smelled cigar smoke. Ming jumped to the floor and sat for a moment looking out of the door towards the terrace. He yawned, then arched his back and stretched, and limbered up his muscles by digging his claws into the thick straw carpet. Then he slipped out to the right of the terrace and glided silently down the long stairway of broad stones to the garden below. The garden was like a jungle or a forest. Avocado trees and mango trees grew as high as the terrace itself, there were bougainvillaea against the wall, orchids in the trees, and magnolias and several camellias which Elaine had planted. Ming could hear birds twittering and stirring in their nests. Sometimes he climbed trees to get at their nests, but tonight he was not in the mood, though he was no longer tired. The voices of his mistress and the man disturbed him. His mistress was not a friend of the man's tonight, that was plain.

Concha was probably still in the kitchen, and Ming decided to go in and ask her for something to eat. Concha liked him. One maid who had not liked him had been dismissed by Elaine. Ming thought he fancied barbecued pork. That was what his mistress and the man had eaten tonight. The breeze blew fresh from the ocean, ruffling Ming's fur slightly. Ming felt completely recovered from the awful experience of nearly falling into the sea.

Now the terrace was empty of people. Ming went left, back into the bedroom, and was at once aware of the man's presence, though there was no light on and Ming could not see him. The man was standing by the dressing table, opening a box. Again involuntarily Ming gave a low growl which rose and fell, and Ming remained frozen in the position he had been in when he first became aware of the man, his right front paw extended for the next step. Now his ears were back, he was prepared to spring in any direction, although the man had not seen him.

'*Ssss-st!* Damn you!' the man said in a whisper. He stamped his foot, not very hard, to make the cat go away.

Ming did not move at all. Ming heard the soft rattle of the white necklace which belonged to his mistress. The man put it into his pocket, then moved to Ming's right, out of the door that went into the big living-room. Ming now heard the clink of a bottle against glass, heard liquid being poured. Ming went through the same door and turned left towards the kitchen.

Here he miaowed, and was greeted by Elaine and Concha. Concha had her radio turned on to music.

'Fish? – Pork. He likes pork,' Elaine said, speaking the odd form of words which she used with Concha.

Ming, without much difficulty, conveyed his preference for pork, and got it. He fell to with a good appetite. Concha was exclaiming 'Ah-eee-ee!' as his mistress spoke with her, spoke at length. Then Concha bent to stroke him, and Ming put up with it, still looking down at his plate, until she left off and he could finish his meal. Then Elaine left the kitchen. Concha gave him some tinned milk, which he loved, in his now empty saucer, and Ming lapped this up. Then he rubbed himself against her bare leg by way of thanks and went out of the kitchen, made his way cautiously into the living-room en route to the bedroom. But now Elaine and the man were out on the terrace. Ming had just entered the bedroom, when he heard Elaine call:

'Ming? Where are you?'

Ming went to the terrace door and stopped, and sat on the threshold.

Elaine was sitting sideways at the end of the table, and the candlelight was bright on her long fair hair, on the white of her trousers. She slapped her thigh, and Ming jumped on to her lap.

The man said something in a low tone, something not nice. Elaine replied something in the same tone. But she laughed a little.

Then the telephone rang.

Elaine put Ming down, and went into the living-room towards the telephone.

The man finished what was in his glass, muttered something at Ming, then set the glass on the table. He got up and tried to circle Ming, or to get him towards the edge of the terrace, Ming realized, and Ming also realized that the man was drunk – therefore moving slowly and a little clumsily. The terrace had a parapet about as high as the man's hips, but it was broken by grilles in three places, grilles with bars wide enough for Ming to pass through, though Ming never did, merely looked through the grilles sometimes. It was plain to Ming that the man wanted to drive him through one of the grilles, or grab him and toss him over the terrace parapet. There was nothing easier for Ming than to elude him. Then the man picked up a chair and swung it suddenly, catching Ming on the hip. That had been quick, and it hurt. Ming took the nearest exit, which was down the outside steps that led to the garden.

The man started down the steps after him. Without reflecting Ming dashed back up the few steps he had come, keeping close to the wall which was in shadow. The man hadn't seen him, Ming knew. Ming leapt to the terrace parapet, sat down and licked a paw once to recover and collect himself. His heart beat fast as if he were in the middle of a fight. And hatred ran in his veins. Hatred burned his eyes as he crouched and listened to the man uncertainly climbing the steps below him. The man came into view.

Ming tensed himself for a jump, then jumped as hard as he could, landing with all four feet on the man's right arm near the shoulder. Ming clung to the cloth of the man's white jacket, but they were both falling. The man groaned. Ming hung on. Branches crackled. Ming could not tell up from down. Ming jumped off the man, became aware of direction and of the earth too late, and landed on his side. Almost at the same time, he heard the thud of the man hitting the ground, then of his body rolling a little way, then there was silence. Ming had to breathe fast with his mouth open until his chest stopped hurting. From the direction of the man, he could smell drink, cigar, and the sharp odour that meant fear. But the man was not moving.

Ming could now see quite well. There was even a bit of moonlight. Ming headed for the steps again, had to go a long way through the bush, over stones and sand, to where the steps began. Then he glided up and arrived once more upon the terrace.

Elaine was just coming on to the terrace.

'Teddie?' she called. Then she went back into the bedroom where she turned on a lamp. She went into the kitchen. Ming followed her. Concha had left the light on, but Concha was now in her own room, where the radio played.

Elaine opened the front door. The man's car was still in the driveway, Ming saw. Now Ming's hip had begun to hurt, or now he had begun to notice it. It caused him to limp a little. Elaine noticed this, touched his back, and asked him what was the matter. Ming only purred.

'Teddie? – Where are you?' Elaine called.

She took a torch and shone it down into the garden, down among the great trunks of the avocado trees, among the orchids and the lavender and pink blossoms of the bougainvillaeas. Ming, safe beside her on the terrace parapet, followed the beam of the torch with his eyes and purred with content. The man was not below here, but below and to the right. Elaine went to the terrace steps and carefully, because there was no rail here, only broad steps, pointed the beam of the light downward. Ming did not bother looking. He sat on the terrace where the steps began.

'Teddie!' she said. *'Teddie!'* Then she ran down the steps.

Ming still did not follow her. He heard her draw in her breath. Then she cried:

'Concha!'

Elaine ran back up the steps.

Concha had come out of her room. Elaine spoke to Concha. Then Concha became excited. Elaine went to the telephone, and spoke for a short while, then she and Concha went down the steps together. Ming settled himself with his paws tucked under him on the terrace, which was still faintly warm from the day's sun. A car arrived. Elaine came up the steps, and went and opened the front door. Ming kept out of the way on the terrace, in a shadowy corner, as three or four strange men came out on the terrace and tramped down the steps. There was a great deal of talk below, noises of feet, breaking the bushes, and then the smell of all of them mounted the steps, the smell of tobacco, sweat, and the familiar smell of blood. The man's blood. Ming was pleased, as he was pleased when he killed a bird and created this smell of blood under his own teeth. This was big prey. Ming, unnoticed by any of the others, stood up to his full height as the group passed with the corpse, and inhaled the aroma of his victory with a lifted nose.

Then suddenly the house was empty. Everyone had gone, even Concha. Ming drank a little water from his bowl in the kitchen, then went to his mistress's bed, curled against the slope of the pillows, and fell fast asleep. He was awakened by the *rr-rr-r* of an unfamiliar car. Then the front door opened, and he recognized the step of Elaine and then Concha. Ming stayed where he was. Elaine and concha talked softly for a few minutes. Then Elaine came into the bedroom. The lamp was still on. Ming watched her slowly open the box on her dressing table, and into it she let fall the white necklace that made a little clatter. Then she closed the box. She began to unbutton her shirt, but before she had finished, she flung herself on the bed and stroked Ming's head, lifted his left paw and pressed it gently so that the claws came forth.

'Oh, Ming – Ming,' she said.

Ming recognized the tones of love.

The Cat and Superstition

Anne Marks

In treating of superstitions associated with the cat, it may safely be asserted (in spite of the fact that some of them favour the animal) that no other four-footed creature has suffered so much from the cruelties incidental to this lamentable offspring of ignorance. In this country, in common with most others, superstition in regard to the animal was great and widespread during the Middle Ages, when many people believed that almost every movement of the cat had some significance. Some of these beliefs linger on even up to the present time, for the idea still survives that a black cat brings good luck, and that a sable stray should never be turned away from the house; it is also believed that, at the completion of a newly-built dwelling, a stray should be brought in 'for luck' – a black, not a white puss, for the latter would be considered a harbinger of ill-fortune. Possibly we have here a variation of the superstition that on removal to a new house a cat or dog should be thrown in before anyone enters; the idea is that whoever first crosses the threshold will be the first to die. In Ireland, however, it is considered most unlucky in removing to a new house to take the cat, and in consequence the animal is turned adrift.

By some authorities the sable puss is credited with miraculous healing powers. For instance, there are districts of this country in which a black cat is supposed to be, in regard to epilepsy, not merely an antidote, but a cure. In Cornwall again, sore eyes in children are said to be cured by the passing of the tail of a black cat nine times over the part affected. There are places (not necessarily in this country) where it is believed that blood from the tail of a cat will cure erysipelas.

In Germany it was at one time believed that the appearance of a black puss on the bed of an invalid presaged death, and one seen on a grave was regarded as a sign that the soul of the departed was in the power of the Devil. Another superstition averred that to dream of a black cat at Christmas foreboded some serious illness during the following year.

Black cats and skulls were the requisite accompaniments of the work of witchcraft; the former were always to be found in the hovels of the sorceress and the wizard, while the steed of a witch was a tomcat, a black one for choice. The apparatus required by the Evil One for the accomplishment of his enchantments including nails from the coffin of a person who had been executed, portions of a goat which had been a woman's pet, and the skull of a cat that had been fed on human flesh.

For a long time black cats were believed to be witches, because they were reported to be seen on the Sabbath in the company of goats and toads. Often, merely as the companion of a witch, puss shared the fate of her mistress and perished in the flames. It was anciently asserted that hags were allowed to take the form of the cat nine times, and it was a common belief that the animal, when it reached the age of twenty, became a witch, and that a witch who lived to be one hundred turned again into a cat.

In Hungary a variation of this superstition was current to the effect that a cat generally became a witch between the ages of seven and twelve years.

In the Middle Ages it was believed that Satan appeared as a black cat, when he desired to torment or show his power over his victims; indeed, this was imagined to be his favourite disguise, and puss therefore became an object of dread. St Dominique in his sermons represented the Devil in the guise of a cat.

In those days a kind of incantation was employed in which the cat was introduced, and by which the reciter of the charm was enabled to see demons. It may be that the connection of black cats with witchcraft was to a large extent due to the great quantity of electricity (more in black than in other cats) liberated from the coat by friction. Apropos of this supposition, it has been remarked that a cat, in moving quickly through an undergrowth of vegetation, produces an appearance of luminosity, and this being more noticeable in frosty weather, it was attributed to uncanny influence. It has also been observed that highly sensitive temperaments experience something akin to an electric shock through the slightest contact with the fur of a black cat; by the way, the Rev. Gilbert White, in 'The Natural History of Selborne', relates that, during two intensely cold days, the fur of his parlour cat was so charged with electricity, that anyone properly insulated, who stroked the animal might have communicated the shock to a whole circle of people.

Black cats were associated with witches in many districts of Southern Europe, and in Norwegian folklore; in the latter they were also believed to inhabit ghost-haunted houses and to indulge in nocturnal revels. It is curious, notwithstanding these delusions, that among the Scandinavians and the people of Northern Europe puss should have been considered as an emblem of love; they used also to believe that cats were possessed of magical powers, and that it was advisable to humour them. In Sicily it was thought that, if one of these sable cat-fiends lived with seven masters, the soul of the last of these was fated to accompany him on his return to Hades.

Although we are told that in China puss is considered to betoken ill-luck, and the display of sudden attachment to a family on the part of a feline stray is supposed to foreshadow poverty and distress, yet a clay likeness of a cat with a bob-tail like those seen in this country is frequently placed on the apex of a roof as a protection against maleficent powers. At the same time the animal is suspected of being in league with the Evil One, and is credited with meterological prescience. For these reasons it is propitiated, and, as in ancient Egypt, its likeness forms a favourite charm.

Amongst other superstitions prevalent in China is the notion that, shortly after the birth of a child, some hairs of cats and dogs should be suspended for eleven days outside the door of the bedroom where the mother is lying. This prevents the noise of the animals from frightening the baby.

In this country also, according to tradition, people sometimes reverence the ghost of a cat. Spiritual communication is established by hanging the cat, after which seven weeks of occasional fasting and prayer are observed in its honour. A bag is suspended by its side, and offerings are made to it. It is asserted that the ghost purloins the neighbours' property, and places the booty in the bag, and it is added, that as a consequence those who serve these cat-deities get rich very quickly. A high official in a certain district discovered that a considerable quantity of his store of rice had disappeared, and also learnt that behind his house dwelt a man who sacrificed to one of these cat-ghosts. He ordered that the devotee and the dead cat should be severely flogged, with the not unexpected result that this particular animal ceased for the future to exercise its power. A similar tale appears in Northern legends.

In consequence of her great powers of endurance puss is said to have nine lives, and perhaps that is a reason why at one time the poor creature was assailed and ill-treated so continually, for if one life was ended, were there not others in reserve? In Scotland it was believed that witches often assumed the feline form to facilitate the exercise of their evil influence over a family. On the other hand, in the West of Scotland that person was considered lucky to whom a male cat, on entering a dwelling, attached himself. In fact, a puss of any kind was always welcomed and petted. If, however, the animal became ill then (for it would have been considered unlucky for him to die inside the house) the custom was to remove poor pussy to an outhouse, put plenty of food there, and leave him alone either to recover or die. In Lancashire also it is believed to be unlucky for a cat to die in the house, but in this country the misfortune is prevented by the simple method of drowning the animal when it becomes ill. There is a peculiar superstition current on the Scottish Border according to which, if a cat or dog pass over a corpse, it is a presage of misfortune; in fact, in Scotland the animals are not allowed to approach a dead body, and to prevent the possibility of such approach the poor things are killed without compunction. In Devonshire, however, it is said that a cat will not remain in a house which contains a corpse, and stories are told of the disappearance of one on the death of an inmate and its reappearance *after* the funeral.

To return to mediaeval superstitions. Certain characteristics were assigned to the second-born of twins – the power of detaching the spirit from the body, and an insatiable appetite. The former helped the latter in that the child was able to take the form of a cat, and so could more easily commit depredations for the purpose of obtaining the particular food desired. Parents of twins were very anxious that puss should not be ill-treated, lest their own child should be a sufferer. After the age of ten or twelve the child ceased to indulge in this practice, and its exercise could have been entirely prevented, if at the time of birth a decoction of onion broth and camel's milk had at once been administered to the infant. This superstition regarding twins existed among the Copts; it was of Egyptian origin, and probably an outcome of the belief in the transmigration of souls.

A very old saying, ascribed to an Athenian oracle, is that when puss 'combs herself it is a sign of rain, because, when she feels the moisture in the air, she smooths the fur to cover her body, and so suffer the inconvenience as little as possible'; on the other hand, it is said that 'she opens her fur in the dry season that she may more easily derive benefit from any humidity in the atmosphere.' The superstition lasted long and was greatly extended, so that for a cat to show more than the ordinary tendency to sit by the fire, and with the tail towards it, to scratch the legs of the table, to sneeze, to lick her feet, to trim the whiskers and the fur of the head, to wash with the paw behind the ears, or to stretch the paw beyond the crown of the head, were severally to be considered as signs of rainy weather; belief in the last named dates from time when the priests of the goddess Pasht flourished. There is a Spanish saying that when the cat's fur looks bright it will be fine the next day.

It may be noticed here that sailors believe, when puss becomes unusually frolicsome, it portends tempestuous weather; the same result would follow should a cat unfortunately be drowned, and they think that if a black cat comes on board it foretells disaster. However, at Scarborough in former days the wives of sailors fancied that by keeping a black cat the safety of the husband while at sea was insured; consequently anyone else had a poor chance of possessing a sable puss, as she was nearly always stolen by one of these women.

The idea that the cat under certain circumstances may be a harbinger of evil is the reason that in many countries it is kept away from children's cradles. Another explanation of the objection that exists to the presence of a cat in a baby's cradle is to be found in the notion that the animal would inhale the infant's breath, and that death might ensue in consequence. It is, perhaps, needless to add that this impression has no real justification. On the other hand, it is current in Russo-Jewish folklore that, if a cat is put into a new cradle, it will be the means of driving away evil spirits from the infant.

The following are further interesting instances of superstition in connection with the cat, and are taken indiscriminately from the traditions of many countries. In some districts it was believed that all cats that wandered over the housetops in the month of February were witches, and therefore to be destroyed. The belief that 'great evil is in store for him who harms or kills a cat' is evidently derived from the Egyptian appreciation of the animal, and in addition, it was doubtless feared that hags would avenge any injury done to their familiars. When a cat washes herself, it is taken as a sign that a guest is coming; but if while so occupied puss looks at anyone, it portends that the unfortunate individual so regarded will be the recipient of a scolding. To keep a cat or dog from the wish to run away, it must be chased three times round the hearth, and afterwards be rubbed against the chimney-shaft; or, according to another mode, when the animal has been bought and brought home, it should be carried into the house tail foremost. It is believed that if a maiden is fond of cats she will have a sweet-tempered husband. Another superstition holds that if a kitten strays into a house in the morning it presages good luck, but if at night, the reverse, unless the kitten remains as a countercharm. If in a house where a person is ill the cats bite each other, it foretells death at an early date. In Tuscany, if a man wishes for death, it is opined that a cat – *i.e.*, the Devil in this form – approaches the bed.

A superstition that originated in Hungary and Tuscany avers that for a cat to be a clever thief, and therefore a good mouser, it must itself have been stolen. In Sicily there is a prevailing superstition to the effect that if a cat mews while the rosary is being counted for the welfare of outward-bound sailors, a tedious voyage will be the result. English folklore informs us that kittens born during the month of May should be drowned; it was thought that if spared they would not catch rats or mice, and, in addition, that they would attract snakes and other reptiles into the house. A saying in Huntingdonshire runs 'A May kitten makes a dirty cat.' At one time it was a common belief that if puss were hungry she would eat coal, and in some districts the idea prevails to the present day. The tongue of the cat is rough, somewhat like a file, and it was supposed that if, by licking a person sufficiently, the animal drew blood, the taste caused it to become mad. A cat-call on the roof used to be considered as a token of death. If puss sneezed, it was said to presage 'good luck' to the bride who was to be married on the following day; but a sneeze was also accepted as an evil omen, which foretold rain, and also colds to every member of the family. It was advisable to look well after pussy's comforts, for it was believed that rain on the wedding-day showed that the cat had been starved, and in this manner the offended messenger of the goddess of love took revenge. Another superstition which connected the cat and weddings warned the credulous that the union would not be happy if, on the way to church, the company met either a hare, a dog, a cat, a lizard, or a serpent; as some people had full belief in such portents, care was taken to prevent the occurrence of such an ominous encounter. There are instances recorded when brides have fainted through terror as a result of meeting under the circumstances either of the above-mentioned creatures.

A gipsy dislikes a sable cat in his dwelling, as he considers it uncanny, and a thing of the Devil; he approves of a white cat, which he deems good, and like the ghost of a fair lady. However, it used to be believed that the bite of a white cat was more dangerous than that of a black one.

A formula for deliverance of a cat from the power of a witch was to make upon its skin an incision in the form of a cross.

Puss has sometimes been accused of want of attachment to people. A suggested ground for this is that the animal eats mice, which are credited with being the source of forgetfulness, and the fear that this imperfection is contagious is responsible for the report that up to the present day in Russia Jewish boys are forbidden even to caress a cat. Apropos of this association of the Jew and the animal, we may ask whether it is reasonable to assume that the dearth of reference to the cat by early Hebrew writers may be accounted for by their probable dislike to it, consequent on its intimate relationship to the religious rites of the Egyptians.

The Cat and the Moon

The cat went here and there
And the moon spun round like a top,
And the nearest kin of the moon,
The creeping cat, looked up.
Black Minnaloushe stared at the moon,
For, wander and wail as he would,
The pure cold light in the sky
Troubled his animal blood.
Minnaloushe runs in the grass
Lifting his delicate feet.
Do you dance, Minnaloushe, do you dance?
When two close kindred meet,
What better than call a dance?
Maybe the moon may learn,
Tired of that courtly fashion,
A new dance turn.
Minnaloushe creeps through the grass
From moonlit place to place,
The sacred moon overhead
Has taken a new phase.
Does Minnaloushe know that his pupils
Will pass from change to change,
And that from round to crescent,
From crescent to round they range?
Minnaloushe creeps through the grass

Alone, important and wise,
and lifts to the changing moon
His changing eyes.

W. B. YEATS

The Cat's Paradise

Emile Zola

I was then two years old, and was at the same time the fattest and most naive cat in existence. At that tender age I still had all the presumptuousness of an animal who is disdainful of the sweetness of home.

How fortunate I was, indeed that providence had placed me with your aunt! That good woman adored me. I had at the bottom of a wardrobe a veritable sleeping salon, with feather cushions and triple covers. My food was equally excellent; never just bread, or soup, but always meat, carefully chosen meat.

Well, in the midst of all this opulence, I had only one desire, one dream, and that was to slip out of the upper window and escape on to the roofs. Caresses annoyed me, the softness of my bed nauseated me, and I was so fat that it was disgusting even to myself. In short, I was bored the whole day long just with being happy.

I must tell you that by stretching my neck a bit, I had seen the roof directly in front of my window. That day four cats were playing with each other up there; their fur bristling, their tails high, they were romping around with every indication of joy on the blue roof slates baked by the sun. I had never before watched such an extraordinary spectacle. And from then on I had a definitely fixed belief: out there on that roof was true happiness, out there beyond the window which was always closed so carefully. In proof of that contention I remembered that the doors of the chest in which the meat was kept were also closed, just as carefully!

I resolved to flee. After all there had to be other things in life besides a comfortable bed. Out there was the unknown, the ideal. And then one day they forgot to close the kitchen window. I jumped out on to the small roof above it.

How beautiful the roofs were! The wide eaves bordering them exuded delicious smells. Carefully I followed those eaves, where my feet sank into fine mud that smelled tepid and infinitely sweet. It felt as if I were walking on velvet. And the sun shone with a good warmth that caressed my plumpness.

I will not hide from you the fact that I was trembling all over. There was something overwhelming in my joy. I remember particularly the tremendous emotional upheaval which actually made me lose my footing on the slates, when three cats rolled down from the ridge of the roof and approached with excited miaows. But when I showed signs of fear, they told me I was a silly fat goose and insisted that their miaowing was only laughter.

I decided to join them in their caterwauling. It was fun, even though the three stalwarts weren't as fat as I was and made fun of me when I rolled like a ball over the roof heated by the sun.

An old tomcat belonging to the gang, honoured me particularly with his friendship. He offered to take care of my education, an offer which I accepted with gratitude.

Oh, how far away seemed all the soft things of your aunt! I drank from the gutters, and never did sugared milk taste half as fine! Everything was good and beautiful.

A female cat passed by, a ravishing she, and the very sight of her filled me with strange emotions. Only in my dreams had I up to then seen such an exquisite creature with such a magnificently arched back. We dashed forward to meet the newcomer, my three companions and myself. I was actually ahead of the others in paying the enchanting female my compliments; but then one of my comrades gave me a nasty bite in the neck, and I let out a shriek of pain.

'Pshaw!' said the old tomcat, dragging me away. 'You will meet plenty of others.'

After a walk that lasted an hour I had a ravenous appetite.

'What does one eat on these roofs?' I asked my friend the tom.

'Whatever one finds,' he replied laconically.

This answer embarrassed me somewhat for, hunt as I might, I couldn't find a thing. Finally I looked through a dormer window and saw a young workman preparing his breakfast. On the table, just above the windowsill, lay a chop of a particular succulent red.

'There is my chance,' I thought, rather naively.

So I jumped on to the table and snatched the chop. But the workingman saw me and gave me a terrific wallop across my back with a broom. I dropped the meat, cursed rather vulgarly and escaped.

'What part of the world do you come from?' asked the tomcat. Don't you know that meat on tables is meant only to be admired from afar? What we've got to do is look in the gutters.'

I have been able to understand why kitchen meat shouldn't belong to cats. My stomach began to complain quite bitterly. The tom tried to console me by saying it would only be necessary to wait for the night. Then, he said, we would climb down from the roofs into the street and forage in the garbage heaps.

Wait for the night! Confirmed philosopher that he was, he said it calmly, while the very thought of such a protracted fast made me positively faint.

Night came every so slowly, a misty night that made me shiver. To make things worse, rain began to fall, a thin, penetrating rain whipped up by brisk howling gusts of wind.

How desolate the streets looked to me! There was nothing left of the good warmth, of the big sun, of those roofs where one could play so pleasantly. My paws slipped on the slimy pavement, and I began to think with some longing of my triple covers and my feather pillow.

We had hardly reached the street when my friend, the tom, began to tremble. He made himself small, quite small, and glided surreptitiously along the walls of the houses, warning me under his breath to be quick about it. When we reached the shelter of a house door, he hid behind it and purred with satisfaction. And when I asked him the reason for his strange conduct, he said:

'Did you see that man with the hook and the basket?'

'Yes.'

'Well, if he had seen us, we would have been caught, fried on the spit and eaten!'

'Fried on the spit and eaten!' I exclaimed. 'Why, then the street is really not for the likes of us. One does not eat, but is eaten instead!'

In the meantime, however, they had begun to put the garbage out on the sidewalks. I inspected it with growing despair. All I found there were two or three dry bones that had obviously been thrown in among the ashes. And then and there I realized how succulent a dish of fresh meat really is!

My friend, the tom, went over the heaps of garbage with consummate artistry. He made me rummage around until morning, inspecting every cobblestone, without the least trace of hurry. But after ten hours of almost incessant rain my whole body was trembling. Damn the street, I thought, damn liberty! And how I longed for my prison!

When day came, the tomcat noticed that I was weakening.

'You've had enough, eh?' he asked in a strange voice.

'Oh, yes,' I replied.

'Do you want to go home?'

'I certainly do. But how can I find my house?'

'Come along. Yesterday morning when I saw you come out I knew immediately that a cat as fat as you isn't made for the joys of liberty. I know where you live. I'll take you back to your door.'

He said this all simply enough, the good, dignified tom. And when we finally got there, he added, without the slightest show of emotion:

'Goodbye, then.'

'No, no!' I protested. 'I shall not leave you like this. You come with me! We shall share bed and board. My mistress is a good woman . . .'

He didn't even let me finish.

'Shut up!' he said brusquely. 'You are a fool. I'd die in that stuffy softness. Your abundant life is for weaklings. Free cats will never buy your comforts and your featherbeds at the price of being imprisoned. Goodbye!'

With these words he climbed back on to the roof. I saw his proud thin shadow shudder deliciously as it began to feel the warmth of the morning sun.

When I came home your aunt acted the martinet and administered a corrective which I received with profound joy. I revelled in being punished and voluptuously warm. And while she cuffed me, I thought with delight of the meat she would give me directly afterwards.

You see – an afterthought, while stretched out before the embers – true happiness, paradise, my master, is where one is locked up and beaten, wherever there is meat.

I speak for cats.

The Cheshire Cat

Lewis Carroll

. . . So she set the little creature down, and felt quite relieved to see it trot away quietly into the wood. 'If it had grown up,' she said to herself, 'it would have made a dreadfully ugly child: but it makes rather a handsome pig, I think.' And she began thinking over other children she knew, who might do very well as pigs, and was just saying to herself 'if one only knew the right way to change them – ' when she was a little startled by seeing the Cheshire-Cat sitting on a bough of a tree a few yards off.

The Cat only grinned when it saw Alice. It looked good-natured, she thought: still it had *very* long claws and a great many teeth, so she felt that it ought to be treated with respect.

'Cheshire-Puss,' she began rather timidly, as she did not at all know whether it would like the name: however, it only grinned a little wider. 'Come, it's pleased so far,' thought Alice, and she went on. 'Would you tell me, please, which way I ought to go from here?'

'That depends a good deal on where you want to get to,' said the Cat.

'I don't much care where – ' said Alice.

'Then it doesn't matter which way you go,' said the Cat.

' – so long as I get *somewhere*,' Alice added as an explanation.

'Oh, you're sure to do that,' said the Cat, 'if you only walk long enough.'

Alice felt that this could not be denied, so she tried another question. 'What sort of people live about here?'

'In *that* direction,' the Cat said, waving his right paw round, 'lives a Hatter: and in *that* direction,' waving the other paw. 'lives a March Hare. Visit either you like: they're both mad.'

'But I don't want to go among mad people,' Alice remarked.

'Oh, you can't help that,' said the Cat: 'we're all mad here. I'm mad. You're mad.'

'How do you know I'm mad?' said Alice.

'You must be,' said the Cat, 'or you wouldn't have come here.'

Alice didn't think that proved it at all: however, she went on: 'And how do you know that you're mad?'

'To begin with,' said the Cat, 'a dog's not mad. You grant that?'

'I suppose so,' said Alice.

'Well, then,' the Cat went on, 'you see a dog growls when it's angry, and wags its tail when it's pleased. Now *I* growl when I'm pleased and wag my tail when I'm angry. Therefore I'm mad.'

'I call it purring, not growling,' said Alice.

'Call it what you like,' said the Cat. 'Do you play croquet with the Queen to-day?'

'I should like it very much,' said Alice, 'but I haven't been invited yet.'

'You'll see me there,' said the Cat, and vanished.

Alice was not much surprised at this, she was getting so well used to queer things happening. While she was still looking at the place where it had been, it suddenly appeared again.

'By-the-bye, what became of the baby?' said the Cat. 'I'd nearly forgotten to ask.'

'It turned into a pig,' Alice answered very quietly, just as if the Cat had come back in a natural way.

'I thought it would,' said the Cat, and vanished again.

Alice waited a little, half expecting to see it again, but it did not appear, and after a minute or two she walked on in the direction in which the March Hare was said to live. 'I've seen hatters before,' she said to herself: 'the March Hare will be much the more interesting, and perhaps, as this is May, it wo'n't be raving mad – at least not so mad as it was in March.' As she said this, she looked up, and there was the Cat again, sitting on a branch of a tree.

'Did you say "pig", or "fig"?' said the Cat.

'I said "pig",' replied Alice; 'and I wish you wouldn't keep appearing and vanishing so suddenly: you make one quite giddy!'

'All right,' said the Cat; and this time it vanished quite slowly, beginning with the end of the tail, and ending with the grin, which remained some time after the rest of it had gone.

'Well! I've often seen a cat without a grin,' thought Alice; 'but a grin without a cat! It's the most curious thing I ever saw in all my life!'

Miss Edith's Modest Request

My papa knows you, and he says you're a man who makes
 reading for books;
But I never read nothing you wrote, nor did papa – I know by
 his looks.
So I guess you're like me when I talk, and I talk, and I talk all
 the day,
And they only say: 'Do stop that child!' or, 'Nurse, take Miss
 Edith away.'

But papa said if I was good I could ask you – alone by myself –
If you wouldn't write me a book like that little one up on the
 shelf.
I don't mean the pictures, of course, for to make *them* you've
 go to be smart;
But the reading that runs all around them, you know – just the
 easiest part.

You needn't mind what it's all about, for no one will see it but
 me
And Jane – that's my nurse – and John – he's the coach-man –
 just only us three.
You're to write of a bad little girl, that was wicked and bold
 and all that;
And then you are to write, if you please, something good –
 very good – of a cat!

This cat she was virtuous and meek, and kind to her parents

and mild,
And careful and neat in her ways, though her mistress was
   such a bad child;
And hours she would sit and would gaze when her mistress –
   that's me – was so bad,
And blink, just as if she would say: 'O Edith! you make my
   heart sad.'

And yet, you would scarcely believe it, that beautiful angelic
   cat
Was blamed by the servants for stealing whatever, they said,
   she'd get at.
And when John drank my milk – don't you tell me! – I know
   just the way it was done –
They said 'twas the cat – and she sitting and washing her face
   in the sun!

And then there was Dick, my canary. When I left his cage open
   one day,
They all made believe that she ate it, though I know that the
   bird flew away.
And why? Just because she was playing with a feather she
   found on the floor,
As if cats couldn't play with a feather without people thinking
   'twas more.

Why, once we were romping together, when I knocked down a
   vase from the shelf,
That cat was as grieved and distressed as if she had done it
   herself;
And she walked away sadly and hid herself, and never came
   out until tea –
So they say, for they sent *me* to bed, and she never came even
   to me.

No matter whatever happened, it was laid at the door of that
   cat.
Why, once when I tore my apron – she was wrapped in it, and
   I called 'Rat!' –

Why, they blamed that on *her*. I shall never – no, not to my
    dying day –
Forget the pained look that she gave me when they slapped *me*
    and took me away.

Of course, you know just what comes next, when a child is as
    lovely as that:
She wasted quite slowly away – it was goodness was killing
    that cat.
I know it was nothing she ate, for her taste was exceedingly
    nice;
But they said she stole Bobby's ice cream, and caught a bad
    cold from the ice.

And you'll promise to make me a book like that little one up on
    the shelf,
And you'll call her 'Naomi,' because it's a name that she just
    gave herself;
For she'd scratch at my door in the morning, and whenever I'd
    call out, 'Who's there?'
She would answer 'Naomi! Naomi! like a Christian I vow and
    declare.

And you'll put me and her in a book. And, mind, you're to say
    I was bad;
And I might have been badder than that but for the example I
    had.
And you'll say that she was a Maltese, and – what's that you
    asked? 'Is she dead?'
  Why, please, sir, *there ain't any cat!* You're to make one up
    out of your head!

BRET HARTE

Below the Mill Dam

Rudyard Kipling

'Book – Book – Domesday Book!' They were letting in the water for the evening stint at Robert's Mill, and the wooden Wheel where lived the Spirit of the Mill settled to its nine-hundred-year-old song: 'Here Azor, a freeman, held one rod, but it never paid geld. *Nun-nun-nunquam geldavit.* Here Reinbert has one villein and four cottars with one plough – and wood for six hogs and two fisheries of sixpence and a mill of ten shillings – *unum molinum* – one mill. Reinbert's mill – Robert's Mill. Then and afterwards and now – *tunc es post et mode* – Robert's Mill. Book – Book – Domesday Book!'

'I confess,' said the Black Rat on the cross-beam, luxuriously trimming his whiskers – 'I confess I am not above appreciating my position and all it means.' He was a genuine old English black rat, a breed which, report says, is rapidly diminishing before the incursions of the brown variety.

'Appreciation is the surest sign of inadequacy,' said the Grey Cat, coiled up on a piece of sacking.

'But I know what you mean,' she added. 'To sit by right at the heart of things – eh?'

'Yes,' said the Black Rat, as the old mill shook and the heavy stones thuttered on the grist. 'To possess – er – all this environment as an integral part of one's daily life must insensibly of course . . . You see?'

'I feel,' said the Grey Cat. 'Indeed, if *we* are not saturated with the spirit of the Mill, who should be?'

'Book – Book – Domesday Book!' the Wheel, set to his work, was running off the tenure of the whole rape, for he knew

Domesday Book backwards and forwards: *In Ferle tenuit Abbatia de Wiltuna unam hidam et unam virgam et dimidiam. Nunquam geldavit*. And Agemond, a freeman, has half a hide and one rod. I remembered Agemond well. Charmin' fellow – friend of mine. He married a Norman girl in the days when we rather looked down on the Normans as upstarts. An 'Agemond's dead? So he is. Eh, dearie me! dearie me! I remember the wolves howling outside his door in the big frost of Ten Fifty-Nine . . . *Essewelde hundredum nunquam geldum reddidit*. Book! Book! Domesday Book!'

'After all,' the Grey Cat continued, 'atmosphere is life. It is the influences under which we live that count in the long run. Now, outside' -she cocked one ear towards the half-opened door – 'there is an absurd convention that rats and cats are, I won't go so far as to say natural enemies, but opposed forces. Some such ruling may be crudely effective – I don't for a minute presume to set up my standards as final among the ditches; but from the larger point of view that one gains by living at the heart of things, it seems for a rule of life a little overstrained. Why, because some of your associates have, shall I say, liberal views on the ultimate destination of a sack of – er – middlings don't they call them – '

'Something of that sort,' said the Black Rat, a most sharp and sweet-toothed judge of everything ground in the mill for the last three years.

'Thanks – middlings be it. *Why*, as I was saying, must I dissarrange my fur and digestion to chase you round the dusty arena whenever we happen to meet?'

'As little reason,' said the Black Rat, 'as there is for me, who, I trust, am a person of ordinarily decent instincts, to wait till you have gone on a round of calls, and then to assassinate your very charming children.'

'Exactly! It has its humorous side though.' The Grey Cat yawned. 'The miller seems afflicted by it. He shouted large and vague threats to my address, last night at tea, that he wasn't going to keep cats who "caught no mice." Those were his words. I remember the grammar sticking in my throat like a herringbone.'

'And what did you do?'

'What does one do when a barbarian utters? One ceases to utter and removes. I removed – towards his pantry. It was a *riposte* he might appreciate.'

'Really those people grow absolutely insufferable,' said the Black Rat. 'There is a local ruffian who answers to the name of Mangles – a builder – who has taken possession of the outhouses on the far side of the Wheel for the last fortnight. He has constructed cubical horrors in red brick where those deliciously picturesque pigstyes used to stand. Have you noticed?'

'There has been much misdirected activity of late among the humans. They jabber inordinately. I haven't yet been able to arrive at their reason for existence.' The Cat yawned.

'A couple of them came in here last week with wires, and fixed them all about the walls. Wires protected by some abominable composition, ending in iron brackets with glass bulbs. Utterly useless for any purpose and artistically absolutely hideous. What do they mean?'

'Aaah! I have known *four*-and twenty leaders of revolt in Faenza,' said the Cat, who kept good company with the boarders spending a summer at the Mill Farm. 'It means nothing except that humans occasionally bring their dogs with them. I object to dogs in all forms.'

'Shouldn't object to dogs,' said the Wheel sleepily . . . 'The Abbot of Wilton kept the best pack in the county. He enclosed all the Harryngton Woods to Sturt Common. Aluric, a freeman, was dispossessed of his holding. They tried the case at Lewes, but he got no change out of William de Warrenne on the bench. William de Warrenne fined Aluric eight and fourpence for treason, and the Abbot of Wilton excommunicated him for blasphemy. Aluric was no sportsman. Then the Abbot's brother married . . . I've forgotten her name, but she was a charmin' little woman. The Lady Philippa was her daughter. That was after the barony was conferred. She rode devilish straight to hounds. They were a bit throatier than we breed now, but a good pack: one of the best. The Abbot kept 'em in splendid shape. Now, who was the woman the Abbot kept? Book-Book! I shall have to go right back to Domesday and work up the centuries: *Modo per omnia reddit burgum tunc – tunc – tunc!* Was it *burgum* or *hundredum*? I shall remember in a minute. There's no hurry.' He paused as he turned over silvered with showering drops.

'This won't do,' said the Waters in the sluice. 'Keep moving.'

The Wheel swung forward; the Waters roared on the buckets and dropped down to the darkness below.

'Noisier than usual,' said the Black Rat. 'It must have been raining up the valley.'

'Floods maybe,' said the Wheel dreamily. 'It isn't the proper season, but they can come without warning. I shall never forget the big one – when the Miller went to sleep and forgot to open the hatches. More than two hundred years ago it was, but I recall it distinctly. Most unsettling.'

'We lifted that wheel off his bearings,' cried the Waters. 'We said, "Take away that bauble!" And in the morning he was five miles down the valley – hung up in a tree.'

'Vulgar!' said the Cat. 'But I am sure he never lost his dignity.'

'We don't know. He looked like the Ace of Diamonds when we had finished with him . . . Move on there! Keep on moving. Over! Get over!'

'And why on this day more than any other,' said the Wheel statelily. 'I am not aware that my department requires the stimulus of external pressure to keep it up to its duties. I trust I have the elementary instincts of a gentleman.'

'Maybe,' the Waters answered together, leaping down on the buckets. 'We only know that you are very stiff on your bearings. Over, get over!'

The Wheel creaked and groaned. There was certainly greater pressure upon him than he had ever felt, and his revolutions had increased from six and three-quarters to eight and a third per minute. But the uproar between the narrow, weed-hung walls annoyed the Grey Cat.

'Isn't it almost time,' she said plaintively, 'that the person who is paid to understand these things shuts off those vehement drippings with that screw-thing on the top of that box-thing.'

'They'll be shut off at eight o'clock as usual,' said the Rat; 'then we can go to dinner.'

'But we shan't be shut off till ever so late,' said the Waters gaily. 'We shall keep it up all night.'

'The ineradicable offensiveness of youth is partially compensated for by its eternal hopefulness,' said the Cat. 'Our dam is not, I am glad to say, designed to furnish water for more than four hours at a time. Reserve is Life.'

'Thank goodness!' said the Black Rat. 'Then they can return to their native ditches.'

'Ditches!' cried the Waters; 'Raven's Gill Brook is no ditch. It is almost navigable, and *we* come from there away.' They slid over solid and compact till the Wheel thudded under their weight.

'Raven's Gill Brook,' said the Rat. '*I* never heard of Raven's Gill.'

'We are the waters of Harpenden Brook – down from under Callton Rise. Phew! how the race stinks compared with the heather country.' Another five foot of water flung itself against the Wheel, broke, roared, gurgled, and was gone.

'Indeed,' said the Grey Cat, 'I am sorry to tell you that Raven's Gill Brook is cut off from this valley by an absolutely impassable range of mountains, and Callton Rise is more than nine miles away. It belongs to another system entirely.'

'Ah yes,' said the Rat, grinning, 'but we forget that, for the young, water always runs uphill.'

'Oh, hopeless! hopeless! hopeless!' cried the Waters, descending open-palmed upon the Wheel. 'There is nothing between here and Raven's Gill Brook that a hundred yards of channelling and a few square feet of concrete could not remove; and hasn't removed!'

'And Harpenden Brook is north of Raven's Gill and runs into Raven' Gill at the foot of Callton Rise, where the big ilex trees are, and *we* come from there!' These were the glassy, clear waters of the high chalk.

'And Batten's Ponds, that are fed by springs, have been led through Trott's Wood, taking the spare water from the old Witches' Spring under Churt Haw, and we – we – *we* are their combined waters!' Those were the Waters from the upland bogs and moors – a porter-coloured, dusky, and foam-flecked flood.

'It's all very interesting,' purred the Cat to the sliding waters, 'and I have no doubt that Trott's Woods and Bott's Woods are tremendously important places; but if you could manage to do your work – whose value I don't in the least dispute – a little more soberly, I, for one, should be grateful.'

'Book – book – book – book – book – Domesday Book!' The urged Wheel was fairly clattering now: 'In Burgelstaltone a monk holds of Earl Godwin one hide and a half with eight villeins.

There is a church – and a monk . . . I remember the monk. Blessed if he could rattle his rosary off any quicker than I am doing now . . . and wood for seven hogs. I must be runing twelve to the minute . . . almost as fast as Steam. Damnable invention, Steam! . . . Surely it's time we went to dinner or prayers – or something. Can't keep up this presure, day in and day out, and not feel it. I don't mind for myself, of course. *Noblesse oblige*, you know. I'm only thinking of the Upper and the Nether Millstones. They came out of the common rock. They can't be expected to – '

'Don't worry on our account, please,' said the Millstones huskily. 'So long as you supply the power we'll supply the weight and the bite.'

'Isn't it a trifle blasphemous, though, to work you in this way?' grunted the Wheel. 'I seem to remember something about the Mills of God grinding "slowly." *Slowly* was the word!'

'But we are not the Mills of God. We're only the Upper and Nether Millstones. We have received no instructions to be anything else. We are actuated by power transmitted through you.'

'Ah, but let us be merciful as we are strong. Think of all the beautiful little plants that grow on my woodwork. There are five varieties of rare moss within less than one square yard – and all these delicate jewels of nature are being grievously knocked about by this excessive rush of the water.'

'Umph!' growled the Millstones. 'What with your religious scruples and your taste for botany we'd hardly know you for the Wheel that put the carter's son under last autumn. You never worried about *him*!'

'He ought to have known better.'

'So ought your jewels of nature. Tell 'em to grow where it's safe.'

'How a purely mercantile life debases and brutalises!' said the Cat to the Rat.

'They were such beautiful little plants too,' said the Rat tenderly. 'Maiden's-tongue and hart's-hair fern trellising all over the wall just as they do on the sides of churches in the Downs. Think what a joy the sight of them must be to our sturdy peasants pulling hay!'

'Golly! said the Millstones. 'There's nothing like coming to the heart of things for information'; and they returned to the song that all English water-mills have sung from time beyond telling:

> There was a jovial miller once
> Lived on the River Dee,
> And this the burden of his song
> For ever used to be.

Then, as fresh grist poured in and dulled the note:

> I care for nobody – no, not I,
> And nobody cares for me.

'Even these stones have absorbed something of our atmosphere,' said the Grey Cat. 'Nine-tenths of the trouble in this world comes from lack of detachment.'

'One of your people died from forgetting that, didn't she?' said the Rat.

'One only. The example has sufficed us for generations.'

'Ah! but what happened to Don't Care?' the Waters demanded.

'Brutal riding to death of the casual analogy is another mark of provincialism!' The Grey Cat raised her tufted chin. 'I am going to sleep. With my social obligations I must snatch rest when I can; but, as your old friend here says, *Noblesse oblige* . . . Pity me! Three functions tonight in the village, and a barn-dance across the valley!'

'There's no chance, I suppose, of your looking in on the loft about two. Some of our young people are going to amuse themselves with a new sacque-dance – best white flour only,' said the Black Rat.

'I believe I am officially supposed not to countenance that sort of thing, but youth is youth. . . . By the way, the humans set my milk-bowl in the loft these days; I hope your youngsters respect it.'

'My dear lady,' said the Black Rat, bowing, 'you grieve me. You hurt me inexpressibly. After all these years, too!'

'A general crush is so mixed – highways and hedges – all that sort of thing – and no one can answer for one's best friends. *I* never try. So long as mine are amusin' and in full voice, and can hold their own at a tile-party, I'm as catholic as these mixed waters in the dam here!'

'We aren't mixed. We *have* mixed. We are one now,' said the Waters sulkily.

'Still uttering?' said the Cat. 'Never mind, here's the Miller coming to shut you off. Ye-es, I have known – *four* – or five is it? – and twenty leaders of revolt in Faenza . . . A little more babble in the dam, a little more noise in the sluice, a little extra splashing on the wheel, and then – '

'They will find that nothing has occurred,' said the Black Rat. 'The old things persist and survive and are recognised – our old friend here first of all. By the way,' he turned toward the Wheel, 'I believe we have to congratulate you on your latest honour.'

'Profoundly well deserved – even if he had never – as he was – laboured strenuously through a long life for the amelioration of millkind,' said the Cat, who belonged to many tile and out-house committees. 'Doubly deserved, as I may say, for the silent and dignified rebuke his existence offers to the clattering, fidgety-footed demands of – er – some people. What form did the honour take?'

'It was,' said the Wheel bashfully, 'a machine-moulded pinion.'

'Pinions! Oh, how heavenly!' the Black Rat sighed. 'I never see a bat without wishing for wings.'

'Not exactly that sort of pinion,' said the Wheel, 'but a really ornate circle of toothed iron wheels. Absurd, of course, but gratifying. Mr Mangles and an associate herald invested me with it personally – on my left rim – the side that you can't see from the mill. I hadn't meant to say anything about it – or the new steel straps round my axles – bright red, you know – to be worn on all occasions – but, without false modesty, I assure you that the re-cognition cheered me not a little.'

'How intensely gratifying!' said the Black Rat. 'I must really steal an hour between lights some day and see what they are doing on your left side.'

'By the way, have you any light on this recent activity of Mr Mangles?' the Grey Cat asked. 'He seems to be building small houses on the far side of the tail-race. Believe me, I don't ask from any vulgar curiousity.'

'It affects our Order,' said the Black Rat simply but firmly.

'Thank you,' said the Wheel. 'Let me see if I can tabulate it pro-

perly. Nothing like system in accounts of all kinds. Book! Book!
Book! On the side of the Wheel towards the hundred of burgelstaltone, where till now was a stye of three hogs, Mangles a freeman, with four villeins and two carts of two thousand bricks, has
a new small house of five yards and a half, and one roof of iron
and floor of cement. Then, how, and afterwards beer in large tan-
kards. And Felden, a stranger, with three villeins and one very
great cart, deposits on it one engine of iron and brass and a small
iron mill of four feet, and a broad strap of leather. And Mangles,
the builder, with two villeins, constructs the floor for the small
mill. There are there also chalices filled with iron and water, in
number fifty-seven. The whole is valued at one hundred and
seventy-four pounds. . .. I'm sorry I can't make myself clearer,
but you can see for yourself.'

'Amazingly lucid,' said the cat. She was the more to be admired
because the language of Domesday Book is not, perhaps the clearest medium wherein to describe a small but complete electric-light
installation, deriving its power from a water-wheel by means of
cogs and gearing.

'See for yourself – by all means, see for yourself,' said the
Waters, spluttering and choking with mirth.

'Upon my word,' said the Black Rat furiously, 'I may be at fault,
but I wholly fail to perceive where these offensive eavesdroppers
– er – come in. We were discussing a matter that solely affected
our order.'

Suddenly they heard, as they had heard many times before, the
Miller shutting off the water. To the rattle and rumble of the
labouring stones succeeded thick silence, punctuated with little
drops from the stayed wheel. Then some water-bird in the dam
fluttered her wings as she slid to her nest, and the plop of a water-
rat sounded like the fall of a log in the water.

'It is all over – it always is all over at just this time. Listen, the
Miller is going to bed – as usual. Nothing has occurred,' said the
cat.

Something creaked in the house where the pig-styes had stood,
as metal engaged on metal with a clink and a burr.

'Shall I turn her on?' cried the Miller.

'Ay,' said the voice from the dynamo-house.

'A human in Mangles' new house!' the Rat squeaked.

'What of it?' said the Grey Cat. 'Even supposing Mr Mangles'
cat's-meat-coloured hovel ululated with humans, can't you see
for yourself – that – ?'

There was a solid crash of released waters leaping upon the
wheel more furiously than ever, a grinding of cogs, a hum like the
hum of a hornet, and then the unvisited darkess of the old mill
was scattered by intolerable white ight. It threw up every cobweb,
every burl and knot in the beams and the floor; till the shadows
behind the flakes of rough plaster on the wall lay clear-cut as
shadows of mountains on the photographed moon.

'See! See! See!' hissed the Waters in full flood. 'Yes, see for
yourselves. Nothing has occurred. Can't you see?'

The Rat, amazed, had fallen from his foothold and lay half-
stunned on the floor. The Cat, following her instinct, leaped nigh
to the ceiling, and with flattened ears and bared teeth backed in a
corner ready to fight whatever terror might be loosed on her. But
nothing happened. Through the long aching minutes nothing
whatever happened, and her wire-brush tail returned slowly to
its proper shape.

'Whatever it is,' she said at last, 'it's overdone. They can never
keep it up, you know.'

'Much you know,' said the Waters. 'Over you go, old man. You
can take the full head of us now. Those new steel axle-straps of
yours can stand anything. Come along, Raven's Gill, Harpenden,
Callton Rise, Batten's Ponds, Witches' Spring, all together! Let's
show these gentlemen how to work!'

'But – but – I thought it was a decoration. Why – why – why it
only means more work for *me!*'

'Exactly. You're to supply about sixty eight-candle lights when
required. But they won't be all in use at once – '

'Ah, I thought as much,' said the Cat. 'The reaction is bound to
come.'

'*And*,' said the Waters, 'you will do the ordinary work of the
mill as well.'

'Impossible!' the old Wheel quivered as it drove. 'Aluric never
did it – nor Azor, nor Reinbert. Not even William de Warrenne or
the Papal Legate. There's no precedent for it. I tell you there's no
precedent for working a wheel like this.'

'Wait a while! We're making one as fast as we can. Aluric and

Co. are dead. So's the Papal Legate. You've no notion how dead they are, but we're here – the Waters of Five Separate Systems. We're just as interesting as Domesday Book. Would you like to hear about the land-tenure in Trott's Wood? It's squat-right, chiefly.' The mocking Waters leaped one over the other, chuckling and chattering profanely.

'In that hundred Jenkins, a tinker, with one dog – *unus canis* – holds, by the Grace of God and a habit he has of working hard, *unam hidam* – a large potato patch. Charmin' fellow, Jenkins. Friend of ours. Now, who the dooce did Jenkins keep? . . . In the hundred of Calltonis one charcoal-burner *irreligiosissimus homo* – a bit of a rip – but a thorough sportsman. *Ibi est ecclesia. Non multum.* Not much of a church, *quia* because, *episcopus* the Vicar irritated the Noncomformists *tunc et post et modo* – then and afterwards and now – until they built a cut-stone Congregational chapel with red brick facings that did not return itself – *defendebat se* – at four thousand pounds.'

'Charcoal-burners, vicars, schismatics, and red brick facings,' groaned the Wheel. 'But this is sheer blasphemy. What waters have they let in upon me?'

'Floods from the gutters. Faugh, this light is positively sickening!' said the Cat, rearranging her fur.

'We come down from the clouds or up from the springs, exactly like all other waters everywhere. Is that what's surprising you!' sang the Waters.

'Of course not. I know my work if you don't. What I complain of is your lack of reverence and repose. You've no instinct of deference towards your betters – your heartless parody of the Sacred volume (the Wheel meant Domesday Book) proves it.'

'Our betters?' said the Waters most solemnly. 'What is there in all this damned race that hasn't come down from the clouds, or – '

'Spare me that talk, please,'the Wheel persisted. 'You'd *never* understand. It's the tone – your tone that we object to.'

'Yes. It's your tone,' said the Black Rat picking himself up limb by limb.

'If you thought a trifle more about the work you're supposed to do, and a trifle less about your precious feelings, you'd render a little more duty in return for the power vested in you – we mean wasted on you,' the Waters replied.

'I have been some hundreds of years laboriously acquiring the knowledge which you see fit to challenge so light-heartedly,' the Wheel jarred.

'Challenge him! Challenge him! clamoured the little waves riddling down through the tail-race. 'As well now as later. Take him up!'

The main mass of the Waters plunging on the Wheel shocked that well-bolted structure almost into box-lids by saying: 'Very good. Tell us what you suppose yourself to be doing at the present moment.'

'Waiving the offensive form of your question, I answer, purely as a matter of courtesy, that I am engaged in the trituration of farinaceous substances whose ultimate destination it would be a breach of the trust reposed in me to reveal.'

'Fiddle!' said the Waters. 'We knew it all along! The first direct question shows his ignorance of his own job. Listen, old thing. Thanks to us, you are now actuating a machine of whose construction you know nothing, that that machine may, over wires of whose ramifications you are, by your very position, profoundly ignorant, deliver a power which you can never realise, to localities beyond the extreme limits of your mental horizon, with the object of producing phenomena which in your wildest dreams (if you ever dream) you could never comprehend. Is that clear, or would you like it all in words of four syllables?'

'Your assumptions are deliciously seeping, but may I point out that a decent and – the dear old Abbot of Wilton would have put it in his resonant monkish Latin much better than I can – a scholarly reserve does not necessarily connote black vacuity of mind on all subjects.'

'Ah, the dear old Abbot of Wilton,' said the Rat sympathetically, as one nursed in that bosom. 'Charmin' fellow – thorough scholar and gentleman. Such a pity!'

'Oh, Sacred fountains!' – the Waters were fairly boiling. 'He goes out of his way to expose his ignorance by triple bucketfuls. He creaks to high Heaven that he is hopelessly behind the common order of things! He invites the streams of Five Watersheds to witness his su-su-su-pernal incompetence, and then he talks as though there were untold reserves of knowledge behind him that he is too modest to bring forward. For a bland, circular, absolutely sincere impostor, you're a miracle, O Wheel!'

'I do not pretend to be anything more than an integral portion of an accepted and not altogether mushroom institution.'

'Quite so,' said the Waters. 'Then go round – hard – '

'To what end?' asked the Wheel.

'Till a big box of tanks in your house begins to fizz and fume – gassing is the proper word.'

'It would be,' said the Cat, sniffing.

'That will show that your accumulators are full. when the accumulators are exhausted, and the lights burn badly, you will find us whacking you round and round again.'

'The end of life as decreed by Mangles and his creatures is to go whacking round and round for ever,' said the Cat.

'In order,' the Rat said, 'that you may throw raw and unnecessary illumination upon all the unloveliness in the world. Unloveliness which we shall – er – have always with us. At the same time you will riotously neglect the so-called little but vital graces that make up Life.'

'Yes, Life,' said the Cat, 'with its dim delicious half-tones and veiled indeterminate distances. Its surprisals, escapes, encounters, and dizzying leaps – its full-throated choruses in honour of the morning star, and its melting reveries beneath the sun-warmed wall.'

'Oh, you can go on the tiles, Pussalina, just the same as usual,' said the laughing Waters. 'We shan't intefere with you.'

'On the tiles, forsooth!' hissed the Cat.

'Well that's what it amounts to,' persisted the Waters. 'We see a good deal of the minor graces of life on our way down to our job.'

'And – but I fear I speak to deaf ears – do they never impress you?' said the Wheel.

'Enormously,' said the Waters. 'We have already learned six refined synonyms for loafing.'

'But (here again I feel as though preaching in the wilderness) it never occurs to you that there may exist some small difference between the wholly animal – ah – rumination of bovine minds and the discerning, well-apportioned leisure of the finer type of intellect?'

'Oh yes. The bovine mind goes to sleep under a hedge and makes no bones about it when it's shouted at. We've seen *that* – in haying-time – all along the meadows. The finer type is wide awake enough to fudge up excuses for shirking, and mean enough to get stuffy when its excuses aren't accepted. Turn over!'

'But, my good people, no gentleman gets stuffy as you call it. A certain proper pride, to put it no higher, forbids – '

'Nothing that he wants to do if he really wants to do it. Get along! What are you giving us? D'you suppose we've scoured half heaven in the clouds, and half earth in the mists, to be taken in at this time of the day by a bone-idle, old hand-quern of your type?'

'It is not for me to bandy personalities with you. I can only say that I simply decline to accept the situation.'

'Decline away. It doesn't make any odds. They'll probably put in a turbine if you decline too much.'

'What's a turbine?' said the Wheel quickly.

'A little thing you don't see, that performs surprising revolutions. But you won't decline. You'll hang on to your two nice red-strapped axles and your new machine-moulded pinions like – a – like a leech on a lily stem! There's centuries of work in your old bones if you'd only apply yourself to it; and, mechanically, an overshot wheel with this head of water is about as efficient as a turbine.'

'So in future I am to be considered mechanically? I have been painted by at least five royal Academicians.'

'Oh, you can be painted by five hundred when you aren't at work of course. But while you are at work you'll work. You won't half-stop and think and talk about rare plants and dicky-birds and farinaceous fiduciary interests. You'll continue to revolve, and this new head of water will see that you do so continue.'

'It is a matter on which it would be exceedingy ill-advised to form a hasty or a premature conclusion. I will give it my most careful consideration,' said the Wheel.

'Please do,' said the Waters gravely. 'Hullo! Here's the Miller again.'

The Cat coiled herself in a picturesque attitude on the softest corner of a sack, and the Rat without haste, yet certainly without rest, slipped behind the sacking as though an appointment had just occurred to him.

In the doorway, with the young Engineer, stood the Miller grinning amazedly.

'Well – well – well! 'tis true-ly won'erful. An' what a power o'dirt! It comes over me now looking at these lights, that I've never rightly seen my own mill before. She needs a lot being' done to her.'

'Ah! I suppose one must make oneself moderately agreeable to the baser sort. They have their uses. This thing controls the dairy.' The Cat, pincing on her toes, came forward and rubbed her head against the Miller's knee'

'Ay, you pretty puss,' he said, stooping. 'You're as big a cheat as the rest of 'em that catch no mice about me. A won'erful smooth-skinned, rough-tongued cheat you be. I've more than half a mind – '

'She does her work well,' said the Engineer, pointing to where the Rat's beady eyes showed behind the sacking. 'Cats and Rats livin' together – see?'

'Too much they do – too long they've done. I'm sick and tired of it. Go and take a swim and larn to find your own vittles honest when you come out, Pussy.'

'My word!' said the Waters, as a sprawling Cat landed all un-announced in the centre of the tail-race. 'Is that you, Mewsalina? You seem to have been quarrelling with your best friend. Get over to the left. It's shallowest there. Up on that alder-root with all four paws. Goodnight!'

'You'll never get any they rats,' said the Miller, as the young Engineer struck wrathfully with his stick at the sacking. 'They're not the common sort. 'They're the old black English sort.'

'Are they, by Jove? I must catch one to stuff, some day.'

Six months later, in the chill of a January afternoon, they were let-ting in the waters as usual.

'Come along! It's both gears this evening,' said the Wheel, kick-ing joyously in the first rush of the icy stream. 'There's a heavy load of grist just in from Lamber's Wood. Eleven miles it came in an hour and a half in our new motor-lorry, and the Miller's rigged five new five-candle lights in his cow-stables. I'm feeding 'em tonight. There's a cow due to calve. Oh, while I think of it, what's the news from Callton Rise?'

'The waters are finding their level as usual – but why do you ask? ' said the deep outpouring Waters.

'Because Mangles and Felden and the Miller are talking of increasing the plant here and running a saw-mill by electricity. I was wondering whether we – '

I beg your pardon,' said the Waters, chuckling. '*What* did you say?'

'Whether *we*, of course, had power enough for the job. It will be a biggish contract. there's all Harpenden Brook to be considered and Batten's Ponds as well, and Witches' Fountain, and the Churt's Hawd system.'

'We've power enough for anything in the world,' said the Waters. 'The only question is whether you could stand the strain if we came down on your full head.'

'Of course I can,' said the Wheel. 'Mangles is going to turn me into a set of turbines – beauties.'

'Oh – er – I suppose it's the frost that has made us a little thick-headed, but to whom are we talking?' asked the amazed Waters.

'To me – the Spirit of the Mill, of course.'

'Not to the old Wheel, then?'

'I happen to be living in the old Wheel just at present. When the turbines are installed I shall go and live in them. What earthly difference does it make?'

'Absolutely none,' said the Waters, 'in the earth or in the waters under the earth. But we thought turbines didn't appeal to you.'

'Not like turbines? Me? My dear fellows, turbines are good for fifteen hundred revolutions a minute – and with our power we can drive 'em at full speed. Why there's nothing we couldn't grind for saw or illuminate or heat with a set of turbines! That's to say if all the Five Watersheds are agreeable.'

'Oh, we've been agreeable for ever so long.'

'Then why didn't you tell me?'

'Don't know. Suppose it slipped our memory.' The Waters were holding themselves in for fear of bursting with mirth.

'How careless of you!' You should keep abreast of the age, my dear fellows. We might have settled it long ago, if you'd only spoken. Yes, four good turbines and a neat brick penstock – eh? This old Wheel's absurdly out of date.'

'Well,' said the Cat, who after a little proud seclusion had returned to her place impenitent as ever. 'Praised by Pasht and Old

Gods, that whatever may have happened *I*, at least, have preserved the Spirit of the Mill!'

She looked round as expecting her faithful ally, the Black Rat; but that very week the Engineer had caught and stuffed him, and had put him in a glass case; he being a genuine old English black rat. That breed, the report says is rapidly diminishing before the incursions of the brown variety.

The Vatican Cat

Judy Martin

Centuries ago, when the nation-states of Europe were constantly
at war, the Vatican in Rome wielded considerable political power.
The Pope and his officials made it their business to chart the shifting patterns of treaties, alliances and conflicts between the states
and to manipulate the political intrigues.

A silent witness to the comings and goings of the politicians
was a slim, sleek cat, an enigmatic presence with her hooded eyes
and sinuous tail. This cat had thoroughly absorbed the conspira-
torial atmosphere and trusted no one. She was a favourite of the
Pope, however, and knowing him to be someone apart from all
the rest, she responded to his favours and made the most of her
privileged position. Many people at the papal court were super-
stitiously afraid of her, and those who knew she was a Scorpio
suspected her of having secret power and possibly of communing
with the forces of darkness. Ignoring such foolishness, the cat
made her way through the court unimpeded and mostly alone.
She loved the dark corners and shadowed corridors of the palace,
the rich furnishings and gold ornament of the ceremonial
chambers, and the swirling colours of the officials' robes.

The cat was, in fact, privy to the highly sensitive political negotiations conducted in the Pope's inner chambers. She had a hiding place in the vast sleeve of the Pope's robe, from where she
spied upon the visiting dignitaries and followed the sometimes
angry, sometimes conciliatory tones of the negotiations.

It was through this privilege that she unwittingly caused a
serious incident which had the most violent repercussions. An
alliance was to be arranged between two of the most powerful

warring states, signified by an important marriage ceremony which was to be conducted by the Pope. Part of the marriage settlement was the largest ruby ever seen, a sumptuous jewel set in gold which would be handed over as the final symbol of the signed treaty of alliance. The Pope had requested to see this important object prior to the marriage. As the glistening jewel was presented to him, the cat shifted her position under his robe and her sleek head momentarily appeared by the hem of his sleeve.

She had never seen anything so beautiful, even in all the treasures around her. The ruby seemed to wink and sparkle enticingly: in that moment she conceived a passion to make it her own. The jewel was well guarded, but no one could think it necessary to protect it from the attentions of a cat. In the dead of night, the cat made her way to the chamber where the ruby was kept in a special box, hidden in a niche in the wall. She started quietly to fiddle with the gold catch on the box until eventually her stealth and patience were rewarded and the catch slipped free. Tipping up the lid she snatched the jewel from its cushion and without hesitation bore it away to a secret hiding place known only to herself.

All hell broke loose next day when the loss of the ruby was discovered. The parties to the alliance both departed quickly and in anger, and war between their countries was resumed to devastating effect. The papal court was thoroughly disrupted. The atmosphere of secrecy and mistrust seemed to increase daily, as the mystery of the missing jewel remain unsolved.

The cat never gave away her secret and spent hours brooding pleasurably on her treasure, oblivious to the havoc she had caused. Those few who suspected the truth, though for the wrong reasons, made her life at the court more precarious, but none could produce an accusation. She lived, in fact, to a ripe old age and saw the downfall of many of her enemies. Rumour has it to this day, that the ruby remains in her secret cache, unseen ever since by human eye.

Ginger

Lady Morgan

The head favourite of my menagerie was a magnificent and very intelligent cat, 'Ginger,' by name, from the colour of her coat, which though almost orange was very much admired. She was the last of a race of cats sacred in the traditions of the Music Hall. Ginger was as much the object of my idolatry as if she had had a temple and I had been a worshipper in ancient Egypt; but, like other deities, she was reprobated by those who were not of my faith. I made her up a nice little cell, under the beaufet, as sideboards were then called in Ireland – a sort of alcove cut out of the wall of our parlour where the best glass and the family 'bit of plate' – a silver tankard – with the crest of the Hills upon it (a dove with an olive branch in its mouth),* which commanded great respect in our family. Ginger's sly attempt to hide himself from my mother, to whom she had that antipathy which animals so often betray to particular individuals, were a source of great amusement to my little sister and myself; but when she chose the retreat of the beaufet as the scene of her accouchment, our fear lest it should come to my mother's knowledge, was as great as if we had been concealing a moral turpitude. It was a good pious custom of my mother's to bear us our prayers every night; when Molly tapped at the parlour door at nine o'clock, we knelt at my mother's feet, our four little hands clasped in her's, and our eyes turned to her with looks of love, as they repeated that simple and beautiful invocation, the Lord's Prayer; to this was always added the supplication, 'Lighten our darkness we beseech Thee'; after

* Perhaps the words 'were kept' are missing here? editor

which we were accustomed to recite a prayer of our affectionate suggestion, calling a blessing on the heads of all we knew and loved, which ran thus, 'God bless papa, mamma, my dear sister, and Molly, and Betty, and Joe, and James, and all our good friends.' One night, however, before my mother could pronounce her solemn 'amen,' a soft muttered 'purr' issued from the cupboard, my heart echoed the appeal, and I added, 'God bless Ginger the cat!' Wasn't my mother shocked! She shook both my shoulders and said, 'What do you mean by that, you stupid child?' 'May I not say, "Bless Ginger"?' I asked humbly. 'Certainly not,' said my mother emphatically. 'Why, mamma?' 'Because Ginger is not a Christian?' '*Why* is not Ginger a Christian?' 'Why? because Ginger is only an animal.' 'Am I a Christian, mamma, or an animal?' 'I will not answer any more foolish questions tonight. Molly, take these children to bed, and do teach Sydney not to ask silly questions.'

So we were sent off in disgrace, but not before I had given Ginger a wink, whose bright eyes acknowledged the salute through the half-open door.

The result of this was that I tried my hand at a poem. The jingle of rhyme was familiar to my ear through my mother's constant recitation of verses, from the sublime Universal Prayer of Pope to the nursery rhyme of Little Jack Horner; whilst my father's dramatic citations, which had descended even to the servants, had furnished me with the tags of plays from Shakespeare to O'Keefe, so that I 'lisped in numbers' though the numbers never came.

Here is my first attempt:

> My dear pussy cat,
> Were I a mouse or rat,
> Sure I never would run off from you
> You're so funny and gay,
> With your tail when you play,
> And no song is so sweet as your 'mew';
> But pray keep in your press,
> And don't make a mess,
> When you share with your kittens our posset;
> For mamma can't abide you,

And I cannot hide you,
Except you keep close in your closet!

To Pangur Ban, my White Cat

Brother artists, he and I
Special crafts elect to ply;
Hunting mice would Pangur choose:
I have different sporting views.

At my books I never tire,
Nor rewards of fame desire:
Proud of inborn talents he
never thinks of envying me.

Snug indoors who roam abroad?
By ourselves we're never bored:
Countless thrilling tests arise
For our keenest faculties.

He, superbly dexterous,
Many a time entraps the mouse:
Truth elusive I pursue –
Sometimes I can trap her too!

Pangur's pupils, full and bright,
Fix the wainscot in their sight:
Through the walls of science I
Seek with feebler shafts to pry.

Pangur glories in his skill
When his claws achieve a kill:

I am overjoyed to gain
Prizes hunted in the brain.

Thus we live from day to day,
Neither in the other's way,
And our pleasures win apart,
Following each his special art.

Perfect use of eye and limb
Daily practice gives to him:
I my task appointed find
Chasing darkness from the mind.

OLD IRISH, TRANSLATED
BY SAMUEL COURTLAND

Three Cats

Colette

THE SIAMESE

'Sacred Cat! Cat of Siam! Royal Cat!' It's all very well to address me like that, and then on top of it to feed me on nothing but rice and fish. Fish is certainly very good; but everlasting fish and rice, rice and fish! Do they suppose my Siamese origins, and maybe my religion too, forbid me to eat like anyone else? My word, if I were to listen to them!

Cat, they called me, though I strive my utmost to be dog-like and follow them along the shore and in the forest, even going as far as the marsh, though it's so swollen with soft shapeless creatures which give under one's paws that it makes my head swim. And I always go to the side of the road, as dogs do, to let cars pass. When our headlights meet, the cars shine white and I, red. Yes, red! At night your cats burn green, like sheep. But I have to teach you everything.

It's true that I've eaten wood pigeons, and a partridge, and a tender rabbit. It's in my nature to track down everything beige, or tawny, or just brownish. Why otherwise should the Lord of Creation have given me this coat the colour of sand and rotting leaves! I can never hide unless I close my flame-blue eyes. If I open them, all things take flight – partridges, voles, and thrushes too. These humbled folk have not the stature to stand up to such a blue.

Ah, here you come, bringing me a fillet of turbot an a bowl of rice, for a change. Well, I hope you enjoy it; I shan't touch it. As it's still daylight it's useless to think of hunting; all the best game

is either in the air or underground at this time of day. But I have
stores that no one knows, and cat or no cat, I have a taste – like
the prince that I am – for low company. A dead jackdaw, for instance, makes my mouth water even to think of it. And a black
and yellow salamander, a bit high, will soon drive away the
memory of this pale fish and that rice, white as a ghost. If the
worst comes to the worst, I'll go and try conclusions with the only
creature that can meet my gaze without blinking, the one who,
since his fall, can't abide the sight of any heavenly blue: my
brother the serpent.

SIMPLETON

My name's Simpleton. And I think I've managed to live up to it,
though I didn't do it all by myself.

You must try and understand what my wedded life has been
like. Married too soon, a mother at eight months, I was already
re-married before I was a year old. And so it went on. I grew
sickly. They gave me sardines, cod-liver-oil and underdone horseflesh. With a diet like that I soon got back my strength and put
it to the best possible use. I needn't make my meaning any
clearer, need I?

We all carry our destinies within us. For nine weeks every so
often mine is in my belly. I eat heartily and I sleep a lot. After all,
you must reserve a little place for dreams when everything is so
terrible real inside you and all round you.

As a mother cat I'm gentle and tender. I'm like those bachelors'
housekeepers who hide their lusts under a modest gown and a
noncommittal smile. I lead my string of kittens about, confusing
them with those of the litter before. I don't do them much harm,
or much good either. And if one day some mysterious hand removes them from me, what of it? I can make some more. My husbands also disappear, unfaithful and oblivious. But what of that?
There'll be others.

You didn't think it was possible to be as dissolute as I am and
yet breathe innocence, did you? As a matter of fact I don't breathe
innocence, or cunning, or even that sacred rage which makes my

fellow she-cats howl prophetically. I don't breathe anything at all, for the simple reason that I'm empty, although I mayn't look it.

What a routine it all is, and how utterly lacking in variety! That's why I sleep as much as I can. And in my sleep the greatest bliss I know is to dream that I'm asleep and dreaming of nothing at all.

THE LITTLE BLACK CAT
(Posthumous Words)

I didn't live long on earth, but when I was there I was black, entirely black, without any white patch on my chest or white star on my forehead. I hadn't even those three or four white hairs which black cats often have below their chins, in the hollow of their throats. My coat was short, smooth and thick, my tail thin and sprightly, my eyes slanting and gooseberry green – a real black cat.

My earliest memory goes back to a house where I met a little white cat walking towards me down a long, dark room. Some instinct I didn't understand made me go to meet him, and we stopped nose to nose. He gave a jump backwards and at the same moment I gave a jump backwards too. If I hadn't jumped that day, perhaps I should still inhabit the world of colours and sounds and shapes you can touch.

But I jumped, and the white cat took me for his black shadow. After that I tried in vain to convince him that I had a shadow of my own. He insisted that I was nothing but his shadow and that I should imitate all his gestures, with no thanks for my pains. I had to dance if he danced, drink if he drank, eat if he ate, and hunt the game he hunted. But what I drank was the shadow of water, what I ate was the shadow of meat, and I would spend hours of boredom lying in wait for the shadow of a bird.

The white cat didn't like my green eyes, because they refused to be the reflection of his blue ones. He would curse them and go for them with his claws. So I used to keep them closed, and accustomed myself to seeing nothing but the darkness which reigned behind my eyelids.

But it was a wretched life for a little black cat. On moonlit nights I used to escape and dance feebly in front of a white wall, just for the pleasure of seeing a shadow that was my own, a thin, horned shadow that with every moon grew thinner and ever thinner, as though it were melting away.

And that was how I escaped from the little white cat. But I can't remember clearly just how I got away. Did I climb up a moonbeam? Did I imprison myself for ever behind my locked eyelids? Was I called by one of the magic cats that emerge from the depths of mirrors? I don't know. But ever since then the white cat thinks he has lost his shadow and he spends his time seeking it and calling it. Yet death has brought me no rest, because I doubt. As time goes on I grow always less and less certain that I was ever a real cat, and not just a shadow, the nocturnal half, the black, reverse side of the white cat.

Mike

Sir Ernest A. Wallace Budge

(The cat who assisted in keeping the main gate of the British Museum from February, 1909, to January 1929)

In the days when that famous and learned man, Sir Richard Garnett, ruled over the Department of Printed Books in the British Museum, he was frequently visited by a cat who was generally known among the staff as 'Black Jack.'

He was a very handsome black creature, with a white shirt front and white paws, and whiskers of great length. He was fond of sitting on the desks in the Reading Room, and he never hesitated to ask a reader to hold open both folding doors when he wanted to go out into the corridor. Being shut in one of the newspaper rooms one Sunday, and being bored, he amused himself by sharpening his claws on the bindings of the volumes of newspapers, and it must be confessed did much damage. This brought down upon him the wrath of the officials, and he was banished from the library; the Clerk of the Works was ordered to get rid of him, and tried to do so, but failed, for Black Jack had disappeared mysteriously. The truth was that two of the members of the staff arranged for him to be kept in safety in a certain place, and provided him with food and milk. An official report was written to the effect that Black Jack had disappeared, and he was 'presumed dead'; the bindings of the volumes of newspapers were repaired, and the official mind was once more at peace. A few weeks later Black Jack reappeared, and everyone was delighted to see him again; and the chief officials asked no questions!

Early in the spring of 1908 the Keeper of the Egyptian cat mum-

mies in the British Museum was going down the steps of his official residence, when he saw Black Jack coming towards the steps
and carrying something rather large in his mouth. He came to the
steps and deposited his burden on the steps at the Keeper's feet
and then turned and walked solemnly away. The something
which he deposited on the steps was a kitten, and that kitten was
later known to fame as 'Mike.' The kitten was taken in and cared
for and grew and flourished, and by great good luck was adopted
as a pal by the two cats already in the house. So all was well.

When Mike was a little older he went and made friends with
the kind-hearted gatekeeper at the main gate, and he began to frequent the lodge. By day and night he was always sure of a welcome, and thus he was the happy possessor of two homes. On
Sunday mornings the house cat taught him to stalk pigeons in the
colonnade. Mike was set to 'point' like a dog, and the house cat
little by little drove the pigeons up into a corner. The pigeons became dazed, and fell down, and then each cat seized a bird and
carried it into the house uninjured. The Housekeeper took the
pigeons from the cats, and in return for them gave a slice of beef
or mutton and milk to each cat. The pigeons were taken into a
little side room, and after they had eaten some maize and drunk
water, they flew out of the window none the worse for their
handling by the cats. The fact was that neither cat liked to eat
game with dirty, sooty, feathers on it; they preferred clean,
cooked meat.

As time went on, Mike, wishing to keep his proceedings during
the hours of night uncriticised by the household, preferred the
lodge to the house, and finally he took up his abode there; the
corner shelf out of the draughts was prepared for him to sleep on,
and he could go out and come in at anytime he pleased both by
day and by night. The Keeper of the Mummied Cats took care to
feed him during the lean years of the war, and whoever went
short, Mike did not. During the last two years he was difficult to
feed because of his decaying teeth, but a diet of tender meat and
fish on alternate days kept him going. He preferred sole to
whiting, and whiting to haddock, and sardines to herrings; for
cod he had no use whatever. He owed much to the three kind-
hearted gatekeepers who cooked his food for him, and treated
him as a man and a brother.

The Blue Dryad

G. H. Powell

'According to that theory' – said a critical friend, *à propos* of the last story but one – 'susceptibility of "discipline" would be the chief test of animal character, which means that the best Dogs get their character from men. If so –'

'You pity the poor brutes?'

'Oh, no. I was going to say that on that principle, cats should have next to no character at all.'

'They have plenty,' I said, 'but it's usually bad – at least hopelessly unromantic. Who ever heard of a heroic or self-denying Cat? Cats do what they like, not what you want them to do.'

He laughed. 'Sometimes they do what you like very much. You haven't heard Mrs Warburton-Kinneir's Cat-story?'

'The Warburton-Kinneirs! I didn't know they were back in England.'

'Oh, yes. They've been six months in Hampshire, and now they are in town. She has Thursday afternoons.'

'Good,' I said. 'I'll go the very next Friday, and take my chance. . . .'

Fortunately only one visitor appeared to tea. And as soon as I had explained my curiosity, he joined me in petitioning for the story which follows:

Stoffles was her name, a familiar abbreviation, and Mephistophelian was her nature. she had all the usual vices of the feline tribe, including a double portion of those which men are so fond of describing as feminine. Vain, indolent, selfish, with a highly cultivated taste for luxury and neatness in her personal appearance, she was distinguished by all those little irritating habits and traits for which nothing but an affectionate heart (a thing in her case conspicuous by its absence) can atone.

It would be incorrect, perhaps, to say that Stoffles did not care for the society of my husband and myself. She liked the best of everything, and these our circumstances allowed us to give her. For the rest, though in kitten days suspected of having caught a Mouse, she had never been known in after life to do anything which the most lax of economists could describe as useful. she would lie all day in the best armchair enjoying real or pretended slumbers, which never affected her appetite at supper time; although in that eventide which is the feline morn she would, if certain of a sufficient number of admiring spectators, condescend to amuse their dull human intelligence by exhibitions of her dexterity. But she was soon bored, and had no conception of altruistic effort. Abundantly cautious and prudent in all matters concerning her own safety and comfort, she had that feline celerity of vanishing like air or water before the foot, hand, or missile of irritated man; while on the other hand, when a sensitive specimen of the gentler sex (my grandmother, for example) was attentively holding the door open for her, she would stiffen and elongate her whole body; and, regardless of all exhibitions of kindly impatience, proceed out of the drawing-room as slowly as a funeral cortege of Crocodiles.

A good-looking Persian Cat is an ornamental piece of furniture in a house; but though fond of animals, I never succeeded in getting up an affection for Stoffles until the occurrence of the incident here to be related. Even in this, however, I cannot conceal from myself that the share which she took was taken, as usual, solely for her own satisfaction.

We lived, you know, in a comfortable old-fashioned house facing the high road, on the slope of a green hill from which one looked across the gleaming estuary (or the broad mud-flats) of Southampton Water on to the rich, rolling woodland of the New Forest. I say *we*, but in fact for some months I had been alone, and my husband had just returned from one of his sporting and scientific expeditions in South America. He had already won fame as a naturalist, and had succeeded in bringing home alive quite a variety of beasts, usually of the reptile order, whose extreme rarity seemed to me a merciful provision of Nature.

But all his previous triumphs were completely eclipsed, I soon learned, by the capture, alive, on this last expedition, of an abominably poisonous Snake, known to those who knew it as the Blue Dryad, or more familiarly in backwoods slang, as the Half-hour striker, in vague reference to its malignant and fatal qualities. The time in which a snake-bite takes effect is, by the way, no very exact test of its virulence, the health and condition not only of the victim but of the Snake, having, of course, to be taken into account.

But the Blue Dryad, sometimes erroneously described as a variety of Rattlesnake, is I understand, supposed to kill the average man, under favourable circumstances, in less time even than the deadly Copperhead – which it somewhat resembles, except that it is larger in size, and bears a peculiar streak of faint peacock-blue down the back, perceptible only in a strong light. This precious reptile was destined for the Zoological Gardens.

Being in extremely delicate health at the time, I need hardly say that I knew nothing of these gruesome details until afterwards. Henry (that is my husband), after entering my room with a robust and sunburned appearance that did my heart good, merely observed – as soon as we had exchanged greetings – that he had brought home a pretty Snake which 'wouldn't (just as long, that is to say, as it couldn't) do the slightest harm,' – an evasive assurance which I accepted – the nervous wife of an enthusiastic naturalist. I believe I insisted on its not coming into the house.

The cook, indeed, on my husband expressing a wish to put it in the kitchen, had taken up a firmer position: she had threatened to 'scream' if 'the vermin' were introduced into her premises; which ultimatum, coming from a stalwart young woman with unimpaired lungs, was sufficient.

Fortunately the weather was very hot (being in July of the ever-memorable summer of 1893), so it was decided that the Blue Dryad, wrapped in flannel and securely confined in a basket, should be left in the sun, on the farthest corner of the verandah, during the hour or so in the afternoon when my husband had to visit the town on business.

He had gone off with a cousin of mine, an officer of Engineers in India, stationed, I think, at Lahore, and home on leave. I remember that they were a long time, or what seemed to me a long time, over their luncheon; and the last remark of our guest as he came out of the dining-room remained in my head as even meaningless words will run in the head of any idle invalid shut up for most of the day in a silent room. What he said was, in the positive tone of one emphasizing a curious and surprising statement, 'D'you know, by the way, it's the *one* animal that doesn't care a rap for the cobra.' And, my husband seeming to express disbelief and a desire to change the subject as they entered my boudoir, 'It's a holy fact! Goes for it, so smart! Has the beggar on toast before you can say, "Jack Robinson!"'

The observation did not interest me, but simply ran in my head. Then they came into my room, only a few moments, as I was not to be tired. The Engineer tried to amuse Stoffles, who was seized with such a fit of mortal boredom that he transferred his attentions to Ruby, the Gordon setter, a devoted and inseparable friend of mine, under whose charge I was shortly left as they passed out of the house. The Lieutenant, it appears, went last, and inadvertently closed without fastening the verandah door. Thereby hangs a tale of the most trying quarter of an hour it has been my lot to experience.

I suppose I may have been asleep for ten minutes or so when I was awakened by the noise of Ruby's heavy body jumping out through the open window. Feeling restless and seeing me asleep, he had imagined himself entitled to a short spell off guard. Had the door not been ostensibly latched, he would have made his way out by it, being thoroughly used to opening doors and such tricks – a capacity which in fact proved fatal to him. That it was unlatched I saw in a few moments, for the Dog on his return forced it open with a push and trotted up in a disturbed manner to my bedside. I noticed a tiny spot of blood on the black side of his nose, and naturally supposed he had scratched himself against a bush or a piece of wire. 'Ruby,' I said, 'what have you been doing?' Then he whined as if in pain, crouching close to my side and shaking in every limb. I should say that I was myself lying with a shawl over my feet on a deep sofa with a high back. I turned to look at Stoffles, who was slowly perambulating the room, looking for flies and other insects (her favourite amusement) on the wainscot. When I glanced again at the Dog, his appearance filled me with horror; he was standing, obviously in pain, swaying from side to side and breathing hard. As I watched, his body grew more and more rigid. With his eyes fixed on the half-open door, he drew back as if from the approach of some dreaded object, raised his head with a pitiful attempt at a bark, which broke off into a stifled howl, rolled over sideways suddenly and lay dead. The horrid stiffness of the body, almost resembling a stuffed creature overset, made me believe that he had died as he stood, close to my side, perhaps meaning to defend me – more probably, since few Dogs would be proof against such a terror, trusting that I should protect him against the *thing coming in at the door*. Unable to resist the unintelligible idea that the Dog had been frightened to death, I followed the direction of his last gaze, and at first saw nothing. The next moment I observed round the corner of the verandah door a small, dark, and slender object, swaying gently up and down like a dry bough in the wind. It had passed right into the room with the same slow, regular motion before I realized what it was and what had happened.

My poor, stupid Ruby must have nosed at the basket on the verandah till he succeeded somehow in opening it, and had been bitten in return for his pains by the abominable beast which had been warranted in this insufficient manner to do no harm, and which I now saw angrily rearing its head and hissing fiercely at the dead dog within three yards of my face.

I am not one of those women who jump on chairs or tables when they see a Mouse, but I have a constitutional horror of the most harmless reptiles. Watching the Blue Dryad as it glided across the patch of sunlight streaming in from the open window, and knowing what it was, I confess to being as nearly frightened out of my wits as I ever hope to be. If I had been well, perhaps I might have managed to scream and run away. As it was, I simply dared not speak or move a finger for fear of attracting the beast's attention to myself. Thus I remained a terrified spectator of the astonishing scene which followed. The whole thing seemed to me like a dream. As the beast entered the room, I seemed again to hear my cousin making the remark above mentioned about the Cobra. *What* animal, I wondered dreamily, could he have meant? Not Ruby! Ruby was dead. I looked at his stiff body again and shuddered. The whistle of a train sounded from the valley below, and then an errand-boy passed along the road at the back of the house (for the second or third time that day) singing in a cracked voice the fragment of a popular melody, of which I am sorry to say I know no more –

'I've got a little cat,
And I'm very fond of that;
But Daddy wouldn't buy me a bow, wow, wow';

the wow-wows becoming fainter and farther as the youth strode down the hill. If I had been 'myself,' as the poor folk say, this coincidence would have made me laugh, for at that very moment Stoffles, weary of patting flies and spiders on the back, appeared gently purring on the crest, so to speak of the sofa.

It has often occurred to me since, that if the scale of things had been enlarged – if Stoffles, for example, had been a Bengal Tiger, and the Dryad a Boa-constrictor or Crocodile, – the tragedy which followed would have been worthy of the pen of any sporting and dramatic historian. I can ony say that, being transacted in such objectionable proximity to myself, the thing was as impressive as any combat of Mastodon and Iguanodon could have been to primitive man.

Stoffles, as I have said, was inordinately vain and self-conscious. Stalking along the top of the sofa-back and bearing erect the bushy banner of her magnificent tail, she looked the most ridiculous creature imaginable. She had proceeded halfway on this pilgrimage towards me when suddenly, with the rapidity of lightning, as her ear caught the sound of the hiss and her eyes fell upon the Blue Dryad, her whole civilized 'play-acting' demeanour vanished, and her body stiffened and contracted to the form of a watchful wild beast with the ferocious and instinctive antipathy to a natural enemy blazing from its eyes. No change of a shaken kaleidoscope could have been more complete or more striking. In one light bound she was on the floor in a compressed, defensive attitude, with all four feet close together, near, but not too near, the unknown but clearly hostile intruder; and to my surprise, the Snake turned and made off towards the window. Stoffles trotted lightly after, obviously interested in its method of locomotion. Then she made a long arm and playfully dropped a paw upon its tail. The Snake wriggled free in a moment, and coiling its whole length, some three and a half feet, fronted this new and curious antagonist.

At the very first moment, I need hardly say, I expected that one short stroke of that little pointed head against the Cat's delicate body would quickly have settled everything. But one is apt to forget that a Snake (I suppose because in romances snakes always 'dart') can move but slowly and awkwardly over a smooth surface, such as a tiled or wooden floor. The long body, in spite of its wonderful construction, and of the attitudes in which it is frequently drawn, is no less subject to the laws of gravitation than that of a Hedgehog. A Snake that 'darts' when it has nothing secure to hold on by, only overbalances itself. With half or two-thirds of the body firmly coiled against some rough object or surface, the head – of a poisonous Snake at least – is indeed a deadly weapon of precision. This particular reptile, perhaps by some instinct, had now wriggled itself on to a large and thick fur rug about twelve feet square, upon which arena took place the extraordinary contest that followed.

The audacity of the Cat astonished me from the first. I had no reason to believe she had ever seen a Snake before, yet by a sort of instinct she seemed to know exactly what she was doing. As the Dryad raised its head, with glittering eyes and forked tongue, Stoffles crouched with both front paws in the air, sparring as I had seen her do sometimes with a large moth.

The first round passed so swiftly that mortal eye could hardly see with distinctness what happened. The Snake made a dart; and the Cat, all claws, aimed two rapid blows at its advancing head. The first missed, but the second I could see came home, as the brute, shaking its neck and head, withdrew farther into the jungle – I mean, of course, the rug. But Stoffles, who had no idea of the match ending in this manner, crept after it, with an air of attractive carelessness which was instantly rewarded. A full two feet of the Dryad's body straigtened like a black arrow, and seemed to strike right into the furry side of its antagonist – seemed, I say to slow-going human eyes; but the latter shrank, literally *fell* back, collapsing with such suddenness that she seemed to have turned herself inside out, and become the mere skin of a Cat. As the Serpent recovered itself, she pounced on it like lightning, driving at least half a dozen claws well home, and then, apparently realizing that she had not a good enough hold, sprang lightly into the air from off the body, alighting about a yard off. There followed a minute of sparring in the air; the Snake seemingly half afraid to strike, the Cat waiting on its every movement.

Now, the poisonous Snake when provoked is an irritable animal, and the next attack of the Dryad, maddened by the scratchings of puss and its own unsuccessful exertions, was so furious, and so close to myself, that I shuddered for the result. Before this stage, I might perhaps, with a little effort have escaped, but now panic fear glued me to the spot; indeed I could not have left my position on the sofa without almost treading upon Stoffles, whose bristling back was not a yard from my feet. At last, I thought – as the Blue Dryad, for one second coiled close as a black silk cable, sprang out the next as straight and sharp as the piston-rod of an engine, – this lump of feline vanity and conceit is done for, and – I could not help thinking – it will probably by my turn next! Little did I appreciate the resources of Stoffles, who without a change in her vigilant pose, without a wink of her fierce green eyes, sprang backwards and upwards on to the top of me and there confronted the enemy as calm as ever, sitting, if you please, upon my feet! I don't know that any gymnastic performance ever surprised me more than this, though I have seen this very beast drop twenty feet from a window sill on to a stone pavement without appearing to notice any particular change of level. Cats with so much plumage have probably their own reasons for not flying.

Trembling all over with fright, I could not but observe that she was trembling too – with rage. Whether instinct inspired her with the advantages of a situation so extremely unplesant to me I cannot say. The last act of the drama rapidly approached, and no more strategic catastrophe was ever seen.

For a Snake, everybody knows, naturally rears its head when fighting. In that position, though one may hit it with a stick it is extremely difficult, as this battle had shown, to get hold of. Now, as the Dryad, curled to a capital S, quivering and hissing, advanced for the last time to the charge, it was bound to strike across the edge of the sofa on which I lay, at the erect head of Stoffles, which vanished with a juggling celerity that would have dislocated the collar-bone of any other animal in creation. From such an exertion, the Snake recovered itself with an obvious effort, quick beyond question, but not nearly quick enough. Before I could well see that it had missed its aim, Stoffles had launched out like a spring released and, burying eight or ten claws in the back of its enemy's head, pinned it down against the stiff cushion of the sofa. The tail of the agonized reptile flung wildly in the air and flapped on the arched back of the imperturbable Tigress. The whiskered muzzle of Stoffles dropped quietly, and her teeth met once, twice, thrice, like the needle and hook of a sewing-machine, in the neck of the Blue Dryad; and when, after much deliberation, she let it go, the beast fell into a limp tangle on the floor.

When I saw that the thing was really dead I believe I must have fainted. Coming to myself, I heard hurried steps and voices. 'Great heavens' my husband was screaming, 'where has the brute got to?' 'It's all right,' said the Engineer; 'just you come and look here, old man. Commend me to the coolness of that Cat. After the murder of your priceless specimen, here's Stoffles cleaning her fur in one of her serenest Anglo-Saxon attitudes.'

So she was. My husband looked grave as I described the scene. 'Didn't I tell you so?' said the Engineer, 'and this beast, I take it, is worse than any Cobra.'

I can easily believe he was right. From the gland of the said beast, as I afterwards learned, they extracted enough poison to be the death of twenty full-grown human beings.

Tightly clasped between its minute teeth was found (what interested me more) a few long hairs, late the property of Stoffles.

Stoffles, however – she is still with us – has a superfluity of long hair, and is constantly leaving it about.

The Black Cat

Edgar Allan Poe

For the most wild, yet most homely narrative which I am about to pen, I neither expect nor solicit belief. Mad indeed would I expect it, in a case where my very senses reject their own evidence. Yet – mad am I not – and very surely I do not dream. But tomorrow I die, and today I would unburden my soul. My immediate purpose is to place before the world plainly, succinctly, and without comment, a series of mere household events. In their consequences these events have terrified – have tortured – have destroyed me. Yet I will not attempt to expound them. To me they have presented little but horror – to many they will seem less terrible than *baroques*. Hereafter, perhaps, some intellect may be found which will reduce my phantasm to the commonplace – some intellect more calm, more logical, and far less excitable than my own, which will perceive in the circumstances I detail with awe, nothing more than an ordinary succession of very natural causes and effects.

From my infancy I was noted for the docility and humanity of my disposition. My tenderness of heart was even so conspicuous as to make me the jest of my companions. I was especially fond of animals, and was indulged by my parents with a great variety of pets. With these I spent most of my time, and never was so happy as when feeding and caressing them. This peculiarity of character grew with my growth, and in my manhood I derived from it one of my principal sources of pleasure. To those who have cherished an affection for a faithful and sagacious dog, I need hardly be at the trouble of explaining the nature or the intensity of the gratification thus derivable. There is something in the unselfish and self-sacrificing love of a brute which goes directly to the heart of him who has had frequent occasion to test the paltry friendship and gossamer fidelity of mere *Man*.

I married early, and was happy to find in my wife a disposition not uncongenial with my own. Observing my partiality for domestic pets, she lost no opportunity in procuring those of the most agreeable kind. We had birds, goldfish, a fine dog, rabbits, and small monkey, and *a cat*.

This latter was a remarkably large and beautiful animal, entirely black, and sagacious to an astonishing degree. In speaking of his intelligence, my wife, who at heart was not a little tinctured with superstition, made frequent allusion to the ancient popular notion which regarded all black cats as witches in disguise. Not that she was ever *serious* upon this point, and I mention the matter at all for no better reason than that it happens just now to be remembered.

Pluto – this was the cat's name – was my favourite pet and playmate. I alone fed him, and he attended me wherever I went about the house. It was even with difficulty that I could prevent him from following me through the streets.

Our friendship lasted in this manner for several years, during which my general temperament and character – through the instrumentality of the Fiend Intemperance – had (I blush to confess it) experienced a radical alteration for the worse. I grew, day by day, more moody, more irritable, more regardless of the feelings of others. I suffered myself to use intemperate language to my wife. At length, I even offered her personal violence. My pets of course were made to feel the change in my disposition. I not only neglected, but ill-used them. For Pluto, however, I still retained sufficient regard to restrain me from maltreating him, as I made no scruple of maltreating the rabbits, the monkey, or even the dog, when by accident, or through affection, they came in my way. But my disease grew upon me – for what disease is like Alcohol? – and at length even Pluto, who was now becoming old, and consequently somewhat peevish – even Pluto began to experience the effects of my ill-temper.

One night, returning home much intoxicated, from one of my haunts about town, I fancied that the cat avoided my presence. I seized him; when, in his fright at my violence, he inflicted a slight wound upon my hand with his teeth. The fury of a demon instantly possessed me. I knew myself no longer. My original soul seemed at once to take its flight from my body, and a more than fiendish malevolence, gin-nurtured, thrilled every fibre of my frame. I took from my waistcoat-pocket a penknife, opened it, grasped the poor beast by the throat, and deliberately cut one of its eyes from the socket! I blush, I burn, I shudder, while I pen the damnable atrocity.

When reason returned with the morning – when I had slept off the fumes of the night's debauch – I experienced a sentiment half of horror, half of remorse, for the crime of which I had been guilty; but it was, at best, a feeble and equivocal feeling, and the soul remained untouched. I again plunged into excess, and soon drowned in wine all memory of the deed.

In the meantime the cat slowly recovered. The socket of the lost eye presented, it is true, a frightful appearance, but he no longer appeared to suffer any pain. He went about the house as usual, but, as might be expected, fled in extreme terror at my approach. I had so much of my old heart left as to be at first grieved by this evident dislike on the part of a creature which had once so loved me. But this feeling soon gave place to irritation. And then came, as if to my final and irrevocable overthrow, the spirit of PER-VERSENESS. Of this spirit philosophy takes no account. Yet I am not more sure that my soul lives, than I am that perverseness is one of the primitive impulses of the human heart – one of the indivisible primary faculties, or sentiments, which gives direction to the character of Man. who has not, a hundred times, found himself committing a vile or a silly action for no other reason than because he knows he should *not*? Have we not a perpetual inclination, in the teeth of our best judgment, to violate that which is *Law*, merely because we understand it to be such? This spirit of perverseness, I say, came to my final overthrow. It was this unfathomable longing of the soul *to vex itself* – to offer violence to its own nature – to do wrong for the wrong's sake only – that urged me to continue and finally to consummate the injury I had inflicted upon the unoffending brute. One morning, in cold blood, I slipped a noose about its neck and hung it to the limb of a tree; – hung it with tears streaming from my eyes; and with the bitterest remorse at my heart; – hung it *because* I knew that it had loved me, and *because* I felt it had given me no reason of offence; – hung it *because* I knew that in so doing I was committing a sin – a deadly sin that would so jeopardise my immortal soul as to place it, if such a thing were possible, even beyond the reach of the infinite mercy of the most Merciful and Most Terrible God.

On the night of the day on which this cruel deed was done, I was aroused from sleep by the cry of fire. The curtains of my bed were in flames. The whole house was blazing. It was with great difficulty that my wife, a servant, and myself, made our escape from the conflagration. The destruction was complete. My entire worldly wealth was swallowed up, and I resigned myself thenceforward to despair.

I am above the weakness of seeking to establish a sequence of cause and effect, between the disaster and the atrocity. But I am detailing a chain of facts, and wish not to leave even a possible link imperfect. On the day succeeding the fire, I visited the ruins. The walls, with one exception, had fallen in. This exception was found in a compartment wall, not very thick, which stood about the middle of the house, and against which had rested the head of my bed. The plastering had here, in great measure, resisted the action of the fire, a fact which I attributed to its having been recently spread. About this wall a dense crowd were collected, and many persons seemed to be examining a particular portion of it with very minute and eager attention. The words 'strange!' 'singular!' and other similar expressions, excited my curiosity. I approached, and saw, as if graven in *bas-relief* upon the white surface, the figure of a gigantic *cat*. The impression was given with an accuracy truly marvellous. There was a rope about the animal's neck.

When I first beheld this apparition – for I could scarcely regard it as less – my wonder and my terror were extreme. But at length reflection came to my aid. The cat, I remembered, had been hung in a garden adjacent to the house. Upon the alarm of fire, this garden had been immediately filled by the crowd, by some one of whom the animal must have been cut from the tree and thrown, through an open window, and into my chamber. This had probably been done with the view of arousing me from sleep. The falling of the other walls had compressed the victim of my cruelty into the substance of the freshly spread plaster; the lime of which,

with the flames and the *ammonia* from the carcass, had then
accomplished the portraiture as I saw it.

Although I thus readily accounted to my reason, if not altogether to my conscience, for the startling fact just detailed, it did
not the less fail to make a deep impression upon my fancy. For
months I could not rid myself of the phantasm of the cat; and
during this period there came back into my spirit a half-sentiment
that seemed, but was not, remorse. I went so far as to regret the
loss of the animal, and to look about me, among the vile haunts
which I now habitually frequented, for another pet of the same
species, and of somewhat similar appearance, with which to supply its place.

One night as I sat half stupefied in a den of more than infamy,
my attention was suddenly drawn to some black object reposing
upon the head of one of the immense hogsheads of gin or of rum
which constituted the chief furniture of the apartment. I had been
looking steadily at the top of this hogshead for some minutes, and
what now caused me surprise was the fact that I had not sooner
perceived the object thereupon. I approached it, and touched it
with my hand. It was a black cat, a very large one, fully as large as
Pluto, and closely resembling him in every respect but one. Pluto
had not a white hair upon any portion of his body; but this cat
had a large, although indefinite, splotch of white, covering nearly
the whole region of the breast.

Upon my touching him, he immediately arose, purred loudly,
rubbed against my hand, and appeared delighted with my notice.
This, then, was the very creature of which I was in search. I at
once offered to purchase it from the landlord; but this person
made no claim on it – knew nothing of it – had never seen it
before.

I continued my caresses; and when I prepared to go home, the
animal evinced a disposition to accompany me. I permitted it to
do so, occasionally stooping and patting it as I proceeded. When
it reached the house it domesticated itself at once, and became immediately a great favourite with my wife.

For my own part, I soon found a dislike to it arising within me.
This was just the reverse of what I had anticipated; but – I know
not how or why it was – its evident fondness for myself rather disgusted and annoyed. By slow degrees these feelings of disgust

and annoyance rose into the bitterness of hatred. I avoided the creature; a certain sense of shame, and the remembrance of my former deed of cruelty, preventing me from physically abusing it. I did not for some weeks strike or otherwise violently ill-use it; but gradually – very gradually – I came to look upon it with un-utterable loathing, and to flee silently from its odious presence, as from the breath of a pestilence.

What added, no doubt, to my hatred of the beast, was the dis-covery, on the morning after I brought it home, that, like Pluto, it also had been deprived of one of its eyes. This circumstance, however, only endeared it to my wife, who, as I have already said, possessed, in a high degree, that humanity of feeling which had once been my distinguishing trait, and the source of many of my simplest and purest pleasures.

With my aversion to this cat, however, its partiality for myself seemed to increase. It followed my footsteps with a pertinacity which it would be difficult to make the reader comprehend. Whenever I sat, it would crouch beneath my chair, or spring upon my knees, covering me with its loathsome caresses. If I arose to walk it would get between my feet, and thus nearly throw me down; or, fastening its long and sharp claws in my dress, clamber in this manner to my breast. At such times, although I longed to destroy it with a blow, I was yet withheld from so doing, partly by a memory of my former crime, but chiefly – let me confess it at once – by absolute *dread* of the beast.

This dread was not exactly a dread of physical evil – and yet I should be at a loss how otherwise to define it. I am almost ashamed to own – yes, even in this felon's cell I am almost ashamed to own – that the terror and horror with which the animal inspired me had been heightened by one of the merest chimeras it would be possible to conceive. My wife had called my attention more than once to the character of the mark of white hair of which I have spoken, and which constituted the sole vis-ible difference between the strange beast and the one I had des-troyed. The reader will remember that this mark, although large, had been originally very indefinite; but by slow degrees – degrees nearly imperceptible, and which for a long time my Reason strug-gled to reject as fanciful – it had at length assumed a rigorous dis-tinctness of outline. It was now the representation of an object that I shudder to name – and for this, above all, I loathed and dreaded and would have rid myself of the monster *had I dared* – it was now, I say, the image of a hideous – of a ghastly thing – of the GALLOWS! O – mournful and terrible engine of Horror and of Crime – of Agony and of Death!

And now was I indeed wretched beyond the wretchedness of mere Humanity. And *brute beast* – whose fellow I had contemptuously destroyed – *a brute beast* to work out for *me* – for me, a man fashioned in the image of the High God – so much of insufferable woe! Alas! neither by day nor by night knew I the blessing of rest any more! During the former the creature left me no moment alone; and, in the latter, I started hourly from dreams of unutterable fear, to find the hot breath of *the thing* upon my face, and its vast weight an incarnate Nightmare that I had no power to shake off – incumbent eternally upon my *heart*!

Beneath the pressure of torments such as these, the feeble remnant of the good within me succumbed. Evil thoughts became my sole intimates – the darkest and most evil of thoughts. The moodiness of my usual temper increased to hatred of all things and of all mankind; while, from the sudden, frequent, and ungovernable outbursts of a fury to which I now blindly abandoned myself, my uncomplaining wife, alas! was the most usual and the most patient of sufferers.

One day she accompanied me, upon some household errand into the cellar of the old building which our poverty compelled us to inhabit. The cat followed me down the steep stairs, and, nearly throwing me headlong, exasperated me to madness. Uplifting an axe, and, forgetting in my wrath the childish dread which had hitherto stayed my hand, I aimed a blow at the animal, which of course would have proved instantly fatal had it descended as I wished. But this blow was arrested by the hand of my wife. Goaded, by the interference, into a rage more than demoniacal, I withdrew my arm from her grasp, and buried the axe in her brain. She fell dead upon the spot, without a groan.

This hideous murder accomplished, I set myself forthwith, and with entire deliberation, to the task of concealing the body. I knew that I could not remove it from the house, either by day or by night, without the risk of being observed by the neighbours. Many projects entered my mind. At one period I thought of cutting the corpse into minute fragments and destroying them by fire. At another, I resolved to dig a grave for it in the floor of the cellar. Again, I deliberated about casting it in the well in the yard – about packing it in a box, as if merchandise, with the usual arrangements, and so getting a porter to take it from the house. Finally I hit upon what I considered a far better expedient than either of these. I determined to wall it up in the cellar – as the monks of the Middle Ages are recorded to have walled up their victims.

For a purpose such as this the cellar was well adapted. Its walls were loosely constructed, and had lately been plastered throughout with rough plaster, which the dampness of the atmosphere had prevented from hardening. Moreover, in one of the walls was a projection, caused by a false chimney, or fireplace, that had been filled up, and made to resemble the rest of the cellar. I made no doubt that I could readily displace the bricks at this point, insert the corpse, and wall the whole up as before, so that no eye could detect anything suspicious.

And in this calculation I was not deceived. By means of a crowbar I easily dislodged the brick; and, having carefully deposited the body against the inner wall, I propped it in that position, while with little trouble I relaid the whole structure as it originally stood. Having procured the mortar, sand, and hair, with every possible precaution, I prepared a plaster which could not be distinguished from the old, and with this I very carefully went over the new brickwork. When I had finished, I felt satisfied that all was right. The wall did not present the slightest appearance of having been disturbed. The rubbish on the floor was picked up with the minutest care. I looked around triumphantly, and said to myself, 'Here at last, then, my labour has not been in vain.'

My next step was to look for the beast which had been the cause of so much wretchedness; for I had at length firmly resolved to put it to death. Had I been able to meet with it at the moment there could have been no doubt of its fate, but it appeared that the crafty animal had been alarmed at the violence of my previous anger, and forebore to present itself in my present mood. It is impossible to describe or to imagine the deep, the blissful sense of relief which the absence of the detested creature occasioned in my bosom. It did not make its appearance during the night; and thus for one night at least since its introduction into the house, I soundly and tranquilly slept – ay, *slept* even with the burden of murder upon my soul!

The second and third day passed, and still my tormentor came not. Once again I breathed as a free man. The monster, in terror, had fled the premises for ever! I should behold it no more! My happiness was supreme! The guilt of my dark deed disturbed me but little. Some few inquiries had been made, but these had been readily answered. Even a search had been instituted; but of course nothing was to be discovered. I looked upon my future felicity as secured.

Upon the fourth day of the assassination, a party of the police came over unexpectedly into the house, and proceeded again to make a rigorous investigation of the premises. Secure, however, in the inscrutability of my place of concealment, I felt no embarrassment whatever. The officers bade me accompany them in their search. They left no nook or corner unexplored. At length, for the third or fourth time, they descended into the cellar. I quivered not in a muscle. My heart beat calmly as that of one who slumbers in innocence. I walked the cellar from end to end. I folded my arms upon my bosom, and roamed easily too and fro. The police were thoroughly satisfied, and prepared to depart. The glee of my heart was too strong to be restrained. I burned to say, if but one word, by way of triumph, and to render doubly sure their assurance of my guiltlessness.

'Gentlemen,' I said at last, as the party ascended the steps, 'I delight to have allayed your suspicions. I wish you all health, and a little more courtesy. By the bye, gentlemen, this – this is a very well constructed house.' (In the rabid desire to say something easily, I scarcely knew what I uttered at all.) 'I may say an *excellently* constructed house. These walls – are you going, gentlemen? – these walls are so solidly put together;' and here, through the mere frenzy of bravado, I rapped heavily, with a cane which I held in my hand, upon that very portion of the brickwork behind which stood the corpse of the wife of my bosom.

But may God shield and deliver me from the fangs of the Arch-Fiend! No sooner had the reverberation of my blows sunk into silence than I was answered by a voice from within the tomb! – by a cry, at first muffled and broken, like the sobbing of a child, and then quickly swelling into one long, loud, and continuous scream, utterly anomalous and inhuman – a howl – a wailing shriek, half of horror and half of triumph, such as might have arisen only out of hell, conjointly from the throats of the damned in their agony and of the demons that exult in the damnation.

Of my own thoughts it is folly to speak. Swooning, I staggered to the opposite wall. For one instant the party upon the stairs remained motionless, through extremity of terror and of awe. In the next, a dozen stout arms were toiling at the wall. It fell bodily. The corpse, already greatly decayed and clotted with gore, stood erect before the eyes of the spectators. Upon its head, with red extended mouth and solitary eye of fire, sat the hideous beast whose craft had seduced me into murder, and whose informing voice had consigned me to the hangman. I had walled the monster up within the tomb!

The Fox and the Cat

The Fox and the Cat, as they travell'd one day,
With moral discourses cut shorter the way:
''Tis great,' says the Fox, 'to make justice our guide!'
'How god-like is mercy!'Grimalkin replied.
Whilst thus they proceeded, a Wolf from the wood,
Impatient of hunger, and thirsting for blood,
Rush'd forth – as he saw the dull shepherd asleep –
And seiz'd for his supper an innocent Sheep.
'In vain, wretched victim, for mercy you bleat,
When Mutton's at hand,' says the Wolf, 'I must eat.'
Grimalkin's astonish'd – the Fox stood aghast,
To see the fell beast at his bloody repast.
'What a wretch,' says the Cat, ''tis the vilest of brutes;
Does he feed upon flesh when there's herbage and roots?'
Cries the Fox, 'While our oaks gives us acorns so good,
What a tyrant is this to spill innocent blood!'
   Well, onward they march'd, and they moraliz'd still,
Till they came where some Poultry pick'd chaff by a mill.
Sly Reynard survey'd them with gluttonous eyes,
And made, spite of morals, a pullet his prize.
A Mouse, too, that chanc'd from her covert to stray,
The greedy Grimalkin secured as her prey.
   A Spider that sat in her on the wall,
Perceiv'd the poor victims, and pitied their fall;
She cried, 'Of such murders, houw guiltless am I!'
So ran to regale on a new-taken Fly.

ALLAN CUNNINGHAM

A Cat Correspondence

Anna Seward & Dr Darwin

From the Persian Snow, at Dr Darwin's to
Miss Po Felina, at the Palace, Lichfield

Lichfield Vicarage.
Sept. 7, 1780.

DEAR MISS PUSSEY

As I sat, the other day, basking myself in the Dean's walk, I saw you, in your stately palace, washing your beautiful round face, and elegantly brindled ears, with your velvet paws, and whisking about, with graceful sinuosity, your meandering tail. That treacherous hedgehog. Cupid, concealed himself behind your tabby beauties, and darting one of his too well aimed quills, pierced, O cruel imp! my fluttering heart.

Ever since that fatal hour I have watched, day and night, in my balcony, hoping that the stillness of the starlight evenings might induce you to take the air on the leads of the palace. Many serenades have I sung under your windows; and, when you failed to appear, with the sound of my voice made the vicarage re-echo through all its winding lanes and dirty alleys. All heard me but my cruel Fair-one; she, wrapped in fur, sat purring with contented insensibility, or slept with untroubled dreams.

Though I cannot boast those delicate varieties of melody with which you sometimes ravish the ear of night, and stay the listening stars; though you sleep hourly on the lap of the favourite of the muses, and are patted by those fingers which hold the pen of science; and every day, with her permission, dip your white whiskers in delicious cream; yet am I not destitute of all advantages of birth, education, and beauty. Derived from Persian kings, my snowy fur yet retains the whiteness and splendour of their ermine.

This morning, as I sat upon the Doctor's tea-table, and saw my reflected features in the slop-basin, my long white whiskers, ivory teeth, and topaz eyes, I felt an agreeable presentiment of my suit; and certainly the slop-basin did not flatter me, which shews the azure flowers upon its borders less beauteous than they are.

You know not, dear Miss Pussey Po, the value of the address you neglect. New milk have I, in flowing abundance, and mice pent up in twenty garrets, for your food and amusement.

Permit me, this afternoon, to lay at your divine feet the head of an enormous Norway Rat, which has even now stained my paws with its gore. If you will do me the honour to sing the following song, which I have taken the liberty to write, as expressing the sentiments I wish you to entertain, I will bring a catgut and cat-call, to accompany you in chorus.

(Air: *Spirituosi*)
Cats I scorn, who sleek and fat,
Shiver at a Norway Rat;
Rough and hardy, bold and free,
Be the cat that's made for me!
He, whose nervous paws can take
My lady's lapdog by the neck;
With furious hiss attack the hen,
And snatch a chicken from the pen.
If the treacherous swain should prove
Rebellious to my tender love,
My scorn the vengeful paw shall dart,
Shall tear his fur, and pierce his heart.

Chorus
Qu-ow wo, quall, wawl, moon.

Deign, most adorable charmer, to purr your assent to this my request, and believe me to be with the profoundest respect, your true admirer,

Snow.

Answer

Palace, Litchfield.
Sept. 8, 1780.

I am but too sensible of the charms of Mr Snow; but while I admire the spotless whiteness of his ermine, and the tyger-strength of his commanding form, I sigh in secret, that he, who sucked the milk of benevolence and philosophy, should yet retain the extreme of that fierceness, too justly imputed to the Grimalkin race. Our hereditary violence is perhaps commendable when we exert it against the foes of our protectors, but deserves much blame when it annoys their friends.

The happiness of a refined education was mine; yet, dear Mr Snow, my advantages in that respect were not equal to what yours might have been; but, while you give unbounded indulgence to your carnivorous desires, I have so far subdued mine, that the lark pours his mattin song, the canarybird warbles wild and loud, and the robin pipes his farewell song to the setting sun, unmolested in my presence; nay, the plump and tempting dove has reposed securely upon my soft back, and bent her glossy neck in graceful curves as she walked around me.

But let me hasten to tell thee how my sensibilities in thy favour were, last month, unfortunately repressed. Once, in the noon of one of its most beautiful nights, I was invited abroad by the serenity of the amorous hour, secretly stimulated by the hope of meeting my admired Persian. With silent steps I paced around the dimly-gleaming leads of the palace. I had acquired a taste for scenic beauty and poetic imagery, by listening to ingenious observations upon their nature from the lips of thy own lord, as I lay purring at the feet of my mistress.

I admired the lovely scene, and breathed my sighs for thee to the listening moon. She threw the long shadows of the majestic cathedral upon the silvered lawn. I beheld the pearly meadows of Stow Valley, and the lake in its bosom, which, reflecting the lunar rays, seemed a sheet of diamonds. The trees of the Dean's Walk, which the hand of Dulness had been restrained from torturing into trim and detestable regularity, met each other in a thousand various and beautiful forms. Their liberated boughs danced on the midnight gale, and the edges of their leaves were whitened by the moonbeams. I descended to the lawn, that I might throw the beauties of the valley into perspective through the graceful arches, formed by their meeting branches. Suddenly my ear was startled, not by the voice of my lover, but by the loud and dissonant noise of the war-song, which six black grimalkins were raising in honour of the numerous victories obtained by the Persian, Snow; compared with which, they acknowledged those of English cats had little brilliance, eclipsed, like the unimportant victories of the Howes, by the puissant Clinton and Arbuthnot, and the still more puissant Cornwallis. It sung that thou didst owe thy matchless might to thy lineal descent from the invincible Alexander, as he derived his more than mortal valour from his mother Olympia's illicit commerce with Jupiter. They sang that, amid the renowned siege of Persepolis, while Roxana and Statira were contending for the honour of his attractions, the conqueror of the world deigned to bestow them upon a large white female cat, thy grandmother, warlike Mr Snow, in the ten thousandth and ninety-ninth ascent.

Thus far their triumphant din was music to my ear; and even when it sung that lakes of milk ran curdling into whey, within the ebon conclave of their pancheons, with terror at thine approach; that mice squealed from all the neighbouring garrets; and that whole armies of Norway rats, crying out amain, 'the devil take the hindmost,' ran violently into the minster-pool, at the first gleam of thy white mail through the shrubs of Mr Howard's garden.

But O! when they sung, or rather yelled, of larks warbling on sunbeams, fascinated suddenly by the glare of thine eyes, and falling into thy remorseless talons; of robins, warbling soft and solitary upon the leafless branch, till the pale cheek of winter dimpled into joy; of hundreds of those bright breasted songsters, torn from their barren sprays by thy pitiless fangs! - Alas! my heart died within me at the ideas of so preposterous a union!

Marry you, Mr Snow, I am afraid I cannot; since, though the laws of our community might not oppose our connection, yet those of principle, of delicacy, of duty to my mistress, do very powerfully oppose it.

As to presiding at your concert, if you extremely wish it, I may perhaps grant your request; but then you must allow me to sing a song of my own composition, applicable to our present situation,

and set to music by my sister Sophy at Mr Brown's the organist's,
thus:

(Air: *Affettuoso*)
He, whom Pussy Po detains
A captive in her silken chains,
Must curb the furious thirst for prey,
Nor rend the warbler from his spray!
Nor let his wild, ungenerous rage
An unprotected foe engage.

O, should cat of Darwin prove
Foe to pity, foe to love!
Cat, that listens day by day,
To mercy's mind and honies lay,
Too surely would the dire disgrace
More deeply brand our future race,
The stigma fix, where'er they range,
That cats can ne'er their nature change.

Should I consent with thee to wed,
These sanguine crimes upon thy head,
And ere the wish'd reform I see,
Adieu to lapping Seward's tea!
Adieu to purring gently praise
Charm'd as she quotes thy master's lays!-
Could I, alas! our kittens bring
Where sweet her plumy favourites sing,
Would not the watchful nymph espy
Their father's fierceness in their eye,

And drive us far and wide away,
In cold and lonely barn to stray?
Where the dark owl, with hideous scream,
Shall mock our yells for forfeit cream,
As on starv'd mice we swearing dine,
And grumble that our lives are nine.

Chorus (Largo)
Waal, woee, trone, moan, mall, oll, moule.

The still too much admired Mr. Snow will have the goodness to pardon the freedom of these expostulations, and excuse their imperfections. The morning, O Snow! had been devoted to this my correspondence with thee, but I was interrupted in that employment by the visit of two females of our species, who fed my ill-starved passion by praising thy wit and endowments, exemplified by thy elegant letter, to which the delicacy of my sentiments obliges me to send so inauspicious a reply.

I am, dear Mr. Snow
Your ever obliged
PO FELINA

Tom Quartz: Miner's Cat

Mark Twain

One of my comrades there – another of those victims of eighteen years of unrequited toil and blighted hopes – was one of the gentlest spirits that ever bore its patient cross in a weary exile: grave and simple Dick Baker, pocket-miner of Dead-House Gulch. – He was forty-six, gray as a rat, earnest, thoughtful, slenderly educated, slouchily dressed and clay-soiled,but his heart was finer metal than any gold his shovel ever brought to light – than any, indeed, that ever was mined or minted.

Whenever he was out of luck and a little down-hearted, he would fall to mourning over the loss of a wonderful cat he used to own (for where women and children are not, men of kindly impulses take up with pets, for they must love something). And he always spoke of the strange sagacity of that cat with the air of a man who believed in his secret heart that there was something human about it – may be even supernatural.

I heard him talking about this animal once. He said:

'Gentlemen, I used to have a cat here, by the name of Tom Quartz, which you'd a took an interest in I reckon – most any body would. I had him here eight year – and he was the remarkablest cat *I* ever see. He was a large gray one of the Tom specie, an' he had more hard, natchral sense than any man in this camp – 'n' a *power* of dignity – he wouldn't let the Gov'ner of California be familiar with him. He never ketched a rat in his life – 'peared to be above it. He never cared for nothing but mining. He knowed more about mining, that cat did, than any man *I* ever, ever see. You couldn't tell *him* noth'n' 'bout placer diggin's – 'n' as for pocket mining, why he was just born for it. He would dig out after me an' Jim when we went over the hills prospetc'n', and he would trot along behind us for as much as five mile, if we went so fur. An' he had the best judgment about mining ground – why you never see anything like it. When we went to work, he'd scatter a glance around, 'n' if he didn't think much of the indications, he would give a look as much as to say, "Well, I'll have to get you to excuse *me*," 'n' without another word he'd hyste his nose into the air 'n' shove for home. But if the ground suited him, he would lay low 'n' keep dark till the first pan was washed, 'n' then he would sidle up 'n' take a look, an' if there was about six or seven grains of gold *he* was satisfied – he didn't want no better prospect 'n' that – 'n' then he would lay down on our coats and snore like a steamboat till we'd struck the pocket, an' then get up 'n' superintend. He was nearly lightnin' on superintending.

'Well, bye an' bye, up come this yer quartz excitement. Every body was into it – every body was pick'n 'n' blas'n' instead of shovelin' dirt on the hill side – every body was put'n down a shaft instead of scrapin' the surface. Noth'n' would do Jim, but *we* must tackle the ledges, too, 'n' so we did. We commenced put'n' down a shaft, 'n' Tom Quartz he begin to wonder what in the Dickens it was all about. *He* hadn't ever seen any mining like that before, 'n' he was all upset, as you may say - he couldn't come to a right understanding of it no way – it was too many for *him*. He was down on it, too, you bet you – he was down on it powerful – 'n' always appeared to consider it the cussodest foolishness out. But that cat, you know, was *always* agin new fangled arrangements – somehow he never could abide 'em. *You* know how it is with old habits. But by an' by Tom Quartz begin to git sort of reconciled a little, though he never *could* altogether understand that eternal sinkin' of a shaft an' never pannin' out any thing. At last he got to comin' down in the shaft, hisself, to try to cipher it out. An' when he'd git the blues, 'n' feel kind o' scruffy, 'n' aggravated and disgusted - knowin' as he did, that the bills was runnin' up all the time an' we warn't makin' a cent – he would curl up on a gunny sack in the corner an' go to sleep. Well, one day when the shaft was down about eight foot, the rock got so hard that we had to put in a blast – the first blast'n' we'd ever done since Tom Quartz was born. An' then we lit the fuse 'n' clumb out 'n' got off 'bout fifty yards – 'n' forgot 'n' left Tom Quartz sound asleep on the gunny sack. In 'bout a minute we seen a puff of smoke bust up out of the hole, 'n' then everything let go with an awful crash, 'n' about four million tons of rocks 'n' dirt 'n' smoke 'n' splinters shot up 'bout a mile 'an a half into the air, an' by George, right in the dead centre of it was old Tom Quartz a goin' end over end, an' a snortin' an' a sneezin', an' a clawin' an' reachin' for things like all possessed. But it warn't no use, you know, it warn't no use. An' that was the last we see of *him* for about two minutes 'n' a half, an' then all if a sudden it begin to rain rocks and rubbage, an' directly he come down ker-whop about ten foot off f'm where we stood. Well, I reckon he was p'haps the orneriest lookin' beast you ever see. One ear was sot back on his neck, 'n' his tail was stove up, 'n' his eye-winkers was swinged off, 'n' he was all blacked up with powder an' smoke, an' all sloppy with mud 'n' slush f'm one end to the other. Well sir, it warn't no use to try to apologize – we couldn't say a word. He took a sort of a disgusted look at hisself, 'n' then he looked at us – an' it was just exactly the same as if he had said - 'Gent, may be *you* think it's smart to take advantage of a cat that 'aint had no experience of quartz minin', but I think *different*' – an' then he turned on his heel 'n' marched off home without ever saying another word.

'That was jest his style. An' may be you won't believe it, but after that you never see a cat so prejudiced agin quartz mining as what he was. An' by an' bye when he *did* get to goin' down in the shaft agin, you'd 'a been astonished at his sagacity. The minute we'd tetch off a blast 'n' the fuse'd begin to sizzle, he'd give a look as much as to say: "Well, I'll have togit you to excuse *me*," an' it was surprisin' the way he'd shin out of that hole 'n' go f'r a tree. Sagacity? It aint no name for it. 'Twas *inspiration!*'

I said, 'Well, Mr Baker, his prejudice against quartz-mining *was* remarkable, considering how he came by it. Couldn't you ever sure him of it?'

'Cure him! No! When Tom Quartz was sot once, he was *always* sot – and you might a blowed him up as much as three million times 'n' you'd never a broken him of his cussed prejudice agin quartz mining.'

The affection and the pride that lit up Baker's face when he delivered this tribute to the firmness of his humble friend of other days, will always be a vivid memory with me.

from THE SPHINX

Dawn follows Dawn and Nights grow old
   and all the while this curious cat
Lies couching on the Chinese mat
   with eyes of satin rimmed with gold.

Upon the mat she lies and leers
   and on the tawny throat of her
Flutters the soft and silky fur
   or ripples to her pointed ears.

Come forth, my lovely seneschal!
   so somnolent so statuesque!
Come forth, you exquisite grotesque!
   half woman and half animal!

OSCAR WILDE

My Cat Jeoffry

from: Rejoice in the Lamb

For I will consider my cat Jeoffery.

For he is the servant of the living God, duly and daily serving him.

For at the first glance of the glory of God in the East he worships in his way.

For this is done by wreathing his body seven times round with elegant quickess.

For when he leaps up to catch the musk, which is the blessing of God upon his prayer.

For he rolls upon a prank to work it in.

For having done duty and received blessing he begins to consider himself.

For this he performs in ten degrees.

For first he looks upon his fore-paws to see if they are clean.

For secondly he kicks up behind to clear away there.

For thirdly he works it upon stretch with the fore-paws extended.

For fourthly he sharpens his paws by wood.

For fifthly he washes himself.

For sixthly he rolls upon wash.

For seventhly he fleas himself, that he may not be interrupted upon the beat.

For eighthly he rubs himself against a post.

For ninthly he looks up for his instructions.

For tenthly he goes in quest of food.

For having consider'd God and himself he will consider his neighbour.

For if he meets another cat he will kiss her in kindness.

For when he takes his prey he plays with it to give it [a] chance.

For one mouse in seven escapes by his dallying.

For when his day's work is done his business more properly begins.

For he keeps the Lord's watch in the night against the adversary.

For he counteracts the powers of darkness by his electrical skin and glaring eyes.

For he counteracts the Devil, who is death, by brisking about the life.

For in his morning orisons he loves the sun and the sun loves him.

For he is of the tribe of Tiger.

For the Cherub Cat is a term of the Angel Tiger.

For he has the subtlety and hissing of a serpent, which in goodness he suppresses.

For he will not do destruction, if he is well-fed, neither will he spit without provocation.

For he purrs in thankfulness, when God tells him he's a good Cat.

For he is an instrument for the children to learn benevolence upon.

For every house is incomplete without him & a blessing is lacking in the spirit.

For the Lord commanded Moses concerning the cats at the departure of the Children of Israel from Egypt.

For every family had one cat at least in the bag.

For the English cats are the best in Europe.

For he is the cleanest in the use of his fore-paws of any quadrupeds.

For the dexterity of his defence is an instance of the love of God to him exceedingly.

For he is the quickest to his mark of any creature.

For he is tenacious of his point.

For he is a mixture of gravity and waggery.

For he knows that God is his Saviour.

For there is nothing sweeter than his peace when at rest.

For there is nothing brisker than his life when in motion.

For he is of the Lord's poor and so indeed is he called by benevolence perpetually – Poor Jeoffrey! poor Jeoffry! the rat has bit thy throat.

For I bless the name of the Lord Jesus that Jeoffry is better.

For the divine spirit comes about his body to sustain it in compleat cat.

For his tongue is exceeding pure so that it has in purity what it wants in musick.

For he is docile and can learn certain things.

For he can set up with gravity which is patience upon approbation.

For he can fetch and carry, which is patience in employment.

For he can jump over a stick which is patience upon proof positive.

For he can spraggle upon waggle at the word of command.

For he can jump from an eminence into his master's bosom.

For he can catch the cork and toss it again.

For he is hated by the hypocrite and miser.

For the former is afraid of detection.

For the latter refused the charge.

For he camels his back to bear the first motion of business.

For he is good to think on, if a man would express himself neatly.

For he made a great figure in Egypt for his signal services.

For he killed the Icneumon-rat very pernicious by land.

For his ears are so acute that they sting again.

For from this proceeds the passing quickness of his attention.

For by stroking of him I have found out electricity.

For I perceived God's light about him both wax and fire.

For the Electrical fire is the spiritual substance, which God sends from heaven to sustain the bodies both of man and beast.

For God has blessed him in the variety of his movements.

For, tho he cannot fly, he is an excellent clamberer.

For his motions upon the face of the earth are more than other quadrupeds.

For he can tread to all the measures upon the musick.
For he can swim for life.
For he can creep.

CHRISTOPHER SMART

An Object of Love

Mary E. Wilkins

A tiny white-painted house, with a door and one window in front, and a little piazza, over which the roof jutted, and on which the kitchen door opened, on the rear corner. Squashes were piled up on the piazza in a great yellow and green heap.

Ann Millet, her shawl pinned closely over her hair and ears, the small oval of her solemn, delicate old face showing almost uncanny beneath it, stood in the doorway, surveying the sky outside.

'There's goin' to be a heavy frost, sure enough', she said. 'I'll hev to git the squashes in. Thar's Mis' Stone comin'. Hope to goodness she won't stop an' hinder me! Lor' sakes! I'd orter hev more patience.'

A tall, stooping figure came up the street, and paused at the gate hesitatingly.

'Good-evenin', Ann.'

'Good-evenin', Mis' Stone.'

'Gettin' in your squashes, ain't you?' Mrs Stone spoke in a very high pitched tone. Ann was somewhat deaf.

'Yes. I didn't dare resk 'em out tonight, it's so cold.'

'Well, it's a good deal colder than I hed any idea of when I come out. Yes, I'd take 'em in. We got ourn in last week. We ain't got more'n half as many as you hev. I shouldn't think you could use 'em all, Ann.'

'Well, I do. I allers liked squashes, an' Willy likes 'em, too. You'd orter see him brush round me, a-roundin' up his back an' purrin' when I'm scrapin' of 'em out of the shell. He likes 'em better'n fresh meat.'

'Seems queer for a cat to like sech things. Ourn won't touch 'em. How nice an' big your cat looks a-settin' thar in the window!'

'He's a-watchin' of me. He jumped up thar jest the minute I come out!'

'He's a good deal of company for you, ain't he?'

'Yes, he is. What on airth I should do this long winter that's comin', without him, I don't know. Everybody wants somethin' that's alive in the house.'

'That's so. It must be pretty lonesome for you anyway.'

'Well, I don't mean to complain. I'd orter be thankful. I've got my Bible an' Willy, an' a roof over my head, an' enough to eat an' wear; an' p'rhaps some other woman ain't lonesome because I am, an' maybe she'd be one of the kind that didn't like cats, an' wouldn't hev got along half as well as me. No, I never orter complain.'

'Well, if all of us looked at our mercies mor'n our trials, we'd be a good deal happier. But, sakes! I must be goin'. Good night, Ann.'

'Good night, Mis' Stone.'

Mrs Stone hitched rapidly down the street to her own home, and Ann went on tugging in her squashes. She was a little woman and had to carry them in one at a time. After they were all in she took off her shawl and hung it on a nail behind the kitchen door. Then she gave her cat his saucer of warm milk in a snug corner by the stove and sat down contentedly to her own supper. The cat was a beautiful little animal, with a handsome dark striped coat on his back, and white paws and face.

When he had finished lapping his milk, he came out and stood beside his mistress' chair while she ate, and purred, and she gave him bits of bread from her plate now and then. She talked to him.

'Nice Willy; nice cat. Got up on the window to see me bring in the squashes, didn't he? There's a beautiful lot of 'em, an' he shall hev some stewed for his dinner tomorrow, so he shall.'

And the cat would purr, and rub his soft coat against her, and look as if he knew just what she meant.

There was a prayer meeting that evening, and Ann Miller went. She never missed one. The minister, when he entered, always found her sitting in the same place. She had a pretty voice when she was young, people said, and she sang now in a sweet thin quiver the hymns which the minister gave out. She listened in solemn enjoyment to the stereotyped prayers and the speaker's remarks.

After the meeting Ann always went up and told him how much she had enjoyed his remarks, and inquired after his wife and children. To her a minister was an unpublished apostle, and his wife and children were set apart on the earth.

When she had reached home and lighted her lamp, she called her cat. She had expected to find him waiting to be let in, but he was not. She stood out on her little piazza, and called, 'Willy! Willy! Willy!'

She thought every minute she would see him bounding around the corner, but she did not. She called over and over, 'Willy! Willy! Kitty! Kitty! Kitty!'

Finally she went into the house and waited awhile, crouching, shivering with cold and nervousness, over the kitchen stove. Then she went outside and called again. 'Willy!' over and over, waiting between the calls trembling, her dull ears alert, her dim old eyes strained. She ran out to the road, and looked and called. Once her heart leaped; she thought she saw Willy coming; but it was only a black cat which belonged to one of the neighbours. Over and over all night long she called the poor little creature which was everything earthly she had to keep her company in the great universe in which she herself was so small.

In the morning she went over to Mrs Stone's, her small old face wild and wan.

'Hev you seen anything of Willy?' she asked. 'He's been out all night, an' I'm afraid somethin's happened to him. I never knowed him to stay out so before.'

When they told her they had not seen him, she went on to the next neighbour to inquire. But no one had seen anything of the cat. All that day and night, at intervals, people heard her plaintive, inquring call, 'Willy! Willy! Willy!'

The next Sunday, Ann was not out at church. Mrs Stone went over to see what was the matter.

'Why, Ann Millet, are you sick?' she asked.

'No, I ain't sick.'

'You wasn't out to meetin', an I didn't know – '

'I ain't never goin' to meetin' agin.'

'Why, what do you mean?'

'I mean jest what I say. I ain't never goin' to meetin' agin. Folks go to meetin' to thank the Lord for blessin's, I s'pose. I've lost mine, an' I ain't goin'.'

'What hev you lost, Ann?'

'Ain't I lost Willy?'

'You don't mean to say you're makin' such a fuss as this over a cat?'

'Yes, I do.'

'Well, I ain't nothin' agin cats, but I must say I'm beat. Why, Ann Millet, it's downright sinful for you to feel so. Of course, you set a good deal by Willy; but it ain't as ef he was a human creature. Cats is cats. For my part, I never thought it was right to set by animals as ef they was babies.'

'I can't hear what you say.'

'I never thought it was right to set by animals as ef they was babies.'

'I don't keer. It's comfortin' to have live creatures about you, an' I ain't never had anything like other women. I ain't hed no folks of my own sense I kin remember. I've worked hard all my life, an' hed nothin' at all to love, an' I've thought I'd orter be thankful all the same. But I did want as much as a cat.'

'Well, as I said before, I've nothin' agin cats. But I don't understand any human bein with an immortal soul a-settin' so much by one.'

'I can't hear what you say.'

I don't understand any human bein' with an immortal soul a-settin' so much by a cat.'

'You've got folks, Mis' Stone.'

'I know I hev; but folks is trials sometimes. But, Ann Millet, I didn't think you was one to sink down so under any trial. I thought the Lord would be a comfort to you.'

'I know all thet, Mis' Stone. But when it comes to it, I'm here an' I ain't thar; an; I've got hands, an' I want somethin' I kin touch.'

Then the poor soul broke down, and sobbed out loud like a baby.

'I ain't – never felt as ef I orter begrutch other – women their homes an' their folks. I thought – p'raps – I could git along better without 'em than – some; an' the Lord knowed it, an' seein' thar wa'n't enough to go round, he gave 'em to them that needed them most. I ain't – never – felt – as ef I'd orter complain. But – thar – was – cats – enough. I might a had – that - much.'

'You kin git another cat, Ann. Mis' Maxwell's got some real smart kittens.'

'I don't want any of Mis' Maxwell's kittens; I don't never want any other cat.'

'P'rhaps yourn will come back.'

'No, he won't. I'll never see him agin. I've felt jest that way about it from the first.'

'Hark! I declar' I thought I heard a cat mew somewhar! But I guess I didn't. Well, I'm sorry, Ann. Why, Ann Millet, whar's your squashes?'

'I throwed 'em out in the field. Willy can't hev none of 'em now, an' I don't keer about 'em myself.'

Mrs Stone looked at her in horror. When she got home she told her daughter that Ann Millet was in a dreadful state of mind, and she thought the minister ought to see her.

The next day the minister called on her. He did not find her so outspoken; her awe of him restrained her. Still, Ann Millet was for the time a wicked, rebellious old woman.

In the course of the call a rap came at the kitchen door.

'Nothin' but a little girl with a Malty cat', said she. 'The children hev got wind of my losin' Willy, an' they mean it all right, but it seem as ef I should fly! They keep comin' and bringin' cats. They'll find a cat they think mebbe is Willy, an' so they bring him to show me. They've brought Malty and white cats, an' cats all Malty. They've brought yaller cats, an' black, an' there wa'n't one of 'em looked like Willy. Then they've brought kittens that they knowed wa'n't Willy, but they thought mebe I'd like 'em instead of him. They mean all right, I know; they're tenderhearted; but it 'most kills me. Why, they brought me two little kittens that hain't got their eyes open yet jest before you came. They was striped and white, an' they said they thought they'd grow up to look like Willy.'

He went away without saying much of anything; he was so afraid that what he said might be out of proportion to the demands of the case.

Going out of the door, he stopped and listened a minute; he thought he heard a cat mew. Then he concluded he was mistaken, and went on. He watched eagerly for Ann the next meeting night, but she did not come.

The day after the meeting, she had occasion to go down the cellar for something. The cellar steps led up to the front part of the house. Ann went through her chilly sitting room, and opened the cellar door, which was in the front entry. There was a quick rush from the gloom below, and Willy flew up the cellar stairs.

'Lor' sakes!' said Ann, with a white shocked face. 'He has been down there all the while. Now I remember. He followed me when I came through here to git my cloak that meetin' night, and he wanted to go down cellar, an' I let him. Lor' sakes!'

She went back into the kitchen, her knees trembling. She poured out a saucer of milk, and watched Willy hungrily lapping. He did not look as if he had suffered, though he had been in the cellar a week.

Ann watched him the white, awed look still on her face.

'I s'pose he mewed an' I didn't hear him. Thar he was all the time, jest whar I put him; an' me a'blamin' of the Lord an' puttin' of it on Him. I've been an awful wicked woman. I ain't been to meetin', an' I've talked, an' -them squashes I threw away. It's been so warm they ain't froze, an' I don't deserve it. I hadn't orter hev one of 'em; I hadn't orter hev anything. I'd orter offer up Willy. Lor' sakes, think of me sayin' what I did, an' him down cellar!'

That afternoon Mrs Stone saw Ann slowly and painfully bringing in the squashes one at a time. The next meeting night Ann was in her place. After meeting, the minister hurried out of his desk to speak to her. When she looked up at him, her old cheeks were flushing.

'The cat has come back', said Ann.

Cats and Dogs

Jerome K. Jerome

I like cats and dogs very much indeed. What jolly chaps they are! They are much superior to human beings as companions. They do not quarrel or argue with you. They never talk about themselves, but listen to you while you talk about yourself, and keep up an appearance of being interested in the conversation. They never make stupid remarks. And they never ask a young author with fourteen tragedies, sixteen comedies, seven farces, and a couple of burlesques in his desk, why he doesn't write a play.

They never say unkind things. They never tell us of our faults, 'merely for our own good.' They do not, at inconvenient moments, mildly remind us of our past follies and mistakes. They never inform us that we are not nearly so nice as we used to be. We are always the same to them. They are always glad to see us. They are with us in all our humors. They are merry when we are glad, sober when we feel solemn, sad when we are sorrowful.

'Hulloa! happy, and want a lark! Right you are; I'm your man. Here I am, frisking round you, leaping, barking, pirouetting, ready for any moment of fun and mischief. Look at my eyes, if you doubt me. What shall it be? A romp in the drawing room, and never mind the furniture, or a scamper in the fresh, cool air, a scud across the fields, and down the hill, and we won't let old Gaffer Goggles's geese know what time o'day it is neither. Whoop! come along.'

Or you'd like to be quiet and think. Very well. Pussy can sit on the arm of the chair, and purr, and purr, and Montmorency will curl himself up on the rug, and blink at the fire, yet keeping one eye on you the while, in case you are seized with any sudden desire in the direction of rats. And when we bury our face in our hands and wish we had never been born, they don't sit up very straight, and observe that we have brought it all upon ourselves. They don't even hope it will be a warning to us.

But they come up softly; and shove their heads against us. If it is a cat, she stands on your shoulder, rumples your hair and says, 'I am sorry for you,' as plain as words can speak; and if it is a dog, he looks up at you with his big, true eyes, and says with them, 'Well, you've always got me, you know. We'll go through the world together, and always stand by each other, won't we?'

He is very imprudent, a dog is. He never makes it his business to inquire whether you are in the right or in the wrong, never bothers as to whether you are going up or down upon life's lad-der, never asks whether you are rich or poor, silly or wise, sinner or saint. Come luck or misfortune, good repute or bad, honor or shame, he is going to stick to you, to comfort you, guard you, and give his life for you, if need be – foolish, brainless, soulless dog!

Ah! old staunch friend, with your deep, clear eyes, and bright, quick glances that take in all one has to say before one has time to speak it, do you know you are only an animal, and have no mind? Do you know that dull-eyed, gin-sodden lout, leaning against the post out there, is immeasurably your intellectual superior?

Do you know that every little-minded, selfish scoundrel, who lives by cheating and tricking, who never did a gentle deed, or said a kind word, who never had a thought that was not mean and low, or a desire that was not base, whose every action is a fraud, whose every utterance is a lie; do you know they are all as much superior to you as the sun is superior to rush-light, you honorable, brave-hearted, unselfish brute?

They are *men*, you know, and *men* are the greatest, noblest, and wisest, and best Beings in the whole vast eternal Universe. Any man will tell you that. Yes, poor doggie, you are very stupid, very stupid indeed, compared with us clever men, who understand all about politics and philosophy, and who know everything in short, except what we are, and where we came from, and whither we are going, and what everything outside this tiny world and most things in it are.

Never mind, though, pussy and doggie, we like you both all the better for your being stupid. We all like stupid things. It is so pleasant to come across people more stupid than ourselves. Ah me! life sadly changes us all. The world seems a vast horrible grinding machine, into which what is fresh and bright and pure is pushed at one end, to come out old and crabbed and wrinkled at the other.

Look even at Pussy Silversides, with her dull sleepy glance, her grave slow walk, and dignified prudish airs; who could ever think that once she was the blue-eyed, whirling, scampering, head-over-heels, mad little firework that we call a kitten.

What marvellous vitality a kitten has. It is really something very beautiful the way life bubbles over in the little creatures. They rush about, and mew, and spring; dance on their hind legs, embrace everything with their front ones, roll over and over, lie on their backs and kick. They don't know what to do with themselves, they are so full of life.

Can you remember when you and I felt something of the same sort of thing? Can you remember those glorious days of fresh young manhood; how, when coming home along the moonlit road, *we* felt too full of life for sober walking, and had to spring and skip, and wave our arms and shout? Oh, that magnificent young *Life!* that crowned us kings of the earth; that rushed through every tingling vein, till we seemed to walk on air; that thrilled through our throbbing brains; and told us to go forth and conquer the whole world; that welled up in our young hearts, till we longed to stretch out our arms and gather all the toiling men and women and the little children to our breast, and love them all – all.

Ah! they were grand days, those deep full days, when our coming life, like an unseen organ, pealed strange, yearnful music in our ears, and our young blood cried out like a warhorse for the battle. Ah, our pulse beats slow and steady now, and our old joints are rheumatic, and we love our easy chair and sneer at boys' enthusiasm. But oh! for one brief moment of that god-like life again.

A Dying Cat

Pierre Loti

An old mangy cat, hunted out of its abode no doubt by its owners, had established itself in our street, on the footpath of our house, where a little November sun once more warmed its body. It is the custom with certain people whose pity is a selfish pity thus to send off as far away as possible and *lose* the poor animals they care neither to tend nor to see suffer.

All day long it would sit piteously in the corner of a window-sill, looking, oh! so unhappy and so humble, an object of disgust to those who passed, menaced by children and by dogs, in continual danger, and sickening from hour to hour. It lived on offal, picked up with great difficulty in the streets, and there it sat all alone, dragging out its existence as it could, striving to ward off death. Its poor head was eaten up with disease, covered with sores, and almost without fur, but its eyes, which remained bright, seemed to reflect profoundly. It must have felt in its frightful bitterness the worst of all sufferings to a cat – that of not being able to make its toilet, to lick its fur, and to comb itself with the care cats always bestow on this operation.

To make its toilet! I believe that to beast, as to man, this is one of the most necessary distractions of life. The poorest, the most diseased, and the most decrepit animals at certain hours dress themselves up, and, as long as they are able to find time to do that, have not lost everything in life. But to be no longer able to care for their appearance because nothing can be done before the final mouldering away – that has always appeared to me the lowest depth of all the supreme agony. Alas for those poor old beggars who before death have mud and filth on their faces, their bodies scarred with wounds that no longer can be dressed, the poor diseased creatures for whom there is no longer even pity.

It gave me so much misery to look at this forsaken cat that I first sent it something to eat in the street, and then I approached it and spoke to it, softly – (animals very soon learn to understand kind actions and find consolation in them). Accustomed to be hunted, it was first frightened at seeing me stop before it. Its first look was suspicious, filled with reproach and supplication. 'Are you also going to drive me away from this last sunny corner?' And then quickly perceiving that I had come from sympathy, and astonished at so much kindness, it addressed to me very softly its poor cat's answer, 'Prr! Prr! Prr!' even rising out of politeness, and attempting to lift its back, in spite of its weariness, and in hopes that perhaps I would go as far as a caress.

No; my pity, even though I was the only body in the world that felt any for it, did not go this length. That happiness of being caressed it would never know again, but as a compensation I imagined that I might give it death – immediately, with my own hand, and in a manner almost pleasant.

An hour afterwards this was done in the stable. Sylvester, my servant, who had first gone and bought some chloroform, had quietly coaxed the cat in, and induced it to lie down on the hot hay at the bottom of a wicker basket, which was to be its mortuary chamber. Our preparations did not disquiet it. We had rolled a carte-de-visite in the shape of a cone, as we had seen the surgeons do in the ambulance. The cat looked at us with a confiding and happy air, thinking it had at last found a home, and people who would take compassion on it, new masters who would heal it.

Meantime, and in spite of my dread of its disease, I leaned down to caress it, having already received from the hands of Sylvester the pasteboard cup all covered with poison. While caressing it I tried to induce it to remain quiet there, to push little by little the end of its nose into the narcotised cup. A little surprised at first, sniffing with vague terror at this unaccustomed smell, it ended by doing as it was asked with such submission that I almost hesitated to continue my work. The annihilation of a thinking animal, even though it be not a human being, has in it something to dumbfound us. When one thinks of it, it is always the same revolting mystery, and death besides carries with it so much majesty, that from the instant its shadow appears it has the power of giving sublimity in an unexpected, exaggerated form to the most infinitesimal scene. At this moment I appeared to myself like some black magician, arrogating to myself the right of bringing to the suffering what I believed to be supreme peace, the right of opening to those who had not demanded it the gates of the great night.

Once it lifted its poor head, almost lifeless, to look at me fixedly. Our eyes met – his, questioning, expressive, asking me with an extreme intensity, 'What are you doing to me, you to whom I confided myself, and whom I know so little? What are you doing to me?' And I still hesitated, but its neck fell; its poor disgusting head now supported itself on my hand, which I did not withdraw. A torpor invaded it in spite of itself, and I hoped it would not look at me again.

But it did, one other last time. Cats, as the poor people say, have their souls pinned to their bodies. In a last spasm of life, it looked at me again across the half-sleep of death. It seemed even to all at once comprehend everything. 'Ah, then it was to kill me and not assist me; I allow it to be done . . . It is too late . . . I am falling asleep.'

In fact, I was afraid that I had done wrong. In this world in which we know nothing of anything, men are not allowed to even pity intelligently. Thus, its look, infinitely sad, even while it descended into the petrifaction of death, continued to pursue me as with a reproach. 'Why did you interfere with my destiny? I might have been able to drag along for a time; to have had still some little thoughts for at least another week. There remained to me sufficient strength to leap on to the window-sill where the dogs could no more torment me, where I was not cold. In the morning, when the sun came there, I had some moments which were not unbearable, looking at the movement of life around me, interested in the coming and going of other cats, conscious at least of something; whilst now, I am about to decompose and be transformed into I know not what, that will not remember me. Soon *I shall no longer be.*"

I should have recollected, in fact, that even the meanest of things love to prolong their life by every means, even to its utmost limits of misery, preferring anything to the terror of being nothing, of no longer *being*.

When I came back in the evening to see it again, I found it stiff and cold, in the attitude of sleep in which I had left it. Then I told Sylvester to close the little mortuary basket, to carry it away far from the city, and throw it away in the fields.

Translated by Ambrose Bierce

Sir Robert Grant – cat

Sir Thomas Gordon

. . . It had been discovered that for twenty-five years past an oral addition to the written standing orders of the native guard at Government House, near Poona, had been communicated regularly from one guard to another, on relief, to the effect that any cat passing out of the front door after dark was to be regarded as His Excellency the Governor, and to be saluted accordingly. The meaning of this was that Sir Robert Grant, Governor of Bombay, had died there in 1838, and on the evening of the day of his death, a cat was seen to leave the house by the front door and walk up and down a particular path, as had been the Governor's habit to do, after sunset. A Hindu sentry had observed this, and he mentioned it to others of his faith, who made it a subject of superstitious conjecture, the result being that one of the priestly class explained the mystery of the dogma of the transmigration of the soul from one body to another, and interpreted the circumstances to mean that the spirit of the deceased Governor had entered into one of the House pets. It was difficult to fix on a particular one, and it was therefore decided that every cat passing out of the main entrance after dark was to be regarded as the tabernacle of Governor Grant's soul, and to be treated with due respect and the proper honours. This decision was accepted without question by all the native attendants and others belonging to Government House. The whole guard, from sepoy to subadar, fully acquiesced in it, and an oral addition was made to the standing orders that the sentry at the front door would 'present arms' to any cat passing out there after dark. The notion was essentially Hindu, yet the Mahomedans and the native Christians and Jews (native Jews are to be found in the Bombay army) devoutly assented to it. Dread of the supernatural overcame all religious objections, and every one scrupulously bowed to the heathen decree.

This sepoy guard was a weekly one, furnished alternately by the two infantry regiments of the garrison. The respective commanding officers at that time were of diametrically different dispositions. The one was of sympathetic temperament and calm judgment; the other impetuous and arbitrary, a rigid disciplinarian and a severe commander. I and others were at pains to discover the truth of the story concerning military honours to the cat, and I mentioned it to both commanding officers, as an interesting subject of wonder at the long continuance of the oral order without it becoming known. The one said he would laugh his native officers out of the idea, the other said he would order them to discontinue the folly, and there would be an end of the absurdity. The latter had the fullest belief in his ability to influence his men to dare the demons of darkness rather than openly disobey him. He set his mind firmly on this, and he assembled the native officers and ordered them to refuse to take over, or countenance in any way, the unwritten order regarding the House cat, warning them of the severe court-martial consequences of disobedience. When the first guard furnished by his regiment after this warning returned from the week's duty at Government House, the subadar in command was questioned regarding the oral order. It then came out that his fear of the supernatural was greater than his fear of the stern, uncompromising colonel, and in his awful presence he meekly said, in a few words, that to act as ordered meant to him a life of terror and a death of horror, and having disobeyed, he was ready to lose his highly-prized commission, and the pension reward of his long and faithful service. The colonel insisted on treating the matter as 'subversive of good order and military discipline,' and placing the subadar in arrest, he prepared an application for his trial by court martial. To me he said, 'I know you will laugh, but my authority must be vindicated.' The brigadier took a sympathetic view of the case, ordered the native officer to be released from arrest, and quietly advised the colonel to contend more gently and patiently with simple superstitions . . .

Mice Before Milk

Lat take a cat and fostre hym wel with milk
And tendre flessch and make his couche of silk,
And lat hym seen a mouse go by the wal,
Anon he weyvith milk and flessch and al,
And every deyntee that is in that hous,
Suich appetit he hath to ete a mous.

FROM *The Manciple's Tale*, BY GEOFFREY CHAUCER

Feline Favourites

Théophile Gautier

MADAME-THÉOPHILE

I pass over a number . . . and I shall come to Madame-Théophile, a red cat, with white breast, pink nose, and blue eyes, so called because she lived with me on a footing of conjugal intimacy. She slept on the foot of my bed, snoozed on the arm of my chair while I was writing, came down to the garden and accompanied me on my walks, sat at meals with me, and not infrequently appropriated the morsels on their way from my plate to my mouth. One day a friend of mine who was going out of town for a few days, entrusted his parrot to me with the request that I would take care of it during his absence. The bird, feeling strange in my house, had climbed, helping himself with his beak, to the very top of his perch, and looking pretty well bewildered, rolled round his eyes, that resembled the gilt nails on armchairs, and wrinkled the whitish membrane that served him for eyelids. Madame-Théophile had never seen a parrot, and she was evidently much puzzled by the strange bird. Motionless as an Egyptian mummy cat in its network of bands, she gazed upon it with an air of profound meditation, and put together whatever she had been able to pick up of natural history on the roofs, the yard, and the garden. Her thoughts were reflected in her shifting glance, and I was able to read in it the result of her examination: 'It is unmistakably a chicken.' Having reached this conclusion, she sprang from the table on which she had posted herself to make her investigations, and crouched down in one corner of the room, flat on her stomach, her elbows out, her head low, her muscular backbone on the stretch, like the black panther in Gérome's painting, watching gazelles on their way to the drinking-place. The parrot followed her movements with feverish anxiety, fluffing out its feathers, rattling its chain, lifting its foot, and moving its claws, and sharpening its beak upon the edge of its seed-box. Its instinct warned it that an enemy was preparing to attack it.

The eyes of the cat, fixed upon the bird with an intensity that had something of fascination in it, plainly said in a language well understood of the parrot and absolutely intelligible: 'Green though it is, that chicken must be good to eat.'

I watched the scene with much interest, prepared to interfere at the proper time. Madame-Théophile had gradually crawled nearer; her pink nose was working, her eyes were half-closed, her claws were protruded and then drawn in. She thrilled with anticipation like a gourmet sitting down to enjoy a truffled pullet; she gloated over the thought of the choice and succulent meal she was about to enjoy, and her sensuality was tickled by the idea of the exotic dish that was to be hers. Suddenly she arched her back like a bow that is being drawn and a swift leap landed her right upon the perch. The parrot, seeing the danger upon him, unexpectedly called out in a deep sonorous bass voice: 'Have you had your breakfast, Jack?'

The words filled the cat with indescribable terror; and she leapt back. The blast of a trumpet, the smash of a pile of crockery, or a pistol-shot fired in her ear would not have dismayed the feline to such an extent. All her ornithological notions were upset.

'And what did you have? – a royal roast,' went on the bird.

The cat's expression clearly meant: 'This is not a bird; it's a man; it speaks.'

'When of claret I've had my fill,
The pot-house whirls and is whirling still,'

sang out the bird with a deafening voice, for it had at once perceived that the terror inspired by its speech was its surest means of defence. The cat looked at me questioningly, and my reply proving unsatisfactory, she sneaked under the bed and refused to come out for the rest of the day. Those of my readers who have not been in the habit of having animals to keep them company, and who see in them, as did Descartes, merely machines, will no doubt think I am attributing intentions to the bird and quadruped, but as a matter of fact, I have merely translated their thoughts into human speech. The next day Madame-Théophile, having somewhat overcome her fright, made another attempt, and was routed in the same fashion. That was enough for her, and henceforth she remained convinced that the bird was a man.

This dainty and lovely creature adored perfumes. She would go into ecstasies on breathing in the patchouli and vetiver used for Cashmere shawls. She also had a taste for music. Nestling upon a pile of scores, she would listen attentively and with every mark of satisfaction to the singers who came to perform at the critic's piano. But high notes made her nervous, and she never failed to close the singer's mouth with her paw if the lady sang the high A. We used to try the experiment for the fun of the thing, and it never failed once. It was quite impossible to fool my dilettante cat on that note.

DON PIERROT DE NAVARRE

Its immaculate whiteness caused it to be named Pierrot, and this appellation, when it grew up, developed into Don Pierrot of Navarre, which was infinitely more majestic and smacked of a grandee of Spain.

Don Pierrot, like all animals that are fondled and petted, became delightfully amiable, and shared the life of the household with that fullness of satisfaction cats derive from close association with the fireside. Seated in his customary place, close to the fire, he really looked as if he understood the conversation and was interested in it. He followed the speakers with his eyes, and every now and then would utter a little cry, exactly as if to object and give his own opinion upon literature, which formed the staple of our talks. He was very fond of books, and when he found one open on the table, he would lie down by it, gaze attentively at the page and turn the leaves with his claws; then he ended by going to sleep, just as if he had really been reading a fashionable novel. As soon as I picked up my pen, he would leap upon the desk and watch attentively the steel nib scribbling away on the paper, moving his head every time I began a new line. Sometimes he endeavoured to collaborate with me, and would snatch the pen out of my hand, no doubt with the intention of writing in his turn, for he was as aesthetic a cat as Hoffmann's Murr. Indeed, I strongly suspect that he was in the habit of inditing his memoirs, at night, in some gutter or another, by the light of his own phosphorescent eyes. Unfortunately these lucubrations are lost.

Don Pierrot of Navarre always sat up at night until I came home, waiting for me on the inside of the door, and as soon as I stepped into the antechamber he would come rubbing himself against my legs, arching his back and purring in gladsome, friendly fashion. Then he would start to walk in front of me, preceding me like a page, and I am sure that if I had asked him to do so, he would have carried my candle. In this way he would escort me to my bedroom, wait until I had undressed, jump up on the bed, put his paws round my neck, rub his nose against mine, lick me with his tiny red tongue, rough as a file, and utter little inarticulate cries by way of expressing unmistakably the pleasure he felt at seeing me again. When he had sufficiently caressed me and it was time to sleep, he used to perch upon the backboard of his bed and slept there like a bird roosting on a branch. As soon as I woke in the morning, he would come and stretch out beside me until I rose.

Midnight was the latest time allowed for my return home. On this point Pierrot was as inflexible as a janitor. Now at that time I had founded, along with a few friends, a little evening reunion called 'The Four Candles Society,' the place of meeting happening to be lighted by four candles stuck in silver candlesticks placed at each corner of the table. Occasionally the conversation became so absorbing that I would forget the time, even at the risk of seeing, like Cinderella, my carriage turn into a pumpkin and my coachman into a big rat. Twice or thrice Pierrot sat up for me until two o'clock in the morning, but presently he took offence at my conduct and went to bed without waiting for me. I was touched by this mute protest against my innocently disorderly way of life, and thereafter I regularly returned home at midnight. Pierrot, however, proved hard to win back; he wanted to make sure that my repentance was no mere passing matter, but once he was convinced that I had really reformed, he deigned to restore me to his good graces and again took up his nightly post in the antechamber.

SÉRAPHITA

Séraphita was of a dreamy and contemplative disposition. She would remain for hours on a cushion, wide awake and following with her eyes, with intensest attention, sights invisible to ordinary mortals. She liked to be petted, but returned caresses in a very reserved way, and only in the case of persons whom she honoured with her approbation, a most difficult thing to obtain. She was fond of luxury, and we were always sure to find her curled up in the newest armchair or on the piece of stuff that best set off her swansdown coat. She spent endless time at her toilet; every morning she carefully smoothed out her fur. She used her paws to wash herself, and every single hair of her fur, having been brushed out with her rosy tongue, shone like brand-new silver. If anyone touched her, she at once removed the traces of the touch, for she could not bear to be rumpled. Her elegance and stylishness suggested that she was an aristocrat, and among her own kind she must have been a duchess at the very least. She delighted in perfumes, stuck her little nose into bouquets, and bit with little spasms of pleasure at handkerchiefs on which scent had been put; she walked upon the dressing-table among the scent bottles, smelling the stoppers, and if she had been allowed to do so would no doubt have used powder. She was Séraphita, and never did a cat bear a poetic name more worthily.

ENJOLRAS GAVROCHE AND EPONINE

Enjolras, who was by far the handsomest of the three, was marked by his big lion-like head and well-whiskered cheeks, by his muscular shoulders, his long back, and his splendid tail, fluffy as a feather duster. There was something theatrical and grandiloquent about him, and he seemed to pose like an actor who attracts admiration. His motions were slow, undulating, and full of majesty; he seemed always to be stepping on a table covered with china ornaments and Venetian glass, so circumspectly did he select the place where he put down his foot. He was not much of a Stoic, and exhibited a liking for food which his namesake would have had reason to blame. No doubt Enjolras, the pure and sober youth, would have said to him, as the angel did to Swedenborg, 'You eat too much.' We rather encouraged this amusing voracity, analogous to that of monkeys, and Enjolras grew to a size and weight very uncommon amongst domestic cats. Then I bethought myself of having him shaved in the style of poodles, in order to bring out completely his leonine appearance. He retained his mane and a long tuft of hair at the end of the tail, and I would not swear that his thighs were not adorned with mutton-chop whiskers like those Munito used to wear. Thus trimmed, he resembled, I must confess, a Japanese monster much more extravagant fancy carried out on the body of a living animal; his closely clipped coat allowed the skin to show through, and its bluish tones, most curious to note, contrasted strangely with his black mane.

Gavroche was a cat with a sharp, satirical loook, as if he intended to recall his namesake in the novel. Smaller than Enjolras, he was endowed with abrupt and comical agility, and in the stead of the puns and slang of the Paris street-arab, he indulged in the funniest capers, leaps and attitudes. I am bound to add that, yielding to his street instincts, Gavroche was in the habit of seizing every opportunity of leaving the drawing-room and going off to join, in the court, and even in the public streets, numbers of wandering cats, 'of unknown blood and lineage low,' with whom he took part in performances of doubtful taste, completely forgetful of his dignified rank as a Havana cat, the son of the illustrious Don Pierrot of Navarre, a grandee of Spain of the first class, and of the Marchioness Séraphita, noted for her haughty and aristocratic manners.

Sometimes he would bring in to his meals, in order to treat them, consumptive friends of his, so starved that every rib in their body showed, having nothing but skin and bones, whom he had picked up in the course of his excursions and wanderings, for he was a kind-hearted fellow. The poor devils, their ears laid back, their tails between their legs, their glances restless, dreading to be driven from their free meal by a housemaid armed with a broom, swallowed the pieces two, three and four at a time, and like the famous dog, Siete Aguas (Seven Waters), of Spanish posadas, would lick the platter as clean as if it had been washed and scoured by a Dutch housekeeper who had served as model to Mieris or Gerard Dow. Whenever I saw Gavroche's companions, I remembered the lettering under one of Gavarni's drawings: 'A nice lot, the friends you are capable of proceeding with!' But after all it was merely a proof of Gavroche's kindness of heart, for he was quite able to polish off the plateful himself.

The cat who bore the name of the interesting Eponine was more lissome and slender in shape than her brothers. Her mien was quite peculiar to herself, owing to her somewhat long face, her eyes slanting slightly in the Chinese fashion, and of a green like that of the eyes of Pallas Athene, on whom Homer invariably bestows the title of χλαυκῶπις, her velvety black nose, of as fine a grain as a Périgord truffle, and her incessantly moving whiskers. Her coat, of a superb black, was always in motion and shimmered with infinite changes. There never was a more sensitive, nervous and electric animal. If she were stroked two or three times, in the dark, blue sparks came crackling from her fur. She attached herself to me in particular, just as in the novel Eponine becomes attached to Marius. As I was less taken up with Cosette then that handsome youth, I accepted the love of my affectionate and devoted car, who is the delight of my hermitage on the confines of the suburbs. She trots up when she hears the bell ring, welcomes my visitors, leads them into the drawing-room, shows them to a seat, talks to them – yes, I mean it, talks to them – with croonings and cooings and whimpers quite unlike the language cats make use of among themselves, and which simulate the articulate speech of man. You ask me what it is she says? She says, in the plainest possible fashion, 'Do not be impatient; look at the pictures, or chat with me, if you enjoy that. My master will be down in a minute.' And when I come in she discreetly retires to an armchair or on top of the piano, and listens to the conversation without breaking in upon it, like a well-bred animal that is used to society.

To My Cat

Half loving-kindliness and half disdain,
Thou comest to my call serenely suave,
With humming speech and gracious gestures grave,
In salutation courtly and urbane;
Yet must I humble me thy grace to gain,
For wiles may win thee though no arts enslave,
And nowhere gladly thou abidest, save
Where naught disturbs the concord of thy reign.
Sphinx of my quiet hearth, who deign'st to dwell
Friend of my toil, companion of mine ease,
Thine is the love of Ra and Rameses;
That men forget dost thou remember well,
Beholden still in blinking reveries
With sombre, sea-green gaze inscrutable.

ROSAMUND MARRIOTT WATSON

Turkish Customs

Charles Nicholas Sigisbert
Sonnini De Manoncourt

. . . the Turks have a great fancy for cats. Mahomet was very partial to them. It is related, that being called upon some important and urgent business, he preferred cutting off the sleeve of his robe, to waking his cat that lay upon it fast asleep. Nothing more was necessary to bring these animals into high request, if, in other respects, their extreme cleanliness, the lustre and polish of their skin, their mild and quiet disposition, their gentle and cautious caresses, did not render them amiable creatures in the eyes of the mussulmans. A cat may even enter a mosque; it is caressed there as the favourite animal of the Prophet, and as the enemy of other troublesome animals . . .

. . . Here, it is true, the cats are very gentle and familiar; they have none of that suspicious and ferocious disposition which, in some parts of France, distinguishes a race of animals more wild than domestic. But these differences are as much the work of man as the effect of the influence of climate. In the department where I reside, as well as in the neighbouring ones, the cats especially in the country, are, next to the farmhorses, the most unfortunate of all animals; masters and servants alike hunt, beat, and throw stones at them, set dogs at them, and keep them without food. If hunger, which their meagre appearance attests, induce one of them to watch and take the smallest morsel, the pretended robber, because nature would not suffer her to die for want, forfeits her life for the dexterity she employed in its support. How can cats, in the houses of such hosts, whose cruelty approaches to barbarity, fail to have a savage look, the mark of ferocity? And if we compare the miserable cats of my country to those kept in

Paris, where, better treated, and free from perpetual fear, they show an amiable familiarity, we shall find this an additional proof, how far the disposition of man can influence that of the animals about him.

I was for a long time the possessor of a very fine Angora she-cat. Her long and thick hair covered her entirely; her bushy tail formed a brush, resembling a beautiful plume of feathers, which she could at pleasure turn upon her back. No spot, no shade tarnished the dazzling whiteness of her coat. Her nose and the turn of her lip were of a pale rose colour. In her round head sparkled two large eyes, the one of a light yellow and the other blue. The graceful notions and attitudes of this charming cat were even surpassed by her amiable disposition. Her aspect was mild, and her gentleness truly interesting. Though ever so much handled, she never exerted her claws from their sheath. Sensible of caresses, she licked the hand that stroked her, or even that by which she was teazed. When travelling, she would lie quietly upon my knees, without the necessity of being held; she made no noise, nor was she at all troublesome while near me, or any other person she was in the habit of seeing. When I was alone, she sat at my side; would sometimes interrupt me with little affectionate caresses, in the midst of my labours or meditations; and she would also follow me in my walks. In my absence she would seek me, and at first cry after me with uneasiness, and if I did not soon make my appearance, she would leave my appartment and attach herself to the person in the house, whom, after me, she most loved. She knew my voice, and seemed to receive me every time with additional satisfaction. Her step was straight, her gait free, and her look as mild as her disposition; in a word, under the brilliant and furry skin of a cat, she possessed the good temper of the most amiable dog.

This animal was for many years my delight. How expressively was her attachment painted in her face! How often have her fond caresses diverted my mind from care, and consoled me in my misfortunes! How often has an animal, of a species accused of treachery, formed, at my house, a striking contrast to a crowd of real traitors, who, under the mask of friendship, beset the door of an honest man, only the better to deceive him; to those serpents that I have so many times fostered in my bosom, only to feel as often their sting! Unfortunately for mankind, the life of the wicked is long. Those audacious, criminal, and execrable men, whose names my pen should trace, were it not reserved to Heaven to signalize against them its justice, are yet alive; while my beautiful and interesting companion is no more. After several days of suffering, during which I never left her, her eyes, constantly fixed on me, closed never again to open – my tears flowed – they now flow. Feeling minds will pardon this digression, the result of grief and gratitude. Those whose souls are rendered callous by egotism and insensibility, give me no disquiet; it is not for them I write.

From the Diary of a Cat
Edwina Stanton Babcock

Monday: very uncertain and lamentable conditions of the weather, much dampness and discomfort. This morning I was forced to rise early, as it appeared that the cook at the house where I occasionally stay wished to use the coal scuttle in which I passed the night. I conveyed to her that she might have it and welcome, that its usefulness to me was, for the time being, over; and intimated that I should be obliged to her if she could furnish me with any suggestions as to where I might obtain a breakfast. She thrust me out of the gate. I turned and surveyed the cook with a look of reproach; the cook had not a graceful foot – yet I determined to accept it as an omen, and I kept on in the same direction in which I had been, as it were, impelled. Thus a calamity often saves us indecision. Being impelled in any direction is better than no progress at all. I proceeded with some deliberation around the edges of many puddles toward an ash barrel which I could dimly make out through the grey dawn. I saw very little that was worthy of my attention, but after acute search, walking slowly around the rim of the barrel, I at last descried a small chicken bone half embedded in the ashes. With some degree of exertion I drew it forth and made a delicious repast. My breakfast completed, and my personal appearance all that I could render it, the weather being so unpropitious, I spent the day in short excursions up and down fire escapes and in an observing ramble down Back Fence Boulevard. At last the sun came out, and I found a convenient porch step, and passed the remainder of the day in quiet reflections.
Tuesday: For a long while I have been very curious about a garden with a spoked fence enclosing it, which I pass daily on my prome-

nades over the roofs. I often pause to look down upon it, and I have three times had the same dream about it. In the dream I thought that I had somehow obtained access to the garden, and that I dwelt there amid scenes of luxury and content. I did not lack for adventure and sport, for there were droves of entrancing white mice tripping here and there; enticing birds flew from tree to tree and played rarely at my favourite game of catching and eating; and besides all this there was a fountain of milk spinning high in the sunlight, with tender goldfish roving about in the great basin and endeavouring to attract my eye. It is not surprising that since my vivid dream I have used every device to effect an entrance into the garden, but I have not discovered a crack nor a crevice where I can creep in. Always, on my tours over the roofs, I have kept this object in mind. I have surveyed the situation carefully and accurately from every possible viewpoint, making estimates and measuring, and at last I think I can gain an entrance to the garden in four jumps. The first three I have essayed and found practicable, but the fourth jump is a feat of peculiar requirements. What agility I command has not yet proved equal to it, yet I am determined to accomplish it.

This fourth jump I have failed in repeatedly. Friends of mine who have unfailingly achieved well-nigh impossible leaps have warned me against the dangers attending this one. But it seems to me that what may not be crawled under must be jumped over, and so far, in practising the jump, though I have invariably fallen, I have invariably alighted upon my feet.

Wednesday: Today I went in to see the grocer to consult with him as to my using one of the barrels in his cellar as a winter habitation. I offered to pay him in dead mice. I produced one as a sample. He asked what he could do with a dead mouse. I thought it a stupid question, for I have observed that he was never able to put live mice to any use, and I suggested that he should sell them, as he had been so successful in selling dead fish. What there was in my bearing that should so have offended the grocer I do not know. As he has no tail, I could not be aware of his rising wrath. I was, therefore, not a little surprised when he seized me by the neck and hurled me into the street. I had no time to remonstrate. My sensations were indescribable. Flying through the air in a revolving manner does away with apperception. It is well-nigh impossible to record one's impressions when one is in doubt as to whether he is upside down or sidewise over and keeps on revolving in a maze of successive inversions. I obtained some exceedingly curious views of my surroundings, and I regret that I cannot recall them more clearly. But as I remember my swift and shameful transit, I see how much we have to depend upon our own uprightness to judge correctly the positions of others. The grocer, as I left his grasp, appeared to me to be standing on his head, but it was in reality I, who stood upon nothing, who mistook his attitude.

As I say, my speed was great, and though I alighted upon my feet, my distance from the grocer was incredibly long. Fortunately, I retained my presence of mind, and I turned, surveying the grocer with intense disapproval. I conveyed to him that from my point of view he had acted with undue haste and under grave error, and that I should trouble him no further. I then went down a side street, regretting that I had left the sample mouse where the grocer would be sure to see it and appropriate it.

Friday: For some time I have been interested in the cultivation of my voice. There are certain tones that I find I can produce with ease, and I have developed them into sounds of extraordinary power. Of late, in the evenings, I have taken up a comfortable position on Back Fence Avenue and practised these tones; I keep to simple exercises, striving for a certain quality of great beauty and sweetness. One or two friends having a like ambition, we have formed an agreeable custom of meeting at the same spot every night and comparing our progress. Our exertions have caused intense curiosity in the inmates of the houses about us, and exclamations of wonder and awe are often heard. We expect to combine our several tones of excellence into a chord which will express great emotion. It will be called the 'Yearn Chord', or the 'Song of Unnumbered Woes', and will be of a plaintive, pleading character, with rising and falling cadences and inflections of great depth and resonance.

Monday: After practising the fourth jump and being unsuccessful, I repaired to the butcher's to try and obtain a portion of meat. I walked in upon him early and with a brisk manner, as one who should say, 'It is necessary that I should eat to live.' 'Are you sure that you do not live to eat?' retorted the butcher.

The butcher is a brief and caustic man. The shortness of his speech is due to the influence of his pursuits upon his character. There is nothing quicker and shorter than a chop or a cut. A butcher might, with great success, found a school of expression for preciseness and brevity. I jumped upon his broad back where he could not reach me.

'Get off, you brute!' cried the butcher, but I dug my claws deeper into his soft, fat flesh. Then he bribed me, and when he tempted me with something worth my while, a red and juicy bit of steak, down I came, and, seizing the meat in my mouth, ran out of the shop and ate the steak behind a garbage can. Poverty, it is said, sharpens the wits, but it is hard to keep the wits as sharp as the hunger, which poverty also grinds out to a pretty point.

Tuesday: After many failures, I have at last discovered a most desirable place in which to sleep. I have adopted one of the large white urns on the gateway of the entrance to the Park. It is a commodious, elegant affair, sheltered by the great oak tree that spreads its branches over the gateway, and I can drop into it from the oak boughs as softly and lightly as a snowflake. There I have solitude and shadowed gloom; the moonlight reveals the cold statues glimmering in the groves and bathes the dead fountain in white streams. Not wishing to be selfish, and sensible of the lack of sleeping places, I invited a chance acquaintance, Speckle Devil by name, to occupy the other urn. He refused in a sullen, dogged manner, saying in a shamefaced way that 'he didn't want to sleep in no Symbol'; but Speckle is of a rough and superstitious nature, given to foolish and groundless prejudices. He and two friends of his, Stealthy Rake and Smutty Sneak, make a strange trio. Careless of appearances, rough and defiant in manner, theirs seem to be characters of intense swagger and bravado; but their adventures and their conversation I find highly interesting. I detect a certain eloquence and clear-cutness in their expressions. I find that their lack of conventionality renders them at once picturesque and convincing. Hence I ask the question – can it be that it is only the vagabond and the social outcast to whom it has been given to utter plain truths? Is it only a rake that can call a spade a spade?

Tuesday: Mild weather. Perhaps spring is coming. I spent the morning wandering through some empty sewer pipes. It is a stealthy mode of travel, and one that much pleases me. Things that I wish to eat I often secrete in these pipes until such time as I can enjoy them. The only difficulty is that the pipes are all very much alike, and are placed end to end in long lines down the different streets, so that it is often hard for me to remember in which pipe I placed the bone or bacon rind that I wished to preserve. I sometimes wander on through miles and miles of pipe in search of the treasure, only to discover at last that I have entered the wrong line of pipes. However, my travels are entertaining, and often bring me out to interesting places. This morning, as I stepped out of the end of the pipe tunnel into the open sunlight, I found myself facing a dog kennel, which I concluded was empty. There was a saucer of milk by the door. I stopped to quench my thirst, when immediately I was set upon by an old blind creature, who flew out of the kennel and hurled furious invective at me. I drew back. 'Madam', said I, 'there is some mistake here.'

'You are the mistake'! retorted the old creature. 'Get out of here'! – uttering horrible imprecations. This unpleasant exhibition of feminine temper completely unnerved me. Though I wished to explain that my interest in the milk had been merely that of endeavouring to test the accuracy of casual observation, I refrained, and, completely disgusted, moved rapidly back into the sewer pipe.

Wednesday: I was in an ailanthus tree in Pigeon Place the other day, devoting my leisure to nature study. I was endeavouring to concentrate upon the innocent gambols of a flock of sparrows, one of whom, by her artless coquetries, particularly engaged my attention. Her fascination for me was exceedingly pleasant, and I cast about for some means of drawing nearer to her, for nothing could have been more coy and retiring than the little sparrows. As I gently advanced along the limb upon which she perched, gazing at me with a pretty shyness, I was startled to perceive someone else climbing the tree. Looking down, I recognized my acquaintance, Speckle Devil, who rapidly ascended. I concealed myself, but the astute Speckle soon discovered me. When he approached, the sparrows ceased their interesting sports and flew away. I was disappointed and could not conceal my chagrin from the clumsy Speckle. He stopped and surveyed me.

'Chasing dicky-birds, hey?' he volunteered, in his coarse way.

I was irritated and did not hesitate to show it. I climbed farther out on the limb. Speckle followed me. 'Don't be mad', he whined, teasingly.

I faced him and surveyed him with cool scorn. 'You look like a shattered ideal, Speckle', I said, trying to make him sensible of his uncouth appearance, for nothing could have been filthier or more shocking than his entire person.

He turned and sharpened his claws on the limb, saying defiantly: 'Oh, get gay, then – wot do I care? You look like an animal cracker, you do. Gee! you look like a leopard that's lost his spots.'

I saw then that the honest fellow was hurt, and in a milder tone I asked him his reason for disturbing me. Speckle chewed a twig or two in silence, then he replied, 'Fight'.

I was interested at once. I hesitated. I had some idea of going to practise the fourth jump, and I disliked the society of Rat Alley. Speckle watched me disdainfully, narrowing his yellow eyes. Finally I said:

No, Speckle, I think I shall stay here. You must understand that is a principle of mine – not to witness a fight.'

Speckle, having reached the ground, turned up his face and eyed me scornfully. Principle?' he sneered. 'Principle! Won't witness a fight, hey? Sits on a limb and witnesses dicky-birds, but he's too good to witness a fight. Oh, Lord!' and he swore violently. Then, saying with intense scorn, 'Yes, you're full of principle, you are!' he ran along the fence towards Rat Alley.

Thursday: Had an interesting debate this morning with an old family friend who used to know my mother. Our talk drifted to serious things, and I asked her if she believed in the theory of nine lives. She replied that she did, that she knew for certain that she hd lived through seven lives, and warned me against such rash ventures as the fourth jump without making sure of at least one life to spare.

Saturday: I spent yesterday afternoon and evening at the home of a young child, whom I followed because she bore a paper of codfish which attracted me. The house where the child lives was exceedingly warm and pleasant, and I reclined in front of the glowing fire and made myself agreeable and attractive, considering meanwhile the advantages of such a home. It has often occurred

to me that sometime in my life I must have been owned. I can recall the feeling of caresses and the scent of soft garments worn by
some gentle person who felt solicitude and affection for me. I
think I can remember, though but dimly, the look of delicate
white hands that cuddled me, and the warmth and sweetness of a
breast to which I was pressed. How I ever became dissevered
from all those comfortable conditions I do not know, but it was
long ago, and has no part in my present life, for now I become
restless in any close environment, and invariably after a short stay
by some hearth of friendliness I feel the spell of the streets – a
spell that draws me away from mere ease and plenty to the thrill
and mystery of a roving life. And so it was yesterday. Half slum-
bering on the little girl's lap after a delicious refreshment of cus-
tard and cold liver, I heard suddenly, or thought I heard, a voice
that called me: and an old desire for vast lonely spaces, for the
Desert of the Roofs, for silent cobbled streets, seized me. I
thought of the vague gutters stretching away into solitude and
night, and the old hungry haunting, the strong longing to go out
and look for something, possessed me. I got down from the little
girl's lap and went out of the door that led to the street.

A Swiss Legend

C. H. Ross

'One day, once upon a time, or thereabouts, the witch-finder of a certain Swiss town – himself secretly a wizard – was taking his afternoon's walk, when he came across a Tom Cat, looking very thin and miserable. This Cat had once been the chief favourite of a rich old lady, who had trained him up in luxurious living. Now she was dead, and Tom's happy days were over: he was as shaggy and meagre, as he had formerly been sleek and plump. Now, you must know that Cats' grease was, in those days, an invaluable ingredient for certain magical preparations, provided the Cat to whom it belonged willingly made a donation of it. This proviso rendered good efficient Cats' grease an exceedingly rare commodity; for though there might be no great difficulty in finding a fat Cat, to find one willing to part with its fat was, of course, difficult enough.

'Here, however, was an animal in desperate circumstances, who might be accessible to reason; therefore, says the magician –
'"How much will you take for your fat?"

'"Why, I haven't got any," replied Tom, who, to tell the truth, was as thin as a hurdle.

'"You may have, though, if you say the word," said the magician; "and I'll tell you how."

'You see, he knew from experience that Tom was a Cat who was capable of making flesh, for he had known him as round as a dumpling; so he made this bargain: "He offered Tom a whole month's luxurious living on condition that at the expiration of that time he should voluntarily lay down his life and yield up all the fat he had acquired during the four weeks. Of course Tom agreed, and the contract was signed on the spot. The apartment provided for Tom's lodging was "fitted up as an artificial land-scape. A little wood was perched on the top of a little mountain, which rose from the banks of a little lake. On the branches of the trees were perched dainty birds, all roasted, and emitting a most savoury odour. From the cavities of the mountain peered forth sundry baked mice, all seasoned with delicious stuffing and ex-quisitely larded with bacon. The lake consisted of the newest milk, with a small fish or two at the bottom. Thus, to the en-joyment of the epicure, was added the excitement of imaginary sportsmanship. Tom ate his fill, and more, and soon became as fat as the magician could wish, but before long he became thoughtful. The month had nearly expired; at the end he was to die if fat enough. Ah! a bright thought, he would get thin again. With a wondrous strength of mind he refrained from eating the luxuries provided, took plenty of exercise on the house-tops, and kept himself in excellent health, but much thinner than suited the wizard's fancy.

'Before long, this gentleman remonstrated with Tom, pointing out to him very plainly, that he was bound by all the laws of honour to get fat by the month's end. To this, Tom had little to urge of any moment, and the magician informed him that he would kill him at the appointed period, let him be in what con-dition he might. Tom, therefore, would gain nothing by being thin, and it was hoped that his good taste, unchecked by other considerations, would induce him to make up for lost time. Time rolled on, Tom behaved worse than ever, and when the fatal day arrived "he looked in worse condition than ever – dissipated, abandoned, shaggy scamp, without an ounce on his bones." The wizard could not stand this, so he thrust Tom into an empty coop and fed him by violence. In course of time, the wizard was satis-fied, and began to sharpen his knife; but no sooner did Tom per-ceive this act, than he began to utter such singular expressions of contrition, that his proprietor paused to ask him to explain them. The Cat in wild terms alluded to a certain sum of ten thousand florins lying at the bottom of a well, and the wizard wanted to know more about them. It appeared then, that Tom's late mis-tress had thrown the sum he named to the bottom of a well, and informed her Cat that "should he find a perfectly beautiful and a penniless maiden, whom a perfectly honest man was inclined to wed in spite of her poverty, then he should empty the contents of the well as a marriage portion.''

'Of course this tale was false. The money existed where Tom had described, but it had been ill-gotten gold, with a curse upon it. But the wizard nibbled at the bait, put a chain round Tom's neck, and went to have a look at the treasure. There it was, sure enough, shining under the water.

'"Are you quite sure that there are exactly ten thousand florins?'' asked the magician.

'"I've never been down to see,'' replied Tom; "I was obliged to take the old lady's word for it.''

'"But where shall I find a wife?'' asked the wizard.

'"I'll find you one,'' said Tom.

'"Will you?''

'"To be sure. Tear up that contract, though, to begin with.''

'The wizard, not without grumbling, drew from his pocket the fatal paper, which Tom no sooner perceived than he pounced on it and swallowed it whole, making at the same time the reflection that he had never before tasted so delicious a morsel in his life.

'In the neighbourhood dwelt an old woman, who was a witch – one of the ugliest old women you ever saw, who every night flew up the chimney on a broom-stick, and played Meg's diversions by the light of the moon. This lady had an owl, who was a bird of loose principles, and had been an associate of Tom's in his gay days. This bright couple consulted together how they should persuade the ancient maiden to marry the old man.

'"She never will,'' said the owl.

'"Then we must make her; but how?''

'"We must catch her first, and take her prisoner, and that is to be done easily enough, with a net, spun by a man of sixty years old, who has never set eyes on the face of woman.''

'"Where are we to find him?''

'"Just round the corner: he has been blind from his birth.''

'"When the net had been procured, they set it in the chimney, and presently caught the old lady, and after much trouble they starved her into compliance. Then, by magical art, she put on an appearance of youth and beauty, and the wizard married her in an ecstacy of delight; but was he not in a fury when, evening approaching, she resumed her pristine ugliness. And was he not disgusted at his bride, in spite of the treasure she had brought him. As for Tom, like many bad people, he lived happy ever afterwards.'

James in Wartime

Oswald Barron, FSA

To tread a pavement that is not greasy with the mud, to walk in dry boots upon dry stones, that is comfortable after those rainy weeks. This was a morning on which a man might live hopefully, remembering that now every morning gains us another dole of daylight. Only another day lies between us and the New Year, the first New Year of the peace.

The little things that comfort us on our pilgrimage! It is certain that a stroll upon the dry pavement has been enough to put me in good humour for the day. Something I shared with my friends the cats: they were all out of doors this morning, well content as I was for the respite from the slow rain which has been falling these many days.

My neighbours the pussycats have shared the perils of wartime with us. I can remember days when frantic souls were writing to the Editor begging that he would join them in demanding the deaths of cats and dogs and canary birds, useless mouths that ought not to be fed in time of war. We had stern folk among us; when I read those letters I knew that there were men who, at a pinch, would look round among their fellow-men to denounce useless mouths. I was glad to think that I could bring evidence for my own war work, a light labour, but enough to save me from the doom of the lethal chamber.

As for the cats, they took these threats calmly enough. The only cat for whom I can answer was at work of national importance; five voters, at least, could testify to her long vigils beside the storeroom door. While Haig and his men were slaying Germans, she was slaying the mice that would have devoured our food. For a warranty of her honest work she would bring the dead mouse upstairs and lay it upon a hearthrug with the air of a cat that has done her duty.

But it never came to a massacre of cats. They and we lived out the war together. We shared our hardships; there were times when we fared on scanty rations. Cats who had lived delicately learned how cats might endure in besieged cities when the rations were doled out in small scales. To the palate of the cat there is nothing so delicious as meat of rabbit, but rabbit has been a dish for munitioners, meat out of reach of any catspaw. Had it not been for those worthy Belgians of the Flemish colony near my house, my cat would have been the leanest of my friends. It was well for her when the horse butchery opened its doors and sold meat upon which a cat might live honourably. Or let me say that it was well for me who, on many a day, carried the best of my own meal to the little black beast that must live at my cost. She lives and is sleek. Of all the cats whom I count my friends, only James has passed away too soon to know the blessedness of peace. Not that the life of James was a troubled life. If there were any war in it it was of his own seeking, for James was that sort of cat to whom adventure calls. He would sidle out of the house at dusk, not to come home again until the morning brought him to the door, a weary cat with the signs of battle upon him.

Pretty it was to see the sleek Pippa welcome back James from his battles, mewing about him, asking how he came by his scratches. James had no story to tell. H had fought and held his own; he desired nothing but sleep. H would doze through the long days, not heeding his wounds, giving no minute to his toilette.

A slovenly cat was James, as ever I saw. Pippa, who will wash herself from ears to tail after eating the tail of a sardine, could never understand the fine carelessness of the male. I have seen her, in distress over his slovenliness, turn to and wash James and sleek out his fur. James bore her with humour; at such times his eye was like the eye of a man who is having his white tie properly tied for him by female hands. Hardy he was and brave; a more amiable warrior I have never known. His purr, when he purred for sheer happiness of life, was as the purr of many kettles. Now he is dead, and I remember James with sorrow. He died as a cat should die, giving up life without murmuring, having lived and loved and fought. His widow goes in rich black, like many another widow, and seems consoled.

The Cats of Piacenza

W. L. Alden

The guide-books seem to have found it difficult to say much concerning Piacenza. In point of fact, there is very little historical interest attached to the place. While great men were born in profusion in other Italian cities, nobody of any consequence appears to have thought of being born in Piacenza. The city was founded by the Romans, who called it Placentia, in accordance with their usual custom of calling Italian cities out of their names. Its ostensible mission was to defend one of the fords of the Po against the Gauls and other undesirable barbarians; though why it was placed a good third of a mile from the river, instead of being planted directly on the south bank, is not clear. During the middle ages Piacenza was evidently popular with the rulers of the neighboring duchies and marquisates, and was frequently besieged and captured by covetous tyrants. Tennyson, in his poem descriptive, or rather reminiscent, of a journey he once made in Italy, found nothing to notice in Piacenze except rain. He briefly remarks that he found –

In Parma rain: Piacenza rain

And to tell the truth, Piacenza is a particularly rainy place in the late autumn and winter. But the one unique and extraordinary feature of Piacenza consists in its cats, and this feature is not so much as hinted at in any guide-book. This may possibly have been due to accident, but it looks like deliberate suppression of the truth, for it is incomprehensible how any guide-book editor could have visited Piacenza without being struck by the overwhelming predominance of cats among its population and the unique social position which they hold.

I entered Piacenza one sunny autumn day, and in accordance with my usual custom I avoided the hotel omnibus and walked into the town. It ought to be generally known that the hotel omnibus is expressly designed to weaken the mind of the passenger, and thereby fit him to undergo with meekness the exactions of the hotel-keeper. To this end a large mirror is always placed against the front partition of the vehicle, and in this mirror the passenger sees the streets and all that is therein reversed. He sees in the mirror an interesting doorway, a picturesque tower, a beautiful statue, or a vigorous dog-fight; but when he leans out of the window and gazes in front of the omnibus in search of them he cannot discover them, and only when it is too late does he remember that the treacherous mirror has led him to look in the wrong direction. It is the same if he sees a pretty girl or some novel and ingenious variety of professional cripple. The mirror always induces him to look from the window in the wrong direction, and brings to him failure and disappointment. A confused state of mind bordering upon imbecility results from this state of things, and when the passenger arrives at the hotel he falls an easy victim to the landlord.

I reached the main street of Piacenza in time to witness what at first sight looked like a popular uprising. A crowd of vociferating men and weeping women and joyous small boys occupied the street from curb to curb. I pushed my way through the throng until I came upon a motor-car with a single occupant. He was sitting in stolid silence, smoking a wooden pipe, and I could not fail to recognise him as an Englishmen. Leaning over the front of the vehicle was a tall and excited man, holding a dead and extremely limp cat by the scruff of its neck, and waving it from time to time before the impassive Englishman's face. A policeman stood by the side of the car, and at intervals addressed what seemed to be remonstrances to its occupant, although the noise of the crowd was so great that I could not hear what he was saying.

Evidently the motor-car had committed some grave contravention of the laws and customs of Piacenza, and as it was equally evident that the Englishman did not understand Italian, and was sitting still and waiting for better times, I felt that it was my duty to proffer assistance.

'What is the matter?' I asked. 'Can I be of service to you?'

He looked at me doubtfully for a moment, evidently suspecting me of being a professional guide. 'You are English?' he said presently, with a note of doubt in his voice.

'I am an American,' I replied, 'which in the circumstances ought to do nearly as well.'

'Glad to see you,' he said. 'I've had the bad luck to run down an old woman and kill a cat. These beggars don't seem to care a hang about the old woman, who, I fancy, isn't much hurt, but they've gone stark mad about the cat. It's the rummiest thing I ever met. This Johnny here' – and he indicated the policeman with a wave of his pipe – 'seems to want something, I don't know what. I should say a lunatic asylum would be about what he ought to want.'

The policeman's face brightened as I spoke to him, and he gladly unfolded his view of the case. The English signore in the motor-car had, he informed me, killed a cat, and naturally the proprietors of the cat were greatly displeased. He had, as was his duty, asked the signore to accompany him to the police office, but the signore smoked always and always, and would not so much as look at him. Could I not kindly explain to my compatriot that it would be a great favor if he would condescend to come to the police office. Otherwise – !' And here the policeman, who was a gentle and peaceable man, shrugged his shoulders in deprecation of the terrible consequences which would follow the Englishman's refusal to comply with the demands of the law.

'I am afraid,' I said to my new acquaintance, 'that you will have to go with this policeman to the police office. If you like, I will go with you, as I may be able to be of some little use.'

'Oh! That's what the matter, is it!' replied the Englishman. 'How was I to know the fellow was a policeman? Where's his helmet and what right has he got to wear a sword? Our policemen don't get themselves up like imitations soldiers.'

I explained that there were sometimes slight differences between the customs of different countries. This seemed to strike the Englishman as an original and forcible idea.

'That's so!' he exclaimed, as he climbed down from the car and prepared to accompany the officer. 'All the same, it's a mighty rum thing to dress a policeman up in that way.'

We made an imposing procession as we marched down the Via Garibaldi. It was headed by the Englishman and myself, closely followed by the policeman. Then followed the motor-car, laboriously pushed by two more policemen, who had arrived in the nick of time. Next came the remains of the cat, borne aloft by the tall man who acted as chief mourner, followed by half a dozen or more other mourners, weeping and gesticulating. The rear of the procession was brought up by citizens generally, without regard to rank or sex. We reached the police office without further incident, and were ushered into the presence of a severe looking magistrate, who regarded us with one eye, while he kept the other on the motor-car, which had come to a halt just in front of the window. He accomplished this feat with perfect ease, for nature has endowed him with eyes expressly constructed to enable him to look in two directions at once. Perhaps it was to this qualification that he owed his elevation to the bench.

After the crowd of witnesses had been reduced to a semblance of order, the policeman gave his evidence. He charged the prisoner with having run over and killed a cat, and with having refused to submit to arrest until the casual arrival of a distinguished compatriot, who had succeeded in making him listen to reason.

The judge bowed to me in recognistion of my good offices, and I was about to ask his permission to make a statement, when he waved his hand, implying that I should wait until the witnesses had been examined. It is only the Italian who can make long and intricate sentences with a wave of the hand. I knew what that magistrate's hand wished to say as well as if he had spoken audibly and at length.

Five men and two women severally swore that they were owners in part of the deceased cat, and that it had been wickedly and purposely killed by the accused. Four other witnesses, who disclaimed any ownership in the cat, sustained the testimony of the seven cat-owners, and described the death of the animal with a wealth of indignation that would have been justified only in the case of the wanton killing of an exceptionally valuable baby. Then the magistrate turned to the Englishman and solemnly said: 'Accused! It is established by the testimony of these good people that you have killed a cat. Moreover, that it was an important cat, belonging to the seven bereaved persons whose names the clerk will now read aloud.'

The seven names were read, and the magistrate asked the Englishman if he had anything to say in his defence.

I replied for him, saying that he did not understand Italian, and wished me to act as interpreter. I said that neither of us could understand how the cat could possibly have seven owners, and that the Englishman wished to have this matter explained.

'Here in Piacenza,' replied the magistrate, gently, 'it is not uncommon for a prominent cat to have several owners. If a person cannot afford to keep an entire cat, he joins with other who take shares in the cat and become its joint owners. This lamented animal who met with such a sudden and painful death was, as I have said, the property of the seven persons now in court, and they are entitled to payment for their sad loss.'

I translated the magistrate's explanation to the Englishman, who received it with an impassive face and the remark that it was 'deuced rum.' To my inquiry as to what he might wish me to say in his defence he replied:

'Oh, I killed the cat straight enough. Tell the beak and I did it because I was trying not to kill an old woman. Tell him I did knock an old woman down and am ready to pay damages for it, but I'm blessed if I'm going to pay for a beastly cat.'

In my translation of this defence I judiciously omitted the refusal to pay for the cat, since I knew that such payment was inevitable. The magistrate waves the matter of the old woman aside as being of trivial importance.

'No complaint has been made as to the complete or partial killing of any old woman,' he remarked. 'What is now before the court is the far more important affair of the cat. I have the most profound respect for the noble English nation, and would gladly show to your friend any possible favor, but justice must be maintained. I therefore decree that he shall pay to each owner of the deceased cat five francs, besides a fine of ten francs more, making in all forty-five francs. Unless this is paid, I must commit him to prison.'

The Englishman, after some little argument on my part, decided that resistance was useless. He paid over the forty-five francs, and was informed that he was at liberty to go where he pleased, provided he abstained from slaughtering cats. The bereaved cat-owners were quite satisfied with their respective five francs, and the magistrate complimented us on the promptness with which Englishmen always pay their debts.

'Tell him,' said the Englishman, 'that he has not heard the last of this outrage. Tell him that I shall write to the *Times*.'

I did not think it worthwhile to translate this dire threat, so I merely informed the magistrate that we were both grateful for his courtesy and consideration. He descended from the bench to shake hands with us 'at the mode of the English,' and again lamented the hard fate which had compelled him to fine an English gentleman.

'But you conceive,' he aded, 'that we cannot permit foreigners even of the most distinguished, to come here and kill our leading cats. It is impossible. If such conduct were to be permitted, there would be a revolution of the most sanguinary.'

We bade the magistrate farewell, and I said to my companion:

'Come with me and have some luncheon. Baedeker says there is a hotel near by where there is a good restaurant, and I should be delighted if you would lunch with me.'

'Right you are,' he replied. 'If you can find anything decent to eat in this country, it's more than I've been able to do. There's one thing: folks that worship cats as they do in this blooming town won't serve them up at a restaurant.'

We drove carefully in the motor-car, keeping a bright lookout for cats, until we reached the hotel. The dining-room was a large square apartment, with a rather dusty cement floor and a quantity of small deal tables, at most of which officers of the garrison in brilliant uniforms and well-to-do citizens were vigorously lunching. We selected a table in a quiet corner, and at the Englishman's request I ordered the luncheon. He was evidently in grave doubt as to what the order might bring forth.

'The food in this country,' he remarked, as the waiter departed, 'is rummer than it is in France, and that's saying a lot. I haven't had a bit of bacon nor a cut of mutton since I left England. I can't see what ails foreigners. They don't seem to have the first idea of what a dinner ought to be.'

But when the luncheon was brought on the table, and the Englishman successively ate *tagliatelle alla Bolognese, fritto misto,* and *polpettone*, washed down by an excellent red wine, and followed by Parmesan cheese that wept under the knife, he magnanimously admitted that it was possible to eat, even in Piacenza.

'I don't fancy,' he added, 'that a man could get any forrader with this wine, even if he drank twice as much as I've had; but I'd really like to know if all the cats I see in this room are real.'

In point of fact, the room swarmed with cats. I counted eleven within sight at one time, and there were many more under the tables and behind the legs of the guests. They were mostly young cats, for they walked with their tails erect and it is an inflexible rule among cats that one must turn one's tail down on attaining fourteen months of age. The cats walked fearlessly among the multitudinous legs of the guests, rubbing themselves against the steel scabbards of the officers, and condescending to eat the morsels of meat that nearly every one made it a rule to offer them. The officers were especially friendly with the cats, and when one of the latter refused a bit of cheese offered by a second lieutenant, the gentle warrior was obviously hurt and ashamed.

'They are real enough,' I said, in reply to the Englishman's question. 'Only I begin to think with you that cats must be worshipped in Piacenza. Perhaps the ancient Egyptian cult of Pasht still survives here.'

Just at the moment there entered four grizzled men in faded red shirts and venerable gray trousers. They were Garibaldian veterans, and at the sight of them I remembered that it was the anniversary of the battle of the Volturno, and I understood that these relics of the great Garibaldian epic had donned their old uniforms to do honor to the day. The officers rose and saluted as the four veterans entered. What if the men had been only privates in the army that gave half the peninsula to United Italy! What if they were evident mechanics, with the stoop of the shoulders that comes to men who toil with their hands! They were still the immortal Red Shirts who had accomplished miracles under their miraculous leader, and the handsomely uniformed and high-bred officers of the Italian army were proud to salute them.

'Who are those Johnnies in their shirt-sleeves? asked my companion. 'They might dress decently before coming into a public place.'

'They are Garibaldian veterans,' I replied, 'and one of them wears the medal of the Thousand.'

'Oh, that's it, is it?', said the Englishman. 'I remember seeing Garibaldi in London when I was a kid. He was as right as they make 'em. When you got on your legs I thought for a minute that you were going to chuck those chaps out.'

A large white cat walked solemnly towards the veteran of the Thousand, sprang into his lap, and reaching up, touched the medal reverently with his lips. Then he gently released himself from the caressing hand of the Garibaldian, and jumping down, seated himself a few feet from the table, and contemplated the four Red Shirts with obvious admiration.

I began to think that there was something uncanny about the cats of Piacenza. I had once heard a cat enthusiast speak of a religious cat whom he claimed to have known, but, since cats were first domesticated, who had ever dreamed of a patriotic cat! And yet here was a cat who saluted the medal of the Thousand; a cat who unquestionably knew the Garibalidan legend and reverenced the symbolic red shirt. I felt uncomfortable in that patriotic animal's presence.

'Come,' I said. 'We must have a look at this town. I want to take the afternoon train for Modena, and that will give us just an hour to see the cathedral and the other objects of interest.'

The Englishman readily acquiesced, and we went in search of the cathedral. Here the fates were unexpectedly good to me. The entire front of the cathedral was covered with straw matting, for it was in the process of restoration. This saved me from admiring a building that Ruskin may have called vile and wicked, or of failing to admire what that tyrannical master may have called beautiful and holy. To tell the truth, I did not then and do not now know Ruskin's opinion of the façade of the Piacenza cathedral, but it is a relief to know that whatever that opinion may have been, there is not the least danger that I shall ever run counter to it, for I shall never see Piacenza again.

There is really very little to see in Piacenza except the narrow streets, which, like nearly all narrow Italian streets, are picturesque. The Piazza Cavalli is rather impressive, although the statue of Ranuzio Farnese, which is intended to be its chief ornament, is little better than the average equestrian statue executed by order of Congress for the embellishment of the Capitol. The

Church of St Antonino has its architectural merits, but as for the rest of the Piacenza churches, they are painfully commonplace.

As we walked up the nave of the cathedral, I noticed a black cat slinking behind a column, and had little doubt that its black coat was purposely worn in imitation of a cassock. We had finished our last tomb and our last picture, and were nearly ready to leave the cathedral, when the Englishman touched my arm and pointed to the pulpit. There, on the reading-desk, sat the black cat, with his head slightly on one side as he watched us.

'Let's get out of here before he begins to preach,' whispered the Englishman, and I hastened to follow his counsel. I had been in Piacenza but three hours, and had seen a dead cat owned in shares by seven persons, a patriotic cat who kissed the Garibaldian medal, and an ecclesiastical cat who gave every reason to suppose that he was ready to preach a sermon from the pulpit of the cathedral. Prudence loudly told me to leave Piacenza without risking any fresh and still more startling evidences of the unique intelligence of its cats.

'Look here,' said the Englishman, when we were once more in the open air. 'You get into my automobile and come with me as far as Modena. I'm, in the automobile-manufacturing business, and I've got to take this machine to a man in Florence who has bought it. I'll take you all the way there if you'll come. Don't say no.'

I thanked him warmly. We stopped at the railway station for my luggage, and presently we were spinning down the old Roman road that runs in almost a straight line from Piacenzi to Rimini. As the fresh air blew on my face and the warm sun filled me with the sense of contentment that we share with other sun-loving animals, I wondered if the cats of Piacenza were not partly the creatures of a dream. But beyond doubt I had been wide awake while in Piacenza; and besides, there was the testimony of my unimaginative English friend, who swore that there was something bally rum about the cats. So I must accept those wierd animals as real, no matter how unaccountable and inexplicable their conduct may have been.

St Jerome And His Lion

St Jerome in his study kept a great big cat,
It's always in his pictures, with its feet upon the mat.
Did he give it milk to drink, in a little dish?
When it came to Fridays did he give it fish?
If I lost my little cat, I'd be sad without it:
I should ask St Jeremy what to do about it:
I should ask St Jeremy, just because of that,
for he's the only saint I know who kept a pussy cat.

ANON

Windsor Cats

Louisa Victoria Barry

In 1891 we left Knapdale to take up our residence in The Cloisters at Windsor. For some time before, I had a favourite black cat who had the distinction of not possessing a single white hair. She was unusually attached to me on account of my having saved her life from a dog, just two minutes before her first kitten was born – she had only one. The shock to the poor thing was so great that it was with difficulty I saved her life, and her terror at every sound was so pitiful that I gave up a small empty room to her and her kitten, locking her in, and allowing no one to go near but myself. I waited on her for a whole month, until she quieted down and allowed her kitten to see the world. Ever after when she had kittens she had the same attack of nerves and required my undivided attention. We were living then in an interesting old manor-house which had belonged to Oliver Cromwell. His daughter, Mrs Ireton, was said to haunt the gallery; the house has always had the reputation of being haunted. I feel I ought to mention this, although I do not know whether it could in any way have affected the cat.

After the Bishop's appointment up to the time of our removal the car was much on my mind, as I dreaded the change and disturbance for her which all ordinary cats without nerves hate. But the gardener was left in the house, to take charge of it for a new tenant, so I made special arrangments that the cat should remain in his care with good board wages till I was quite settled, when I was to write for it and he would see her safely on her journey to Windsor.

Time went on, and I did not worry about my cat and was waiting until all was ready, when one night I had a dream. I was walking – as I thought – in the garden at Knapdale, in a path under the wall, which was a favourite place of mine, and where the black cat used to follow me up and down, when I heard a piteous cry, and looking up saw my Puss, standing on the top of the wall, in a lamentable plight, evidently starved to death and very weak. I awoke much disturbed, but went to sleep again, and this appearance of the cat came to me three times that night.

In the morning I told the Bishop that I intended to go off immediately to fetch my cat. He did his best to dissuade me from doing so, as he said I could telegraph to the gardener and the cat would arrive without any trouble. But I could not feel satisfied, and started off immediately after breakfast.

On my arrival at Knapdale I found the house in the possession of workmen. On entering, no gardener was to be seen, and no cat. Filled with anxiety, I asked every man I met if a black cat had been seen, but with no result. At last a woman in a house nearby told me that the gardener had been dismissed summarily, and being no doubt unwilling I should know it, had departed and left the cat to its fate. This woman had heard the poor thing crying and had tried to get at it and give it milk, but it was always terrified and too wild to come near her. It occured to me to go and walk under the wall I had seen in my dream, and which the cat had no doubt always associated with me, and call her. In a few minutes I saw a wild, haggard face appear, gazing at me as if it could not believe the evidence of its senses, then down she came and rushed into my arms, and clung to me frantically. I carried her into the room we both remembered, and found her nothing but skin and bone, and very weak. I went into the village and fed her with milk and fish, bought a hamper into which she crawled of her own accord, and during the many hours' journey home she lay quite still and purred whenever I stroked her. She took a fancy to her new home and settled down at once.

This story is perfectly true; who can explain the fact of the cat spirit being able to make an impression on a human spirit so as to induce me to act as I did and only just in time to save her life?

A Poor Black Cat

George Borrow

The house or cottage, for it was called a cottage though it consisted of two stories, in which my wife had procured lodgings for us, was situated in the Northern suburb. Its front was towards a large perllan or orchard, which sloped down gently to the banks of the Dee; its back was towards the road leading from Wrexham, behind which was a high bank, on the top of which was a canal called in Welsh the Camlas, whose commencement was up the valley about two miles west. A little way up the road, towards Wrexham, was the vicarage, and a little way down was a flannel factory, beyond which was a small inn, with pleasure grounds, kept by an individual who had once been a gentleman's servant. The mistress of the house was a highly respectable widow, who, with a servant maid, was to wait upon us. It was as agreeable a place in all respects as people like ourselves could desire.

As I and my family sat at tea in our parlour, an hour or two after we had taken possession of our lodgings, the door of the room and that of the entrance to the house being open, on account of the fineness of the weather, a poor black cat entered hastily, sat down on the carpet by the table, looked up towards us, and mewed piteously. I never had seen so wretched a looking creature. It was dreadfully attenuated, and being little more than skin and bone, and was sorely afflicted with an eruptive malady. And here I may as well relate the history of this cat previous to our arrival which I subsequently learned by bits and snatches. It had belonged to a previous vicar of Llangollen, and had been left behind at his departure. His successor brought him dogs and cats, who, conceiving that the late vicar's cat had no business at

the vicarage, drove it forth to seek another home, which, however, it could not find. Almost all the people of the suburb were
dissenters, as indeed were the generality of the people of Llangollen, and knowing the cat to be a church cat, not only would not
harbour it, but did all they could to make it miserable; whilst the
few who were not dissenters, would not receive it into their
houses, either because they had cats of their own, or dogs, or did
not want a cat, so that the cat had no home and was dreadfully
persecuted by nine-tenths of the suburb. Oh, there never was a
cat so persecuted as that poor Church of England animal, and
solely on account of the opinions which it was supposed to have
imbibed in the house of its late master, for I never could learn that
the dissenters of the suburb, nor indeed of Llangollen in general,
were in the habit of persecuting other cats; the cat was a Church
of England cat, and that was enough: stone it, hang it, drown it!
were the cries of almost everybody. If the workmen of the flannel
factory, all of whom were Calvinistic-Methodists, chanced to get a
glimpse of it in the road from the windows of the building, they
would sally forth in a body, and with sticks, stones, or for want of
other weapons, with clots of horse dung, of which there was
always plenty on the road, would chase it up the high bank or
perhaps over the Camlas; the inhabitants of a small street between our house and the factory leading from the road to the
river, all of whom were dissenters, if they saw it moving about
the perllan into which their back windows looked, would shriek
and hoot at it, and fling anything of no value, which came easily
to hand, at the head or body of the ecclesiastical cat. The good
woman of the house, who though a very excellent person, was a
bitter dissenter, whenever she saw it upon her ground or heard it
was there, and would make after it, frequently attended by her
maid Margaret, and her young son, a boy about nine years of age,
both of whom hated the cat, and were always ready to attack it,
either alone or in company, and no wonder, the maid being not
only a dissenter, but a class teacher, and the boy not only dissenter, but intended for the dissenting ministry. Where it got its
food, and food it sometimes must have got, for even a cat, an
animal known to have nine lives, cannot live without food, was
only known to itself, as was the place were it lay, for even a
cat must lie down sometimes; though a labouring man who

occasionally dug in the garden told me he believed that in the springtime it ate freshets, and the woman of the house once said that she believed it sometimes slept in the hedge, which hedge, by-the-bye, divided our perllan from the vicarage grounds, which were very extensive. Well might the cat after having led this kind of life for better than two years look mere skin and bone when it made its appearance in our apartment, and have an eruptive malady, and also a bronchitic cough, for I remember it had both. How it came to make its appearance there is a mystery, for it had never entered the house before, even when there were lodgers; that it should not visit the woman, who was its declared enemy, was natural enough, but why if it did not visit her other lodgers, did it visit us? Did instinct keep it aloof from them? Did instinct draw it towards us? We gave it some bread-and-butter, and a little tea with milk and sugar. It ate and drank and soon began to purr. The good woman of the house was horrified when on coming in to remove the things she saw the church cat on her carpet.'What impudence!' she exclaimed, and made towards it, but on our telling her that we did not expect that it should be disturbed, she let it alone. A very remarkable circumstance was, that though the cat had hitherto been in the habit of flying, not only from her face, but the very echo of her voice, it now looked her in the face with perfect composure, as much as to say, 'I don't fear you, for I know that I am now safe and with my own people.' It stayed with us two hours and then went away. The next morning it returned. To be short, though it went away every night, it became our own cat, and one of our family. I gave it something which cured it of its eruption, and through good treatment it soon lost its other ailments and began to look sleek and bonny.

How the First Cat was Created
An Irish Legend

Douglas Hyde

One day Mary and her Son were travelling the road, and they heavy and tired, and it chanced that they went past the door of a house in which there was a lock of wheat being winnowed. The Blessed Virgin went in, and she asked an alms of wheat, and the woman of the house refused her.

'Go in again to her,' said the Son, 'and ask for it in the name of God.'

She went, and the woman refused her again.

'Go in to her again,' said He, 'and ask her to give leave to put your hand into the pail of water, and to thrust it down into the heap of wheat, and to take away with you all that shall cling to your hand.'

She went, and the woman gave her leave to do that. When she came out to our Saviour, He said to her, 'Do not let one grain of that go astray, for it is worth much and much.'

When they had gone a bit from the house they looked back, and saw a flock of demons coming towards the house, and the Virgin Mary was frightened lest they might do harm to the woman. 'Let there be no anxiety on you,' said Jesus to her; 'since it has chanced that she has given you all that of alms, they shall get no victory over her.'

They travelled on, then, until they reached as far as a place where a man named Martin had a mill. 'Go in,' said our Saviour to His mother, 'since it has chanced that the mill is working, and ask them to grind that little grain-*een* for you.'

She went. 'O musha, it's not worth while for me,' said the boy who was attending the querns, 'to put that little *lockeen* a-grinding for you.' Martin heard them talking and said to the lout, 'Oh then, do it for the creature, perhaps she wants it badly,' said he. He did it, and he gave her all the flour that came from it.

They travelled on then, and they were not gone any distance until the mill was full of flour as white as snow. When Martin perceived this great miracle he understood well that it was the Son of God and His Mother who chanced that way. He ran out and followed them, at his best, and he made across the fields until he came up with them, and there was that much haste on him in going through a scunce of hawthorns that a spike of the hawthorn met his breast and wounded him greatly. There was that much zeal in him that he did not feel the pain, but clapt his hand over it, and never stopped until he came up with them. When our Saviour beheld the wound upon poor Martin, He laid his Hand upon it, and it was closed, and healed upon the spot. He said to Martin then that he was a fitting man in the presence of God; 'and go home now,' said He, 'and place a fistful of the flour under a dish, and do not stir it until morning.'

When Martin went home he did that, and he put the dish, mouth under, and the fistful of flour beneath it.

The servant girl was watching him, and thought that maybe it would be a good thing if she were to set a dish for herself in the same way, and signs on her, she set it.

On the morning of the next day Martin lifted his dish, and what should run out from it but a fine sow and a big litter of bonhams with her. The girl lifted her own dish, and there ran out a big mouse and a clutch of young mouselets with her. They ran here and there, and Martin at once thought that they were not good, and he plucked a big mitten off his hand and flung it at the young mice, but as soon as it touched the ground it changed into a cat, and the cat began to kill the young mice. That was the beginning of cats. Martin was a saint from that time forward, but I do not know which of the saints he was of all who were called Martin.

To A Cat

Cat! who has pass'd thy grand climacteric,
  How many mice and rats has in thy days
  Destroy'd? – How many tit bits stolen? Gaze
With those bright languid segments green, and prick
Those velvet ears – but pr'ythee do not stick
  Thy latent talons in me – and upraise
  Thy gentle mew – and tell me all thy frays
Of fish and mice, and rats and tender chick.
Nay, look not down, nor lick thy dainty wrists –
  For all the wheezy asthma, – and for all
Thy tail's tip is nick'd off – and though the fists
  Of many a maid have given thee many a maul,
Still is that fur as soft as when the lists
  In youth thou enter'dst on glass bottled wall.

JOHN KEATS

The Demon Cat

Lady Wilde

There was a woman in Connemara, the wife of a fisherman; as he had always good luck, she had plenty of fish at all times stored away in the house ready for market. But, to her great annoyance, she found that a great cat used to come in at night and devour all the best and finest fish. So she kept a big stick by her, and determined to watch.

One day, as he and a woman were spinning together, the house suddenly became quite dark; and the door was burst open as if by the blast of the tempest, when in walked a huge black cat, who went straight up to the fire, then turned round and growled at them.

'Why, surely this is the devil,' said a young girl, who was by, sorting fish.

'I'll teach you how to call me names,' said the cat; and, jumping at her, he scratched her arm till the blood came. 'There, now,' he said, 'you will be more civil another time when a gentleman comes to see you.' And with that he walked over to the door and shut it close, to prevent any of them going out, for the poor young girl, while crying loudly from fright and pain, had made a desperate rush to get away.

Just then a man was going by, and hearing the cries, he pushed open the door and tried to get in; but the cat stood on the threshold, and would let no one pass. On this the man attacked him with his stick, and gave him a sound blow; the cat, however, was more than a match in the fight, for it flew at him and tore his face and hand so badly that the man at last took to his heels and ran away as fast as he could.

'Now, it's time for my dinner,' said the cat, going up to examine the fish that was laid out on the tables. 'I hope the fish is good today. Now, don't disturb me, nor make a fuss; I can help myself.' With that he jumped up, and began to devour all the best fish, while he growled at the woman.

'Away, out of this, you wicked beast,' she cried, giving it a blow with the tongs that would have broken its back, only it was a devil; 'out of this; no fish shall you have today.'

But the cat only grinned at her, and went on tearing and spoiling and devouring the fish, evidently not a bit the worse for the blow. On this, both the women attacked it with sticks, and struck hard blows enough to kill it, on which the cat glared at them, and spit fire; then, making a leap, it tore their heads and arms till the blood came, and the frightened women rushed shrieking from the house.

But presently the mistress returned, carrying with her a bottle of holy water; and, looking in, she saw the cat still devouring the fish, and not minding. So she crept over quietly and threw holy water on it without a word. No sooner was this done than a dense black smoke filled the place, through which nothing was seen but the two red eyes of the cat, burning like coals of fire. Then the smoke gradually cleared away, and she saw the body of the creature burning slowly till it became shrivelled and black like a cinder, and finally disappeared. And from that time the fish remained untouched and safe from harm, for the power of the evil one was broken, and the demon cat was seen no more.

The Cat By The Fire

Leigh Hunt

A blazing fire, a warm rug, candles lit and curtains drawn, the
kettle on for tea (nor do the 'first circles' despise the preference of
a kettle to an urn, as the third or fourth may do), and finally, the
cat before you, attracting your attention, – it is a scene which
everybody likes unless he has a morbid aversion to cats; which is
not common. There are some nice inquirers, it is true, who are apt
to make uneasy comparisons of cats with dogs, – to say they are
not so loving, that they prefer the house to the man, etc. But
agreeably to the good old maxim, that 'comparisons are odious,'
our readers, we hope, will continue to like what is likable in anything, for its own sake, without trying to render it unlikable from
its inferiority to some thing else, – a process by which we might
ingeniously contrive to put soot into every dish that is set before
us, and to reject one thing after another, till we were pleased with
nothing. Here is a good fireside, and a cat to it; and it would be
our own fault if, in removing to another house and another fireside, we did not take care that the cat removed with us. Cats cannot look to the moving of goods, as men do. If we would have
creatures considerate towards us, we must be so towards them. It
is not to be expected of everybody, quadruped or biped, that they
should stick to us in spite of our want of merit, like a dog or a
benevolent sage. Besides, stories have been told of cats very
much to the credit of their benignity; such as their following a
master about like a dog, waiting at a gentleman's door to thank
him for some obligation overnight, etc. And our readers may remember the history of the famous Goldophin Arabian, upon
whose grave a cat that had lived with him in the stable went and

stretched itself, and died.

The cat purrs, as if it applauded our consideration, – and gently moves its tail. What an odd expression of the power to be irritable and the will to be pleased there is in its face, as it looks up at us! We must own, that we do not prefer a cat in the act of purring, or of looking in that manner. It reminds us of the sort of smile, or *simmer* (*simper* is too weak and fleeting a word) that is apt to be in the faces of irritable people when they are pleased to be in a state of satisfaction. We prefer, for a general expression, the cat in a quiet, unpretending state, and the human countenance with a look indicative of habitual grace and composure, as if it were not necessary to take any violent steps to prove its amiability, – the 'smile without a smile,' as the poet beautifully calls it.

Furthermore (in order to get rid at once of all that may be objected to poor Pussy, as boys at school get down their bad dumpling as fast as possible before the meat comes), we own we have an objection to the way in which a cat sports with a mouse before she kills it, tossing and jerking it about like a ball, and letting it go, in order to pounce upon it with the greater relish. And yet what right have we to apply human measures of cruelty to the inferior reflectability of a cat? Perhaps she has no idea of the mouse's being alive, in the sense that we have, – most likely she looks upon it as a pleasant movable toy, made to be eaten, – a sort of lively pudding, that oddly jumps hither and thither. It would be hard to beat into the head of a country squire of the old class that there is any cruelty in hunting a hare; and most assuredly it would be still harder to beat mouse-sparing into the head of a cat. You might read the most pungent essay on the subject into her ear, and she would only sneeze at it.

As to the unnatural cruelties, which we sometimes read of, committed by cats upon their offspring, they are exceptions to the common and beautiful rules of nature, and accordingly we have nothing to do with them. They are traceable to some unnatural circumstances of breeding or position. Enormities as monstrous are to be found among human beings, and argue nothing against the general character of the species. Even dogs are not always immaculate; and sages have made slips. Dr Franklin cut off his son with a shilling for differing with him in politics.

But cats resemble tigers? They are tigers in miniature? Well, –

and very pretty miniatures they are. And what has the tiger himself done, that he has not a right to eat his dinner as well as Jones?
A tiger treats a man much as a cat does a mouse; – granted; but we
have no reason to suppose that he is aware of the man's sufferings, or means anything but to satisfy his hunger; and what have
the butcher and poulterer been about meanwhile? The tiger, it is
true, lays about him a little superfluously sometimes, when he
gets into a sheepfold, and kills more than he eats; but does not the
Squire or the Marquis do pretty much like him in the month of
September? Nay, do we not hear of venerable judges, that would
not hurt a fly, going about in that refreshing month, seeking
whom they may lame? See the effect of habit and education! And
you can educate the tiger in no other way than by attending to his
stomach. Fill that, and he will want no men to eat, probably not
even to lame. On the other hand, deprive Jones of his dinner for a
day or two, and see what a state he will be in, especially if he is by
nature irascible. Nay, keep him from it for half an hour, and
observe the tiger propensities of his stomach and fingers, – how
worthy of killing he thinks the cook, and what boxes of the ear he
feels inclined to give the footboy.

Animals, by the nature of things, in their present state, dispose
of one another into their respective stomachs, without ill-will on
any side. They keep down the several populations of their neighbours, till time may come when superfluous population of any
kind need not exist, and predatory appearances may vanish from
the earth, as the wolves have done from England. But whether
they may or not is not a question by a hundred times so important
to moral inquirers as into the possibilities of human education
and the nonsense of ill-will. Show the nonentity of that, and we
may all get our dinners as jovially as we can, sure of these three
undoubted facts, – that life is long, death short, and the world
beautiful. And so we bring our thoughts back again to the fireside, and look at the cat.

Poor Pussy! she looks up at us again, as if she thanked us for
those vindications of dinner; and symbolically gives a twist of a
yawn and a lick to her whiskers. Now she proceeds to clean herself all over, having a just sense of the demands of her elegant
person, beginning judiciously with her paws, and fetching amaz-
ing tongues at her hind-hips. Anon, she scratches her neck with a

foot of rapid delight, leaning her head towards it, and shutting her eyes, half to accommodate the action of the skin, and half to enjoy the luxury. She then rewards her paws with a few more touches; – look at the action of her head and neck, how pleasing it is, the ears pointed forward, and the neck gently arching to and fro. Finally, she gives a sneeze, and another twist of mouth and whiskers, and then, curling her tail towards her front claws, settles herself on her hind quarters, in an attitude of bland meditation.

What does she think of? – of her saucer of milk at breakfast? or of the thump she got yesterday in the kitchen for stealing the meat? or of her friend the cat next door, the most impassioned of serenaders? or her little ones, some of whom are now large, and all of them gone? Is *that* among her recollections when she looks pensive? Does she taste of the noble prerogative-sorrows of man?

She is a sprightly cat, hardly past her youth; so, happening to move the fringe of the rug a little with our foot, she darts out a paw, and begins plucking it and inquiring into the matter, as if it were a challenge to play, or something lively enough to be eaten. What a graceful action of that foot of hers, between delicacy and petulance! – combining something of a thrust out, a beat, and a scratch. There seems even something of a little bit of fear in it, as if just enough to provoke her courage, and give her the excitement of a sense of hazard. We remember being much amused with seeing a kitten manifestly making a series of experiments upon the patience of its mother, – trying how far the latter would put up with positive bites and thumps. The kitten ran at her every moment, gave her a knock or a bite of the tail; and then ran back again, to recommence the assault. The mother sate looking at her, as if betwixt tolerance and admiration, to see how far the spirit of the family was inherited or improved by her sprightly offspring. At length, however, the 'little Pickle' presumed too far, and the mother, lifting up her paw, and meeting her at the very nick of the moment, gave her one of the most unsophisticated boxes of the ear we ever beheld. It sent her rolling half over the room, and made her come to a most ludicrous pause, with the oddest little look of premature and wincing meditation.

The lapping of the milk out of the saucer is what one's human thirst cannot sympathise with. It seems as if there could be no satisfaction in such a series of atoms of drink. Yet the saucer is soon emptied; and there is a refreshment to one's ears in that sound of plashing with which the action is accompanied and which seems indicative of a like comfort to Pussy's mouth. Her tongue is thin, and can make a spoon of itself. This however, is common to other quadrupeds with the cat, and does not, therefore, more particularly belong to our feline consideration. Not so the electricity of its coat, which gives out sparks under the hand; its passion for the herb valerian (did the reader ever see one roll in it? it is a mad sight) and other singular delicacies of nature, among which, perhaps, is to be reckoned its taste for fish, a creature with whose element it has so little to do that it is supposed even to abhor it; though lately we read somewhere of a swimming cat, that used to fish for itself. And this reminds us of an exquisite anecdote of dear, dogmatic diseased, thoughtful, surly, charitable Johnson, who would go out of doors himself, and buy oysters for his cat, because his black servant was too proud to do it! Not that we condemn the black, in those enslaving, unliberating days. He had a right to the mistake, though we should have thought better of him had he seen farther, and subjected his pride to affection for such a master. But Johnson's true practical delicacy in the matter is beautiful. Be assured that he thought nothing of 'condescension' in it, or of being eccentric. He was singular in somethings, because he could not help it. But he hated eccentricity. No: in his best moments he felt himself simply to be a man, and a good man too, though a frail – one that in virtue as well as humility, and in a knowledge of his ignorance as well as his wisdom, was desirous of being a Christian philosopher; and accordingly he went out, and bought food for his hungry cat, because his poor negro was too proud to do it, and there was nobody else in the way whom he had a right to ask. What must anybody that saw him have thought, as he turned up Bolt Court! But doubtless he went as secretly as possible, – that is to say, if he considered the thing at all. His friend Garrick could not have done as much! He was too grand, and on the great 'stage' of life. Goldsmith could; but he would hardly have thought of it. Beauclerc might; but he would have thought it necessary to excuse it with a jest or a wager, or some such thing. Sir Joshua Reynolds, with his fashionable, fine-lady-painting hand, would certainly have shrunk from it. Burke would have reasoned himself into its propriety, but he would have reasoned himself out again. Gibbon! Imagine its being put into the head of Gibbon!! He and his bag-wig would have started with all the horror of a gentleman-usher; and he would have run the bell for the cook's-deputy's-under-assistant-errand-boy.

Cats at firesides live luxuriously, and are the picture of comfort; but least they should not bear their portion of trouble in this world, they have the drawbacks of being liable to be shut out of doors on cold nights, beatings from the 'aggravated' cooks, over-pettings of children (how should we like to be squeezed and pulled about in that manner by some great patronising giants?) and last, not least, horrible merciless tramples of unconscious human feet and unfeeling legs of chairs. Elegance, comfort, and security seem the order of the day on all sides, and you are going to sit down to dinner, or to music, or to take tea, when all of a sudden the cat gives a squall as if she was mashed; and you are not sure that the fact is otherwise. Yet she gets in the way again, as before; and dares all the feet and mahogany in the room. Beautiful present sufficingness of a cat's imagination! Confined to the snug circle of her own sides, and the two next inches of rug or carpet.

The Cat and the Mice

Aesop

A cat, grown feeble with age, and no longer able to hunt for mice as she was wont to do, sat in the sun and bethought herself how she might entice them within reach of her paws.

The idea came to her that if she would suspend herself by the hind legs from a peg in the closet wall, the mice, believing her to be dead, no longer would be afraid of her. So, at great pains and with the assistance of a torn pillow case she was able to carry out her plan.

But before the mice could approach within range of the innocent-looking paws a wise old gaffer-mouse whispered to his friends: 'Keep your distance, my friends. Many a bag have I seen in my day, but never one with a cat's head at the bottom of it.'

Then turning to the uncomfortable feline, he said: 'Hang there, good madam, as long as you please, but I would not trust myself within reach of you though you were stuffed with straw.'

Application HE WHO IS ONCE DECEIVED IS DOUBLY CAUTIOUS.

The love affairs of an English cat

Honoré de Balzac

I was born in the house of a clergyman in Catshire, near the little town of Miaulbury. The fertility of my mother condemned nearly all her children to a cruel fate, for you know that no one has been able to assign a cause for the maternal intemperance of English cats, which threatens to populate the entire world. Both toms and tabbies in turn attribute this result to their amiability and to their own special virtues. But some irreverent observers say that toms and tabbies in England are subject to such utterly boring rules, that they find their only amusements in these little family diversions. Others believe that matters of business and high policy are involved, because of English rule in India; but such considerations are hardly appropriate for my paws, and I leave them to the *Edinburgh Review*.

I was saved from the statutory drowning because of my pure white coat. And they called me 'Beauty'. But alas, the poverty of the clergyman, who had a wife and eleven daughters, prevented him from keeping me. An elderly spinster noticed that I had some sort of affection for the rector's Bible; I always sat on it, not because I was religiously inclined, but one morning, I, poor little child of Nature, was attracted by the cream in a bowl, across which lay a muffin. I knocked off the muffin with my paw, and I lapped up the cream; then in my satisfaction and also perhaps as the result of the weakness of my youthful organs, I gave myself up, on the waxed floor, to the most imperious demand experienced by kittens. On perceiving what she called my intemperance and my lack of education, she seized me and beat me soundly with a birch, declaring that she would make a lady of me, or she would abandon me.

'Here's a nice thing,' said she. 'Understand, Miss Beauty, that English cats wrap in the deepest mystery things of Nature which could offend English dignity, and they banish everything that is improper, by applying to the creature, as you have heard the Rev Doctor Simpson say, the laws made by God for the Creation. You must learn to suffer a thousand deaths rather than reveal your desires; it is in this that lies the virtue of Saints. It is the fairest privilege of cats to depart with their characteristic grace, and to go, no one knows whither, to perform their little toilets. You will thus only show yourself when looking your best. Deceived by appearances, everyone will take you for an angel. In future, when seized by a similar desire, you should gaze at the window, with an air of wanting to go for a walk, and then make for the bushes or go into a gutter.'

'And when I am in the gutter?' I thought, gazing at the old lady.

'Once you are alone and sure of being seen by no one, well then, Beauty, you can sacrifice decorum with all the more charm, that you were so much more restrained in public. It is thus that the perfection of English morality shines most clearly, since it is wholly concerned with appearances, this world being, alas, one of appearance and deceit.'

From that moment I habitually hid my favourite tit-bits under beds. No one ever saw me either eating or drinking or making my toilet. I was regarded as a pearl among cats.

When ladies and gentlemen used to pick me up, in order to stroke my back and make the sparks fly from my fur, the maiden lady said with pride: 'You can hold her without the least fear for your dress; she is beautifully brought up!' Everybody said I was an angel, and lavished tit-bits and the most delicate dishes on me; but I declare I was profoundly bored. I understood very well how a young cat in the neighbourhood had come to run away with a tom. The word 'tom' seemed to bring on a sort of sickness in my soul, that nothing would cure, not even the compliments which I received – or rather which my Mistress paid to herself.

'Beauty is completely moral, she is a little angel,' she would say. 'Although she is very lovely, she appears not to be aware of it. She never looks at anyone, which is the very height of the best aristocratic education; it is true that she lets herself be seen very willingly, but she is above all completely unaffected, a quality which we demand of our young girls, but which is very hard to develop. She waits to approach until she is wanted, she never jumps up on you in a familiar manner, no one sees her when she eats, and certainly that monster Lord Byron would have adored her. Like a true Englishwoman she loves tea, sits gravely by when you are explaining the Bible, and thinks evil of no one – and so hears it spoken!'

One evening my Mistress begged one of the young ladies to sing. As soon as this young girl sat down at the piano and began to sing, I immediately recognized the Irish melodies which I had learnt in my childhood, and I realized that I too was a musician. I therefore joined my voice to that of the young girl, but I received an angry smack, whereas the young lady was complimented. This signal act of injustice revolted me, and I took refuge in the attics. Oh sacred love of my country, what a delicious night! I realized what gutters meant. I heard hymns sung by toms to other tabbies, and these adorable elegies made me despise the hypocrisies which my Mistress had forced me to learn. Some of the tabbies then perceived me, and appeared to take umbrage at my presence, when a tom, his fur on end, with a magnificent beard and of a fine bearing, came to look me over, and said to the company, 'It is a child'. At these scornful words, I began to leap on the tiles, and to prance with the agility which distinguishes us, dropping on my paws in that soft and flexible fashion, which no other animal can imitate, in order to prove I was no mere child. But these dainty ways went for nothing.'When will they sing hymns to me?', I thought to myself. The appearance of these bold toms, their melodies, which no human voice will ever rival, had moved me profoundly, and led me to compose little poems which I sang on the stairs.

But an event of immense importance was about to take place, which tore me away roughly from this innocent existence. I was carried off to London by a niece of my Mistress, a rich heiress, who became crazy about me. She would kiss and pet me in a sort of frenzy, which pleased me so much, that contrary to my usual habit I became attached to her. We were always together, and I was able to observe the best society in London during the Season. It was there that I was to learn about the perversity of English manners, which had spread even to the animals, and to recognize the cant which Lord Byron had denounced, and of which I was a victim as well as he, without having ever published my 'Hours of Idleness'.

Arabella, my Mistress, was a young woman like many others in England; she did not know what sort of husband she wanted. The complete liberty allowed young girls in their choice of a husband drives them almost mad, particularly when they ponder on the stiffness of English manners, which precludes any intimate conversation after marriage. I was far from realizing that the cats of London had adopted this severe code, that English laws would be cruelly applied to me, and that I should undergo sentence at the terrible court of Doctors Commons.

At last one day, an elderly English Peer said to her on seeing me: 'You have a very pretty cat; she is like you, she is white, she is young, she needs a husband; let me introduce to her a magnificent Angora which I have at home'.

Three days later, the Peer brought in the handsomest tom of his lordly house, Puff, black as night, with the most magnificent green and yellow eyes, though cold and proud. His tail, which had yellowish stripes, swept the carpet with its long silky hairs. Perhaps he came from the Imperial House of Austria since he wore, as you perceive, its colours. His manners were those of a cat which had been to Court and lived in the best society. His bearing was so strict, that he would never have scratched his head with his paw, in the presence of anyone. Puff had travelled on the continent. In fine he was so handsome, that the Queen herself had expressed her admiration for him and had actually caressed him. Naively and simply I flung myself round his neck to induce him to play with me. But he refused on the pretext that we were in the presence of other people. I then perceived that this English peer of cats, owing to age and over-eating, had succumbed to that forced and false gravity which the English call respectability. His stoutness, which men admired, hampered his movements. This was the real reason for his refusal to reply to my blandishments; he remained calm and cold, sitting on his posterior, twiddling his whiskers, looking at me and sometimes closing his eyes. In the highest society of English cats, Puff was a splendid match for a cat born in a parsonage; he had two valets to look after him, he ate off Chinese porcelain, he drank tea without milk, he drove in a carriage to Hyde Park, and he attended Parliament.

My Mistress kept him in her house. Unknown to me, the whole feline population of London learnt that Miss Beauty of Catshire was to marry the illustrious Puff, who bore the Austrian colours. During the night I heard a concert in the street; I went down, accompanied by his lordship, who because of his gout, proceeded slowly. We found the cats of the district had come to congratulate me and to beg me to join their Ratophil Society. They explained to me that it was thoroughly common to chase rats and mice. The words 'shocking', 'vulgar', were on every lip. Finally they had formed, for the glory of their country, a Temperance Society. A few nights later, his lordship and I went on the roof at Almack's, to hear a grey cat speak on the question.

'They are our brothers,' he said. And he painted so exquisitely the sufferings of a rat caught in the jaws of a cat, that I was moved to tears. Seeing me the dupe of this speech, Lord Puff told me confidentially that England was hoping for an enormous trade in rats and mice; that if other cats no longer ate them, rats would be cheaper; that behind English morality there was always some economic reason; and that this alliance of morals and commerce was the sole alliance on which England really depended.

Puff seemed to me too much of a politician ever to make a good husband.

My Lord fell asleep. When the Meeting broke up, I heard these delicious words spoken by a young tom from the French Embassy, whose accent proclaimed his nationality:

'Dear Beauty. It will be long before Nature can produce a cat as perfect as you. The cashmeres of Persia and India are like the hides of a camel, compared with your fine and brilliant silk. You breathe a perfume to make Angels swoon with happiness, and I scented it in Prince Talleyrand's drawing-room, which I only left in order to listen to this flood of folly that you call a Meeting. The fire of your eyes lights up the night. Your ears would be perfection itself, if my sighs were to soften them. There is no rose in all

England, which is as rosy as the rosy rim of your rosy mouth. A fisherman would search in vain the caverns of Ormus for pearls to rival your teeth. Your dear fine soft muzzle is the prettiest thing produced in England. The Alpine snows would appear brown beside your heavenly coat. Ah, such furs can only be seen in your fogs. Your paws carry softly and gracefully the body which epitomizes the miracles of the Creation; were it not surpassed by your tail, the elegant interpreter of your heart; yes, never did any other cat own a curve so elegant, a rounded shape more perfect, movements more delicate. Abandon this silly old Puff, who goes to sleep like an English Lord in Parliament; besides, the wretch has sold himself to the Whigs, and, through living too long in Bengal, has lost all power to please a lady.'

Without appearing to observe him, I then had a good look at this charming French tom; he was shaggy, small, dashing, not the least like an English cat. His gallant air, as well as the way he shook his ears, proclaimed him a careless rogue. I must confess I was bored by the mere bodily cleanliness of English cats as well as by their solemnity. . . .

However, I woke his lordship and made him understand that it was very late, and that we must go in. I showed no sign of having heard Brisquet's declaration, and my manner appears to have been so frigid that it petrified him. He remained behind, all the more taken aback because he believed himself to be extremely handsome. I learned later that he seduced all tabbies who 'showed willing'. I watched him out of the corner of my eye; he went off in a series of short bounds and came back again in a similar manner, just like a French cat in despair; a true Englishman would have behaved decently and not allowed his feelings to be so obvious. . . .

One night I heard the voice of my French tom in the street. No one could see us; I climbed the chimney and having reached the top of the house, I called out to him: 'To the gutters!' This response lent him wings. He was after me in the twinkling of an eye. Would you believe it? This French tom had the ill-bred audacity, in reply to my modest little call, to exclaim: 'Come to my paws, darling!' Without any sanction at all, he actually dared to 'darling' me – ME, a cat of distinction!

I looked at him very coldly and, to teach him a lesson, I told him that I belonged to the Temperance Society.

'I see, my dear boy,' I said to him, 'from your accent and the laxity of your principles, that, like most Catholic cats, you are light-minded and would be guilty of a thousand idiocies in the fond belief that you have only to say you're sorry, to get out of the mess. In England, we are more moral; we are respectable in everything, even our pleasures.'

Brisquet was struck dumb by the magnificence of our English cant and listened to me with such close attention that I actually began to hope that I had a convert and that he would become a Protestant cat. He said in a most gentlemanly way, that he would do whatever I wished – provided that I let him adore me! I gazed at him unable to reply; his beautiful, splendid eyes were shining like stars, lighting up the whole night. Encouraged by my silence, he boldly exclaimed: 'Darling Minette!'

'What's this new impertinence?' I cried, though I knew how flippantly French cats talked.

Brisquet explained that on the Continent, everyone, even the King himself, would call his daughter 'Minette, my love!' or 'My little Puss,' as a sign of affection; many women, even the prettiest and most aristocratic, were in the habit of calling their husbands 'Kitten', often even when they were no longer in love with them. If I wanted to make him happy, he said, I would call him 'Mani-kin'. And upon that he raised his paws with irresistible charm. For fear of yielding to him, I made myself scarce. Brisquet promptly began to sing 'Rule, Britannia!', he was so thrilled; next day, his dear voice was still echoing in my ears.

Meanwhile, a scene was taking place which was to have dreadful consequences for me. Puck, one of Puff's nephews, who had ex-pectations under will and who was living at that time in Welling-ton Barracks, met my beloved Brisquet. Captain Puck slyly com-plimented the Attaché on his success with me; according to him, I had resisted all the most charming toms in England. Brisquet, vain Frenchman that he was, said that he would be very happy to attract my attention, although he detested cats who were always talking of temperance and the Bible and such things.

'Aha!' said Puck; 'so she does speak to you!'

My dear French Brisquet had fallen a victim to English diplomacy! And he went on to make one of those idiotic mistakes which outraged all the well-bred tabbies in England. What did the inconsistent young donkey do but greet me in the park and try to talk to me in a familiar manner, as if we knew each other! My instant reaction was to remain cold and distant. The coachman saw Brisquet and gave him a lash with his whip which nearly killed him. Brisquet received the blow without flinching and continued to gaze at me with such courage that my heart was melted. I adored him for seeing only me, while letting himself be beaten and for feeling simply happiness in my presence and for standing his ground in spite of the strong natural instinct of cats to run from the slightest sign of hostility. He did not guess that my outward coldness concealed a feeling that I was going to die. From that moment I made up my mind to elope with him.

'Darling,' I said to him, 'have you enough capital to pay Puff damages?'

'I haven't a bean,' said Brisquet with a laugh, 'except the hairs of my moustache, my four paws and this tail.' And with that he swaggered arrogantly along the gutter.

'No capital!' I exclaimed. 'Why, darling, you're just an adventurer!'

'I dote on adventures!' he said with a languishing look. 'In France, in circumstances like ours, cats spruce themselves up and rely on their claws, not their cash!'

'Poor country! And how on earth do people "without a bean" get assigned to your embassies abroad?'

'Our new government,' said Brisquet, 'isn't interested in its servants' pockets, only in their brains.'

Dear Brisquet's little smirk as he spoke made me think he had too good a conceit of himself.

'It's nonsense to think of love on a shoe-string,' I told him. 'You wouldn't pay much attention to me if you were running about looking for food all the time, my sweet.'

My scamp's only answer was that he was descended on his grandmother's side from Puss-in-Boots. Also, he knew of ninety-nine ways of borrowing money and that we should need only one way of spending it. Finally he said he was musical and could give lessons. And most meltingly he sang me one of his country's national songs, 'Au clair de la lune'.

At this very moment, a number of toms and tabbies, brought along by Puck, caught sight of me just when, overcome by so many arguments, I was promising my beloved Brisquet to follow him anywhere – as soon as he had the means to keep a wife in comfort.

'I'm in for it now,' I groaned.

The very next day, Puff brought an action for 'Criminal conversation' before the Court of Doctors' Commons. Puff was deaf and his nephews traded on it. When they asked him questions, he told them one night I had charmed him by calling him 'Manikin'. This was one of the most damaging accusations against me, as I simply could not explain where I had learnt such an amorous expression. His lordship had without realizing it been my undoing. But then, as I have said before, he was in his second childhood. He had no suspicion of the shabby intrigues of which I was the victim. Several young cats, who did their best to defend me against public opinion, told me that he sometimes asked for his angel, the light of his eyes, his darling, his Beauty. My own Mother, when she came to London, wouldn't see me or listen to me; she said that an English lady cat should be above suspicion, and that I was causing her unhappiness in her old age. My sisters were jealous of my position in Society and sided with my accusers. Even the servants gave evidence against me. I now saw very clearly the sort of situation that made everyone in England lose their heads. The moment there is a question of criminal proceedings, everyone suppresses their natural feelings. A mother is no longer a mother, a nurse repudiates her foster-child, every cat howls in the streets. And what was still more disgusting, my Counsel was won over by Captain Puck – my Counsel, who in his time had actually believed in the innocence of the Queen and to whom I had given every detail. He even assured me that I had nothing to worry about. I thought it was proof of my innocence that I had no idea what the words 'criminal conversation' meant. I told him this and he said that the offence was so named just because it meant nothing but small-talk. Anyhow, the result was that his defence of me was so weak that my cause seemed utterly lost and so I plucked up courage to appear in person before Doctors' Commons.

'My Lords,' said I, 'I am an English cat. I swear that I am in-

nocent. What will they say of the justice of Old England if. . . .' I had scarcely pronounced these words than horrible growls
of rage drowned the rest of my speech, so violently had the feelings of the public been aroused by the *Cat-Chronicle* and Puck's friends.

'She is casting doubt on the justice of England, the creator of trial by jury!' they cried.

'She wishes to explain to the Court,' shouted the horrible counsel for the plaintiff, 'how she went on the tiles with a French tom, to convert him to the Anglican Faith, while in fact she went to learn how to say "Manikin" to her unsuspecting husband! To listen to the abominable principles of Popery and to learn to disparage the laws and customs of England!' Well, when the English public hears this sort of farrago of nonsense, it goes potty. Thunders of applause greeted Counsel's words and I was found guilty, at the age of 26 months, although I could prove that I still did not know what a tom was. However, I could now understand why they called England 'Perfidious Albion'.

I fell into a deep hatred of my kind, due less to my divorce than to the death of my beloved Brisquet. Puck had had him killed in a riot, thinking he might try to take his revenge. Besides, nothing infuriated me more than to hear people boasting of the loyalty of English cats.

And so you see, Animals of France, what happens when we get to know men; we copy their vices and adopt their evil institutions. Let us go back to the wilds, where we shall follow only our own instincts and where customs are not opposed to the holy dictates of nature. . . .

I forgot to tell you that although Brisquet had a bullet wound in his back, the revolting hypocrite of a Coroner 'found' that he had poisoned himself with arsenic – as if a tom, so gay, so crazy, so scatter-brained could ever have reflected on life enough to have entertained such a serious idea. How *could* a cat whom *I* loved ever have had the faintest desire to quit this life?

True, – or is it? – they founds stains on a plate, by using Marsh's apparatus. . . .

Midshipman, The Cat

John Coleman Adams

This is a true story about a real cat who, for aught I know, is still alive and following the sea for a living. I hope to be excused if I use the pronouns 'who' and 'he' instead of 'which' and 'it,' in speaking of this particular cat; because although I know very well that the grammars all tell us that 'he' and 'who' apply to persons, while 'it' and 'which' apply to things, yet this cat of mine always seemed to us who knew him to be so much like a human being that I find it unsatisfactory to speak of him in any other way. There are some animals of whom you prefer to say 'he,' just as there are persons whom you sometimes feel like calling 'it.'

The way we met this cat was after this fashion: It was back somewhere in the seventies, and a party of us were cruising east from Boston in the little schooner-yacht *Eyvor*. We had dropped into Marblehead for a day and a night, and some of the boys had gone ashore in the tender. As they landed on the wharf, they found a group of small boys running sticks into a woodpile, evidently on a hunt for something inside.

'What have you in there?' asked one of the yachtsmen.

'Nothin' but a cat,' said the boys.

'Well, what are you doing to him?'

'Oh, pokin' him up! When he comes out we'll rock him,' was the answer, in good Marblehead dialect.

'Well, don't do it anymore. What's the use of tormenting a poor cat? Why don't you take somebody of your size?'

The boys slowly moved off, a little ashamed and a little afraid of the big yachtsman who spoke; and when they were well out of sight the yachtsmen went on, too, and thought no more about the cat they had befriended. But when they had wandered about the tangled streets of the town for a little while, and paid the visits which all good yachtsmen pay, to the grocery and the post office and the apothecary's soda fountain, they returned to the wharf and found their boat. And behold, there in the stern sheets sat the little gray-and-white cat of the woodpile! He had crawled out of his retreat and made straight for the boat of his champions. He seemed in no wise disturbed or disposed to move when they jumped on board, nor did he show anything but pleasure when they stroked and patted him. But when one of the boys started to put him ashore, the plucky little fellow showed his claws; and no sooner was he set on his feet at the edge of the wharf than he turned about and jumped straight back into the boat.

'He wants to go yachting,' said one of the party, whom we called 'the Bosn'n.'

'Ye might as wal take the cat,' said a grizzly old fisherman standing on the wharf. 'He doesn't belong to anybody, and ef he stays here the boys'll worry him t'death.'

'Let's take him aboard,' said the yachtsmen. 'It's good luck to have a cat on board ship.'

Whether it was good luck to the ship or not, it was very clear that pussy saw it meant good luck to him, and curled himself down in the bottom of the boat, with a look that meant business. Evidently he had thought the matter all over and made up his mind that this was the sort of people he wanted to live with; and, being a Marblehead cat, it made no difference to him whether they lived afloat or ashore; he was going where they went, whether they wanted him or not. He had heard the conversation from his place in the woodpile, and had decided to show his gratitude by going to sea with these protectors of his. By casting in his lot with theirs he was paying them the highest compliment of which a cat is capable. It would have been the height of impoliteness not to recognize his distinguished appreciation. So he was allowed to remain in the boat, and was taken off to the yacht.

Upon his arrival there, a council was held, and it was unanimously decided that the cat should be received as a member of the crew; and as we were a company of amateur sailors, sailing our own boat, each man having his particular duties, it was decided that the cat should be appointed midshipman, and should be named after his position. So he was at once and ever after known as 'Middy.' Everybody took a great interest in him, and he took an impartial interest in everybody – though there were two people on board to whom he made himself particularly agreeable. One was the quiet, kindly professor, the captain of the *Eyvor*; the other was Charlie, our cook and only hired hand. Middy, you see, had a seaman's true instinct as to the official persons with whom it was his interest to stand well.

It was surprising to see how quickly Middy made himself at home. He acted as if he had always been at sea. He was never seasick, no matter how rough it was or how uncomfortable any of the rest of us were. He roamed wherever he wanted to, all over the boat. At mealtimes he came to the table with the rest, sat up on a valise, and lapped his milk and took what bits of food were given him, as if he had eaten that way all his life. When the sails were hoisted it was his especial joke to jump upon the main gaff and be hoisted with it; and once he stayed on his perch till the sail was at the masthead. One of us had to go aloft and bring him down. When we had come to anchor and everything was snug for the night, he would come on deck and scamper out on the main boom, and race from there to the bowsprit end as fast as he could gallop, then climb, monkey-fashion, halfway up the masts, and drop back to the deck or dive down into the cabin and run riot among the berths.

One day, as we were jogging along, under a pleasant southwest wind, and everybody was lounging and dozing after dinner, we heard the Bos'n call out, 'Stop that, you fellows!' and a moment after, 'I tell you, quit! Or I'll come up and make you!'

We opened our lazy eyes to see what was the matter, and there sat the Bos'n, down in the cabin, close to the companionway, the tassel of his knitted cap coming nearly up to the combings of the hatch; and on the deck outside sat Middy, digging his claws into the tempting yarn, and occasionally going deep enough to scratch the Bos'n's scalp.

When night came and we were all settled down in bed, it was Middy's almost invariable custom to go the rounds of all the berths, to see if we were properly tucked in, and to end his inspection by jumping into the captain's bed, treading himself a comfortable nest there among the blankets, and curling himself down to sleep. It was his own idea to select the captain's berth as the only proper place in which to turn in.

But the most interesting trait in Middy's character did not appear until he had been a week or so on board. Then he gave us a surprise. It was when we were lying in Camden harbor. Everybody was going ashore to take a tramp among the hills, and Charlie, the cook, was coming too, to row the boat back to the yacht.

Middy discovered that he was somehow 'getting left.' Being a prompt and very decided cat, it did not take him long to make up his mind what to do. He ran to the low rail of the yacht, put his forepaws on it, and gave us a long, anxious look. Then as the boat was shoved off he raised his voice in a plaintive mew. We waved him a good-bye, chaffed him pleasantly, and told him to mind the anchor, and have dinner ready when we got back.

That was too much for his temper. As quick as a flash he had dived overboard, and was swimming like a water spaniel, after the dinghy!

That was the strangest thing we had ever seen in all our lives! We were quite used to elephants that could play at seesaw, and horses that could fire cannon, to learned pigs and to educated dogs; but a cat that of his own accord would take to the water like a full-blooded Newfoundland was a little beyond anything we had ever heard of. Of course the boat was stopped, and Middy was taken aboard drenched and shivering, but perfectly happy to be once more with the crew. He had been ignored and slighted; but he had insisted on his rights, and as soon as they were recognized he was quite contented.

Of course, after that we were quite prepared for anything that Middy might do. And yet he always managed to surprise us by his bold and independent behavior. Perhaps his most brilliant performance was a visit he paid a few days after his swim in Camden Harbor.

We were lying becalmed in a lull of the wind off the entrance to Southwest Harbor. near us, perhaps a cable's-length away, lay another small yacht, a schooner hailing from Lynn. As we drifted along on the tide, we noticed that Middy was growing very restless; and presently we found him running along the rail and looking eagerly toward the other yacht. What did he see – or smell –

over there which interested him? It could not be the dinner, for they were not then cooking. Did he recognize any of his old chums from Marblehead? Perhaps there were some cat friends of his on the other craft. Ah, that was it! There they were on the deck, playing and frisking together – two kittens! Middy had spied them, and was longing to take a nearer look. He ran up and down the deck, mewing and snuffing the air. He stood up in his favorite position when on lookout, with his forepaws on the rail. Then, before we realised what he was doing, he had plunged overboard again, and was making for the other boat as fast as he could swim! He had attracted the attention of her company, and no sooner did he come up alongside than they prepared to welcome him. A fender was lowered, and when Middy saw it he swam toward it, caught it with his forepaws, clambered along it to the gunwale, and in a twinkling was over the side and on the deck scraping acquaintance with the strange kittens.

How they received him I hardly know, for by that time our boat was alongside to claim the runaway. And we were quite of the mind of the skipper of the *Winnie L.*, who said, as he handed our bold midshipman over the side, 'Well, that beats all *my* going a-fishing!'

Only a day or two later Middy was very disobedient when we were washing decks one morning. He trotted about in the wet till his feet were drenched, and then retired to dry them on the white spreads of the berths below. That was quite too much for the captain's patience. Middy was summoned aft, and, after a sound rating, was hustled into the dinghy which was moored astern, and shoved off to the full length of her painter. The punishment was a severe one for Middy, who could bear anything better than exile from his beloved shipmates. So of course he began to exercise his ingenious little brain to see how he could escape. Well under the overhang of the yacht he spied, just about four inches out of water, a little shoulder of the rudder. That was enough for him. He did not stop to think whether he would be any better off there. It was a part of the yacht, and that was home. So overboard he went, swam for the rudder, scrambled on to it, and began howling piteously to be taken on deck again; and, being a spoiled and much-indulged cat, he was soon rescued from his uncomfortable roosting place and restored to favor.

I suppose I shall tax your powers of belief if I tell you many more of Middy's doings. But truly he was a strange cat, and you may as well be patient, for you will not soon hear of his equal. The captain was much given to rifle practice, and used to love to go ashore and shoot at a mark. On one of his trips he allowed Middy to accompany him, for the simple reason, I suppose, that Middy decided to go, and got on board the dinghy when the captain did. Once ashore, the marksman selected a fine large rock as a rest for his rifle, and opened fire upon his target. At the first shot or two Middy seemed a little surprised, but showed no disposition to run away. After the first few rounds, however, he seemed to have made up his mind that since the captain was making all the racket it must be entirely right and proper, and nothing about which a cat need bother his head in the least. So, as if to show how entirely he confided in the captain's judgment and good intentions, that imperturbable cat calmly lay down, curled up, and went to sleep in the shade of the rock over which the captain's rifle was blazing and cracking about once in two minutes. If anybody was ever acquainted with a cooler or more self-possessed cat I should be pleased to hear the particulars.

I wish that this chronicle could be confined to nothing but our shipmate's feats of daring and nerve. But, unfortunately, he was not always blameless in his conduct. When he got hungry he was apt to forget his position as midshipman, and to behave just like any cat with an empty stomach. Or perhaps he may have done just what any hungry midshipman does under the circumstances; I do not quite know what a midshipman does under all circumstances and so I cannot say. But here is one of this cat midshipman's exploits. One afternoon, on our way home, we were working along with a head wind and sea toward Wood Island, a haven for many of the small yachts between Portland and the Shoals. The wind was light and we were a little late in making port. But as we were all agreed that it would be pleasanter to postpone our dinner till we were at anchor, the cook was told to keep things warm and wait till we were inside the port before he set the table. Now, his main dish that day was to be a fine piece of baked fish; and, unfortunately, it was nearly done when we gave orders to hold back the dinner. So he had closed the drafts of his little stove, left the door of the oven open, and turned into his bunk for a quiet doze – a thing which every good sailor does on all possible occasions; for a seafaring life is very uncertain in the matter of sleep, and one never quite knows when he will lose some, nor how much he will lose. So it is well to lay in a good stock of it whenever you can.

It seems that Middy was on watch, and when he saw Charlie fast asleep he undertook to secure a little early dinner for himself. He evidently reasoned with himself that it was very uncertain when we should have dinner and he'd better get his while he could. He quietly slipped down to the stove, walked coolly up to the oven, and began to help himself to baked haddock.

He must have missed his aim or made some mistake in his management of the business, and, by some lucky chance for the rest of us, waked the cook. For, the first we knew, Middy came flying up the cabin companionway, followed by a volley of shoes and spoons and pieces of coal, while we could hear Charlie, who was rather given to unseemly language when he was excited, using the strongest words in his dictionary about 'that thief of a cat!'

'What's the matter?' was all shouted at once.

'Matter enough, sir!' growled Charlie. 'That little cat's eaten up half the fish! It's a chance if you get any dinner tonight, sir.'

You may be very sure that Middy got a sound wigging for that trick, but I am afraid the captain forgot to deprive him of his rations as he threatened. He was much too kindhearted.

The very next evening Middy startled us again by a most remarkable display of coolness and courage. After a weary thrash to windward all day, under a provokingly light breeze, we found ourselves under the lee of the little promontory at Cape Neddick, where we cast anchor for the night. Our supply of water had run very low, and so, just after sunset, two of the party rowed ashore in the tender to replenish our water keg, and by special permission Middy went with them.

It took some time to find a well, and by the time the jugs were filled it had grown quite dark. In launching the boat for the return to the yacht, by some ill luck a breaker caught her and threw her back upon the beach. There she capsized and spilled out the boys, together with their precious cargo. In the confusion of the moment, and the hurry of setting matters to rights, Middy was entirely forgotten, and when the boat again was launched, nobody thought to look for the cat. This time everything went well, and in a few minutes the yacht was sighted through the dusk. Then somebody happened to think of Middy! He was nowhere to be seen. Neither man remembered anything about him after the capsize. There was consternations in the hearts of those unlucky wights. To lose Middy was almost like losing one of the crew.

But it was too late and too dark to go back and risk another landing on the beach. There was nothing to be done but to leave poor Middy to his fate, or at least to wait until morning before searching for him.

But just as the prow of the boat bumped against the fender on the yacht's quarter, out from under the stern sheets came a wet, bedraggled, shivering cat, who leaped on board the yacht and hurried below into the warm cabin. In that moist adventure in the surf, Middy had taken care of himself, rescued himself from a watery grave, got on board the boat as soon as she was ready, and sheltered himself in the warmest corner. All this he had done without the least outcry, and without asking any help whatever. His self-reliance and courage were extraordinary.

Well, the pleasant month of cruising drew to a close, and it became a question what should be done with Middy. We could not think of turning him adrift in the cold world, although we had no fears but that so bright and plucky a cat would make a living anywhere. But we wanted to watch over his fortunes, and perhapstake him on the next cruise with us when he should have become a more settled and dignified Thomas. Finally, it was decided that he should be boarded for the winter with an artist, Miss Susan H-, a friend of one of our party. She wanted a studio cat, and would be particularly pleased to receive so accomplished and traveled a character as Middy. So when the yacht was moored to the little wharf at Annisquam, where she always ended her cruises, and we were packed and ready for our journey to Boston, Middy was tucked into a basket and taken to the train. He bore the confinement with the same good sense which had marked all his life with us, though I think his feelings were hurt at the lack of confidence we showed in him. And, in truth, we were a little ashamed of it ourselves, and when once we were on the cars somebody suggested that he be released from his prison just to see how he would behave. We might have known he would do himself credit. For when he had looked over his surroundings, peeped above the back of the seat at the passengers, taken a good look at the conductor, and counted the rest of the party to see that none of us was missing, Middy snuggled down upon the seat, laid his head upon the captain's knee, and slept all the way to Boston.

That was the last time I ever saw Middy. He was taken to his new boarding place in Boylston Street, where he lived very pleasantly for a few months, and made many friends by his pleasing manners and unruffled temper. But I suppose he found it a little dull in Boston. He was not quite at home in his aesthetic surroundings. I have always believed he sighed for the freedom of a sailor's life. He loved to sit by the open window when the wind was east, and seemed to be dreaming of faraway scenes. One day he disappeared. No trace of him was ever found. A great many things may have happened to him. But I never could get rid of the feeling that he went down to the wharves and the ships and the sailors, trying to find his old friends, looking everywhere for the staunch little *Eyvor*; and, not finding her, I am convinced that he shipped on some East Indianman and is now a sailor cat on the high seas.

The Achievement of the Cat

Saki

In the political history of nations it is no uncommon experience to
find States and peoples which but a short time since were in bitter
conflict and animosity with each other, settled down comfortably
on terms of mutual goodwill and even alliance. The natural
history of the social developments of species affords a similar instance in the coming-together of two once warring elements, now
represented by civilized man and the domestic cat. The fiercely
waged struggle which went on between humans and felines in
those far-off days when sabre-toothed tiger and cave lion con-
tended with primeval man, has long ago been decided in favour
of the most fitly equipped combatant – the Thing with a Thumb –
and the descendants of the dispossessed family are relegated
today, for the most part, to the waste lands of jungle and veld,
where an existence of self-effacement is the only alternative to ex-
termination. But the *felis catus*, or whatever species was the ancestor of the modern domestic cat (a vexed question at present), by a
master-stroke of adaptation avoided the ruin of its race, and 'captured' a place in the very keystone of the conqueror's organiza-
tion. For not as a bond-servant or dependent has this proudest of
mammals entered the human fraternity; not as a slave like the
beasts of burden, or a humble camp-follower like the dog. The cat
is domestic only as far as suits its own ends; it will not be ken-
nelled or harnessed nor suffer any dictation as to its goings out or
comings in. Long contact with the human race has developed in it
the art of diplomacy, and no Roman Cardinal of mediaeval days
knew better how to ingratiate himself with his surroundings than
a cat with a saucer of cream on its mental horizon. But the social

smoothness, the purring innocence, the softness of the velvet paw may be laid aside at a moment's notice, and the sinuous feline may disappear, in deliberate aloofness, to a world of roofs and chimney-stacks, where the human element is distanced and disregarded. Or the innate savage spirit that helped its survival in the bygone days of tooth and claw may be summoned forth from beneath the sleek exterior, and the torture-instinct (common alone to human and feline) may find free play in the death-throes of some luckless bird or rodent. It is, indeed, no small triumph to have combined the untrammelled liberty of primeval savagery with the luxury which only a highly developed civilization can command: to be lapped in the soft stuffs that commerce has gathered from the far ends of the world; to bask in the warmth that labour and industry have dragged from the bowels of the earth; to banquet on the dainties that wealth has bespoken for its table, and withal to be a free son of nature: a mighty hunter, a spiller of life-blood. This is the victory of the cat. But besides the credit of success the cat has other qualities which compel re-cognition. The animal which the Egyptians worshipped as divine, which the Romans venerated as a symbol of liberty, which Euro-peans in the ignorant Middle Ages anathematized as an agent of demonology, has displayed to all ages two closely blended characteristics – courage and self-respect. No matter how unfa-vourable the circumstances, both qualities are always to the fore. Confront a child, a puppy, and a kitten with a sudden danger; the child will turn instinctively for assistance, the puppy will grovel in abject submission to the impending visitation, the kitten will brace its tiny body for a frantic resistance. And disassociate the luxury-loving cat from the atmosphere of social comfort in which it usually contrives to move, and observe it critically under the adverse conditions of civilization – that civilzation which can im-pel a man to the degradation of clothing himself in tawdry ribald garments and capering mountebank dances in the streets for the earning of the few coins that keep him on the respectable, or non-criminal, side of society. The cat of the slums and alleys, starved, outcast, harried, still keeps amid the prowlings of its adversity the bold, free, panther-tread with which it paced of yore the temple courts of Thebes, still displays the self-reliant watchfulness which man has never taught it to lay aside. And when its shifts and clever managings have not sufficed to stave off inexorable fate, when its enemies have proved too strong or too many for its defensive powers, it dies fighting to the last, quivering with the choking rage of mastered resistance, and voicing in its death-yell that agony of bitter remonstrance which human animals, too, have flung at the powers that may be; the last protest against a destiny that might have made them happy – and has not.

'They live in contentment . . .'

Domestic and fond, see
   The kitten and cat;
Clear houses of vermin,
   The mouse and the rat:
They live in contentment,
   And keep you in peace,
Or these foes in number
   Would greatly increase.

ANON